MW00606659

The Rise of the Representative

Representation is integral to the study of legislatures, yet virtually no attention has been given to how representative assemblies developed and what that process might tell us about how the relationship between the representative and the represented evolved. *The Rise of the Representative* corrects that omission by tracing the development of representative assemblies in colonial America. Peverill Squire demonstrates that the rise of representation in the colonies was a practical response to governing problems rather than the imposition of an imported model or an attempt to translate abstract philosophy into a concrete reality. By examining the expectations set at the establishment of the various colonies, he shows that initially there were competing notions of representation. But over time the pull of the political system as it came to operate across the colonies moved lawmakers toward behaving as delegates, even in places where they were originally intended to operate as trustees. By looking at the rules governing who could vote and who could serve, how representatives were apportioned within each colony, how candidates and voters behaved in elections, how expectations regarding the relationship between the representative and the represented evolved, and how lawmakers actually behaved, Squire demonstrates that the American political system that emerged following independence was strongly rooted in colonial-era developments.

Peverill Squire is Hicks and Martha Griffiths Chair in American Political Institutions at the University of Missouri.

LEGISLATIVE POLITICS & POLICY MAKING

Series Editors

Janet M. Box-Steffensmeier, Vernal Riffe Professor of Political Science,
The Ohio State University

David Canon, Professor of Political Science, University of Wisconsin, Madison

THE RISE OF THE REPRESENTATIVE

*Lawmakers and Constituents
in Colonial America*

Peverill Squire

University of Michigan Press
Ann Arbor

Copyright © 2017 by Peverill Squire
All rights reserved

This book may not be reproduced, in whole or in part, including illustrations, in any form
(beyond that copying permitted by Sections 107 and 108 of the U.S. Copyright Law and
except by reviewers for the public press), without written permission from the publisher.

Published in the United States of America by the
University of Michigan Press
Manufactured in the United States of America
♾ Printed on acid-free paper

2020   2019   2018   2017   4   3   2   1

A CIP catalog record for this book is available from the British Library.

Library of Congress Cataloging-in-Publication Data

Names: Squire, Peverill.
Title: The rise of the representative : lawmakers and constituents in colonial America /
    Peverill Squire.
Description: Ann Arbor : University of Michigan Press, 2017. | Series: Legislative
    politics and policy making series | Includes bibliographical references and index.
Identifiers: LCCN 2016053324| ISBN 9780472130399 (hardcover : alk. paper) |
    ISBN 9780472122929 (e-book)
Subjects: LCSH: Legislative bodies—United States—History. | Legislative bodies—
    United States—States—History. | Legislators—United States—History. |
    United States—Politics and government.
Classification: LCC JK1021 .S7 2017 | DDC 328.7309/033—dc23
LC record available at https://lccn.loc.gov/2016053324

For Janet

Contents

Acronyms

AHRN	*Ancient Historical Records of Norwalk*
AM	*Archives of Maryland*
ANJ	*Acts of the General Assembly of the Province of New Jersey*
APC	*Acts of the Privy Council*
ATMR	*Andover Massachusetts Town Meeting Records*
ATR	*Ancient Town Records, New Haven Town Records*
AWM	*American Weekly Mercury*
BEP	*Boston Evening-Post*
BG	*Boston Gazette*
BPB	*Boston Post Boy*
CAAA	*A Collection of All the Acts of Assembly, of the Province of North Carolina*
CBWP	*Correspondence between William Penn and James Logan*
CC	*Connecticut Courant*
CLNY	*Colonial Laws of New York*
CORTD	*Copy of the Old Records of the Town of Duxbury, Mass.*
CRNC	*Colonial Records of North Carolina*
CRSC	*Colonial Records of South Carolina*
CRSG	*Colonial Records of the State of Georgia*
CSP	*Calendar of State Papers, Colonial Series*
CTR	*Concord Town Records*
CVSP	*Calendar of Virginia State Papers*
DCLC	*Diary of Colonel Landon Carter*

DRNH	*Documents and Records Relating to the Province of New Hampshire*
DRNJ	*Documents Relating to the Colonial History of the State of New Jersey*
DRNY	*Documents Relating (Relative) to the Colonial History of the State of New York*
DRRT	*Documents and Records Relating to Towns in New Hampshire*
EG	*Essex Gazette*
ERC	*Extracts from the Records of Colchester*
ERL	*Early Records of Londonderry, Windham, and Derry*
ERTD	*Early Records of the Town of Dedham*
ERTL	*Early Records of the Town of Lunenburg*
ERTPo	*Early Records of the Town of Portsmouth*
ERTPr	*Early Records of the Town of Providence*
ERTWa	*Early Records of the Town of Warwick*
ERTWo	*Early Records of the Town of Worcester*
GG	*Georgia Gazette*
JBTP	*Journals of the Board of Trade and Plantations*
JCH	*Journal(s) of the Commons House of Assembly of South Carolina*
JHB	*Journals of the House of Burgesses of Virginia*
JHHR	*Journal of the Honorable House of Representatives, Massachusetts-Bay*
JVNY	*Journal of the Votes and Proceedings of the General Assembly, New-York*
JVPA	*Journal of the Votes and Proceedings of the House of Representatives, Pennsylvania*
LGD	*Laws of the Government of New-Castle, Kent, and Sussex, Upon Delaware*
LNH	*Laws of New Hampshire*
LPCC	*The Letters and Papers of Cadwallader Colden*
LW	*Letters to Washington and Accompanying Papers*
MAG	*Massachusetts Gazette*
MCCNY	*Minutes of the Common Council of New York*
MCCP	*Minutes of the Common Council of the City of Philadelphia*
MDG	*Maryland Gazette*
MPCP	*Minutes of the Provincial Council of Pennsylvania*
MRBR	*Muddy River and Brookline Records*
MS	*Massachusetts Spy*
NEWJ	*New-England Weekly Journal*
NHG	*New-Hampshire Gazette*

NLG	*New-London Gazette*
NM	*Newport Mercury*
NYEP	*New-York Evening Post*
NYG	*New York Gazette*
NYJ	*New-York Journal*
NYM	*New-York Mercury*
NYWJ	*New-York Weekly Journal*
OLAS	*Official Letters of Alexander Spotswood*
ORTF	*Old Records of the Town of Fitchburg*
PA	*Pennsylvania Archives*
PAG	*Pennsylvania Gazette*
PC	*Pennsylvania Chronicle*
PRCC	*Public Records of the Colony of Connecticut*
PRG	*Providence Gazette*
PSWJ	*The Papers of Sir William Johnson*
RCNH	*Records of the Colony of New Haven*
RCNP	*Records of the Colony of New Plymouth*
RCRI	*Records of the Colony of Rhode Island and Providence Plantations*
RGC	*Records of the Governor and Company of the Massachusetts Bay*
RRCB	*Report of the Record Commissioners of the City of Boston*
RRSM	*Report of the Record Commissioners of the City of Boston, Selectmen*
RTB	*Records of the Town of Braintree*
RTC	*Records of the Town of Cambridge*
RTN	*Records of the Town of Newark*
RTP	*Records of the Town of Plymouth*
SCG	*South-Carolina Gazette*
SLP	*Statutes at Large of Pennsylvania*
SLSC	*Statutes at Large of South Carolina*
SLV	*The Statutes at Large; Being a Collection of All the Laws of Virginia*
SRRC	*Second Report of the Record Commissioners of the City of Boston*
TRDM	*Town Records of Dudley*
TRM	*Town Records of Manchester*
TRS	*Town Records of Salem*
TRT	*Town Records of Topsfield*
VG	*Virginia Gazette*
VPDE	*Votes and Proceedings of the House of Representatives, Delaware*
VPMD	*Votes and Proceedings of the Lower House of Assembly of the Province of Maryland*

VPNJ	*Votes and Proceedings of the General Assembly of the Province of New-Jersey*
VPNY	*Votes and Proceedings of the General Assembly of the Colony of New-York*
VPPP	*Votes and Proceedings of the House of Representatives of the Province of Pennsylvania*
WJ	*Winthrop's Journal*
WR	*Watertown Records*
WTR	*Worcester Town Records*

Acknowledgments

This book grew out of a paper I delivered at a 2013 conference held at Vanderbilt University's Center for the Study of Democratic Institutions. I thank the conference organizers and participants for their encouragement. The University of Missouri awarded me research leave for the 2014–15 academic year to develop the book manuscript, for which I am grateful. The final product benefited greatly from the thorough and thoughtful comments offered by the anonymous readers.

The Rise of the Representative

ONE

Introduction

Representation is the elemental concept in the study of legislatures. The literature devoted to it is voluminous. In almost every examination, however, scholars take the existence of representative institutions as a given. Little attention has been given to how representative assemblies developed and what that process might tell us about how the relationship between the representative and the represented evolved. Pitkin's (1967) study of the concept of representation has deservedly stood as a standard work on the topic for a half century, yet it breezes by the rise of representative institutions. Miller and Stokes (1963, 45) ground their celebrated examination of constituency influence in Congress in the expectations expressed by the founders during the writing of the US Constitution. But their approach misses not only a decade of experience with the Congress under the Articles of Confederation and the original 13 state legislatures but also the 157-year history of representational activities in the colonial assemblies. That colonial experience informed the founders' thoughts because of the 39 who signed the US Constitution 18 had served in an assembly (Squire and Hamm 2005, 19).

In this book I trace the rise of representative assemblies in colonial America and detail the early expectations for representation. My focus is on the experiences of the 16 assemblies that evolved into the original 13 state legislatures. The number of assemblies is greater because Connecticut absorbed New Haven in 1664 while Massachusetts annexed Plymouth in 1692. Both New Haven and Plymouth had assemblies. During the latter part of the seventeenth century New Jersey was separated into East Jersey and West Jersey, each with an assembly. The story developed here includes the assemblies that disappeared because they, too, played a role in launching the relationship between representatives and the represented.

In this introduction I present my argument that the rise of representation in the colonies was a practical response to governing problems rather than the imposition of an imported model or an attempt to translate abstract philosophy into a concrete reality. Over time colonial representatives came to focus more on promoting the interests and concerns of their constituents than on some larger notion of the common good. The representational system evolved in the direction of a mass democracy of the sort more commonly identified with nineteenth-century America.

Representative Assemblies in the Seventeenth Century

Representative assemblies first emerged in medieval Europe when monarchs called together representatives from those segments of society from which they needed tax revenue and military personnel. By the beginning of the seventeenth century such assemblies were established throughout the continent. But most did not fare well over the course of the following 100 years.

Across Europe assemblies disappeared. The French Estates General, called in 1614, was the last one to be held for the next 175 years. Most of that country's provincial estates did not meet again after 1650. The provincial German assemblies, the *Landtags*, generally failed to meet during the second half of the century. The same story prevailed in Spain where only 6 of the 22 *cortes* survived. Naples lost its parliament in 1642 (Huntington 1966, 386; Jansson 2007, 5–13). It is noteworthy that the American colonial assemblies were established and survived at what was an unpropitious time for such institutions.

England, of course, began and ended the 1600s with a parliament. But the institution was not static: no parliament was held between 1629 and 1640; the Short Parliament met for three weeks; the Long Parliament was in session for 19 years but was interrupted by the Rump Parliament, Barebone's Parliament, and several protectorate parliaments; the Cavalier Parliament met for 18 years; and the Glorious Revolution finally cemented parliament's governing status. By the century's end, Parliament differed from what it had been at the beginning. The fact that it existed throughout is of importance to the assemblies' story. The fact that it changed over the course of the century also matters because the assemblies failed to follow suit. As will be shown, representation in the colonies largely harkened back to what it had been in England during the Tudor era.

The Rise of Representative Assemblies in America

The notion of political representation was firmly rooted in England by the time that country began to colonize North America early in the seventeenth century. Claims asserting Parliament's standing surfaced in response to attempts by the Crown to limit the body's influence. In the 1621 "Protestation of the House of Commons," a response to a letter from the king diminishing the institution's authority, it was declared "That the Liberties, Franchises, Privileges, and Jurisdictions of Parliament are the ancient and undoubted Birth-right and Inheritance of the Subjects of England" (Rushworth 1682, 53). The claim of a right to representation had been made explicitly in a 1604 document in which the House of Commons noted that first among "The Rights of the Liberties of the Commons of *England*" was "That the Shires, Cities, and Boroughs of *England*, by Representation to be present, have free Choice of such Persons as they shall put in Trust to represent them" (Petyt 1739, 235). The entitlement of English subjects to be represented in a lawmaking body by representatives of their own choosing was, by the time the colonies were settled, well established.

That might suggest that a representative assembly in the likeness of the House of Commons was simply transplanted into each colony as it came under English rule. Though appealing, such a claim fails to take into account the fact that the assemblies were created through different legal mechanisms, at different times, by different people, and for different reasons. None was created in Parliament's image. Indeed, the assemblies and the representative systems they embodied were distinct not only from Parliament but from each other as well. Among the notable ways in which they differed was in who could vote for their members, who could serve as a member, how seats were apportioned, their election calendars, and their election mechanics. These differences influenced how representatives came to relate to the represented.

It is worth reflecting on the different legal mechanisms used to create the colonies (Kellogg 1903). Both Virginia and Massachusetts started with corporate charters through which the Crown allowed their self-governing corporations to pursue private gain under an assumption that their profits would redound to England's greater good. Virginia had its charter revoked relatively quickly and was put under the Crown's direct control as a royal colony. Its assembly would be the colony's only elective office. Massachusetts had its original charter replaced toward the end of the seventeenth century with the new one putting it under royal control but with an important modification: the Crown appointed the colony's governor, but the assembly elected his council. Both Connecticut and Rhode Island came to operate under charters giving each a right to complete self-government with an elected governor and council as well as assembly. Charter status, then, had consequences for the way colonial representation functioned, but it was not the same for each charter colony. Moreover, a charter could be revoked and replaced.

The other colonies established during the seventeenth century began as proprietary colonies, meaning that the Crown gave title to large swaths of land to a particular person or group of people, allowing them to govern their landholding. Pennsylvania stayed a proprietary colony throughout the colonial era (as did its spinoff, Delaware), while Maryland fell under royal control for a period before being returned to its proprietor. For all intents and purposes, the proprietary colonies were governed like royal colonies with the exception that the proprietor, not the Crown, selected the governor. The remaining colonies that began as proprietorships— Georgia, New Hampshire, New Jersey, New York, North Carolina, and South Carolina—all eventually became royal colonies. Representation in them focused exclusively on their elected assemblies.

The one constant transmitted to all the colonists was that electing representatives to an assembly was their birthright. Just before the Revolution, a former governor of two colonies wrote that the colonists were convinced they had "by an inherent, essential right, the right of representation and legislature, with all the powers and privileges, as possessed in England" (Pownall 1766, 31). Evidencing such expectations, colonists at a 1768 Boston town meeting, riled about the parent country's abuses, adopted a report asserting their innate right to be governed by policies made only with "the consent of the People, in person" or "by Representatives of their own free Election" (*RRCB* 1886, 262–63). Such notions were universal in colonial America.

What representation meant in practice varied, both across the colonies and over time. As shown in table 1.1, a trustee orientation initially took root in assemblies that were conceived as representative bodies. Clear signals were sent to their members that their mission was to promote the larger general welfare, what is called a trustee orientation. A delegate orientation was associated with the assemblies that emerged from meetings of all of a colony's freemen. In these places representative assemblies only emerged for pragmatic reasons, and when they did they featured expectations that representatives would do as their voters wished. There was also a curious third category of hybrid assemblies that combined features of the other two groups, muddling their initial orientations.

The weight of the historical record compiled in this book suggests that two significant developments regarding representation took place during the colonial era. The first involved the question of what interests a representative was to pursue. Over time lawmakers in places that initially favored a trustee orientation came to behave as delegates, pursuing their constituents' interests over what they may have thought was in the larger interest of the colony. The second development involved who was represented. Counter to the direction of England's representational system, which leaned heavily in favor of the elite to the exclusion of the multitudes, the American system moved toward the sort of mass democracy that would be celebrated by Tocqueville in the 1830s.

Trustees and Delegates

The notion of a representational dilemma between delegate and trustee behavior was famously articulated by Edmund Burke in his 1774 speech to the voters of Bristol, England, who had just elected him to represent them in the House of Commons. Burke presented his constituents with what he saw as a binary choice in his representational role. One was the use of

TABLE 1.1. Representational Orientation of Assemblies Established in the Seventeenth Century

Decade	Assembly Created as a Representative Body (trustee)	Representative Assembly Emerged from Assembly of All Freemen (delegate)	Assembly Created as Mixed System (hybrid)
1610–19	Virginia (1619)		
1620–29			
1630–39	New Haven (1639)	Massachusetts (1634) Connecticut (1637) Plymouth (1639)	Maryland (1638)
1640–49		Rhode Island (1647)	
1650–59			
1660–69	North Carolina (1665) New Jersey (1668)		
1670–79	South Carolina (1671)		
1680–89	New Hampshire (1680) West Jersey (1682) New York (1683)		Pennsylvania (1682)
1690–99			

"*authoritative* instructions; *mandates* issued, which the member is bound blindly and implicitly to obey, to vote, and to argue for." The other, which is how Burke viewed his own service, was to be a member of "a *delibera- tive* assembly of *one* nation, with *one* interest, that of the whole; where, not local purposes, not local prejudices ought to guide, but the general good, resulting from the general reason of the whole" (*Works of Edmund Burke*, vol. II 1792, 15–16). Thus a representative's dilemma was to either faith- fully represent the views of a majority of one's constituents, or be guided by one's own understanding of the right or best answer for the good of the entire polity.

Burke's quandary has structured almost every academic examination of representation. Attempts have been made to refine it. Wahlke and his colleagues proposed a third representational role, a politico who, depend- ing on the issue, acts as either a delegate or a trustee (Wahlke et al. 277– 80). Pitkin (1967, 145–46) posited a continuum running from a mandate (delegate) orientation at one end to an independence (trustee) orientation at the other extreme, allowing for politico-type behavior in between. A more elaborate categorization, with eight representational types based on whether a lawmaker pursues republican or pluralist aims, is self-reliant in terms of judgments or is dependent on others and is more or less responsive to sanctions was advanced by Rehfeld (2009). Among other behaviors, this approach allows for instructed trustees and independent delegates. Even the notion of representation itself has been expanded beyond the policy congruence angle embedded in Burke's dilemma. Pitkin (1967) introduced descriptive and symbolic representation, while Eulau and Karps (1977) broke representation into four components: policy; service; allocation; and, again, symbolic.

All these efforts improve our understanding of representation as a theoretical concept. And they speak to observed realities surrounding the behavior of modern representatives operating in complex electoral systems and representing heterogeneous constituencies. But they do not tell us about how those representational systems developed or how expectations about the behavior of representatives or the represented evolved. The his- tory of the rise of representation in the American experience documented here reveals that Burke had it right; colonial lawmakers wrestled with his dilemma decades before he articulated it. They viewed their choices in his stark, binary terms. Only rarely can the nuances advanced by modern theo- rists be seen in the colonial representational experience.

Early American lawmakers saw themselves as acting either as trustees or as delegates. But, as will be documented, representatives in colonies that began with trustee orientations moved away from a single-minded pursuit of the larger good in favor of promoting their constituents' expressed preferences. This change occurred for several reasons. First, in every colony most assembly members came to seek reelection. Because they wanted to continue to serve they were motivated to act in such a way as to appeal to their constituents. Second, for colonial lawmakers assembly service was their highest political aspiration. There were few, if any, higher offices for them to seek—almost all the governorships and council positions were appointed and often filled by nonresidents. Consequently, assembly members exhibited static political career ambitions that promoted a constituency focus. Finally, members were well anchored in their electoral districts. Almost all were elected from the towns, parishes, or counties where they resided or, in some colonies, where they held extensive estates. When they ceased assembly service, those were the places to which they returned and the people they would be motivated to keep happy. Consequently, while the seeds of what we call the Burkean dilemma were planted during the colonial era, the clear pull over time was toward delegate behavior.

Intriguingly, the terms *trustee* and *delegate* were used in the context of representation at the time. *Delegate* surfaced more frequently, both as a label for those serving in some of the assemblies and more generically in terms of the powers granted by the voters to those they elected. *Trustee* was less commonly employed. As will be seen, it was applied in passing as a name for West Jersey representatives. On a theoretical level, it came up in a 1722 election sermon given by John Hancock, grandfather of the revolutionary era figure of the same name. Preaching to Massachusetts assembly members before they elected the council, Hancock told them, "The *Providence* of GOD and your *Principals* have put this Honor upon you who are the Trustees and Representatives of the People, and you may be very Serviceable to this People by choosing out from among our Tribes, *able Men* . . . Men of Truth, able to support the Authority of their Places, and equal to their solemn Trust and Charge" (Hancock 1722, 27–28).

Representation and Movement toward Mass Democracy

The first words in Tocqueville's *Democracy in America* signal his most striking observation: "No Novelty in the United States struck me more vividly . . . than the equality of conditions." He argued that this mattered because "It gives a particular turn to public opinion and a particular twist to the laws, new maxims to those who govern and particular habits to the governed" (1969, 9). The implicit contrast drawn was to political conditions in Europe, where the relationship between the governed and the governors was more distant and inequitable.

The story developed here documents harbingers of the mass democracy that captured Tocqueville's attention in the 1830s. Although the formal rules governing who could vote and who could serve in America were similar in most details to those in England at the time, their impact played out differently. The percentage of the population eligible to vote was much higher in the colonies and the social and economic barriers to serving much lower. Moreover, on an episodic basis assembly elections were hotly contested, with substantial proportions of the potential voter pool mobilized by contentious issues and rowdy campaigns. Colonial America made substantial moves toward Jacksonian democracy.

Making Sense of the Historical Record

The story of the development of representative institutions and representational expectations in America has only been lightly touched on by historians and ignored almost altogether by political scientists. In this book I draw on a wide range of original sources—town and colony records, legislative journals, personal diaries and letters, newspapers, broadsides, and contemporary analyses—to derive an account of how American representative assemblies came to be established and how connections between the representative and the represented developed. Working from Raymond Wolfinger's aphorism "the plural of anecdote is data," I weave bits of relevant information into a coherent pattern. I consider an anecdote or story as a datum and try to find multiple examples of each behavior in order to have greater confidence in my observations about the rise of representation in America. Thus this effort is largely inductive. Where systematic data were gatherable they are used to test relevant hypotheses, notably in chapter 8.

Two complementary sets of lessons emerge from this study. The first set comes from cross-sectional analyses, looking at how each assembly's approach to representation evolved. These lessons emphasize the distinctiveness of the process that unfolded in each colony. The second set of lessons is drawn from the 157 years of representational development. These findings identify commonalities that emerged over time across the colonies.

The Progression of the Book

The process by which representative assemblies emerged in the American colonies is the focus of chapter 2. Their development followed different story lines in each of the colonies with all of them experiencing fits and starts. Representation was a feature from the beginning in some of them, while in others it only emerged for practical reasons. Importantly, none of the assemblies was modeled on the House of Commons. This independence allowed for competing notions of representation to develop across the colonies.

With the rise of representative institutions, several important questions had to be addressed. In chapter 3 the questions of who could vote for representatives and who could serve as a representative are investigated. The rules developed across the colonies were similar but not uniform. Over time, qualifications for voting and serving were tightened. But because economic and social circumstances in the colonies differed from those found in England, even with tighter qualifications a much larger percentage of the white male population was able to both vote and serve than in the parent country. This made colonial officials distrustful of the quality of voters and assembly members. But it also set the stage for the rise of mass democracy.

Chapter 4 tackles the other important question that had to be addressed: how was representation to be apportioned? Almost all the seats were distributed on the basis of geographic units—predominately towns, counties, and parishes—and most sent multiple members. All this was consistent with English norms. Again, however, there were important variations across the colonies, with implications for how representation developed. Colonial politicians understood the importance of how seats were apportioned and occasionally attempted to manipulate the schemes to their political advantage.

Chapters 5 and 6 explore the election process. Chapter 5 looks at election mechanics, notably election schedules and the process of voting, both of which diverged among the colonies and differed in their details from English practices, and again these differences impacted representation. The somewhat mysterious process of candidate emergence is traced, highlighting the power of deference but noting how over time candidacies became more overt and public. Campaigns and voters are the focus of chapter 6. Assembly campaigns are shown to have been more vigorous and issue based than is often thought. Demonstrating these points are close examinations of three New York contests about which detailed information is available. Taken together these two chapters reveal that assembly members came to seek reelection, giving them an incentive to hew to constituent preferences, and that, although they did not always face competitive contests, there were sufficient electoral pressures on them to keep them informed on their voters' desires. Collectively, they supply further evidence that a move toward a mass democracy was well under way by the last few decades of the colonial era.

How the relationship between the representative and the represented evolved is examined in chapter 7. The colonies varied in the mechanics of representation. Some held regularly scheduled elections on a semiannual or annual basis, enhancing the opportunities for voters to keep a tight rein on those they elected. Other colonies held elections irregularly, which built distance between their voters and representatives. In New England, the electoral system operated in such a fashion that voters were well positioned to issue instructions to their representatives, guiding the actions they were to take in the assembly. Elsewhere instructions were less common, but expectations that constituents would be consulted still existed. This forced assembly members outside New England to grapple with the Burkean dilemma well before Burke articulated it. Assembly members began to feel the tug of constituent opinion, pressuring them to take their preferences into greater account. Further pressure was brought to bear by advances such as newspapers and printed legislative journals, which provided constituents with information about assembly actions, thereby giving them the means by which they could hold their representatives accountable for their decisions.

How representation occurred in practice is investigated in chapter 8. First in New England and then elsewhere, lawmakers came to pursue direct representational activities intended to provide particularized policies of benefit to their constituents. Perhaps even more important, assembly agendas swelled as populations and economies grew and diversified, leading to increased demands being made of representatives by the voters. A variety of evidence that representatives came to provide policy representation is presented. Much is anecdotal. But data on the sorts of bills passed over time in five colonies, and on a controversial Massachusetts excise tax for which there was a recorded roll call vote and about which towns held special meetings and took positions on the measure, provide more systematic proof concerning representation. Additionally, analysis of recorded roll call votes in several assemblies shows that multimember delegations voted together at levels that allow us to infer that their members did what their constituents wanted.

My arguments are tied together in chapter 9. The assemblies started with different representational orientations, but over time the electoral rules and structures under which the lawmakers operated combined with a desire among members to seek reelection diminished any push toward trustee behavior. Instead, the incentives that came to be in place pulled members toward the adoption of a delegate orientation. Lawmakers still struggle with this representational dilemma, although political realities continue to draw them toward delegate behavior.

There are a two more comments to make regarding the story laid out here. First, I quote language as it is given in the original source, with a few exceptions. I replace a long *s* with an *s* and shorthand symbols that are not easily reproduced with the letters they represent. I have also taken the liberty to change where necessary the letters *u*, *v*, and *j* to current usage. Italicized words are as in the original. Presenting the original language is vital because it allows a more direct and less interpretative understanding of colonial actions and behaviors.

Second, much of that original language is archaic. But it is less challenging to understand than might be feared because the politics it describes is remarkably familiar. Colonial politicians behaved in the same ways current politicians behave and for the same reasons. Thus, with regard to representation, the questions faced by the political system then are the same as those that face the political system today. Understanding the story of how they arose and were addressed in the past, will, I hope, help us better understand where we are in addressing them now.

TWO

The Emergence of Representative Assemblies in the Colonies

It would be easy to assume the colonial assemblies were all fashioned out of the same English mold. But nothing could be further from the truth. The assemblies were established at different times, by different groups of people, for different reasons, using different legal mechanisms. Their unique histories had significant implications for the representational orientations they initially adopted.

Virginia and the Trustee Model

The first assembly in the Americas was established in Virginia in 1619. Unlike those that would be created in the other early colonies, Virginia's assembly was always intended to be a representative body. According to a contemporary account, the Virginia Company, a commercial enterprise, had determined "that they might have a hande in the governinge of themselves, it was granted that a general assemblie should be helde yearly once, wherat were to be present the Govr and Counsell with two Burgesses from each Plantation freely to be elected by the inhabitants thereof" (*JHB 1619– 1915*, 36). A 1621 ordinance "for Council and Assembly in Virginia" provides a similar account and offers a glimpse of what the now lost 1619 ordinance likely stated: "The other Counsell more generall to bee called by the Governor and yeerly . . . shall consist for present of the said Counsell of State and of Tow Burgesses out of ev[ery] towne hunder and other particuler planta[ti]on to bee respetially Chosen by the inhabitants" (*Records of the Virginia Company* 1933, 483).

It would be a mistake, however, to assume that Virginia's assembly was modeled on the English House of Commons. The failing colony's directors hoped an assembly would help foster much needed economic vitality, and consequently they shaped it to fit their corporate needs (Billings 2004, 5–7; Kukla 1985, 284). In the directors' minds the representatives were to act on behalf of their fellow stakeholders in pursuit of the colony's interests. Their charge makes this clear: "[T]his assembly [is] to have power to make and ordaine whatsoever laws and orders should by them be thought good and proffittable for our subsistence" (*JHB 1619–* 1915, 36). A 1620 letter sent to London officials by a colonist offers a comparable take, noting that a directive had "caused Burgesses to be chosen in all plac[es] who mett at James City, where all matters . . . were debated . . . and lykewise such other lawes enacted, as were held expedient & requisite for the wellfare and peaceable goverm^t of this Com[m]on-weale" (*Records of the Virginia Company* 1933, 241). The assembly's corporate orientation disappeared in 1624 after the Virginia Company was dissolved and the colony fell under royal control. But the representative body was continued, in part because the council and assembly told the Privy Council, "Nothing can be more conducive to our satisfaction or the public utility" (*CSP* 1860, 58).

A trustee orientation was also maintained. Evidence of this comes from the oath sworn by the burgesses, which appeared occasionally in the legislative journals. It confirms a focus on the larger colony good. The oath taken in 1652—the earliest recorded—stated, "You and every of you shall swear upon the holy Evangelist, and in the sight of God to deliver your opinions faithfully and honestly, according to your best understanding and conscience, for the generall good and prosperitie of this country and every perticular member thereof, and to do your utmost endeavor to prosecute that without mingling with it any perticular interest of any person or persons whatsoever" (*JHB 1619–* 1915, 82).

The following year the oath was condensed, and an intriguing change was made to the opening line: "You shall swear to act as a Burgesse for the place you serve for in this Assembly, with the best of your judgment and advice, for the generall good." This suggests a shift toward a delegate model, but every subsequent time the oath appeared over the following century it used the 1652 wording, dropping any reference to "the place you serve" (*JHB 1619–* 1915, 86, 115; *1659/60–* 1914, 25, 120; *1727–* 1910,

382). Thus, the burgesses were sworn to pursue policies for the greater good and forbidden to consider any financial or other implications for themselves or their associates. The idea that their constituents might have distinct preferences they were to promote was recognized only transiently in the 1653 oath.

The New England Colonies and the Delegate Model

In contrast to Virginia, most of the other early assemblies did not begin as representative bodies. The governmental structure put in place in these settlements also consisted of a governor and council, but each assembly was comprised of all the colony's freemen. The intent was for these entities to make decisions jointly. Thus, their original governmental design incorporated direct democracy.

The freemen assemblies, however, were transformed into representative bodies within a brief period of time. In Massachusetts the path was a bit roundabout. The charter the first settlers brought with them held that the governor was authorized to "from tyme to tyme . . . order for the assembling of the saide Company, and calling them together to consult and advise of the businesses and affaires of the said Company." The directive was to hold "foure Generall Assemblies" to be called the "Greate and Generall Court," and this body was to make "lawes and ordi[na]nces for the good and welfare of the saide Company" (RGC, vol. I 1853, 11–12).

The first General Court met in 1630 and was attended "not by a representative, but by every one, that was free of the corporation, in person" (Hutchinson 1765, 25). It opted to delegate lawmaking powers to an elected group of assistants. For a few years the assistants made all laws in consultation with the governor. But in the wake of a controversy over the apportionment of taxes among the colony's towns it was decided to have each community appoint two representatives to discuss the matter with the assistants. In turn that led to a 1634 decision to return to the system of quarterly assemblies called for in the charter. At the same time it was also decided "that it shalbe lawfull for the ffreemen of [every] planta[ti]on to chuse two or three of each towne before e[ver]y Gen[er]all Court . . . & that such p[er]sons as shalbe here-after soe deputed by the ffreemen of [the] se[ver]all planta[ti]ons, to deale in their behalf, in yᵉ publique affayres of the co[mm]onwealth, shall have the full power & voyces of all the said ffreemen, deryved to them for the makeing & establishing of lawes" (RGC, vol. I 1853, 79–80, 93, 118; WJ, vol. I 1908, 74–75, 122–25). The final provision is noteworthy in that it called for representatives to act on behalf of the freemen who elected them.

This decision did not fully establish a representative system. The annual elections court still required that "e[ver]y freeman is to gyve his owne voyce." That requirement was loosened in 1636 when it was ordered that "the townes of Ipsw^{ch}, Neweberry, Salem, Saugus, Waymothe, & Hingham shall have libertie to stay soe many of their ffreemen att home." Those who did not attend in person were entitled to "send their voices by p[ro]xy." Mandatory attendance was removed for the rest of the colonists in 1638 when the court determined that all freemen could vote by proxy. A few years later proxies were determined to be "subject to many miscarriages, & losse of oportunityes for advice in the choyse," so it was decided that "ev^{r}y ten freemen" would "choose one, to bee sent to the Court wth power to make election for all the rest" (*RGC*, vol. I 1853, 118–19, 166, 188, 333–34). Figuring out the mechanics of representation was challenging and it took some time to work out the kinks, but the decision to pursue it was never reversed.

Consequently, a representative assembly emerged in Massachusetts, but for practical rather than philosophical reasons. There were two motives for the move away from reliance on mass assemblies. The 1636 decision allowing for proxies was tied explicitly to the need for a few freemen to stay home to protect "the safty of their towne." The same rationale was offered for the 1638 decision, with the "Courte, takeing into serious consideration the greate danger & damage that may accrue to the state by all the free-mens leaveing their plantations to come to the place of elections" (*RGC*, vol. I 1853, 166, 188). The second reason was the challenging dynamics of lawmaking by large bodies. According to Winthrop, the governor observed that "the number of freemen was supposed to be (as in like corporations) so few, as they might well join in making laws; but now they were grown to so great a body, as it was not possible for them to make or execute laws, but they must choose others for that purpose" (*WJ*, vol. I 1908, 122). An early rendering of Massachusetts history blended these explanations, arriving at the apt conclusion "that this representative body was a thing of necessity" (Hutchinson 1765, 36).

A slightly different sequence of events unfolded with Plymouth's General Court, a body that, like its Massachusetts counterpart, also met several times a year. Although executive and judicial powers were vested in the hands of the governor and a small group of elected assistants, it was initially specified that "the lawes . . . be made onely by the ffreemen." The first hint of a representative body came in a 1636 decision to expand the number of assistants by eight new members from three towns, to act "as Comittees for the whole body of this Comon weale," with the word *committees* meaning "representatives." The major structural change came two years later, again for practical reasons: "Wheras Complaint hath bine made that the ffreemen were put to many Inconveniencyes and great expences by theire Continewall attendances att the Courts It is therefore enacted by the Court and the Authoritie thereof for the ease of the severall townes of this Gou'ment; that every towne shall make Choise of two of theire freemen and the towne of Plymouth of foure to bee Comittes or Deputies to joyne with the bench to enact and make all such lawes and ordinances as shalbee Judged to bee good and wholsome." Freemen, however, were still expected to attend the annual elections court. In 1649, the General Court eased this requirement for one community on the colony's periphery: "It is enacted that the towne of Rehoboth shall have liberty yearely to make choice of 2 freemen of their inhabitants to be assistant[s]." The privilege was shortly thereafter extended to all Plymouth towns, making the assembly a full-fledged representative body (*RCNP* 1861, 6, 11, 55, 59, 91).

Developments along much the same lines occurred elsewhere in New England. The three original Connecticut towns were settled by Massachusetts transplants. Their earlier experiences informed the approach they took to government in the new colony. The first General Court with representatives from each town was held in 1637. In January 1639 the system was elaborated in the Fundamental Orders, which stated, "Wyndsor, Hartford and Wethersfield shall have power . . . to send fower of their freemen as their deputyes to every Generall Courte." The orders said that these elected representatives "shall have the power of the whole Towne to give their voats and alowance to all such lawes and orders as may be for the publike good, and unto wch the said Townes are to be bownd" (*PRCC* 1850, 9, 22–24).

In New Haven, a 1639 "generall meeting of all the free planters" convened to contemplate the sort of governmental structure they should adopt. They arrived at a representational system, relying in part on Bible passages—among them Deuteronomy 1:13, "Take you wise men, and understanding, and known among your tribes, and I will make them rulers over you." Accordingly, the planters reached a "foundamentall agreem^{t}" that only church members could be free burgesses and only free burgesses could "chuse among them sleves" officials to exercise "the power of transacting all publique civill affayres." Unlike the other early New England colonies, New Haven's representatives were given a broad, trusteelike charge rather than one associated with a delegate perspective. They were told, "[T]he worde of God shall be the onely rule to be attended unto in ordering the affayres of government in this plantatio[n]." Deputies were chosen and the first General Court held a few months later. Attendance at the annual election court was mandatory for the freemen until 1643, when "for the ease of those free burgesses, especially in the more remote plantatio[n] s," proxy voting was permitted (*ATR* 1917, 212, 240, 484; *RCNH* 1857, 13–17, 20–21, 113).

The rise of a representative assembly in Rhode Island occurred several years later than in the other early New England colonies. Perhaps because of that lag, the assembly's development phase was, by comparison, compressed. A 1647 meeting at which "the major parte of the Colonie was present" decided that one week prior to any General Court each of the colony's four towns would "chuse a Committee for the Transaction of the affaires there." It was agreed "that six men of each Towne shall be the number of the Committee premised, and to be freely chosen." At the same time they decreed freemen would not have to attend the election court, allowing that "such as go not, may send their votes sealed." This system was declared to be "Democraticall; that is to say, a Government held by ye free and voluntarie consent of all, or the greater parte of the free Inhabitants." Problems with this structure quickly developed, however, leading Newport and Portsmouth to elect a separate assembly from the one chosen by Providence and Warwick. It would take several years before a single assembly composed of representatives from all four towns reemerged (*RCRI* 1856, 147, 149, 156, 233–35, 245, 262–64, 268, 277–78).

How Rhode Island's early representative system was intended to work in practice was made clear by actions at the local level. The Providence town meeting convened to select its first set of representatives—Roger Williams was the "Moderatour"—sent them to the assembly "ffirst, to Acte, and Voate for us . . . as if we our selves were in person" (*ERTPr*, vol. XV 1899, 9–10). Portsmouth issued similar charges, authorizing its representatives to "act in . . . All such matters as shalbe presented as thay shall Judg to bee for the good of the Collonie with full power as if the towne were present" (*ERTPo* 1901, 62, 64, 67). The unambiguous expectation was that the representatives' interests and votes were to mirror those of the people they represented.

Mid-Atlantic Hybrids

The Virginia and New England representational models were blended in two mid-Atlantic colonies. The call for Maryland's first official assembly in 1638 made representation optional: "and to give free power & liberty to . . .

the said freemen either to be p[rese]nt at the said assembly if they so please; or otherwise to elect and nominate such and so many persons as they or the major part of them so assembled shall agree upon to be the deputies or burgesses for the said freemen, in their name and steed." Over 20 representatives responded to their election summons and appeared at the initial assembly meeting. But, because it was considered a general assembly of the freemen, after the representatives' elections were formally acknowledged, "Then was proclaymed, that all freemen omitted in the writ of summons, that would clayme a voyce in this g[en]rall assembly, should come & make their clayme." The offer was immediately accepted: "Whereupon clayme was made by John Robinson, carpent[r] & was admitted." He was later joined by other freemen who for one reason or another desired to participate. Thus, "Came John Langford of the [Island] of Kent, . . . who had given a voice in the choice of Robert Philpott gent to be one of the Burgesses for the freemen of that Iland; and desired to revoke his voice and to be personally p[rese]nt in the Assembly; and was admitted" (*AM*, vol. I 1883, 1–8). During the session some 90 different individuals participated. More than half were gentlemen or planters, but among the others were two more carpenters, five mariners, three priests, a brick mason, and a cooper (Streeter 1876, 57–61).

The assembly's operations were further complicated by the use of proxies. A freeman who did not wish to participate gave his proxy to a representative to act on his behalf. Among the proxies held by elected member Richard Garnett was one from freeman Richard Lustheed. After a few meetings it was recorded that "Richard Lustheed, desired to revoke his proxie; and was admitted and made Rob[t] Clerke his proxie." Not surprisingly, with elected members holding proxies for various freemen and with those proxies being shifted among members or withdrawn in favor of a freeman's personal participation, decision making was complicated. One vote on whether some proposed laws should be read again or considered immediately found 4 members "being in all, 18 voices: wth their proxies" wanting another reading losing out to 7 members "being in all 33 voices" who wanted an immediate vote. The proposed laws were then voted down, being backed by 2 members "being 14 voices" and "denied by all the rest of the Assembly; being 37 voices" (*AM*, vol. I 1883, 4, 8–9, 11).

Proxies proved controversial. A Jesuit missionary informed Lord Baltimore, "Others complaine very much that by the many Proxies w[ch] the Governor, M[r] Lugar, and there instruments had gotten, they did what they would, w[th]out any restraints at all." He went on to vent his fear that "noe man shall . . . never be sure of what he hath, but he that canne git most proxis in every assembly shall dispose of any mans estate that he pleaseth"

(*Calvert Papers* 1889, 160–61, 164). Still, proxies continued to be used off and on for ten years.

Maryland's proprietor attempted to avoid the chaos induced by allowing an ever changing roster of members and proxies by issuing a request that each community "chuse from amongst themselves two or more discreet honest men to be their deputies or Burgesses during the next assembly." But that assembly's elected members could not resist appeals from aggrieved freemen. Consequently, "Cuthbert Fennick claimed a Voice as not assenting to the Election of Saint Marys Burgesses and was admitted." Another freeman was admitted after making the same contention. The assembly later passed an act restricting participation to those who were elected, and several years later the journals reveal that a freeman "demanding to have voice in his own person was Refused" (*AM*, vol. I 1883, 27, 32, 74–75, 105). Not until the late 1640s did the assembly fully jettison the trappings of a freemen's body and complete its transformation into a representative body (Jordan 1987, 20–21; *AM*, vol. 426 1979, 15–21).

The other hybrid assembly, Pennsylvania's, was not as peculiar as Maryland's. The colony's 1682 frame of government held that "the General Assembly shall or may for the first year consist of all the freemen of and in the said province." After the initial freeman's meeting, "[E]ver after it shall be yearly chosen . . . which number of two hundred shall be enlarged as the country shall increase in people, so as it do not exceed five hundred at any time." This optimism evaporated quickly; a revised frame issued the following year stated that the "Assembly shall consist of thirty six persons, being six out of each county" (*MPCP* 1838, xxvii, xxxv). William Penn's explanation for this developmental sequence was given in a 1684 letter. He wrote, "Only this first time y^t ye Freemen may come in Person. The reason of ye Liberty was ye freeness of ye people & ye apprehension we had in England y^t ye people might meet to chuse in some one place, but considering ye mighty distance they are at, & ye season of ye year, I am of opinion that 12 out of a county, 4 like our English Knights of Shires for ye Provincial councel, & 8 for the assembly, will be a fitt company for our magnitude" (*PA*, second series, vol. VII 1890, 6). Thus, as with the New England colonies, the shift to representative systems in Maryland and Pennsylvania was made for pragmatic reasons.

The Later Colonies and the Return of the Trustee Model

With the exception of Pennsylvania, all the later seventeenth-century assemblies were established as representative bodies from the outset. And their members were directed to focus on the larger interests of the colony. But the story lines behind the assemblies and their developmental paths varied in extraordinary ways.

A 1663 charge in Carolina—a distinction between north and south would take several decades to become formalized—empowered the freeholders or "their deputies or assembly-men, to be by them chosen out of themselves, viz.: two out of every tribe, division, or parish . . . to make their own laws . . . for the common defence of the whole." But the institution anticipated in these instructions, or in a similar set of 1665 instructions, never assembled. In its place a different set of representational assemblies was conceived late in 1665, with the freemen of each of the three counties in the colony (one of which would eventually emerge as North Carolina, the others as South Carolina) directed "to make choice of twelve Deputyes or representatives from amongst themselves." These elected representatives would join with the governor and council of their county "for the makeing of such Lawes Ordinances and Constitutions as shalbe necessary for the present good and welfare of the severall Countyes." It appears that the proprietors saw this assembly as temporary because the same instructions held, "but as soone as Parishes Divisions tribes or distric[ti]ons of ye Countyes are made" the freeholders would vote annually to select representatives. The few surviving records indicate that some sort of assembly met in 1665; possibly another in 1667; and, with greater certainty, one in 1669. How they were chosen is not known (*CRNC*, vol. I 1886, 45, 79–81, 104–6, 167, 183–87; Phillips 1921, 201–3).

We do know that the proprietors continued to tinker with the governmental structure. In 1669 they adopted "The Fundamental Constitution of Carolina," which had been written at their request by John Locke. This document was designed to protect the monarchy's interests and "avoid creating a numerous democracy." Among its provisions was one creating a unicameral assembly to be composed of the proprietors or their deputies, the "Landgraves and Casiques," and "one freeholder out of every precinct, to be chosen by the freeholders of the said precinct." Ostensibly, Locke's system governed the colony for two decades, but effectively it was never put into operation. In 1670 the proprietors confessed that, although they had agreed to Locke's plan, they were not "able at present to putt it full in practise by reason of the want of Landgraves and Cassiques and a sufficient number of people." A makeshift system was adopted instead. The new procedures issued to the "Governor and Councell of Albemarle" required that the four precincts in that county would "elect five freeholders to be their representatives to whom the five persons chosen by us being added and who for the present represent the Nobillity are to be your Assembly." In turn, that assembly would "elect five persons which being joyned to those five deputed by us are to be your Councell." The governor was told "You are by and with the Consent of the Assembly to make such laws as you shall from time to time find necessary, which laws being ratified by you and any three of our five deputys." Several more institutional iterations occurred before the "Grand Assembly of Albemarle" emerged as what we take to be North Carolina's representative assembly in the 1690s (*CSP* 1889, 51–52; 1893, 472–73; 1896, 323–24; 1901, 565–66; *CRNC*, vol. I 1886, 181–82, 187–205, 333; vol. II 1886, 852–58; Kammen 1969, 32–34).

Although South Carolina shared a legal taproot with North Carolina— everything discussed in relation to North Carolina up to 1670 applies equally to both—representation in it sprouted in a different fashion. Early efforts to establish the mandated representational system in the south foundered on a lack of population to represent. A 1670 letter to London authorities claimed that in 1669 the governor "would have cal'd a Parliam[t] amongst us allthough wee could not make 20 ffreemen in the Colony, besides the Councell . . . had not wee . . . and some few of the Councell vigorously withstood it." Having agreed "the Number of ffreehould[rs] in the Colony nott neere sufficient to Electe a Parliam[t]," shortly thereafter the governor and council called the colony's freemen together and read to them two orders they alone had promulgated to deal with pressing matters "for ye better keeping of the Sabbath day, & for preserving our [live]stock this yeare." The orders were not well received, and in response "some hot spirited persons . . . spurned at all order & good Governm[t]." The leading "hot spirited" person, William Owen, argued "that w[th]out a Parliam[t] noe such orders ought, or could passe." Owen then "p'swaded the people, to Elect a Parliam[t] among themselves, w[ch] they did." He convinced his fellow colonists to take such a radical step by warning them "that the great seale of the Province nott beinge in the Collony, whatever land they had or should take up, & their Improvem[ts] therein, would not bee assuered to them, butt might bee taken away att pleasure, unlesse a parliam[t] be forth[wth] chosen to p'vent the same" (*CSP* 1893, 144–45; *Collections of the South Carolina Historical Society*, vol. V 1897, 36, 176–77, 202–4, 290–96, 322–24).

Known today as "Owen's Parliament," this unofficial 15-member body could be considered South Carolina's first representative assembly. But it did not survive. The governor subsequently convinced enough freemen that their land titles were safe and "that hee did intend to sum'ons the people for the Election of a parliam[t] when opp'tunity did serve or necessity of makeing lawes did requier" that Owen lost popular support. The governor and council then took revenge by ordering that Owen and one of his collaborators "bee & deemed incapable of bearing any Publick office." By 1671 a legal assembly had been formed. But, as with North Carolina, it would take two decades for a functioning body to become institutionalized (*CSP* 1901, 567; *Collections of the South Carolina Historical Society*, vol. V 1897, 294; Kammen 1969, 35).

A representative assembly was established in New Jersey at roughly the same time as in the Carolinas. But its evolution took yet another strikingly different path. A 1665 concession—nearly identical to that given Carolina—decreed that the colony's freemen were authorized to "make choice of twelve Deputies or Representatives from amongst themselves." They were to meet with the governor and council "for the making of such Laws, Ordinances, and Constitution as shall be necessary for the present good and wellfare of the said Province" (*Grants, Concessions* 1758, 15). In 1668 Governor Carteret issued a proclamation calling for the first meeting of the assembly and asking the freeholders in each town "To make Choice and appoint Two able men that are freeholders and dwellers W[th]in the said Limits to be your Burgesses and Representatives for you." They were to meet with the governor and council to "advise in the Management of the affaires that are needful and Necessary for the Orderly & Well Governing of the Said Province." Great weight was attached to this directive; members were admonished that "you may not faile as You and Every of You Will answere your Contempt to the Contrary" (*DRNJ*, vol. I 1880, 57).

But neither the colony nor its representative assembly developed smoothly. Political battles over landownership rights prompted a split. The existing colonial government morphed into the government of East Jersey, while a new governing structure was instituted in West Jersey. In West Jersey, the proprietors' 1677 Concessions and Agreements proposed that the new province be divided into 100 "proprieties" with the "Inhabitants, Freeholders, and Proprietors" to "choose one Proprietor or Freeholder for each respective Propriety . . . to be Deputies, Trustees or Representatives," thereby creating a 100-member assembly. In a novel twist, the proprietors and freeholders were to give their elected representatives "their Instructions at large, to represent their Grievances, or for the improvement of the Province." Further, "the Persons chosen, do . . . covenant and oblige themselves to Act nothing in that Capacity but what shall tend to the fit Service and Behoof of those that send and employ them, and that in case of failer of Trust, or breach of Covenant, that they be questioned upon complaint made, in that or the next Assembly, by any of their respective Electors" (*Grants, Concessions* 1758, 404–6). This guidance suggests that the proposed assembly would employ a delegate model of representation. Although the Concessions and Agreements were never put into effect, it appears that they influenced both the West Jersey assembly that did eventually meet and, because of William Penn's involvement in putting together both documents, Pennsylvania's Frame of Government (Kammen 1969, 38–39).

East Jersey revisited its assembly structure in a 1683 "Fundamental Constitutions." It was proposed that there would be a "great Council" consisting of 24 proprietors or their proxies and "One Hundred Forty four to be chosen by the Freemen of the Province." But the colony was not large enough to support such a massive body; consequently, it was decided that "at present Four and Twenty shall be chosen for the eight Towns that are at present in being, and Eight and Forty for the County, making together Seventy two." An inventive aspect of this plan was the institution of term limits: "[T]he first chosen shall remain for three Years, and they that go out shall not be capable to come in again for two Years after, and therefore they shall not be put in the Ballot in Elections for that Year" (*Grants, Concessions* 1758, 154). It does not appear that these provisions were ever put into effect. In any event, the representational characteristics of assemblies in both Jerseys continued to evolve before they were reunited in 1702.

Unlike the other colonies, all of which got representative assemblies soon after they fell under English control, New York had to wait several decades before gaining one. The delay was not because there had been no experience with elected representative bodies under Dutch rule. In fact, although no ongoing assembly had been established, on several occasions temporary representative consultative groups were convened, notably "the twelve men," "the eight men," and "the nine men." And in 1653 and 1664, "Landtdags" with elected representatives were called (Brodhead 1853, 570–75, 728–31; *Documents Relating to the History of the Early Colonial Settlements* 1883, 109, 112; *Narratives of New Netherlands* 1909, 214, 226, 327, 333, 341). Thus, the Dutch inhabitants of New York were familiar with the concept of representation.

Once the English took over the colony there was an initial move toward establishing a representative body. In early 1665, the newly installed deputy governor called for a "Gen^all Meeting of Deputyes at Hempsteed" on Long Island. He instructed that in each town or precinct two deputies be "chosen by the major part of the freemen only, which is to be understood, of all Persons rated according to their Estates, whether *English*, or *Dutch*." This assembly was designed to reduce any friction generated by the transition from one governing regime to another and to "Settle good and knowne Laws within this government for the future." Accordingly, 34 deputies representing 17 communities met and declared their support for English rule (*DRNY*, vol. III 1853, 91; vol. XIV 1883, 564–65). The assembly, however, was only a one-time event.

The duke of York, who controlled the colony as its proprietor, resisted the creation of a permanent representative institution. In a 1675 letter to the governor, the duke wrote, "First y^n, touching Generall Assemblyes wch ye people there seeme desirous of in imita[ti]on of their neighbor Colonies, I thinke you have done well to discourage any mo[ti]on of y^t kind." He went on to note that his instructions had never allowed for calling such a body and that he believed one was not "necessary for ye ease or redresse of any grievance y^t may happen." Early the following year, in another letter to the governor, the Duke expressed what we may take to be his real reservation. He started by noting, "I have formerly writt to you touching Assemblyes in those conntreys and have since observed what severall of your lattest letters hint about that matter." With, from a historical perspective, great prescience, the Duke went on to object that unless "what qualifica[ti]ons are usuall and proper to such Assemblyes" were imposed, "I cannot but suspect they would be of dangerous consequence, nothing being more knowne then the aptness of such bodyes to assume to themselves many priviledges wch prove destructive to, or very oft disturbe, the peace of ye governm^t wherein they are allowed" (*DRNY*, vol. III 1853, 230, 235).

Public pressure for an assembly built, however. By 1681 unhappiness with New York's situation was such that the colony's top administrator reported to London that the existing governmental structure "is much disliked by the People who generally cry out for an Assembly" (*Journal of the Legislative Council* 1861, ix). At roughly the same time, financial problems caused the duke to eye the colony as a revenue source. A 1682 letter to the acting governor written on the duke's behalf by a high official said that, although assurances could not be given, "I may hint to you y^t we believe his R^{ll} H^s will condescend to ye desires of y^t Colony in granting y^m equall priviledges, in chooseing an Assembly." The following month the duke confirmed his intention to allow New York to enjoy, as "other planta[ti]ons in America doe enjoy, . . . in chooseing of an Assembly." Within a year, instructions were issued to the governor authorizing the calling of an assembly "of all the Freeholders, by the p^{r}sons who they shall choose to rep^{r}sent y^m." Together with the governor and council the representatives were to determine "what laws are fitt and necessary to be made and established for the good weale and governem^t of the said Colony and its Dependencyes, and all of the inhabitants thereof" (*DRNY*, vol. III 1853, 317, 331). Once more a trustee model of representation was the goal.

The body that met in response to this call was notable for three reasons. First, the electoral system used to elect its members was mixed. In most communities the freemen were directed to meet and choose their representatives. But the freemen in two larger communities, Long Island and Esopus (Ulster County), were instructed to, as in the language directed to communities in the latter stated, "chose foure of themselves in Town, as a Committee for themselves, & those four out of each Town to meet at the Sessions howse, then to chose two to be Representatives for *Esopus*." This mechanism is a form of electoral college. Second, among the communities directed to elect and send a representative were "*Martins* [Martha's] *Vineyard, Nantucket, Elizabeth Island* & all other Islands from the Eastward of *Long Island* to *Nantucket Shoals*" (*DRNY*, vol. XIV 1883, 770–71). Thus the assembly's geographic reach was impressive.

Finally, and most important, the assembly passed a historic measure, *The Charter of Libertys and Privileges granted by his Royal Highness to the Inhabitants of New-York and its Dependencies* (Brodhead 1871, 659–61). The measure contained a bold assertion of the assembly's legislative powers. Although it initially appeared to meet with the Crown's approval—the colony came under royal control with the duke's accession to the throne—it was eventually overturned, and in new instructions to the governor, the assembly was abolished (*DRNY*, vol. III 1853, 357, 377–78). In the time it took to send the laws passed by the first session of the initial assembly to England and receive the official response to them, another session of the first assembly had been held and the second elected. But from 1686 to 1690 no assembly met and all laws adopted were promulgated by the governor and council. The lack of a representative assembly contributed to Leisler's Rebellion, a movement that took control of much of the colony. Leisler established an elected assembly—a "Revolutionary Assembly" in London's eyes—which met in two sessions and passed some laws. But its representative credentials were dubious; one contemporary account stated, "Suffolke County would not meddle with it, from the other Counties came Representatives onely chosen by a few people." By 1691 the Crown had regained control over the colony. But the message behind the unrest had been received. Indeed, when first alerted to the rebellion in 1689, instructions had been handed to a new governor, allowing him to "call generall Assemblies of the Inhabitants being Freeholders within your Government, according to the usage of our other Plantations in America" (*CSP* 1901, 250, 328; *DRNY*, vol. III 1853, 623–24, 717; *Journal of the Legislative Council* 1861, xv–xxv). A representative assembly was elected in 1691 and met that year, and one continued to meet under these instructions until the Revolution.

Because New Hampshire was cleaved out of Massachusetts, the creation of its representational system differed from those of its contemporaries. New Hampshire towns had been represented in the Massachusetts assembly more or less continuously since 1641. In the year before it became a separate colony, four New Hampshire towns had sent representatives, one of whom served as the speaker (*DRNH*, vol. I 1867, 369–72). Thus, upon its removal from "the shadow" of Massachusetts government, there was a tradition of representation on which the new colony could draw (*CSP* 1896, 381, 557–58).

The initial call for a general assembly took that experience into account. The colonists were told to employ "such rules and methods (as to the persons who are to chuse their Deputies and ye time and place of meeting) as they shall judge most convenient." Working with the governor and council, the assembly was instructed to adopt "such Acts, Laws, and Ordinances, as may most tend to ye establishing them in . . . good Governm^t" (*DRNH*, vol. I 1867, 379). This charge indicates that New Hampshire's assembly was pointed toward a trustee model, counter to its experiences under Massachusetts' delegate orientation.

Any hope that the development of a new representative assembly with roots in an established one would go smoothly was quickly dashed. Even from the outset the fledgling body's representative character was suspect. The writs issued for the first election named the specific individuals deemed qualified to vote (Belknap, vol. I 1831, 91). A 1681 "Narrative on the proceedings in New Hampshire," complained that the council "issued summons for the choice of Deputies for a General Assembly, but published also an order forbidding any men to vote but such as they nominated." The consequences of this edict were profound: "In towns of two hundred houses, not twenty men were allowed to vote. The people complained, but were denied, and threatened with punishment for disobedience. So the Council in effect chose the Deputies." To make matters worse, on several occasions during the 1680s the New Hampshire council and governor enacted laws without the consent or even the participation of any assembly. In a 1684 letter to London officials, the colony's governor and council admitted, "Though in obedience to your orders we have called an Assembly, we have not thought it prudent or safe to let them sit" (*CSP* 1898, 110–11, 640; *LNH*, vol. one 1904, 77–142). A representative assembly in New Hampshire would not become institutionalized until the 1690s.

Conclusion

The stories behind the establishment of assemblies in the colonies are important for two reasons. First, they dispel any notion that a single model was imposed across the colonies. If there had been, the assemblies would have looked alike and once they were in place there would have been little reason for them to suffer any discontinuities. But the historical record reveals that they were established at different times with different mechanisms put in place, and their developmental histories diverged dramatically.

It also is critical to appreciate that the rise of representation was largely driven by practical rather than philosophical reasons. This fact was appreciated at the time. A 1770 analysis of representation in the colonies stated, "It will, I presume, be readily admitted, that the Device of enacting Laws by Representation, owes its Origin to the Inconvenience of deliberating on public Affairs in numerous popular Assemblies. The unweildly Multitude of Legislators when collectively met, and the Difficulty of preserving among them the Order and Regularity requisite for the Dispatch of Business, experimentally convinced the People of the Expediency of delegating their Authority to a competent Number of Deputies" (*NYG* 1770c). This matters because it allowed alternative views of representation to take root.

The second reason this story is important is that it demonstrates that the presence of representative assemblies became obligatory. The evidence for this claim is more extensive than just the stories given to this point. There were additional representative assemblies in the colonies established during the seventeenth century. They were formed in seven other English colonies that did not eventually become part of the United States (Kammen 1969). But even within the territory that was later integrated into the country, other representative bodies were created. The governmental status of the territory partly encompassed today by Maine was unsettled until the final quarter of the century. In the 1640s, the freeholders there elected two deputies per county to a representative body that was fashioned the General Assembly of the Province of Lygonia. That assembly disappeared by 1650, but it was replaced a decade later by an assembly for the province of Maine. That body continued in existence until Maine fell under Massachusetts' control (*CSP* 1880, 90–91; Folsom 1830, 60–61, 146; *History of York County* 1880, 26–27, 46–47; Williamson 1832, 281, 303, 394, 430). Mainers were then represented in that colony's General Court. The notion that a representative assembly was required for the governance of any new polity was so well established that when in the early part of the eighteenth century a "Royall Province of Georgeia" was proposed for the "lands and islands between Nova Scotia and Maine" it was to include a "Lower House to consist of freeholders annually chosen by freeholders and other inhabitants" (*CSP* 1930a, 308).

Along the same lines, when the colony of Georgia was floundering toward the end of the colonial era, its trustees turned to the same solution that their predecessors in Virginia had looked to more than a century before: "That an Assembly be form'd." Because lawmaking powers were vested in the trustees, the assembly they created could "only propose, debate, and represent to the Trustees What shall appear to them to be for the Benefit, not only of each particular Settlement, but of the Province in general." Seats in this body were apportioned on a roughly proportional basis. It is best remembered for the curious qualifications required for those to be chosen as representatives: in 1751 a member had to have "One hundred Mulberry trees planted and properly fenc'd upon every fifty Acres he possesses," while by 1753 a member was to have the requisite proportion of white servants and black slaves, "at least one Female in his Family instructed in the Art of reeling Silk," and land that produced 15 pounds of silk for every 50 acres (*CRSG*, vol. II 1904, 498–500). This body did not last long; the trustees surrendered their charter in 1752, and in 1754 the Crown appointed a governor who was given the authority to call a regular assembly, which he quickly did.

But arguably the strongest evidence of the power of representation came when New England colonists lost their assemblies during the Andros administration in the late 1680s. In strenuous terms, they pushed back. Missives were sent to the Crown, protesting that being "without an Assembly, seemed grievous to many here" and requesting "That no lawes may be made nor mony raised there, without the Consent of a generall Assembly, as it is in the other plantations" (*CSP* 1901, 212–13; *Andros Tracts*, vol. third 1874, 137–38). The colonists clearly believed they had a right to representation. But what that meant in practice still had to be sorted out.

THREE

Who Could Vote and Who Could Represent

With the rise of representation, two critical questions had to be addressed. First, who could vote for the assembly? Second, who could serve in it? Standards for voting and service were largely lifted from English practices but applied loosely. Who could vote and serve differed across the colonies. Over time qualifications were generally tightened. Paradoxically, because of the economic success the colonists enjoyed, tighter standards failed to limit their ability to vote for and serve in the assembly to the same extent similar rules did in the parent country. This difference put Americans on a course toward mass democracy.

Formal Qualifications for Voting

A universal qualification for voting in the colonies and England was that voters had to be male. Women were explicitly forbidden to vote only in a 1699 Virginia law. Statutes specifying that men held the right to vote were adopted in Delaware, Georgia, and South Carolina. In the other colonies, the use of the pronoun *he* or title *freemen* in laws was effectively exclusionary (*LGD* 1763, 119; McKinley 1905, 172, 473–74; *SLSC*, vol. second 1837, 688; *SLV*, vol. III 1823, 172). There were only a few instances in which women voted or even attempted to do so (Clarke 1943, 151; Dinkin 1977, 30).

Another voter qualification found everywhere was the age of majority, which for assembly elections was always set at 21 years, although no age was specified by law in Maryland or New Jersey. The rule in England was the same (Blackstone, vol. I 1771, 173). An effort early in New Hampshire's history to establish 24 years as the voting age was rejected by the Crown (*LNH*, vol. one 1904, 25–26, 45). Even with 21 years being universally accepted, there were occasional claims that those too young were allowed to vote.

The most discriminating voter qualification among males 21 years or older was that of being a freeholder. It was the fundamental standard under English law and a staple in instructions issued to colonial governors (*AM*, vol. VIII 1890, 273; *CSP* 1910b, 671; Labaree 1935, 93; *SLV*, vol. II 1823, 425). The rationale behind it was that only property owners were thought to have a stake in the long-term prosperity of society, and therefore only they should be entitled to vote (Dickinson 2007, 25–26; Pole 1966, 25). But property qualifications actually had an intriguing history. One was first imposed in early-fourteenth-century England as a way to quell the "man-slaughters, riots, batteries, and divisions among the gentlemen" that typically pervaded voting (Stephens, vol. I 1838, 142–43). By the colonial era another rationale had surfaced, with Blackstone (vol. I 1771, 171) asserting, "The true reason of requiring any qualification with regard to property, in voters, is to exclude such persons as are in so mean a situation that they are esteemed to have no will of their own. If these persons had votes, they would be tempted to dispose of them under some undue influence or other." Thus property qualifications were intended to calm elections by only allowing the participation of those who were invested in their communities and considered incorruptible.

Despite its centrality, freehold status was not clearly delineated in many colonies, leaving assemblies to fill in the blanks. Over time requirements requiring specific levels of property, wealth, and taxes paid elaborated it, though not always in a consistent fashion. Thus property qualifications for voting varied both across the colonies and over time within each colony.

In fact freehold status was not initially required in several early colonies. Although the first qualifications for voting in Virginia are not known, it appears that a "manhood" standard was used, meaning that any male who was not an indentured servant could participate. This is implied by the colony's earliest surviving election legislation, a 1646 measure that stated, in reference to a penalty for not voting, "ffreemen being covennt. servants being exempted from the said fine." In 1655 the criterion was tightened so that "all house keepers whether ffreeholders, lease holders, or otherwise tenants, shall only be capeable to elect Burgesses," with an additional proviso that only one person in each household could be deemed the householder, a limitation consistent with English practices. That law held for only one year. Admitting that "we conceive it something hard and unagreeable to reason that any persons shall pay equall taxes and yet have no votes in elections," the assembly reversed itself so that "soe much of the act for choosing Burgesses be repealed as excludes freemen from votes." Another statute enacted two years later confirmed that all freemen were entitled to vote (Blackstone vol. I 1771, 173; *SLV*, vol. I 1809, 334, 403, 412, 475).

Qualifications were again stiffened in 1670. Asserting that "the usuall way of chuseing burgesses by the votes of all persons who haveing served their tyme are ffreemen of this country who haveing little interest in the country doe oftner make tumults at the election to the disturbance of his majesties peace," the assembly drew on English practices to justify its decision that "none but ffreeholders and housekeepers who only are answerable to the publique for the levies shall hereafter have a voice in the election of any burgesses in this country." During Bacon's Rebellion in the mid-1670s, the assembly again eased the franchise by allowing all freemen to vote. After the uprising ended that act was rescinded, and the Crown informed the governor that voting was to be restricted to freeholders (*SLV*, vol. II 1823, 280, 356, 380–81, 425).

Although landholding was now required, no set amount of property was specified. A 1684 law relaxed the interpretation of landholding to include those who held leases "for his owne life, for the life of his wife, or for the life of any other person or persons," allowing them "to vote in Election of Burgesses for the county where such lands, tenements, &c. doe lye." A measure passed 15 years later illuminated the understanding of voting rights, specifying that "no person or persons shall be enabled to give a vote for the election of a burgeses or burgeses to serve in the generall assembly . . . but those who are freeholders in the respective county or towne for which the said burgess or burgesses shall be elected and chosen." Further restrictions were put in place in 1736. Voters were required to have "an estate of freehold . . . in one hundred acres of land, at least, if no settlement be made upon it; or twenty five acres with a house and plantation." Allowances were made for those whose land straddled counties and for town dwellers. Laws to ease landholding requirements were passed in 1762 and 1769 but were rejected by London officials, leaving the 1736 measure in place up to the Revolution (Chandler 1901, 17; *SLV*, vol. III 1823, 26, 172; vol. IV 1820, 475–76).

Qualifications were also tightened over time in other colonies. Maryland's experience was much like Virginia's in that it initially employed a "manhood" standard. As noted in chapter 2, early assembly calls required the colony's freemen to participate in elections. The assembly applied a liberal interpretation of such status. In a 1642 case, "Mr Thomas Weston being called [before the assembly for not voting] pleaded he was no freemen because he had no land nor certain dwelling here." The assembly determined otherwise, and "it was voted that he was a Freeman and as such bound to his appearance by himself or proxie." Maryland's standard was changed around 1670, with election writs requiring "Visible seated Plantations of fifty Acres of Land at the least or Visible personal Estates to the Value of forty Pounds Sterling at the least" if one was to be allowed to vote (*AM*, vol. I 1883, 1, 170; vol. V 1887, 77). Unlike the vacillating sequence of decisions that unfolded in Virginia, this standard held throughout the rest of the colonial era.

In the New England colonies, the focus was on freeman standing, which required admission by the town and colony rather than freeholder status. There, too, standards were tightened over time. Plymouth Colony determined in 1638 that, because each town had to cover the costs of its representatives, "such as are not ffreemen but have taken the Oath of fidelitie and are masters of famylies and Inhabitant of the said Townes as they are to beare their p[ar]t in the charges of their Committees so to have a vote in the choyce of them." Thus, because they were liable to help pay the cost of their town's representatives, nonfreemen taxpayers were allowed to vote for them but not to serve in those positions themselves. In 1669 the standards were toughened, with only "ffreemen or ffreeholders of twenty pounds ratable estate" being allowed to vote (*RCNP* 1861, 31, 223). Connecticut's initial qualification held that "said Deputyes shall be chosen by all that are admitted Inhabitants in the sev[r]all Townes and have taken the oath of fidellity." In 1656 it was specified that the term *inhabitants* "meant only housholders that are one & twenty yeares of age, or have bore office, or have 30 [pounds] estate" (*PRCC* 1850, 23, 293, 331). Rhode Island had the loosest freeholder standard; according to a 1665 royal directive, voting was to apply to "all men of competante estates." In 1723 the colony adopted a more precise qualification, requiring voters to "be a Freeholder of Lands, Tenaments, or Hereditraments, in such Town where he shall be admitted Free, of the Value of *One Hundred Pounds*, or to the Value of *Forty Shillings* per Annum." The 40 shillings income standard was based on English precedent and was used at times in several New England colonies and, briefly, in New York. In a unique twist, the Rhode Island law extended voting rights to a freeholder's eldest son, something allowed in England but nowhere else in America (*Acts and Laws, Connecticut* 1702, 40; *Acts and*

Laws, Rhode-Island 1730, 131; *Charter Granted* 1692, 7; *CLNY*, vol. I 1894, 245, 405; McKinley 1905, 454–55, 478–79; *RCRI* 1857, 110).

There were other differences in who was allowed to vote across the colonies. In South Carolina, nonfreeholders who paid taxes were given the right. A 1704 law required voters to have no less than a freehold of 50 acres of land or the value of ten pounds "in money, goods, chattels or rents." In 1721 a measure passed keeping the 50-acre freehold standard but also qualifying anyone who had paid 20 shillings in taxes in the current or previous year. By 1759 the landholding qualification had been increased to a freehold estate of 100 acres on which taxes had been paid the previous year, while the taxpaying standard was lowered to "the sum of ten shillings proclamation money for his own proper tax the preceding year" (*SLSC*, vol. second 1837, 249; vol. third 1838, 136; vol. fourth 1838, 99). The fact that this approach was contrary to royal instructions was noted by South Carolina council members, one of whom called it a source "of great Inconveniences," and by the Board of Trade, which encouraged the governor to get the law changed (Greene 1961, 76, 80). But it was never altered.

As towns gained representation the question of voter qualifications for their residents was raised. Land requirements put in place to determine qualified voters in rural areas did not translate well for those who dwelled in towns. Thus separate but comparable standards were devised. The law granting Williamsburg, Virginia, the right to send a burgess held that "no person shall vote . . . unless he has an estate of freehold in one whole lot of land within the said city; and that there be standing upon the said lot, a house of such dimensions as is required by law, for saving such lot, in tenantable repair, at the time of giving such vote." Joint ownership rights were recognized with the proviso that "no more than one vote shall be given, or allowed, in right of such freehold, and that only in case all the parties interested, can agree; otherwise no vote shall be allowed to be given" (*SLV*, vol. V 1819, 205). Given different specifications for the required lot sizes across Virginia's towns, what was needed to qualify to vote varied by community (McKinley 1905, 39). Lot size was an indirect measure of wealth and therefore akin to landholdings, and it was also used as a standard in several other colonies. North Carolina's law setting the qualification for voters in the town of Brunswick held that "every Tenant of any Stone or habitable House of [20 by 16 feet] Dimensions . . . within the Bounds of the said Town, who at the Day of Election, and for Three Months next before, inhabited such House, shall be intitled to vote in the Election for the Representative of the said Town" (*CAAA* 1764, 201). Some colonies set explicit wealth standards for their town dwellers. Pennsylvania required Philadelphia voters to have "a freehold estate, or be worth fifty pounds, clear personal estate within the same city" (*SLP*, vol. II 1896, 213–14). Similarly, South Carolina's law required "houses, lands or town lots or parts thereof, of the value of sixty pounds proclamation money" on which taxes had been paid the previous year for those who lived in towns with representation (*SLSC*, vol. fourth 1838, 99).

Voters were required to be citizens, which was the expectation under English common law (McKinely 1905, 474–75). In Delaware voting was limited to "natural-born Subjects of *Great Britain*" or those who had been naturalized in England, Delaware, or Pennsylvania (*LGD* 1763, 119). That language had been lifted from Pennsylvania's election law (*SLP*, vol. II 1896, 25). North Carolina's 1715 election law prohibited those "born out of the Allegiance of his Majesty" from voting in assembly elections (*CRNC*, vol. II 1886, 214). But even when it was not directly incorporated into statutes, voters were always expected to be citizens, and assemblies passed both individual (or private) bills and general laws to naturalize aliens and thereby grant them voting status.

In some colonies voters were required to belong to certain faiths or churches. To vote in Connecticut one had to be a freeman, and the freeman's oath testified to one's religious affiliation. Thus a voter had to be a member of the Congregational (or Puritan) church (*PRCC* 1850, 23, 25, 62–63). Massachusetts instituted a similar law (*RGC*, vol. I 1853, 87). So, too, did New Haven. In 1643 the town of Milford was discovered to have admitted as freemen "six planters who are nott in church fellowshipp," thereby allowing them to participate in elections. The assembly's solution was to prohibit the six planters from serving as deputies or from voting for members of the upper house. They could, however, continue to "vote in the electio[n] of deputyes" as long as "wch deputyes so to be chosen & sent, shall allwayes be church members" (*RCNH* 1857, 110–11). In 1650 the Plymouth assembly decided that anyone attending a church established without the approbation of the colony's government "shalbe suspended from having any voyce in towne meetings," thereby disenfranchising them (*RCNP* 1861, 57).

Several colonies passed measures to specifically exclude adherents of certain faiths. In 1663 Massachusetts adopted a measure stating that "all persons, Quakers or others, wch refuse to attend upon the publick worship of God established here . . . whither freemen or others . . . hereby are made uncapable of voting . . . during theire obstinate persisting in such wicked ways" (*RGC*, vol. IV, part II 1854, 88). Plymouth also prohibited

Quakers from having a "voat in choise of publicke officers" (*RCNP* 1861, 101). A 1699 Virginia statute held that that "no . . . recusant convict being freeholders shall be enabled to give a vote or have a voice in the election of burgeses," thereby preventing Catholics from voting (*SLV*, vol. III 1823, 172). South Carolina adopted provisions mandating that only those "professing the Christian religion" could qualify as a voter, leaving out Jewish freeholders among others. Catholics were added to the colony's excluded list by a 1759 election law that narrowed the language to those "professing the Protestant religion" (*SLSC*, vol. second 1837, 688; vol. fourth 1838b, 99). They were disenfranchised in New York by a 1701 law holding that "no Papist or Popish Recusant" would be allowed to vote for representatives (*CLNY*, vol. 1 1894, 453). In 1737 the New York assembly further tightened the franchise when it not only tossed out votes cast by Jews in a contested race but went on to resolve that "it is the unanimous Opinion of this House, That they ought not to be admitted to vote for Representatives in this Province" (*JVNY* 1737, 32). Even religiously tolerant Rhode Island eventually restricted the franchise on the basis of faith with legislation limiting those who could be admitted to freeman status, and therefore entitled to vote, to "all men professing Christianity . . . [who] are obedient to the civil magistrate though of different judgements in Religious Affairs (Roman Catholics only excepted)." That wording surfaced in 1719 and was enforced in 1730 (McKinley 1905, 451–52; Rider 1889).

Race was first mentioned in a 1715 North Carolina law stating that "no Negro Mullatto or Indians shall be capable of voting for Members of Assembly" (*CRNC*, vol. II 1886, 214–15). South Carolina followed suit two years later, limiting the right to vote to "every white man (and no other)" (*SLSC*, vol. third 1838, 3). A 1723 Virginia measure used North Carolina's wording, while Georgia later adopted South Carolina's language (Bishop 1893, 281; *SLV*, vol. IV 1820, 133–34).

Still others were excluded from voting. South Carolina's 1717 law held that "no servant for a term of years . . . nor any seafaring or other transient man, who has neither freehold nor is liable to pay tax . . . shall be deemed capable of voting, or electing a representative" (*SLSC*, vol. third 1838, 3). That, too, followed on an earlier North Carolina law that banned voting by persons "not made free" (*CRNC*, vol. II 1886, 214–15). Drunkenness and fornication were grounds for disenfranchisement in Massachusetts (*RGC*, vol. I 1853, 112; vol. IV, part II 1854, 143). Plymouth not only prevented voting by freeholders guilty of those two violations but also by those deemed "lyers," "swearers," "abettors and entertainers of Quakers," or "a manifest opposer of the lawes of the govment" (*RCNP* 1855a, 132; 1855b,

167, 176–77, 189). Some colonies preferred to accentuate the positive. A 1659 Connecticut statute held that those admitted as freemen, and therefore eligible to vote, should be of "honest and peaceable conversation." The admitted goal of this provision was "to pʳvent tumult and trouble at the Court of Election" (*PRCC* 1850, 331).

Although exclusions generally targeted relatively small slices of the population, when enforced they could swing elections. In 1654 Maryland officials were told to call an assembly "For which Shall be disabled to give any Vote or to be Elected Members" anyone who "doe profess the Roman Catholick Religion." Rebelling against this requirement, two members elected from "St. Maries and Potomack County" refused to swear their subjection to the government, choosing instead to vacate their seats. The impact of the decision not to allow Catholics to vote was demonstrated by the results of the following special election in which the new members were "Chosen Burgesses by the unanimous Consent of the ffreemen Inhabiting the said County." Both of the newly elected members "freely offered themselves to the Service of the Commonwealth in this Assembly" (*AM*, vol. I 1883, 339–40; vol. III 1885, 313).

Because voting rights were usually attached to property ownership, laws could be written so a freeholder could cast votes in more than one place, possibly even in more than one colony, assuming that he met the qualification standards in each jurisdiction. In 1684 Virginia passed a measure confirming that "it is the undoubted Right of every [per]son who holds Lands tenements . . . to vote in Elec[ti]on of Burgesses for yᵗ County where such Lands . . . doe lye (*JHB 1659/60–* 1914, 234). Both New Hampshire and New York had similar laws (*CLNY*, vol. I 1894, 405; *JVNY* 1737, 32–33; *LNH*, vol. two 1913, 402–3).

A length of residency requirement was established in some colonies. South Carolina's 1704 election law required voters to "reside and dwell in the county and precinct for which he doth vote for, or pretend to choose members of Assembly, by the space of three months before the dates of the writts for election." In 1716 the required length of residency was increased to six months. A 1745 measure motivated by a belief that "it may be of evil consequence to give a right to any person or persons to vote for Representatives of the people of this Province in Assembly, who are late residents" extended the requirement to one year. Although that law was disallowed by the Privy Council, a one-year residency requirement was later reimposed (*SCG* 1748; *SLSC*, vol. second 1837, 249, 688; vol. third 1838, 656–57; vol. fourth 1838, 99). North Carolina required voters to be residents and taxpayers for one year prior to an election. That requirement was later relaxed; to vote a freeholder had to be an inhabitant of the colony for six months and have possessed 50 acres of land for at least three months prior to the election (*CAAA* 1764, 199; *CRNC*, vol. II 1886, 214–15). Georgia instituted a six-month residency requirement along with 50 acres of land "in his own right" in the district where the election was being held (Bishop 1893, 281). The most stringent residency requirements were imposed in Delaware and Pennsylvania, each of which required a voter to live in the colony for two years prior to gaining the right to vote (*LGD* 1763, 119; *SLP*, vol. II 1896, 213).

London officials approved of residency requirements. A 1693 South Carolina elections bill was rejected by the proprietors largely on the question of residency, with their veto message stating, "We think that electors ought to be freeholders and as the Act does not even provide that electors should be resident, thus possibly giving every pirate a vote, we disallow this Act" (*CSP* 1903, 85). Such requirements were another device intended to allow only colony stakeholders to vote.

Contemporary Assessments of Assembly Voters

Even with qualifications tightened over the years, colonial executives held low opinions of the voter pool. Lieutenant Governor Alexander Spotswood of Virginia, a well-born Englishman, was the most strident on this score, complaining that the loose rules governing voter qualifications in his colony "allows to everyone tho but just out of the condition of a servant that can but purchase half an acre of land, an equal vote with the men of the best estates in the countrey." He warned London officials of the political consequences of this lapse: "I must always have to do w'th ye Representatives of ye Vulgar People . . . for so long as half an Acre of Land, (which is of small value in this Country,) qualifys a man to be an Elector, the meaner sort of People will ever carry ye Elections" and "the Votes and humours of the lowest Mob do at present decide who shall be the Representatives in Assembly." Time in the colony did not soften Spotswood's views. Toward the end of his stay he complained that "the bulk of electors of Assemblymen, consists of the meaner sort of people" (*CSP* 1926, 70, 277; 1928, 318; *OLAS*, vol. II 1885, 50, 124).

Spotswood was not alone in his low opinion of colonial voters. Pennsylvania's powerful secretary, James Logan, wrote to William Penn that he expected "little good from the present representatives till another election" because "the honest being so much out-voted by the men of deep designs or shallow sense" (*CBWP*, vol. II 1872, 2). Thomas Hutchinson, a leading Massachusetts figure, regretted that of those among the "needy part of the province . . . One of their votes will go as far in popular elections as one of the most opulent" (Hutchinson 1767, 394).

Their assessments were accurate. According to recent estimates, up to 80 percent of white males 21 years and older may have held the franchise (Zagarri 2000, 665). This was a far higher percentage than in the parent country, where perhaps 20 percent of adult males were eligible (Dickinson 2007, 20; Morgan 1988, 175; Williamson 1960, 38–39). The difference was not driven by appreciably lower standards in the colonies; rather it was a product of the plentiful cheap land and opportunities for economic success the colonists enjoyed, allowing them to meet the qualifications. The fact that a sizable percentage of the adult white male population could participate coupled with ongoing efforts to further expand the electorate set the stage for nineteenth-century America's mass democracy.

Formal Qualifications for Assembly Service

Moral aspirations were the early standard for assembly service in some colonies. Connecticut's representatives were to be "men of an honest and peaceable conversation" (*PRCC* 1850, 290, 331). A Plymouth law charged freemen with choosing "fitt and able" persons for assembly service (*RCNP* 1861, 79). Pennsylvania's frame of government admonished electors to select "men of most note for their virtue, wisdom, and ability" (*MPCP* 1838, xxxv). Virginia required burgesses to be "persons of knowne integrity and of good conversation" and prohibited those convicted of the "odious sinnes of drunkenesse, blasphemous swearing and curseing, scandalous liveing in adultery and ffornication" (*SLV*, vol. I 1809, 412, 433).

Such standards met with some pushback. A New Hampshire requirement that members be "not vitious in life, but of honest & good conversation" was part of a law the Crown overturned (*LNH*, vol. one 1904, 25, 45). When a Pennsylvania assembly speaker expressed his belief that "the highest places in government should be supplied with officers of most virtuous & exemplarie Life," the governor countered that "it is hard for a false step, in drinking a cup perhaps too much, a man should be deprived of his birthright, which is that hee be uncapable to elect or be elected; this is too severe." He cautioned, "I believe if this bill You have proposed wer applied to this present assemblie in the strictness of it, Wee should have but a thin House" (*PA*, fourth series, vol. I 1900, 164–65).

In time the colonies focused on more enforceable standards. Because only men could vote, only they could serve. One woman tried. In Maryland in 1648, "Came Mrs Margarett Brent and requested to have vote in the howse for her selfe." Although she was an attorney, "The Govr denied that the s^d Mrs Brent should have any vote in the howse." His decision was not well received, "And the s^d Mrs Brent protested agst all proceedings in this p[rese]nt Assembly, unlesse shee may be p[rese]nt. and have vote as afores^d" (*AM*, vol. I 1883, 215).

The age of 21 was the standard for legislative service in both England and the colonies. This was true even in Maryland where it was not specified in law. After Thomas Frisby was elected to that colony's assembly in 1702, doubts were raised about his age. When the speaker inquired, "Mr Frisby readily acknowledged himselfe not to be of full age till December next." The assembly then deemed him unqualified. The voters returned Frisby to office in the next election, by which time he had attained the required age (*AM*, vol. XXIV 1904, 298, 338).

In some colonies the rule was that anyone who was entitled to vote for the assembly was also qualified to serve as a member. In New York the standard for voting and serving was "Land or Tenem'ts Improved to ye vallue of fforty pounds in free hold free from all Incumbrances," while in Maryland it was "a freehold of fifty Acres of Land or a visible personall Estate of forty pounds starling att least" (*AM*, vol. VII 1889, 61; *CLNY*, vol. I 1894, 405). Over time service standards changed in two ways, first by diverging from those required for voting and second by becoming more stringent. Early in New Hampshire's history, qualified voters were "Freeholders of the value or income of Forty Shillings Per Annum or upwards in Land, or worth Fifty Pounds Sterling at the least in personal Estate." Meeting that criterion also meant a freeholder was "capable of being Elected to Serve in the General Assembly." But the colony's standards for voters and representatives split in 1728, with the latter being required to have "a real Estate within this Province of a value of three hundred pounds" (*LNH*, vol. one 1904, 658–59; vol. two 1913, 402–3). Higher qualifications for assembly service than for voting became the norm. In 1760 North Carolina mandated that voters have 50 acres of land, while representatives had to have 100 acres (*CAAA* 1764, 199). More stringent qualifications were consistent with changes in Great Britain, where the Landed Qualification Act of 1711 confirmed that only landowners of substance were appropriate candidates for the House of Commons (Dickinson 2007, 26–28).

Landholding and wealth qualifications for service became quite detailed in some colonies. In Delaware a member had to be "a Freeholder . . . and have Fifty Acres of Land or more well settled, and twelve Acres thereof cleared and improved, or be otherwise worth *Forty Pounds* lawful Money of this Government clear Estate" (*LGD* 1763, 119). Pennsylvania's law was much the same, the difference being that it required "fifty pounds lawful money" as the alternative standard (*SLP*, vol. II 1896, 24–25). In South Carolina "every person who . . . hath a freehold of five hundred acres of land . . . or has in his own proper person, and in his own right, to the value of one thousand pounds, in houses, buildings, town lots or other lands . . . or that hath one thousand pounds in cash or stock" could stand for election (*SLSC*, vol. third 1838, 3).

Complex standards created enforcement problems. Occasionally, concerns about whether a member-elect met the stated property qualifications surfaced. In 1753 the Virginia assembly determined that a recently elected member did not have a sufficient freehold to qualify and denied him a seat (*JHB 1752– 1909*, 160). A similar case arose in Georgia, and Massachusetts fined two towns for electing nonfreemen as deputies (*CRSG*, vol. XIV 1907, 156; *RGC*, vol. I 1853, 118, 174, 221). There were also accusations that a member's qualifications had been fraudulently obtained. In New York at the turn of the eighteenth century, it was alleged by a group of merchants that, "Abra. Governeur, a Dutchman, so indigent as never to be assessed in the public taxes, and who, as is reasonably to be supposed, had a deed of some land made to him of purpose to qualify him for it, because he never had any land before, was chosen an Assembly man and is since made Speaker" (*CSP* 1910a, 117).

Qualifications were enforced only when there was a willingness to do so, with political considerations sometimes intervening. In 1707 New Jersey's governor requested that a method be devised to "inquire into the quallifications of Members returned to serve in Generall Assembly." He was agitated "because as this House is quallified, the Ringleaders among them dont inquire if the other Members are quallified according to the Queen's Instructions, but whether they will join with them in refusing to give a Revenue, if so, then noe matter whether they are quallified according to the Queen's Instructions or not" (*CSP* 1916b, 613). Property and wealth standards also proved problematic because when strictly applied they could result in too few candidates being eligible to serve. In 1667 the Plymouth assembly had to "p[er]mitt the towne of Sandwich, in regard of their scarcitie of men fitt for publicke imployment, to send but one deputie to the Generall Courts" rather than the larger number to which they were entitled (*RCNP* 1855c, 159).

Stringent standards could also skew the candidate pool in undesirable ways. When the two Jerseys reunited, the Crown stipulated that representatives had to own 1,000 acres. Claims were made that politics underlay this demanding criterion, with one official alleging, "This Instruction was contrived by the Scotch of East Jersey for att least three yeares past, since which time they have been buying up land to quallify themselves and to exclude all others from having a share in the Government for want of such a quantity of land." The consequence of this "Scotch trick" was that "in some Countys there is scarce a man that hath 1,000 acres of land, people formerly not coveting great tracts of land." More troubling was that "very few [holdings] exceeded from 300 acres to 800 acres, and yett these men's improvements and stock may be ten times more valuable then those that have great tracts of land, and far better qualified in all respects, and yett they are rendred incapable by this Instruction to serve H[er] M[ajesty] or the countrey." The governor's assessment was similarly scathing: "[S]everal persons very well qualified to serve could not be elected, because they had not 1,000 acres of land, though at the same time they had twice the value of that land, in money or goods, they being trading men; on the other hand, some were chosen because they have 1,000 acres of land and at the same time have not 20*s.* in money, drive no trade and can neither read nor write, nay they cannot answer a question that is asked them" (*CSP* 1913, 644–45; 1916a, 11).

The counterposition was advanced by the Western Division proprietors. They favored the 1,000-acre qualification, "which we looked upon to be the chief security of our estates in the Province," building their argument around the notion of laws being made only by those with a long-term stake in the community. They backed the standard as being "most agreeable to the Constitution of England, where the electors of knights of shires must have certaine fix'd freehold, and the elected are generally the principall landed men of their respective countys." In their view, these "persons are fittest to be entrusted with choosing and being legislators, who have a valuable and permanent interest in lands, and must stand and fall with their country." They protested that "money is an uncertaine interest, and if it be admitted as a qualification equal to land, an Assembly may be pack'd of strangers and beggars, who will have little regard to the good of the country from whence they can remove at pleasure, and may oppresse the landed men with heavy taxes." Such arguments were conventional in England. But with the governor's support the New Jersey assembly passed a bill loosening the requirement, so that "we shall be able to have the men of the best substance chosen" (*CSP* 1916a, 11, 383, 486; Reid 1989, 34–35).

As with voter qualifications, separate standards for town representatives were fashioned. In the case of Brunswick, North Carolina, it was held that "no Person shall be deemed qualified to be a Representative for the said Town . . . unless on the Day of the Election he be, and for Three Months next before . . . in Fee-simple, of a Brick, Stone, or framed House, in the said Town, of the Dimensions of Twenty Feet by Sixteen, with one or more Brick or Stone Chimney or Chimnies" (*CAAA* 1764, 201). This was the same qualification as for voting in the town, the only distinction being the detail with which the dwelling was described. Similar language was used when Wilmington was granted a representative (*Acts of Assembly* 1751, 99–101). In Pennsylvania both voters and representatives from the counties had to have 50 acres of land, at least 12 of which were "cleared and improved," while their town counterparts had to have a freehold estate or a "clear personal estate within the same city" worth 50 pounds (*SLP*, vol. II 1896, 213–14). The charter authorizing Norfolk, Virginia, to send a burgess to be "present, sit and vote" in the assembly specified that any resident elected had to have a "freehold or visible estate" worth 200 pounds, while any nonresident had to be worth at least 500 pounds (*Revised Ordinances* 1866, 7).

There was in one instance a novel mechanism used to determine a town's representatives. When Annapolis was made Maryland's seat of government in 1708, it was granted the right to send two delegates to the assembly, as St. Mary's, its predecessor, had been. But, as had been the case with St. Mary's, Annapolis's members were to be chosen by "the Mayor Recorder Aldermen and the five Senior or first common Coûncill Men of the s^d City" and not by the freeholders. Annapolis officials petitioned to change the election process, requesting that "all persons being freeholders in this Citty (that is to say owning a whole Lott of land with a house built thereon according to Law) and that all persons actually resideing and Inhabitting in this Citty haveing a visible Estate of the Vallue of twenty pounds ster[ling] and allsoe that all persons that hereafter shall serve five years to any Trade within this Citty and shall after the Expiracon of their Time be actually house keepers and Inhabittants in the same . . . may have a free vote in the Ellecting such representatives or Burgesses to serve hereafter in all g[ene]rall assembly." The petition was granted and Annapolis's voting standards were changed to be similar to those enjoyed by other towns with representation (*AM*, vol. VII 1889, 62; vol. XIII 1894, 543; vol. 748 2008, 593, 595–96).

As was the English custom, citizenship was required for assembly service (Blackstone vol. I 1771, 175). Thus in South Carolina "every person who shall be elected . . . to serve as a member of the Commons House of

Assembly . . . shall be a free-born subject of the Kingdom of Great Britain, or of the dominions thereunto belonging, or a foreign person naturalized by Act of Parliament in Great Britain or Ireland" (*SLSC*, vol. third 1838, 3). Delaware's standard was comparable; members had to be "natural-born subjects of *Great Britain*" or have been naturalized in England, Delaware or Pennsylvania (*LGD* 1763, 119).

At times the absence of laws detailing citizenship status created difficulties. In 1692 Craven County was issued an election writ to send six members to the South Carolina assembly, a number that constituted one-third of that body's total membership. The problem this caused centered on the disputed status of the large number of French Huguenots that the proprietors had encouraged to settle in the county. Unhappy colony residents elsewhere opposed their participation, posing the rhetorical question, "Shall the Frenchmen who cannot speak our language, make our laws?" (Rivers 1856, 176). When the newly elected assembly met, the Craven County delegation was composed of Huguenots; the legislative journal gave the names of three of them prefaced by "Monsr" (monsieur) rather than the "M^r" used before the names of the other two counties' members (*JCH* 1907, 3). Over the next few years there were attempts to prevent the French from serving. But a 1696 law granting "all Aliens" the same rights enjoyed by residents born of English parents ended the controversy (McKinley 1905, 133–35; *SLSC*, vol. second 1837, 131–33).

Questions about citizenship status surfaced elsewhere. In 1698 Virginia's governor dissolved his assembly because it had admitted "a member not born in England, Ireland or the Plantations, contrary to Act of Parliament." The lawmaker in question was a native of Scotland. In a coincidence, the legal authorities in London had recently determined in a Barbados assembly case that, contrary to the Virginia governor's legal interpretation, Scots were considered "natural-born subjects of England" (*CSP* 1905, 294, 516). A few years later the New York assembly became embroiled in a citizenship dispute. A lawmaker whose residency status was under challenge turned the tables on his accuser by charging that "you, Mr. Speaker, are not born the King's Natural subject, and so not qualified to be in the Chair." The charge split the body. Eventually a majority supported the speaker, who was of Dutch origin, finding that he was "within an Act of Naturalization which passed in the Province [in] 1683, which expressly naturalizeth all persons . . . within the Province at the passing [of] that Act" (*CSP* 1910b, 429, 580–81, 706). In 1725 questions were raised about a member who had been born in France and naturalized in England, but after he produced satisfactory documentation the assembly deemed him qualified (*Votes of the*

General Assembly 1725, 3–4, 10). The New Jersey assembly refused to seat a recently naturalized member in 1740. He was elected again in 1745, was seated, and served for 30 years (Davis 1904–5; *VPNJ* (April) 1745, 15–16). In the early 1770s, the Maryland assembly determined that Jonathan Hagar, who had emigrated from Germany, was "not a natural born Subject nor descended from a natural born Subject: That he came into America and was naturalized some Time before the said Election." The assembly declared Hagar ineligible and called for a new election. But it also quickly passed a new law "vesting in such foreign Protestants as are now naturalized or shall be hereafter naturalized in this Province all the Rights and Privileges of natural born Subjects." Hagar was subsequently returned by the voters and seated (*AM*, vol. LXIII 1946, 89, 92–93, 100, 107, 174–75; vol. 426 1979, 379).

Arguably, the most consequential issue raised regarding assembly service involved persons holding two or more paid government positions simultaneously. Holding multiple offices was considered a problem for two reasons. The less common one, a personal conflict of interest, surfaced in Maryland. In the early eighteenth century the governor reported that "many of the County Court Justices for many years last past, having been return'd as Delegates to the Generall Assembly, on all occasions have sought to corroborate and establish their jurisdiction by severall Acts of Assembly." He claimed that "when any of them are in the House of Delegates, they leave no stone unturn'd . . . by referring ye settlement of a competent sallary to enable the four provinciall Justices to performe their duty, and by severall other crafty evasions, looking upon their honour and grandeur to be highly eclipsed and impair'd by the provinciall Justices" (*CSP* 1922, 251).

A different case occurred in Georgia. John Simpson was elected to represent the town of Frederica and parish of St. James. Initially, he "declined taking his Seat Having a Commission for being Clerk of this House" because it was improper to hold both positions. But Simpson made a deal with the assistant clerk to act in his place, saying he had decided "to resign the [clerk] Commission for a time rather than his Constituents should Want a Representative for the Parish." The disputed financial terms under which Simpson agreed to allow his assistant to act in his place caused an ugly disagreement between the two, which the assembly had to resolve (*CRSG*, vol. XIV 1907, 494–95, 599, 622–27).

The second, and more common, reservation about multiple office-holding revolved around an institutional conflict of interest. The issue was whether a lawmaker's loyalties were to the Crown or his constituents.

In some colonies members could not serve in the assembly while holding another paid public office. New Jersey passed a law holding that "if any Person, being chosen a Member of the House of Representatives of this Province, shall accept of any Office of Profit from the Crown, or from the Governor . . . his Election shall be and is hereby declared to be void" (*ANJ* 1776, 83). But the matter was treated in different ways for different offices in different colonies.

Almost always sheriffs were not allowed to serve in the assembly because in most places they controlled election mechanics. But it took time for precedents on this point to be established. Virginia expelled six sitting members for serving as sheriffs in the mid-1690s but only formally passed an act disallowing such dual officeholding in 1730. That law stated that it was "found inconvenient, and may prove of evil consequence to this government, if any person shall accept the office of sheriff, or of any place of profit in this government, during the time he shall be a member of the house of burgesses" (*SLV*, vol. IV 1820, 292). It was invoked frequently (*JHB 1695* 1913, 46, 104; *1727* 1910, 110, 119, 173, 323, 392; *1752–* 1909, 107, 321, 322, 403; *1758–* 1908, 135, 138; *1761–* 1907, 205, 315, 317; *1766–* 1906, 143, 147; *1770–* 1906, 6, 67, 121). Maryland first grappled with the issue in 1678, and by 1681 it was settled that sheriffs could not serve in the assembly. But problems continued well into the future. The colony held three special elections in 1753 because members had "accepted the office of Sheriff" (*AM*, vol. VII 1889, 17, 114, 134, 451, 531; vol. XVII 1898, 16; vol. XXXIV 1914, 64; vol. XXXV 1915, 318–19; *MDG* 1753a; *VPMD* 1745, 34, 43). North Carolina regularly removed members for the same reason (*CRNC*, vol. V 1887, 245; vol. VI 1888, 674–75; vol. IX 1890, 756, 759). The situation arose in New England as well. In 1715 the New Hampshire assembly dismissed Jabez Dow for "being constable of Hampton" (*LNH*, vol. two 1913, 191). In Boston in 1742, Jerimiah Allen stepped down as constable to serve as a representative because "it had not been the Practice of the Town to choose any such Person to be a Constable" (*RRCB* 1885b, 6). All of this was consistent with English practices (Blackstone, vol. I 1771, 175; Hulme 1929; *Proceedings in Parliament 1614* 1988, 38).

Simultaneous service in other government posts also caused concern. In Maryland two years had to elapse before those who had served as tobacco inspectors were allowed to run for the assembly; additionally they were not supposed to "intermeddle . . . with any Election of a Delegate or Delegates, otherwise than by giving his Vote (*Abridgement and Collection* 1759, 249–50)." Over the years, several who were elected failed to qualify because of this prohibition (*MDG* 1750b, 1751a, 1751b). Assembly members were also barred from serving simultaneously as attorney general, county clerk, county prosecutor, deputy commissary, deputy naval officer, deputy surveyor, keeper of the rent rolls, naval officer, or prosecutor (*AM*, vol. LIX 1942, 20–21; *MDG* 1755b, 1755c, 1756b; *VPMD* 1746, 6; 1747, 3; 1750, 3; 1755, 11; 1757, 3; 1770, 209, 215). Virginia passed a similar measure because "inspectors have busied themselves in the election of burgesses, and used the power of their offices, in influencing such elections, as well for procuring themselves, as others, to be elected, to the hinderance of the freedom of voting" (*SLV*, vol. IV 1820, 481–82). As in Maryland, inspectors had to be out of office for two years before they could serve as burgesses (*SLV*, vol. V 1819, 153). Over the years burgesses were forced to resign upon accepting a range of governmental posts: attorney general, assistant surveyor, collector, county clerk, county coroner, deputy attorney, general court clerk, naval officer, receiver-general, and surveyor (*JHB* 1727– 1910, 119, 174, 392, 439; *1742*– 1909, 64, 77, 236; *1752*– 1909, 126, 167, 178, 179, 190, 233, 285, 322, 403, 496; *1758*– 1908, 135, 187; *1761*– 1907, 67, 205, 229, 315; *1766*– 1906, 143, 147; *1770*– 1906, 6, 67, 120, 121). In the mid-1750s, North Carolina passed an act prohibiting inspectors of "Pork, Beef, Rice, Indigo, Tar, Pitch, Turpentine, Staves, Headings, Shingles and Lumber" from simultaneously holding assembly seats. The assembly declared five seats vacant in 1759 because members had accepted such posts (*CRNC*, vol. VI 1888, 109; *State Records of North Carolina*, vol. XXV 1906, 313–19).

Colonial executives defended multiple officeholding because they valued having leverage over lawmakers. After four Maryland delegates were discharged for having "received Places of Trust and Profit from the Government" the governor dissolved the assembly, telling them, "It has always been the Custom of our Mother Country to keep up . . . that necessary Dependance, which One Part of the Legislature has and ought to have upon Others, to the End that Publick Interest may be carried on by the united Endeavours of all the Parts of the Legislature" (*AM*, vol. XXXIX 1919, 149–50, 159). North Carolina's governor was more candid when he informed the Board of Trade that he had rejected a bill on multiple officeholding that would have prevented "several of his Majesty's friends from sitting in future assemblies" (*CRNC*, vol. V 1887, 947).

At times, the line determining which government offices could be held simultaneously and which could not was blurred. For many years John Robinson served simultaneously as a Virginia burgess, usually as speaker, and as the colony's treasurer. The holder of the seat representing William and Mary College often served concurrently as the colony's attorney general. And at times the question could be awkward. As part of a larger battle over control of the New York assembly in the late 1760s, lawmakers voted to deny a seat to a member who was also serving as a judge on the colony's Supreme Court. During a debate on the matter, one lawmaker suggested that "it was as reasonable to excludge all other Officers of the Crown" and offered a motion to that effect. It was rejected when "Mr. Thomas who was a Judge of the County of West Chester put and carried the previous Question by a Majority." Among others agreeing to quash the motion were two members who were serving as county clerks and another who was a sitting justice of the peace (*Historical Memoirs* 1956, 66).

The decision to refuse to seat the New York judge raised an additional issue. He complained to a London official, "During the violent opposition on account of my claim to a seat in the house of Assembly, which has now lasted for three years, with no small warmth on both sides, no objection has ever been made to me on account of my behaviour as a Judge (*DRNY*, vol. VIII 1857, 320). His opponents conceded that point—one wrote, "Nor is it easy for a Judge warmly engaged in Politics, who is not endowed with Judge Livingston's cool unbiased Temper" (*Observations on Mr. Justice Livingston's* 1769, 4)—but he was not allowed to take the seat to which he had been elected. His rejection was driven by politics, not his behavior in office.

Where multiple officeholding was customary, its propriety was still drawn into question. Arguing against Massachusetts judges holding assembly seats, a writer noted that they "are paid a salary by the province in order that they may leave all other business and engagements, and devote themselves wholly to the study of the laws. . . . Now to take off their attention for so great a part of the year as the General Assembly sits, from so important a study, to engage it in political disputes . . . Is it not destroying with one hand the good done by the other?" (*Considerations* 1761, 4). A New York broadside touted as one candidate's virtue that there was "indubitable Evidence of his lately refusing a Post of great Profit, merely as an Acceptance of it would have been incompatible with his invariable Attachment to the Liberty and Interest of America" (*New-York, March 8, 1768* 1768). Although the Crown was comfortable with allowing multiple officeholding, many colonists were not.

Other occupations were occasionally at issue with regard to assembly service. In 1663 Massachusetts adopted a measure stating that "no person who is a usuall & com[m]on atturney in any inferiour Court shall be admitted to sitt as a deputy in this Court" (*RGC*, vol. IV, part II 1854, 87). Rhode Island briefly passed a similar law, a 1729 measure stating that "no practitioner of the law, whatsoever, shall be chosen a deputy for any town," but it was repealed during the following session (*RCRI* 1859, 430). The explanation for the Massachusetts exclusion centered on an inherent conflict between lawyers' interests and the General Court's judicial responsibilities. It appears that the law was effective. A contemporary observer claimed that no lawyer represented Boston until 1738 (Hutchinson 1828, 104). Legislative service by lawyers was controversial throughout the colonial era, with the most vocal opposition to it surfacing during New York assembly elections in the late 1760s. The concern expressed at that point was, as a conspiratorial analyst put it, "Lawyers, in my Opinion, should not be elected to represent you because they are the first Men to perplex Law, and make themselves Work in the Interpretation" (*NYJ* 1768d).

Sometimes assemblies did not accept the membership of those who held what were thought to be seedy occupations. In 1657 Hugh Gunison was elected to the Massachusetts assembly but, "upon information agaynst him, was judged unmeet for y^t service, & so dismist ye Court" (*RGC*, vol. III 1854, 431). Gunison's offense was his job as a licensed rum seller (Bourne 1875, 96). Maryland's law prohibited "no Ordinary [tavern] Keeper within this Province" from serving. Accordingly, in 1751 the assembly refused to seat Abraham Falconar because he was "an Ordinary keeper." Falconar, who was also a planter, was later reelected to the seat (*AM* vol. 426 1979, 316; *Laws of the Province* 1718, 186; *MDG* 1751b). Even professions usually considered honorable could keep someone from serving. In 1692 the Maryland assembly concluded that "Mr Hewett" was "a person unquallified to Sitt as a Member of this house by reason of his being in sacred Orders." Immediately after announcing their decision the members allowed that they did "desire m^r Hewett to give them a Sermon to Morrow being Sunday." A few years later another Maryland delegate was found unqualified for "having been in the Holy Orders" (*AM*, vol. XIII 1894, 364; vol. XXVII 1907, 270–71). Virginia's assembly had reached the same decision in 1653, arguing that a minister could not serve as a burgess because it "m[a]y produce bad consequence." At the end of the 1600s the assembly enforced the prohibition, determining that one member-elect "being a Clergyman is disabled for Serving as a Burgess" (*JHB 1695–* 1913, 140; *SLV*, vol. I 1809, 378). Such rules were not uncommon; clergymen were not allowed to serve in the House of Commons at the time (Blackstone vol. I 1771, 175).

Religious qualifications were imposed in many colonies. Massachusetts adopted such a measure in 1654—even though becoming a freeman, and therefore qualified to serve in the assembly, already required belonging to the church—reasoning that "the safety of the com[m]onwealth, the right administra[ti]on of justice, the preservation of the peace, and the puritye of the churches of Christ therein . . . doth much depend uppon the piety, wisdome, and soundnes of the Generall Court, not only [the upper house] Majistrates, but Deputyes." It decreed that "no man, although a freeman, shallbe accepted as a deputy in the Gennerall Court that is unsound in judgment concerning the mayne points of Christian religion." This requirement was enforced, with one member-elect being rejected for "blasphemy" (*RGC*, vol. IV, part I 1854, 206, 244–45, 263). In Plymouth several who had been elected were not seated because of their willingness to tolerate Quakers (Freeman 1860, 233; *RCNP* 1855b, 162). South Carolina imposed a religious qualification in 1703 because "it hath been found by experience that the admitting of persons of different persuasions and interest in matters of religion to sitt and vote in the Commons House of Assembly, hath often caused great contentions and animosities in this Province." Any person elected who had not taken communion within the previous year had to "receive the Sacrament of the Lord's Supper, according to the rites and usage of the Church of England, in some publick church" and present the speaker with a certificate attesting to that fact. A 1747 measure relaxed that standard in deference to "Protestant dissenters," permitting them to make an affirmation instead of taking an oath (*SLSC*, vol. second 1837, 232–33; vol. third 1838, 692–93).

Laws imposing religious qualifications did not enjoy universal support. Opponents of one such measure adopted in North Carolina in the early 1700s complained to the Crown that an "Act was passed to incapacitate every Person from being a Member of any General Assembly . . . unless he had taken the Sacrament of the Lords Supper according to the Rites of the Church of England." Their apprehension was that "all Protestant Dissenters are made Uncapable of being of the said Assembly." In later years their fears would be confirmed; in 1747 a Quaker was not seated because he refused to take the required oath, and the Council denied his request to accept his "solemn affirmation" in its place (*CRNC*, vol. I 1886, 639; vol. IV 1886, 855–57).

A consequential contrast among the colonies emerged on the matter of residency. At the time the early assemblies were established the prevailing political wisdom held that a residential requirement encouraged parochialism and impeded gathering the best talent available (Kammen 1969, 8–9). England had a residency requirement but did not enforce it. According to Blackstone (vol. I 1771, 175), "in strictness, all members ought to be inhabitants of the places for which they are chosen: but this is entirely disregarded." A prerequisite that a representative reside in the place from which he had been elected was in place throughout the colonial era in Delaware, Maryland, New Hampshire, New Haven, Pennsylvania, and Plymouth.

Residency was not required in Connecticut, Georgia, Rhode Island, and South Carolina, and constituents might be represented by someone who did not live among them (Phillips 1921). But, because residency rules were often hard to interpret, only loosely enforced, or changed, the same was occasionally true in most of the colonies.

Effectively, South Carolina did not have a residency rule. Just prior to the Revolution a visitor to its assembly observed that "a great majority of the house are dwellers in Charlestown, where the body of planters reside during the sickly months" (Quincy 1915–16, 454). The colony's statutes on the matter were convoluted. A 1717 elections bill tied a 500-acre qualification to serve in the assembly to "the said parish wherein he resides." At the same time, an alternative property qualification of 1,000 pounds in houses, buildings, or town lots could be "in any part of this Province." Further confusing matters, another section of the law held that "any person whatsoever, who shall have in his own right . . . a settled plantation of five hundred acres of land . . . and not having less than ten able working negro slaves, living on the same, under the care of at least one white man, in any parish in the Province . . . and the said parish in situated within the bounds of the county where such person is then a resident . . . then it shall be lawful for such person to be chosen a member of the Commons House . . . for such parish, although he is not an actual resident in the same" (SLSC, vol. third, 1838, 3–4).

One consequence of South Carolina's rules was that a wealthy individual with property throughout the colony could be elected in more than one parish, not just the one where he resided. This was a common occurrence. In 1760, for example, five individuals were elected from more than one parish. The member-elect would have to select which parish he wished to represent or decline to serve from any of them. When a member chose a different parish to represent, there could still be a representational silver lining for the orphaned parish or parishes. After Thomas Wright opted to represent St. John Parish in 1762 because he "was under a kind of promise" to those voters, he wrote to the electors of Prince-George Parish that, although his selection by them was "unmerited and unsolicited," he thanked them for their "good opinion of [his] fitness" and promised "with zeal and great readiness to do all in [his] power for [their] parish" (CRSC 1952, 11; SCG 1751, 1752, 1754b, 1760c, 1762c, 1762e).

South Carolina was not the only colony to confront this problem. Georgia and North Carolina often saw someone chosen to represent more than one place too (CRNC, vol. IV 1886, 533–34, 817; CRSG, vol. XIII 1907, 482; vol. XV 1907, 327, 344). On occasion it even happened in colonies that ostensibly had residency rules. In 1756 William Allen was elected to Pennsylvania's assembly from both Cumberland and Northampton counties; he chose to represent the former (*VPPP* 1757, 5). It also occurred in Maryland and Virginia (*AM* vol. XL 1921, 173; *JHB 1702/3–* 1912, 6; *1712–* 1912, 322; *1727–* 1910, 14; *1758–* 1908, 12). A death notice in the Annapolis, Maryland, newspaper provides a glimpse of the sort of career a colonial lawmaker could enjoy: "We had advice of the Death of Mr. Edward Dorsey, an eminent Attorney, of this City, one of our Common Council, and a Representative for *Frederick* County." Dorsey held a local office in Annapolis and practiced law there while representing a county some 70 miles distant where he owned a substantial amount of land (*AM* vol. 426 1979, 274–75; *MDG* 1760).

Residency rules in some colonies either changed at some point or were murky. Representatives in North Carolina were required to live in the places they represented until 1743, at which time nonresidency was allowed. New Jersey permitted nonresidency representation briefly between 1702 and 1710. Virginia required residency except between 1676 and 1692. But the rule was not always enforced; George Washington was elected from Frederick County and Patrick Henry from Louisa County where they did not reside. A similar situation obtained in New York. The colony required residency, but a 1769 investigation found that over the years there had been at least 21 instances of members having been elected from certain counties, although they "did not actually reside within the same" (*JVNY* 1769, 64). It is worth noting that the battle over the residency requirement that triggered the investigation was not prompted by a debate over representational theory but was an offshoot of a struggle between two leading families for political control. Ultimately, the assembly opted to enforce the residency requirement for service but not for voting. An opponent noted that this left lawmakers "urging the Absurdity of a different Interpretation of the same Words in the Law relating to the Elector and the Elected" (*Historical Memoirs* 1956, 51–52, 62, 64).

Initially, Massachusetts did not have a residency requirement. Its operating assumption was encapsulated in a 1644 proposal: "[T]o ye end ye ablest gifted men may be made use of in so weighty a worke, it shalbe at ye liberty of ye freemen to choose them, in their own sheires, or elsewhere, as they shall see best" (*RGC*, vol. II 1853, 88). Consequently, it was common to have members representing towns where they did not live (Bailey 1880, 14; Burt 1898, 34; Corey 1899, 181, 255; Daniels 1892, 13; *Early Records of Lancaster* 1884, 332; Merrill 1880, 18, 30; Sewall 1868, 44–45). This made possible the legislative career enjoyed by John Hull, a Boston merchant and the colony's mint master. In 1668 Hull, "after much persuasion" by two ministers "and sundry other friends," agreed to represent Wenham. In 1671 Westfield selected him as both its representative and the captain of its artillery company, leaving him beseeching, "The Lord make me diligent and humble!" Hull served as Westfield's member for several years and then represented Concord and Salisbury. In a 12-year period he served for four different towns, in none of which he resided (*Diaries of John Hull* 1857, 121, 158–61). So many Bostonians served as nonresident lawmakers that one historian characterized them as a cadre of "professional representatives" for hire (Phillips 1921, 23–25). Many towns were content with nonresident representation; in 1670 Billerica presented its member, Boston's John Davey, with "a fatt oxe," which cost the town 25 acres of land to purchase, while in 1674 Woburn voted "tenne cord of wood gotten at the town's charge, and delivered on the wharf at boston as a gratuity for the good sarvise Mr. Humphary Davie hath dune this Towne at the genearll Courte" (Hazen 1883, 43: Sewall 1868, 45).

Massachusetts adopted a residency requirement in 1693 at the behest of Governor William Phips, who, according to a contemporary observer, found that most of his "opposers were gentlemen, principally of Boston, who were too near Sir William to think well of him, but served in the house for several towns and villages, at some distance" (Hutchinson 1765, 79–80). According to a council member's diary, 21 representatives opposed the bill, "alledging the vote was contrary to Charter, Custom of England, of the Province, hind[e]red men of the fairest estates from Representing a Town where their Estates lay, except also resident." They feared its passage "might prove destructive to the Province" ("Diary of Samuel Sewall," vol. 1 1878, 386). But the governor persuaded a majority to agree that "not any Town in this Province shall chuse any Representative, unless such be a Freeholder and Resident in that Town or Towns, such are chosen to Represent" (*Acts and Laws, Massachusetts* 1693, 47). The law proved controversial. Protests were lodged against it with officials in London. Springfield elected a nonresident representative from Boston and told him "to lay before the Genll Co^{r}te the Clause in the Charter that the Representatives for ye Genll Co^{r}te may be acepted when chosen In the Province." During the assembly's next session the governor rejected the election of five members for nonresidency, in one case coming to the assembly floor "in fury without his hat" to enforce the prohibition (*Acts and Resolves*, vol. VII 1892, 44–45; Burt 1899, 334; *CSP* 1903, 209, 294). Rejections for nonresidency were rare in later years (*JHHR* 1725, 6).

Throughout the colonies arguments were made in both support of and opposition to residency requirements. Those who were against them centered their complaints on an assumption that the geographic distribution of governing talent within a colony was skewed. In 1723 the governor of Massachusetts lamented his colony's residency rule, writing, "This House consists of about one hundred, who by an Act of Assembly must be persons residing in the respective towns, which they represent: whereby it happens that the greatest part of them are of small fortunes, and mean education; men of the best sense and circumstances generally residing in or near Boston." He claimed, "Were it not for this Act, the Assembly would certainly consist of men of much better sense temper and fortune than they do at present" (*CSP* 1934, 325). Another observer of Massachusetts politics took the same position, writing that "a gentleman of good natural interest and resident in the province; a man of reading, observation, and daily conversant with affairs of policy and commerce, is certainly better qualified for a legislator, than a retailer of rum and small beer called a tavern keeper, in a poor obscure country town, remote from all business" (Douglass, vol. I 1755, 507). After his assembly enforced the residency requirement, New York's governor called it "repugnant both, to reason and Justice, as those persons whose usual residence is in this City, and are in general best qualified for representatives in the House of Assembly, are precluded from being chosen in any [county] or Borough, notwithstanding they may have a considerable Estate there" (*DRNY*, vol. VIII 1857, 168).

Residency supporters countered by pointing to the virtues of having representatives drawn from the people they represented. Their thoughts were eloquently distilled in a 1763 election sermon preached before the Connecticut assembly: "Our Rulers are from among our selves, well known in our Towns, and not Strangers; they are of our own choosing, and have the same common Interests with us, so interwoven, that they can't be separated" (White 1763, 25). A Massachusetts election sermon touched on the same theme, referring to lawmakers "chosen by ourselves; and consisting of those who are our neighbors and brethren,—this we esteem an important privilege, and great security of our invaluable liberties" (Tucker 1771, 44). Supporters of New York's rule argued that "it is highly necessary that the Representatives Chosen to serve in General Assembly . . . be Inhabitants and actual residents amongst them to the end that they might be perfectly acquainted with the true State and Circumstances of the People they are to represent" (*CLNY*, vol. IV 1894, 1095).

Both lines of argument surfaced during a New Jersey debate over requiring colony residency. In passing such a law the assembly rationalized, "Whereas nothing can conduce more to the honour, safety & advantage of this Province, than the Members elected to serve in the General Assembly be perfectly acquainted with the true state and Circumstances of this Province" (*Acts Passed* 1710, 31). Urging the Lords of Trade to disallow the measure, the governor asserted that it "was meant and Intended Only to Exclude some persons of the best Estates and figure in the provinces from the Assembly, who for the Sake of their Childrens Education or other Conveniencys reside att [New] York" (*DRNJ*, vol. IV 1882, 235).

What did the voters think about residency? As the earlier Massachusetts examples suggest, they did not appear to be troubled by it. In a contentious 1701 battle over the status of a New York representative, a legislative majority concluded that he was not a resident of the county that had chosen him and the speaker issued a warrant for a writ to elect a new member in his place. The deposed member's constituents wrote back that they found the writ to be "an infringement of our Libertyes, not allowing us to chuse whome we think fittest to trust in that affair." They opted to leave the seat vacant (*CSP* 1910b, 429, 579). In 1753 a Massachusetts town unanimously elected a candidate "who is lately become an Inhabitant here, to the general Acceptance of the Town," because of the "raised Expectations of his Usefulness amongst us" (*BG* 1753). While residency had theoretical virtues, concrete advantages overrode them with the voters.

A less prominent residency rule also stoked controversy. Maryland imposed a requirement that only freeholders who had lived in the colony for three years could hold government office. One governor complained, "This discourages all ingenious men to seeke their fortunes in Maryland," with the consequence "that the natives who are ignorant and raw in business, and naturally proude and obstinate, are . . . the Representatives in Assembly" (*CSP* 1922, 250). Georgia required a year's residency, and several members-elect had to decline because they failed to meet the standard (*CRSG*, vol. XIV 1907, 159, 599). Again voters were not troubled by newcomers. After an Annapolis delegate was disqualified for not having been a three-year resident, the voters waited a few weeks until he crossed that threshold and then returned him to office (*AM*, vol. XXVII 1907, 414, 432).

Contemporary Assessments of Assembly Members

Colonial officials were even harsher in their judgments of assembly members than they were of their voters. As might be expected, Virginia's Lieutenant Governor Spotswood was contemptuous, at one point telling the burgesses in a complaint about some laws they had passed, "I cannot but

Attribute those Miscarriages to the Peoples Mistaken Choice of a Set of Representatives, whom Heaven has not generally endowed with the Ordinary Qualifications requisite to Legislators" (*JHB 1712– 1912*, 170). He told London officials, "I cannot yet see what will be the temper of the next Assembly, the inclinations of the Country being rendered more misterious by a new and unaccountable humour which hath obtained in several countys of excluding the Gentlemen from being Burgesses, and chusing only persons of mean figure and character" (*CSP* 1924, 234).

Other elites registered similar sentiments. A Maryland governor protested that "there are too many Instances of the lowest Persons . . . Men of small fortunes no Soul & very mean Capacities appearing as representatives of their respective Counties" (*AM*, vol. VI 1888, 68). One North Carolina governor grumbled that in two counties "there are neither Persons fit for Magistrates nor Burgesses" while another groused, "The whole lower House . . . consists of forty six & it is impossible to pick out in the whole Province so many fitt to do business" (*CRNC*, vol. III 1886, 207; vol. IV 1886, 177). A prominent New Yorker complemented an assembly speaker's cleverness by commenting that "his Skill lay in the low arts of gaining & surprising the Weak & ignorant part of that house as many of the Country representatives are such." He regretted, "Such may be the state of popular Governments that the turn of Affairs of the greatest consequence may depend upon the Vote of a single man of so litle Credit or Reputation that no man would trust Any of his private affairs of the least consequence to his Arbitration" (*LPCC*, vol. IX 1937, 355). A New York governor asserted that "the Assembly of this Province, as all the others in North America, consists of ordinary Farmers & Shop keepers of no education or knowledge in publick Affairs, or the World." He denigrated his own lawmakers, griping that "in this Province the greatest numbers are Foreigners, or of Foreign Extract, many of which do not understand the English Language and are generaly led by some cunning Attourney or Reader of pamphlets." In his view they were "ignorant, illiterate people, of Republican principles" (*DRNY*, vol. VI 1855, 462, 671). Another New York governor was kinder in his criticism, observing that "the greatest part of the Assembly is composed of plain well meaning Men, whose notions from their education, are extremely confined" (*DRNY*, vol. VIII 1857, 143). But the greatest hyperbole was used by a South Carolina governor, who in unsuccessfully pleading with his assembly to extend its session, told them, "[Y]ou can't but be sensible that I have an Acco^t: of what Sort of Men are intended to be Chosen . . . which if ever Accomplish'd the Country may date their Ruin from the Time" (*JCH* 1944, 43, 47).

Massachusetts representatives fared no better. A former chief justice sneered that the assembly was composed of too many "Innkeepers, Retailers, & yet more inferior Orders of Men" (*Peter Oliver's* 1961, 27). A governor wrote to the Council of Trade and Plantations, "The House of Representatives generally consist of persons (better adapted to their farming affairs than to be Representatives of the Province)." A few years later he maintained that "some of the country members, who are many of them of low fortune, parts and education, are prevented from having the affairs depending before the Assembly, sett in a true light, and free'd from the misrepresentations of the leading men in the House of Representatives." Responding to these insults, the assembly speaker pointed out the obvious in his own letter to London officials: "Tho' many of our Members are men of low fortunes, parts and education, yet they have a sufficiency to qualify them to sit" (*CSP* 1933, 329; 1936, 51, 211).

A "sufficiency to qualify" meant that colonial lawmakers differed from their counterparts in the British House of Commons. Although they were disproportionally drawn from the upper echelons of American society, by the mid-eighteenth century there were substantial numbers of farmers, as well as lawyers, merchants, and other self-made men, among them (Main 1966, 393–97). This, too, evidences the early stirrings of mass democracy.

FOUR

The Apportionment of
Assembly Seats

Another question that had to be addressed with the rise of representative systems was how representation would be apportioned within each colony. Geography was the usual basis of representation in England. The House of Commons also used multimember districts, with two or three members from each shire, town, or borough. Multimember districts had developed in the thirteenth century for pragmatic reasons. Because travel was onerous and fraught with dangers—bandits being the most unnerving of them—it was decided there was safety in numbers. The shift to single-member districts did not occur until the nineteenth century (Klain 1955, 1112).

The experience in the American colonies bore some but not a complete resemblance to that in England. Representation within the colonies was almost always based on geographic units, usually towns, counties, or parishes. Multimember districts were common. There was often rough proportionality to population. In 1638 Connecticut's three largest towns were each granted four deputies while the number for other communities was left to be determined by the assembly, taking into account "a resonable p^{r}portion to the nū[m]ber of Freemen that are in the said Townes." Proportionality, however, was not a hard and fast rule. By 1661 the assembly had reconsidered seat allocations, holding that because of the "great cost and burthen y^t lies upon this Collony by the great number of Deputies that attend ye Gen^{ll} Courts; . . . it is desired y^t ye number may be lessened one halfe in each Towne" (*PRCC* 1850, 24, 372). When reductions were proposed there was often pushback from communities that did not want to see their number of representatives cut (*ERTPo* 1901, 165). But, as will be discussed below, cost played a role in apportioning representatives in many colonies.

The assemblies did not uniformly enjoy control over the creation of new constituencies (Greene 1963, 381–87). The Lords Justice reminded a New Hampshire governor, "[W]hereas the Right of sending Representatives to the said Assembly was founded originally on the Commissions and Instructions given by the Crown to the respective Governors of the Province . . . His Majesty may therefore lawfully extend the Privilege of sending Representatives to such New Towns as His Majesty shall judge to be worthy thereof" (*Miscellaneous Provincial* 1890, 340). One consequence of this reality was that newer communities on the peripheries were often left unrepresented (Haw 2002; Lincoln 1899). Many "backwoodsmen" had to wait for the creation of the provincial congresses during the interregnum between the colonial regimes and their successor state governments to gain representation (Main 1966; Squire 2012, 76–78).

It was also the case that colonial boundaries were often unsettled. The New York assembly had members from Martha's Vineyard in the 1680s and Bennington and the southern tier of Vermont in the early 1770s. Towns were shuffled among New England colonies (Douglass, vol. I 1755, 504). In 1747 five towns were transferred to Rhode Island from Massachusetts, and each was allowed to send two deputies to the former's assembly. They had earlier been represented in the Plymouth and Massachusetts assemblies (Bicknell 1898, 7–8, 182; *RCRI* 1860, 204–5). The question of where a town was to be represented occasionally became contentious. A noteworthy case occurred when Connecticut officials disrupted an election in Rye where voters were selecting representatives to the New York assembly. Only after protracted diplomacy was the town officially placed within New York's borders (Baird 1871, 115–19; *CSP* 1910a, 124; *PRCC* 1868, 335).

Various approaches to apportionment were pursued during the colonial era, which can be demonstrated by examining how seats were allocated in Virginia, New York, and Massachusetts. Over time apportionment schemes changed in each of these colonies. More important, the general approach adopted by each was distinctive, with implications for representation.

Apportionment in Virginia

The initial distribution of seats in the Virginia assembly revolved around plantations or settlements, with eleven of them being given two seats each, as shown in table 4.1 (*JHB 1619– 1915*, 3–4). Over the following two decades the number of plantations represented and the number of seats in the assembly both grew, although at times some geographic areas within the expanding colony were unrepresented (Miller 1907, 40–41).

In the 1630s two developments reshaped the way seats were apportioned. At some point—exactly when has never been pinned down—parishes were granted the right to send representatives. In 1632 burgesses from Elizabeth City's upper and lower parishes appear in the records. A decade later parishioners in Linhaven and Upper Norfolk were granted "the free liberty and priviledge of electing and choosing Burgesses for the said parish" (*SLV*, vol. I 1809, 250). There also appear to have been parish burgesses from the Isle of Wight. But by 1660 problems with parish representation had surfaced; parishes were told that they had to cover the expenses of any members they sent, and sheriffs were warned that they had to convene elections for parish burgesses if a vestry requested it. Around this time parish representation ended, again for unknown reasons (*JHB 1619– 1915*, 108; *SLV*, vol. I 1809, 154, 179, 277, 374, 421, 520–21, 545).

More important in the long run was a 1634 law dividing the colony "into 8 shires . . . to be governed as the shires in England." The shires, or counties, first appeared as electoral units in 1643. A 1645 measure, passed because of a lack of a "certain rule" governing the number of members each county could send, held that James City County could send five members plus another for James City. The other counties could only send at most four members (*SLV*, vol. I 1809, 224, 239, 299–300). By 1649 ten counties were represented. James City County sent its full six-member delegation, while Henrico County sent only one representative. None of the other counties sent the full four-member delegation to which it was entitled.

A bill to reduce the number of burgesses sent by each county failed in 1658, but three years later a revised measure holding that each county could send no more than two members passed. Because it was "the metropolis of the country" James City was granted "the priviledge to elect a Burgesse for themselves." A few years later, after several counties sent only one member, it was decided that each county would be required to send two members (*SLV*, vol. I 1809, 498; vol. II 1823, 20, 272–73). With the colony's growth, by 1684, 20 counties were represented in the assembly, each by two members, and James City by one. In 1710, 25 counties were represented by two members and James City by one.

Over the following decades the apportionment system changed only at the margins. The number of members grew with the number of counties; unlike many of its counterparts, the Virginia assembly retained control over

TABLE 4.1. Virginia House of Burgesses Apportionment, Various Sessions

1619 Electoral Unit	Seats	1649 Electoral Unit	Seats	1684 Electoral Unit	Seats	1710–12 Electoral Unit	Seats	1742–47 Electoral Unit	Seats
Argall's Gift	2	Charles City	2	Accomac	2	Accomack	2	Accomack	2
Charles City	2	Elizabeth City	2	Charles City	2	Charles City	2	Albemarle	2
Flowerdieu Hundred	2	Henrico	2	Elizabeth City	1	Elizabeth City	2	Amelia	2
Henricus	2	Isle of Wight	2	Gloucester	2	Essex	2	Brunswick	2
James City	2	James City	6	Henrico	2	Gloucester	2	Caroline	2
Kiccowtan	2	Lower Norfolk	3	Isle of Wight	1	Henrico	2	Charles City	2
Lawne's Plantation	2	Nansemond	2	James City	2	Isle of Wight	2	Elizabeth City	2
Martin's Brandon[a]	2	Northumberland	2	James City County	2	Jamestown	1	Essex	2
Martin's Hundred	2	Yorke	2	Lancaster	2	James City County	2	Frederick	2
Captain Warde's Plantation	2	Warwick	2	Lower Norfolk	2	King and Queen County	2	Gloucester	2
Smythes Hundred	2			Middlesex	2	King William	2	Goochland	2
				Nansemond	2	Lancaster	2	Hanover	2
				New Kent	2	Middlesex	2	Henrico	2
				Northampton	2	Nansemond	2	Isle of Wight	2
				Northumberland	2	New Kent	2	James City County	2
				Rappahannock	2	Norfolk	2	King & Queen	2
				Stafford	2	Northampton	2	King George	2
				Surrey	2	Northumberland	2	King William	2
				Warwick	2	Prince George	2	Lancaster	2
				Westmoreland	2	Princess Anne	2	Louisa	2
				York	2	Richmond	2	Middlesex	2
						Stafford	2	Nansemond	2
						Surrey	2	New Kent	2
						Warwick	2	Norfolk	2
						Westmoreland	2	Northampton	2
						York	2	Northumberland	2

Orange	2
Prince George	2
Prince William	2
Princess Anne	2
Richmond	2
Spotsylvania	2
Stafford	2
Surrey	2
Warwick	2
Westmoreland	2
York	2
Jamestown	1
Norfolk	1
Williamsburg	1
William and Mary College	1

Source: JHB 1619– 1915, vii, xx; *1659/60– 1914*, xi; *1702/3– 1912*, ix; *1742– 1909*, vii.

ªPlantation's representatives not allowed to serve

the creation of new districts, and it was responsive to the representational needs of its western inhabitants (Greene 1963, 172–74). Two additional towns gained representation: Norfolk in 1736 and Williamsburg in 1742 (*SLV*, vol. IV 1820, 541–42; vol. V 1819, 204–5). An unusual apportionment feature was instituted when a seat was given to the College of William and Mary. The right to such a seat had been granted in the college's 1693 charter, which gave the "President, and masters, or professors of the said college, full and absolute power, liberty, and authority to nominate, elect, and constitute one discreet and able person of their own number, or of the number of the said visitors, or governors, or lastly, of the better sort of inhabitants of our colony of Virginia, to be present in the house of Burgesses, of the General Assembly of our colony of Virginia, and there to act and consent to such things, as by the common advice of our said colony shall (God willing) happen to be enacted" (*History of the College* 1874, 16).

The William and Mary seat was modeled on those given in the House of Commons to Oxford and Cambridge universities. Their charters had similar language; they were, for example, directed to select as representatives "two of the more discreet and efficient men of the university." The idea behind such seats was that universities were impacted by government policies and therefore ought to have representatives to speak on their behalf (Porritt 1911, 8–10).

It took considerable time for William and Mary to get a representative seated. The first attempt, in 1695, failed when "the President and onely one Master did appear to elect" and no burgess was named (*JHB 1695–* 1913, 6). The college finally elected a representative in 1715, but the assembly refused to seat him, stating that, as "for want of a Sufficient number of Masters and for want of the College of being transfferred by the Trustees to the President and Masters that they may Act as a body Pollitick according to the Charter We are of Opinion the Said Election cannot be made at this time" (*JHB 1712–* 1912, 127, 138). In the following assembly, a college burgess was finally seated but only after the president was forced to testify before the lawmakers. A representative was seated again in 1720, but none was admitted in 1723. In 1730 the assembly determined that control of the college had been transferred to the president and masters, and from that point on its representative was always seated and considered entitled to the same pay as other members (*JHB 1712–* 1912, 178, 180–81, 257; *1727–* 1910, 62, 85, 87). William and Mary was the only college to be given representation in a colonial assembly, although in the early 1770s New Hampshire contemplated granting Dartmouth College a seat (Chase 1891, 249).

As Virginia's apportionment scheme evolved, equal representation of counties became its centerpiece. Proportional representation was provided only to the extent that three cities were granted representatives. As will be discussed below, one of them degenerated into a rotten borough. And an interest constituency, the College of William and Mary, was allowed to send a burgess.

Apportionment in New York

New York's apportionment scheme was more complicated than Virginia's. A 1691 act set an initial allocation for "the severall Cittys, Towns, Countys, Shires, Divitions or Mannors of this province" (*CLNY*, vol. I 1894, 245). In addition to the complex array of districts, there was a second notable feature of this system, as can be seen in table 4.2. It maintained a measure of proportionality, with more populous New York City and County being giving the largest delegation.

The most distinctive feature of New York's plan was the granting of representatives to three manors. The 1691 law provided that the "Collony of Renslaerswick" would be entitled to send one representative (*CLNY*, vol. I 1894, 245). The Manor of Rensselaerswyck would maintain its seat throughout the colonial era. Unlike the other manors that gained representation, its right was established by the 1691 act and not by the granting of a family title (Pepper 1846, 25–26). In 1697 a grant was given to "Stephanus van Cortlandt and to his heirs" stating that after 20 years their manor would be entitled to send "a Discreet Inhabitant in and of the said manour to be a Representative of the said Mannour in every Assembly." The member was to "Enjoy such priviledge as the other Representatives Returned and Sent from any other County and Mannours of this our said province" (Scharf 1886, 118). The original 1686 Livingston Manor patent did not provide for a representative. It took a successful petition for a confirmatory patent in 1715 to grant "Robert Livingston . . . and his heirs" the right to send "one fitt person being a freeholder within the limitts and bounds of the said Manor, to be their representative, and to serve in General Assembly of the province of New York." All the manor representatives were granted the same wages as other assembly members (*CLNY*, vol. I 1894, 584–85, 915–16; vol. II 1894, 835–37; *Documentary History*, vol. III 1850, 622–28, 685–86, 696).

These manor seats were an American variant of the English "pocket borough." The manor lord or lords determined who would be elected to

TABLE 4.2. New York Assembly Apportionment, Various Sessions

1691–92		1716–26		1737–38		1752–58		1769–75	
Electoral Unit	Seats	Electoral Unit	Seats	Electoral Unit	Seats	Electoral Unit	Seats	Electoral Unit	Seats
Albany	2	Albany	3	Albany	2	Albany	2	Albany	2
Kings	2	Dutchess	2	Cortlandt Manor	1	Cortlandt Manor	1	Cortlandt Manor	1
New York	4	Kings	2	Dutchess	2	Dutchess	2	Cumberland	2
Queens	2	Livingston Manor	1	Kings	2	Kings	2	Dutchess	2
Rensselaer–Wyck Manor	1	New York	4	Livingston Manor	1	Livingston Manor	1	Kings	2
Richmond	2	Orange	2	New York	4	New York	4	Livingston Manor	1
Suffolk	2	Queens	2	Orange	2	Orange	2	New York	4
Ulster and Dutchess	2	Rensselaer–Wyck Manor	1	Queens	2	Queens	2	Orange	2
Westchester	1	Richmond	2	Rensselaer–Wyck Manor	1	Rensselaer–Wyck Manor	1	Queens	2
		Suffolk	2	Richmond	2	Richmond	2	Rensselaer–Wyck Manor	1
		Ulster	2	Schenectady Township	1	Schenectady Township	1	Richmond	2
		Westchester	2	Suffolk	2	Suffolk	2	Schenectady	1
		Westchester Borough	1	Ulster	2	Ulster	2	Suffolk	2
				Westchester	2	Westchester	2	Tryon	2
				Westchester Borough	1	Westchester Borough	1	Ulster	2
								Westchester	2
								Westchester Borough	1

Source: Lincoln 1906, 150–51; New York Red Book 1909, 370–79.

represent the manors, their freeholders having little incentive to challenge their decisions (Bonomi 1971, 190; Kip 1872, 16–19). One lieutenant governor admitted, with regard to the manors' assembly representation, that "the Proprietors are become hereditary Members of that House" (*DRNY*, vol. VII 1856, 654). The claim was accurate. The nine men elected to represent Livingston Manor all shared the Livingston surname (Livingston 1910, 159). Cortlandt Manor first exercised its right to send a representative in 1734 when it chose Philip Verplanck, who had married into the Van Cortlandt family. He served for the next 34 years. When Verplanck stepped down he was replaced by Pierre Van Cortlandt, who held the seat until independence (Shonnard and Spooner 1900, 189–190). Between 1691 and 1761, Rensselaerswyck was almost always represented by a Van Rensselaer, and from 1762 through 1775 its seat was held by a Van Rensselaer in-law.

There were claims that manor residents were little troubled by this system. Supporters of the Livingston Manor seat acknowledged that, although most of its representatives were nonresident Livingstons, the voters "thought that the Interests of the Public, as well as their own, would by that Means be more effectually served" (*Case of the Manor* 1769, 1). There was some resistance to entitling manors to seats. New York governor Lord Bellomont told London officials that the granting of such rights was "very irregular and illegal in my apprehension" (*CSP* 1910b, 4–5). Although some asked that other manors, of which there were a number, also be granted representatives, none was ever added (*Ne quid falsi* 1734, 2; Scharf 1886, 90–91). The question rarely surfaced elsewhere. An effort to grant a representative to a Connecticut manor failed, and the representation of a Massachusetts manor was brief (Banks, vol. I 1911, 195–99; vol. II 1911, 17–23; Larned 1874, 197–98).

There were additional twists to New York's apportionment. The 1696 charter creating the borough of Westchester granted it the right to send a representative separate from the county's (Scharf 1886, 647). The township of Schenectady was represented by a member from 1726 to independence. Thus New York had representatives from counties, a city and county, manors, a borough, and a township. But its assembly grew more slowly than Virginia's because it only added new counties at a leisurely pace.

Apportionment in Massachusetts

Unlike Virginia and New York, Massachusetts apportioned only by town. Some minimal proportionality was eventually built into the system. Initially, all the towns represented in the assembly sent three deputies. But in 1636 it was "ordered, that, hereafter, no towne in the plantation that hath not 10 freemen resident in it shall send any deputy to the Gen[er]all Courts; those that have above 10, & under 20, not above one; betwixt 20 & 40, not above two; & those that have above 40, three, if they will, but not above." Following that decision Weymouth, "being a very small towne," immediately withdrew two of its three deputies (*RGC*, vol. I 1853, 178–79).

As the number of towns expanded, the number of deputies did as well. This created political complications because the number of assembly members quickly swamped the number of council members (which did not change) in the unicameral General Court. Consequently, in 1639 it was agreed that no town would send more than two deputies (*RGC*, vol. I 1853, 254). This proved controversial because voters feared that "the [upper house] magistrates intended to make themselves stronger, and the deputies weaker, and so, in time, to bring all power into the hands of the magistrates" (*WJ*, vol. I 1908, 302–3). But within a few years differences between the council and the assembly led to their members agreeing to sit apart and reach decisions separately, thereby establishing a bicameral legislature (Squire 2012, 17–18). From that point on the size of the assembly relative to the size of the council did not matter, leaving the number of representatives free to grow again.

As can been seen in table 4.3, by 1644 the towns represented in the assembly were sending one or two deputies. In 1645 the assembly decreed that towns bore the responsibility to pay their representatives (*RGC*, vol. II 1853, 140). Because this imposed a financial burden on small communities, the assembly subsequently determined that "such townes as haue not more then thirty ffreemen shall henceforth be at lib[er]tie for sending, or not sending, deputyes to the Gen^{ll} Court" (*RGC*, vol. III 1854, 320, 352–53). Thus for small towns representation became optional.

Throughout much of the 1600s proportionality was muted. As the colony's metropolis, Boston suffered the most on this score, and the town regularly complained (*RRCB* 1881, 26, 110, 133–35, 142). In 1681 the assembly declared, "In answer to the petition of the comissioners and selectmen of Boston in behalfe of the sayd toune, this Court judgeth it meete to grant to the said toune liberty for the future to send three deputyes to the Gennerall Court" (*RGC*, vol. V 1854, 305). Boston immediately did so.

Massachusetts was given a new charter in 1691. Towns were allowed to "elect and depute Two Persons and no more to serve for and represent them." But lawmakers were granted the power to "declare what number each County, Town and Place shall elect and depute to serve for, and represent them" (*Charter Granted* 1692, 7). They seized the opportunity and passed an act requiring every town with "Forty Freeholders and other Inhabitants qualified by Charter to Elect" to send a representative. In addition it was decreed that every town with 120 "Freeholders and other Inhabitants . . . may send Two such Representatives" while towns "under Forty, are at liberty to send, or not; but may Choose and send one Representative, if they think fit." An exception to the two-member limit was made for Boston, which was "granted to choose and send four" (*Acts and Laws, Massachusetts* 1692, 75). Although some proportionality was attained, it was limited and did not change over the rest of the colonial era. In 1755 a commentator noted, "The charter says, each place is impowered to depute two persons and no more; Boston is allowed to send four; it is true, that equitably, considering their taxes and number of inhabitants in proportion to the whole colony representation; they might be allowed to send twenty" (Douglass, vol. I 1755, 488).

Because towns had to cover the cost of their representatives, they had an incentive to save taxpayer money by not sending any. To discourage such behavior, all but the smallest towns were subject to fines if they failed to send a representative. During the 1753 session, 15 towns were fined from 5 (Dudley and Sunderland) to 26 (Plymouth) pounds for this violation. Fines imposed the previous year were remitted to two towns while requests for remittances from six other towns were rejected (*JHHR* 1753, 13, 30, 31, 35). An analyst calculated, "The townships that have precepts sent to them, but make no returns, are liable to be fined at the discretion of the House; but are generally excused, and perhaps out of 50 delinquents . . . very few are fined" (Douglass, vol. I 1755, 516). This overstates the prospects for evading a fine, but some towns did have their money returned (Brooks 1855, 145; Hobart 1839, 133). Remittances were treated as budgetary windfalls and often used to fund minister salaries or schools (Benedict and Tracy 1878, 55; Biglow 1830, 58–59; Clarke 1912, 182).

TABLE 4.3. Massachusetts House of Representatives Apportionment, Various Sessions

Number of Towns Sending Representatives	1644	1684	1716	1740	1769
Four members			1	1	1
Three members		1			
Two members	15	1	4	2	5
One member	9	24	77	103	115
No members			6	51	83
Number of towns allowed to send members	24	26	88	157	204

Source: JHHR 1740, 4; 1769, 4; *Journal of the House of Representatives* 1717, 1; *RGC*, vol. III 1854, 1–2; vol. V 1854, 437.

Many small towns opted to go without representation. Typically, there was debate on the question, but the verdict was usually clear. During a 1768 Chelsea town meeting, a proposal to send a member "Passed in the Negative by a great Majority" (Chamberlain 1908, 536; see also *CTR* 1894, 20, 41, 64). Occasionally it was close: in 1730 Mendon voted 43 to 39 not to send anyone (Metcalf 1880, 215). Deliberations could be argumentative; a reverend wrote in his diary that, during Milton's 1683 meeting, "Sargeant Badcock did publicly oppose me, was not for sending a deputy" (Teele 1887, 650). Generally, small towns only sent a representative when two conditions were met: they anticipated that the assembly would tackle an issue of local significance and they had sufficient financial resources to cover the costs. Over the years many communities experienced gaps in representation (Allen 1860, 54; Bailey 1880, 136; Benedict and Tracy 1878, 810; Chaffin 1886, 645; Chamberlain 1908, 685; Daniels 1892, 271–72; *History of Brookline* 1906, 250; Hobart 1839, 125; Hyde 1879, 355; Jameson 1886, 80; Nason 1877, 212; Nourse 1894, 414–15; Perley 1880, 390; Pierce 1879, 421; Sanford 1870, 44; Stevens 1891, 45; Tobey and Andros 1872, 54; Wells and Wells 1910, 484; Wright 1917, 58).

At times a town had a good excuse for not sending a member. Bellingham had a fine remitted because its population had been decimated "by so many of their men going on the [military] expedition to Crown Point" (Partridge 1919, 119). A smallpox epidemic was cited by Marblehead; Weymouth mentioned a "terrible throat distemper" (Nash 1885, 50–51; Roads 1880, 62). But the most common justification was poverty (Fox 1846, 136; Pierce 1862, 95; Sheldon 1879, 117). Several decades after its soldiers returned, Bellingham asked to have another fine remitted because "one third of the Inhabitants are Really Poor" (Partridge 1919, 123). Deerfield pleaded, "The scarcity of Money Amongst us and the Apprehension of an Heavier Tax this year so influenced the Town that we had not a vote for a Representative" (Sheldon 1895, 577). Some towns described their dire circumstances at length. In 1754 Hardwick hired an agent to persuade the assembly to rescind its fine. He presented a story bemoaning that the town had been settled on "lands in poor and low circumstances," requiring the residents to "expend yearly large sums in making and repairing their highways . . . beside several large Bridges they are obliged to build and maintain." Making matters worse, "their crops of Indian corn [had] been for several years cut short to that degree that they have been obliged to buy and bring from the Towns upon [the] Connecticut River near half the Corn necessary for their subsistence" while "there were not much above eighty families in the said Town, many of which were extremely poor." This litany of woe proved convincing, and the fine was returned (Paige 1883, 48–49). Sometimes a town admitted that its decision had been driven by competing priorities. Topsfield once voted against sending a member because of "their Being other Things to be Done" (*TRT* 1920, 76).

Although costs were usually the true reason smaller towns opted to forgo sending a representative, many justified their decision by claiming that they were legally excused because of their tiny populations (Daggett 1894, 88–89; Jameson 1886, 48; Nourse 1894, 414; Sanford 1870, 44; *TRDM, 1754–1794* 1894, 66; *TRM* 1889, 154, 164, 170, 173–74). Manchester made such a claim while also confessing the real motive, voting one year "Not to send any person to Represent us at said Gennarl Court as haveing the Liberty by Law so to Do & not being able to support the [representative's] Charges (*TRM*, vol. II 1891, 23). A similar defense was mounted by Truro, "First, because we are not obliged by law to send one; Second, because the [General] Court has rated us so high, that we are not able to pay one for going" (Rich 1883, 220–21). Some small communities sought to sidestep the problem altogether. When Palmer was established in 1752, the law did not grant it the usual right to representation because "said Inhabitants are not at present desirous of" it (*Acts and Laws* 1752, 424). Several small towns never sent a member even though they were entitled to do so (Parmenter 1898, 502; Pease 1917, 69).

Larger towns worried about costs, too, and many that could send two representatives cut back to one for budgetary reasons (Currier 1902, 678; Hazen 1883, 198; *RTB* 1886, 201; *TRS* 1868, 153). Again, such decisions were usually popular. Plymouth's records reveal that in 1758 "a vote was Called to know if the Town would Choose more then one Representative at the Genl Court this present year. There was no hand held up." The town later devised a sly solution to the problem when they "Voted to choose two Representatives the presant year, they both to draw the pay of one Representative" (*RTP* 1903, 108, 289).

When towns were unrepresented but had matters they wanted addressed, there were two alternatives they could pursue. First, they could ask representatives from neighboring towns to advocate on their behalf. In 1744 Greenfield appointed a committee to beg the Hadley, Hatfield, and Northampton members to ask the assembly to reduce the town's tax burden (Willard 1838, 30–31). But a more common solution was to hire an agent to lobby lawmakers. In 1740 Dudley "voted and chose Esqr Vinton to go down to adrees Great and General Court to see whether their Honours will abate som thing of our provinc Tax and fine." The town was often unrepresented and regularly resorted to hiring agents (*TRDM* 1893,

92, 121, 177). Many communities pursued this tactic (Biglow 1830, 40; Fox 1846, 136; *History of Concord, New Hampshire*, vol. I 1903, 152; Metcalf 1880, 216; Sheldon 1879, 320; Smith 1899, 49; Temple and Sheldon 1875, 321; *TRM* 1889, 99).

Apportionment in other New England colonies was also based on towns, and they experienced similar representational struggles (*ATR* 1919, 137, 139; *ERL* 1908, 70). Some excuses for being unrepresented were compelling. After Simsbury, Connecticut, was torched during Philip's War the damage was so extensive that the town was unable to send representatives for the next 12 years (Phelps 1845, 29). Westerly did not send a deputy to the Rhode Island assembly for five years for the same reason (Denison 1878, 53). At other times no explanation was given. In 1709 the New Hampshire assembly issued "warrants to summon all the select men" from Exeter "to appear before them and shew cause" why they had failed to elect anyone (*DRNH*, vol. III 1869, 393). As in Massachusetts, towns in Connecticut (Orcutt 1880, 797–99; 1882, 814–16; Phelps 1845, 156–59) and New Hampshire (Read 1892, 207) experienced gaps in representation.

Eventually, some New England colonies employed a system of joint seats, in which small communities that would not otherwise enjoy representation were combined to elect a representative. By 1769 there were 20 joint constituencies in Massachusetts. New Hampshire also made heavy use of them; in 1768, 7 out of the 34 members represented such districts (*DRNH*, vol. VII 1873, 171). Sometimes more than two communities were combined. In 1748 five New Hampshire towns joined together to elect a single member (*Miscellaneous Provincial* 1890, 355). There were two motivations for establishing joint seats. First, they provided representation to freeholders who might otherwise have had to do without it. Second, they helped "prevent the inconveniency of multiplying representatives" by keeping assemblies from growing too large (Douglass, vol. I 1755, 501).

Managing joint representation was tricky. Some problems were anticipated and attempts made to minimize them. When Carlisle and Concord, Massachusetts, shared a seat it was with the proviso that the residents of Concord "as often as they shall call a meeting for the choice of a representative, shall give seasonable notice to the clerk of [Carlisle], for the time being, of the time and place of said meeting, to the end that [Carlisle] may join them therein." To participate Carlisle had to continue to "pay their proportionable part of all such town, county, parish and province charges" (Bull 1920, 5–6). Such conditions set the ideal for cooperation among communities sharing a representative (Bigelow 1898, 261–74; *ORTF*, 1898, 1–2; Smith 1899, 45).

One difficulty that was never surmounted was the place from which a joint representative would hail. An ineffectual solution was to suggest that it did not matter. When Whately, Massachusetts, was separated from Hatfield, the act included a line stating that their joint representative should be chosen "indifferently" between the two towns (Crafts 1899, 137). The reality was that the member almost always came from the larger or largest community, leaving the smaller or smallest communities feeling aggrieved (Draper 1841, 30–31; Judd 1863, 417). No rotation among towns was ever mandated, and only a few arrived at such an arrangement (Bicknell 1898, 291).

The mechanics of joint representation did not always operate smoothly. Occasionally the problems were comical. In 1774, wrote one Bedford, New Hampshire, resident, "I went to Amherst to the choosing a representative for Amherst and Bedford [and] we met with a great misput by Reason that john Bell our Clerk left our Warrant at home and had to send to his house for it" (*Diary of Matthew Patten* 1903, 320). More serious, complaints were sometimes made that one of the communities involved was not notified about an impending election or that a voting place favored one community because it was inconvenient for the other or others (*DRNH*, vol. VII 1873, 363; Parsons 1905, 32).

Another pitfall of town-based representation was the fact that a community could grow too big and need to be split. In 1730 Providence petitioned the Rhode Island assembly, "setting forth the ill-conveniency of the said town's being so large." The following year an act "erecting and incorporating the out-lands of the town of Providence, into three towns" passed. Each of the new towns—Smithfield, Scituate, and Glocester—was allowed to send two deputies to the next assembly. Sometimes such efforts met with opposition. When in 1765 it was again proposed that Providence be split, some objected, saying it would "be the means of creating more deputies to sit in the General Assembly, when, in our opinion, the number ought to be lessened rather than multiplied" (*RCRI* 1859, 439, 442–44; 1861, 437). Not all communities split from existing towns received representation. After the "Parrish of Greenland," New Hampshire, was "set of[f]" from Portsmouth, its residents complained that "for severall years past" they had not "had the Benefit of having a voat in makeing choice of any person to sit in the Gen^ll Assembly." They felt "much Grieved in not having any person to Represent them in Gen^ll Assembly nor any Vote in the choice of any other." In this case the assembly and governor agreed to allow them to send a member (*DRRT* 1875, 327–28).

Systemic shortcomings of town-based apportionment were alleged. One Massachusetts governor argued that it afforded too much representation (*Correspondence of William Shirley*, vol. I 1912, 473–74). But the real catch was the possibility of too little representation. As one contemporary observer noted, "Incorporating of townships with all other town privileges, excepting that of sending Representatives" was problematic because "(that as we have no county-representatives) persons of good estates real and personal should in no manner be represented, as if they were aliens, servants, or slaves" (Douglass, vol. I 1755, 489, 504). Apportionment by county assured that all, except those in newly settled frontier lands, had representation. The town system often produced situations in which nontrivial numbers of freeholders were left without any members speaking on their behalf.

Additional Apportionment Schemes

The Virginia, New York, and Massachusetts apportionment schemes did not exhaust those pursued during the colonial era. When the two Jerseys were reunited, the plan put in place was built around equal representation of the east and west divisions, mimicking the earlier split. The trouble with this approach was that the voting place was "the center of each division . . . wch. is the most equitable way that coulde be thought on." This made it hard to vote because "yett many men must goe neere 80 miles to the center and be forced to lay in the woods when they come for want of accommodation, which will discourage most people from going" (*CSP* 1913, 645; 1916a, 12). In light of these difficulties the plan was soon changed to allow two members to be elected from each of the five counties and the town of Perth Amboy in the eastern division and two members from each of the four counties and the towns of Burlington and Salem in the western (*DRNJ*, vol. III 1881, 97).

Similarly, in the early South Carolina assembly, seats were apportioned by county but all voting took place in Charleston (*JCH* 1914, 5). In 1716 the assembly concluded that the "far greatest part of the inhabitants in their respective counties of this Province, are at a considerable distance from the stated places of election, whereby they are at great expense of time and money, besides all other hazards, in coming to choose members of the Commons House of Assembly." Given that "the several counties of this Province are divided into distinct parishes," it decided that "in them elections for members of the Commons House of Assembly may be managed." In 1721 the assembly concluded that "the choosing of members . . . by parishes or precincts, has been found by experience to be the most just and least expensive method that can be devised" (*SLSC*, vol. second 1837, 250, 683–85; vol. third 1838, 135). While parishes would continue to be used through the rest of the colonial era, the distribution of seats was unequal. Although the assembly created new parishes against the Crown's wishes, numerical power within the body always rested with the more established Tidewater region (Greene 1963, 173–74).

Apportionment plans were not always the product of plotting or planning. Without intending to do so, North Carolina evolved a system with both county and borough or town seats (Allen 1918, 21; Cooper 1916, 44–45). In passing a 1715 bill "for appointing a Town in the County of Bath," lawmakers had "PROVIDED *always,* That this Election for Members of Assembly to serve for the Town of *Bath,* or any other Town whatsoever, shall not begin or commence till such Town shall have at least Sixty Families." The measure allowed New Bern to continue to send a representative even though it did not have 60 families (*Acts of Assembly* 1751, 31, 37). Under this law, once any town claimed the required population it sent a member to the assembly, even if the community was not chartered by the Crown. In 1760 Halifax even sent a member without so much as an election writ from the governor (*CRNC*, vol. VI 1888, 364–65). The assembly also allowed small towns to gain representation, as it did in 1754 with Brunswick—"a Sea-Port Town, where the King's Ships lie"—which only had 20 families (*Anno regni Georgii II* 1754, 400; *CRNC* vol. V 1887, 158). By 1773, nine towns along with 35 counties enjoyed assembly seats. In what was a slap at the governor, that year the assembly refused to seat a representative from Tarborough, a chartered town that lawmakers argued did not have the requisite 60 resident families (*CRNC*, vol. IX 1890, 348, 746–47, 823, 989; *North Carolina Government* 1981, 55–56).

It was common in colonies apportioned by county for towns where the assembly met to be given separate representation. In Maryland, Annapolis had that right, as did Burlington and Perth Amboy in New Jersey, Philadelphia in Pennsylvania, and Williamsburg in Virginia. Other towns were not always similarly blessed. When the Maryland assembly passed "An Act for the Enlargement of Baltimore Town" it included a proviso that nothing "herein contained, shall extend, or be construed to extend, to enable, or capacitate . . . the said town, to elect or choose Delegates or Burgesses to sit in the General Assembly of this Province as Representatives." Baltimoreans had to be content with representation through their county members (*VPMD* 1747, 51).

Apportionment Complications

Representatives' political calculations influenced apportionment decisions. In 1710 Virginia's Lieutenant Governor Spotswood told London officials, "There is one thing in which I have not been able to surmount the private interests of particular members of the House of Burgesses, and that is the making a more equal division of the countys between York and James Rivers." He elaborated:

> I thought it a fitt time to try the temper of the house of Burgesses in that particular, and did with the unanimous concurrence of the Council propose such a division of the several countys between those two rivers as would have made them all very commodious for the inhabitants, and pretty near an equality in their tithables, and consequently in their county levys and publick charges: but when this came to be debated in the House of Burgesses, the private ends of the Representatives of those countys overswayed the publick benefite of the people, and more particularly through the dilligence of one leading man, who by the alteration proposed, would have lost many of his old friends that had voted for him in former elections, and got others into his county of whose friendship he was no ways confident, that project came to be rejected. (*CSP* 1924, 313–14)

In defending his plan Spotswood highlighted two problems with how seats were distributed. One was malapportionment. With representation allocated equally by county, Spotswood noted, "Some of the countys have 16[00] or 1700 tithables, while others have little more than 500." The other was the difficulty of voting. Because there was only one polling place in each county, he argued, "[T]hose inconveniencys are become intollerably burthensome to the country; some countys are now 90 miles in length, and the inhabitants are obliged in some places to travell 30 or 40 miles to their own Court house, tho' they live within six miles of the Court house of another county" (*CSP* 1924, 315). His plan would have made representation more equal and voting easier. Lawmakers rejected it based on their own political interests.

Another problem was that it was not always clear whether a specific geographic unit was entitled to representation. In 1707 East Haven, Connecticut, was separated from New Haven, but left uncertain was whether the new community was to have a representative. Starting with the following year, East Haven sent a deputy for seven straight sessions. But in 1710 the assembly concluded that it never intended "to give the said village liberty of choosing deputies distinct from the town of New-haven." In 1713 East Haven tried again to send a deputy, but the assembly refused to seat him (*PRCC* 1870, 24, 66, 90, 107, 114, 141, 162, 169, 176–77, 364).

A different twist was presented by another Connecticut case. Towns were uniformly allowed to send two deputies, but when in 1734 East Haddam was separated from Haddam each community was told, "[D]o not send more than one Deputy to this Assembly at any time for the future on the publick charge of this colony." During the early 1740s East Haddam always sent one deputy, but Haddam rebelled and sent two deputies for several sessions before reverting to the one deputy to which it was entitled. A few decades later Redding and Chatham were separated from existing towns, and each was allowed to send only one deputy. In 1768 the representatives from Haddam, East Haddam, Redding, and Chatham united to promote legislation asking that the restriction of only sending one deputy "be taken off, as unequal." The assembly agreed that these communities could send two deputies "in the same manner as the other towns in this Colony" (*PRCC* 1873, 508; 1874, 486, 511, 552; 1881, 580, 633; 1885, 95).

Because the Crown rather than the colony often had final say in apportionment matters, representation was not always provided to all settled areas. A 1704 South Carolina election law filled the gap by allowing "any person or persons not inhabiting within any county for which writts of election are issued forth" to "have liberty to vote for members . . . in the county or precinct next adjoining to his personal residence." But this opportunity did not lessen the desire for direct representation. New communities on the colony's fringe linked it to taxation. A 1768 complaint asserted that "the inhabitants of the upper part of the province have a *right* to be *represented* . . . nor can any public taxes be taken from them, with justice, until members are allowed" (*SCG* 1768a; *SLSC*, vol. second 1837, 250).

Such claims were common because taxation was often tied to representation. If Connecticut towns did not pay taxes, they were not entitled to representation. In 1720 residents of the "east parish of Greenwich" asked the assembly to exempt them from paying taxes for four years so they could use that money "to maintain a gospel ministry." It was decided that they could do so, but in return the colony would only cover the cost of one deputy for the town rather than the normal two. If they wished to send a second representative, "then the town of Greenwich shall defray the whole charges of such deputy." In 1725 Ashford asked to be excused from paying taxes for two years; permission was granted as long as "they neither send deputies nor draw money for their school during said term." An appeal from New Milford residents that they be exempted from taxes for two years because "they labour under in building and finishing their meeting-house, and abundance of other charges" was granted, again with the proviso that they "do not send any representatives to serve as members of this Assembly on the publick cost" (*PRCC* 1872, 221, 565; 1873, 140–41). The New Hampshire assembly negotiated a creative deal with the "Town of Kingstown," voting in 1712 to excuse them "from Sending a Representative & paying any part of the province Charge for the present Year; provided they Assist the Scouts with [boat] pilots at their Own Charge when Ever required" (*LNH*, vol. two 1913, 115).

In New Hampshire, towns were often left unrepresented even though they did pay taxes. In 1773, 46 towns elected the assembly's 34 members and paid roughly 63 percent of the colony's taxes. The other 37 percent was paid by the 101 towns without representation (Belknap, vol. II 1812, 373–75). This led to a complaint that "The Town of Nottingham has never had [representation]; and it is now one of the primary Towns in the Province . . . in short near one Third of the Province is unrepresented; yet are annually taxed" (*NHG* 1774a). Nottingham's petition noted, "For a Long Time Past the inhabitants thereof have been Constantly Taxed toward the Support and Maintenance of the Government of this His Majesty's Province and have always freely and cheerfully Paid the same tho they have Never Enjoy'd the Inestimable Darling Privilege and Liberty of Being Represented in the House of Commons here which other Towns and Parishes Less Opulent and Not so Numerous or ancient have been Indulg[d] with; the Liberty of sending Representatives" (*DRRT* 1875, 642).

When unrepresented New Hampshire towns asked to be allowed to send a member to the assembly, they touted the taxes they were paying (*DRRT* 1875, 47, 321–22, 455, 663–64). But, as will be discussed below, apportionment in the colony hinged on a town's support for the governor rather than on the taxes it paid.

Governors and Apportionment

Colonial governors were not above trying to manipulate the apportionment of assembly seats to increase legislative support for their agendas. In 1699 a group of New York merchants charged that their governor, "To secure a majority of Assembly men such as he desired . . . added two [seats] to the former number, one for the City and County of Albany, and one for the County of Orange, which . . . has not twenty inhabitants freeholders, and never before had a distinct Representative." The assembly tried to play that game too. A few years later lawmakers rushed through their own apportionment scheme just before the arrival of a new governor. According to a report, they planned "to add five members to the Assembly (in those counties where they hope they may carry it) with a clause that it shall not be in the power of a succeeding Governor to add any more members or diminish those that are." Not surprisingly, once he arrived the governor overturned the apportionment plan (*CSP* 1910a, 116–17; 1912, 291–92, 645).

Many colonies were prone to such ploys. Early in the eighteenth century, a Virginian lamented about "poor James City, that hath had the priviledge of electing a burgess ever since we have had Assemblies, and that confirmed by a Law now in force." But the city was "now refused a writ, upon pretence that the State House being gone from thence, it is not the Metropolis; but the true reason is, [the lt. governor] doth not expect a Burgess from thence for his turn." With the arrival of a new lieutenant governor a year later, James City regained its seat (*CSP* 1916a, 107, 625; *SLV*, vol. III 1823, 236). But due to its tiny population, two families controlled the selection of its member (*Colonial Virginia Register* 1902, 9).

James City was not the only rotten borough in the colonies. New Jersey's governor thought Salem fell into that category: "As the town of Salem obtained members mainly for no other reason than because there was one county less in West [New Jersey] than in [East] New Jersey, so now that reason eeasing, it seems unreasonable that they should any longer have so great a priviledge above their neighbours, for this town of Salem is a very poor fishing village of about twenty houses and not above 7 or 8 voters." Again the governor's efforts to take away Salem's representation were motivated by politics, not theory. His message admitted that Salem's "members have been the ring-leaders in the opposition to the Government, and are the more insolent because they are sure of being re-elected" (*CSP* 1933, 378).

The biggest apportionment battle occurred in North Carolina. Not long after Governor Gabriel Johnston arrived in the mid-1730s he expressed a concern that representation in the assembly was lopsided in favor of the northern part of the colony. He observed, "The six Precincts in the County of Albemarle have in each five Members making thirty, & the number of People in it is I am sure not fifteen thousand, which is by much too large a Representation." In contrast, the newer precincts in the southern part of the colony were each allowed to send only two representatives. Unfortunately, to correct this malapportionment Johnston undertook a shady legislative gambit. He called for the assembly to convene in Wilmington, far from its traditional meeting places. Northern representatives complained that it was "the most inconvenient Place that any Assembly had theretofore been held at being not only the most Expensive Town in the Province." Making matters worse, the session was called for November, leaving northerners fuming that they would have to make the trip at a time when the weather was "extremely intemperate" and would have "many broad Ferries to Pass from Seven to ten miles over that are very ill provided with Boats."

The result was that the northern members did not attend. Seizing on their absence, the governor prevailed on the nine southern representatives who did participate to swear in six new members. Although it was clear that the required quorum was not present, the governor leaned on the rump assembly to pass a reapportionment bill that would limit each county to only two representatives. When the governor next called an election, the northern part of the colony refused to cooperate, submitting the usual five names for each precinct instead of the two mandated on the writ. The assembly voided their elections. Since the northerners effectively opted to forego representation, they also decided not to pay taxes. This impasse lasted for eight years until London officials determined that "the [apportionment] Act was not proper to be confirmed." (The Board of Trade advised the Crown that the measure had been "passed by management precipitation & surprise when [few] Members were present.") The repeal arrived in the colony along with a new governor, and the electoral system reverted to the old unequal distribution of seats, which was then maintained through the rest of the colonial era. But the colony's governors continued to try to manipulate the process. In 1760 the assembly raged about its governor "not granting a writ of Election for Tyrell an Ancient County till After the Present Assembly had sat and passed several Bills and the Granting another to Bertie County for fewer Members than they have usually sent to represent them in Assembly." The members told London that "it remained no longer a secret that the Governor Intended to modell the Assembly for his own particular Purposes" (CRNC, vol. IV 1886, 177, 857–58, 1158–59, 1173, 1199–1201; vol. V 1887, 91, 108, 117; vol. VI 1888, 412, 415).

Arguably, the most egregious apportionment abuses occurred in New Hampshire. The colony's governors had a history of rewarding supporters with seats while denying representation to those who opposed them (Fox 1846, 136; History of Concord, vol. I 1903, 251; Wilderson 1994, 223–24). This can be seen in the handling of a 1762 election dispute between two towns, Dunstable and Hollis, which shared joint representation. For years the towns held meetings to elect their representative in Dunstable, the older and, until recent years, larger of the two communities. The person chosen always hailed from Dunstable. Once Hollis became bigger, it petitioned to become an alternate election site. When Dunstable balked, Hollis voters mobilized—they "left at home scarcely man or horse"—so they could take control. Seeing they were outnumbered, Dunstable voters held a separate meeting. Each town ended up electing its own representative. The assembly chose to seat only the Dunstable member. In response the Hollis representative "took measures to acquaint the Governor with what had transpired." To the assembly's shock, it was soon informed that the governor had dissolved it and new election writs had been issued. In the next assembly only Hollis was given a seat (*Collections, Topographical*, vol. I 1831, 57; *DRNH*, vol. VI 1872, 800–809).

That outcome prevailed in each subsequent assembly. In a 1774 petition requesting the right to send a representative, Dunstable noted that it had been "under the Jurisdiction of the Province of Mass[a] Bay and for very many years were priviledged by that Province to send a Person to represent them in the General assembly anualy Convened at Boston untill the Divisionall line between the said Province took place." Then "for several years [following] the said Town of Dunstable enjoyed the Priviledge of voting for a Person to Represent them in the General Assembly for this Province." But "For about Twelve years last past the Freeholders of said Town have for reason to them unknown been Excluded from their ancient Priviledge" (*DRRT* 1875, 225). It appears the town was punished for not supporting the governor (Fox 1846, 170).

Other towns were similarly aggrieved. By 1775 there was pushback to what was seen as an abuse of power. The New Hampshire provincial congress rejected the governor's call for representatives to be elected from "three new Towns that had never sent members before," asserting that "the Governor's Assuming the Right of sending to such new Towns as he thinks fit without concurrence, of the other Branches of the Legislature is unconstitutional & subversive of the rights and Privileges of the good People of this Colony." Their concern was straightforward: "Establishing such a precedent may leave room for some designing Governor to occasion a very partial Representation of the People by sending to small Towns and omitting large ones." The assembly refused to seat the disputed representatives (*DRNH*, vol. VII 1873, 506–7). At the same time, a number of towns that had been unrepresented were allowed to send members, among them Dunstable (Stearns 1906, 70).

Sometimes gubernatorial interference in apportionment was benign; at other times it was malevolent. Regardless, its impact was consequential.

While Josias Fendall served as Maryland's governor (1657–60), his writs called for the election of "fower discreete Burgesses" in each county. During the brief tenure of his successor, Philip Calvert (1660–61), writs "Committed that the number of persons to be Elected was in the expresse words left to the Sherriffe." Calvert was followed by his nephew Charles, who initially issued writs leaving it to each county's freemen whether to elect "one two three or foure discreete Burgesses." By 1670 his writs called for the election of "four several sufficient freemen . . . to be deputy and Delegate."

The younger Calvert leaned toward the manipulative end of the spectrum. Around 1672 St. Mary's, the seat of government, was given the right to send two members to the assembly. But its delegates were to be elected by the mayor and other city officials, not by the town's freeholders. Calvert's intent was to keep a tight rein on the selection process. In a letter to his father, he intimated that he had secured St. Mary's seats for his own ends: "Mr Nottly is now Speaker of o^r Assembly, hee and Mr John Moorcroft beinge Chossen Burgesses for the Citty of St. Maries, And by that Meanes I gott him into the Assembly . . . Dr Morecroft is much more for our purpose, being the best Lawyer in the Country, and has alwayes been (upon other Assemblyes) A great Asserter of yor Lo^{pps} Charter and the Rights & privilidges thereof, I durst not putt it to an Election in the Countyes Butt tooke this way which I Knew would Certainely doe what I desired."

Additionally, although Calvert's writs called for four members to be elected from each county, he did not always summon all four members-elect. In some counties only two were called. When assembly members asked why some elected members had not been invited, the governor told them it was "because the respective Sherriffs of the said Countys at the time when they made their respective Returns desired the Governour . . . not to charge their poor and newly erected Countys with more Delegates than formerly they used to have." In 1676 a "humble" petition to Calvert from "the Cittizens & deputies of the Lower House of Assembly" acknowledged his "Prerogative to Call what number of Delegates or Deputies . . . as your Lord^p shall think fitt to Summons." But they did say that summoning fewer members than were elected "meanes Some of the Inhabitants of this your Lord^{ps} Province Seem dissatisfied and that they have not theire free Vote." They asked that he call every member elected, which he agreed to do.

Subsequently, at the next assembly, in 1678, four members were summoned from each county, along with two members from St. Mary's. That assembly passed a bill specifying that each county would elect four members and St. Mary's two, all of whom would attend without a gubernatorial summons. But the proprietor rejected it because of "The Inconveniency whereof in burdening every County with the charge of four Delegates."

Declaring that "the true intent of the said Act was onely to assure the ffree-men of this our Province that all persons by them elected for their Del-egates and Representatives, should be called to sitt and vote in our said general Assembly," he mandated that "for the future two Delegates onely shall be elected and chosen for every County to sitt and vote in succeed-ing Assemblies." As long as the colony remained under Calvert's control, the assembly kept pushing unsuccessfully for the election of four members from each county. Once the colony passed into the Crown's hands in 1692, the assembly wrote a new law requiring the election of four deputies from each county, a number that held through the Revolution (*AM*, vol. I 1883, 381, 398, 425; vol. II 1884, 240–41, 507–8; vol. V 1887, 77–78; vol. VII 1889, 60–65, 133–34, 407; vol. XIII 1894, 541–42; vol. XV 1896, 378–79; *Calvert Papers* 1889, 264–65).

There was an instance when pressure caused an executive to alter the way a colony was apportioned. Georgia's seats were distributed in a compli-cated fashion. Among the constituencies in 1768 were the "Town of Savan-nah, four members," the "Sea Islands, one Member," the "Village of Acton, one Member," the "District of Little-Ogechee, one Member," and "Ebene-zer and Parish of St. Matthew, three Members" (*GG* 1768a). This distri-bution allocated to bigger populations a proportionally larger number of seats. But it only came about after the assembly pressed the issue. In 1757 it had charged that "through [the executive's] means and for Selfish purposes to secure a Majority in the General Assembly, was made the unequal and Injurious division of the Colony into Districts." It calculated that "by the present regulation near three fourths of the Colony in respect to extent of Country or number of Inhabitants sends but four Members to serve in Gen-eral Assembly." A measure to reduce malapportionment by adding "some Members to those parts of the Province which have considerably encreased and improved since the first distribution of Members were made" passed but was vetoed by the governor for encroaching on his prerogatives. But by 1768 he had addressed the assembly's concerns by creating a new district and redistributing seats within the existing ones to better reflect the popula-tion (*CRSG*, vol. XIII 1907, 129, 409; Greene 1963, 185).

Apportionment and the Shape of the Future States

In two cases, apportionment disputes shaped the way the colonies were organized and, in turn, the boundaries of the future states. A 1699 pro-posal to unite East Jersey and New York foundered over representation. Among the demands made by the East Jersey proprietors was that "the same number of counties be continued in East Jersey, and each county send as many Representatives to the General Assembly as any county in New York" (*CSP* 1908, 325). That was unacceptable to New York, and the two colonies never joined.

Representation drove Pennsylvania and Delaware apart. In 1700 the Pennsylvania assembly was apportioned as it always had been, with equal numbers of members from the three provincial counties in Pennsylvania and the three territorial or lower counties in Delaware. Delaware's representatives, however, sensed that the colony's population dynamics were running against them. They understood that because of geography their county structure was unlikely to change—Delaware operates with the same three counties today—while Pennsylvania was poised to grow westward and in doing so would have to add counties. Consequently, Delaware's representatives proposed either to maintain the status quo in perpetuity or to separate: "[A]t no Time hereafter the Number of Representatives of the People in Legislation in this Province, shall exceed them of the annexed Counties, but if hereafter more Counties be made in the Province, and thereby more Representatives be added, that then the Union [between Pennsylvania and Delaware] shall cease." Pennsylvania's members refused to agree to equal representation but did not press disunion. The dispute festered for several years. In 1701 Delaware's representatives suggested that "they might have Liberty to enter their Dissent to the bill for confirming of the Laws, and that nothing may be carried over their Heads by overvoting them," but the plan was spurned. Despite good faith efforts by both sides to overcome their differences, they were unable to do so. In 1704 Delaware's members again proposed the adoption of rules "so that our Representatives may be equal in Number." In rejecting that idea the Pennsylvania members reminded their lower county colleagues that "by this [1701] Charter [of Privileges] you still have the Opportunity of forming yourselves into a distinct Assembly." With that the two sides amicably agreed to split, Pennsylvania's final message closing "[W]e hope it will prove satisfactory to you, from your real Friends and Wellwishers" (*VPPP*, vol. the First 1752, 123, 130–31, 156; vol. [the First] part the second 1752, 4–5).

Apportionment and Representation

Colonists were cognizant of the political impact of apportionment schemes. In a message to London officials, New York's governor placed the blame for his failure to get a trade bill repealed on the distribution of assembly seats, writing, "[T]he only reason I can give for it is, that the Members for the country are more numerous, then those for the city, they don't care what becomes of the city, provided they have goods cheap." The governor proposed that the Crown "allow the City of New York to chuse as many Representatives to serve in the Generall Assembly, as all the rest of the Province does." Beyond the politics of the moment, the larger rationale he offered revolved around taxes: "[I]f the city of New York is to bear half the burthen, the city ought to bear a proportionable share in the Legislature." Nothing came of this idea. Within a few years another apportionment controversy flared. This time residents of "Nassau Island" complained about "the unequall numbers of Representatives," again linking it to the distribution of taxes. Lawmakers defended the recent adjustments that had triggered the complaint, noting, "The additions then made and complain'd of have been agreable to the laws and practice of this Province," with Orange County having been given one seat and Dutchess County two seats because they were "large countys and daily increasing in people, and by that addition were made but equal to the smallest county in the Province" (*CSP* 1922, 10–11; 1930b, 301).

Representation's importance was demonstrated by its absence. Areas that were unrepresented or underrepresented failed to have their interests protected. Discussing a bill governing when county courts could be held, Virginia's Lieutenant Governor Spotswood observed that residents on the periphery could not "obtain redress in the Assembly unless it happen that the Burgesses of the County be chosen out of that remote precinct" (*CSP* 1928, 86). Suffield residents petitioned the Massachusetts assembly, complaining that "in the year 1739 the Representative for the Town of Springfield moved to the Gen^ll Court for a new Establishment greatly hurtfull to the Town of Suffield, and wee having that year no Representative in Court . . . The Town of Springfield obtained the order of Court for a new Establishment according to their Petition" (Sheldon 1879, 320). In Pennsylvania in 1764, "[T]he Frontier Counties of Lancaster, York, Cumberland, Berks, and Northampton" collectively elected ten assembly members, while the city of Philadelphia and counties of Bucks, Chester, and Philadelphia elected 26. The frontier counties protested that this apportionment scheme was "oppressive, unequal and unjust, the Cause of many of our Grievances and an infringement of our natural Privileges of Freedom and Equality." They were particularly incensed by the passage of a bill that would move the trial of anyone charged with killing an Indian out of the frontier county where it was alleged to have occurred to one of the more established counties. By their calculations, the bill, which "received the assent of a Majority of the House," would not have done so "had our Frontier Counties been equally represented in Assembly" (Mombert 1869, 192–93; *NYG* 1764).

Geographic distance was an impediment to assembly attendance and representation. Members from far-flung areas found it difficult to get to and from the meeting place. Sometimes they left early to start their journeys home. In 1668 Massachusetts records show that two deputies from Springfield, then on the colony's western fringe, "on their request, having binn long absent from their homes, are dismist the service of this Court" (*RGC*, vol. IV, part II 1854, 385). In 1771 the New Hampshire assembly collected data on the distance to the meeting place in Portsmouth and member attendance. Representatives who lived within 50 miles of Portsmouth attended between 10 days and the full 19 during which the assembly met while those from the three towns that were 95 miles or more away failed to attend at all (*DRNH*, vol. VII 1873, 286).

Multimember districts provided one potential remedy for attendance problems by increasing the chances a constituency would have at least one representative present during a session. They also offered a second benefit: multiple members could keep tabs on one another. This improved a constituency's prospects for monitoring lawmaker behavior.

Finally, it is worth noting that colonial lawmakers represented fewer constituents than did their counterparts in Parliament; assemblies in New Hampshire, New Jersey, New York, North Carolina, Rhode Island, and South Carolina are estimated to have had one member for every 1,187 constituents while the House of Commons had one member for every 14,362 constituents (Clarke 1943, 268; Pole 1962, 638). By the mid-eighteenth century the number of constituents per representative was rising in many colonies, notably in Maryland, New Jersey, New York, and Pennsylvania, where populations were growing rapidly. Growth in assembly membership failed to keep pace (Greene 1981, 461). Still, colonial districts were sufficiently small that members could be expected to have tight connections with their constituents.

FIVE

Election Mechanics and Candidate Emergence

Assembly elections were seen as consequential events. Much was published hyping their significance and urging voters to participate. Rhode Island's governor counseled that there was a "very greate neede that the Persons Elected as Deputies for to sitt in the said Assembly bee Prudent & able Persons that may advise in a Business of soe great concern to the whole Colony" (*ERTPr*, vol. XV 1899, 133). A Maryland writer reminded fellow freeholders that these contests were "A Business of the highest Concern to yourselves, and of no less Import to the Province" (*MDG* 1767). One New Yorker declared, "In Reality the Rights and Liberties of every one among us, our Lives and Properties, every Thing dear and valuable, are entrusted to the Care and Disposal of our Representatives," while another called it "the noblest Privilege of a *Free People*, in electing their Representatives" (*To the Freeholders and Freemen of the City and County of New-York, in Communion* 1769; *NYJ* 1769d). A Massachusetts essayist asserted that "among those [Rights and] Privileges, *the Choice of Gentlemen to represent us in the Great and General Court*, I apprehend to be none of the least" (*BEP* 1759). A Rhode Island pamphlet agreed that much was at stake: "You are free, my dear Countrymen, and it is in your own Power to make an Assembly, that will redress your Grievances, and lend their Attention to the greatest Objects of Government" (*Letter to the Common People* 1763, 4).

Because of their significance a New Hampshirite opined that "the *Election of Representatives*, can at no time be justly deemed a light and trifling affair; that to treat it with indifference, must be . . . censurable as a criminal negligence" (*NHG* 1762). A Pennsylvania pamphleteer similarly scolded, "But this great concern of Elections is become too important to be dallied with, and tis' necessary, that All who are interested, should be fully acquainted with their Rights, and with the Measures taken to Pervert and Elude our greatest Securities in them" (*Advice and Information* 1727, 2). The most hyperbolic appeal appeared in a Massachusetts pamphlet, which asserted that "there scarce ever was a Time since this Country was settled, that required more able and faithful PATRIOTS to sit in the General Assembly, than at this juncture, but especially in the *House of Representatives*, who are the *Guardians of the People's Liberty.*" This plea was issued not in 1775 but in 1722 (*English Advice* 1722, 1). Each generation believed its choices were pivotal.

We might conjecture that elections would make colonial lawmakers sensitive to their constituents' preferences. Such a hypothesis would be premised on evidence that incumbents sought reelection, with the notion being that as members increasingly wanted to be reelected they had to pay greater deference to what their voters wanted. But we might also expect that elections would have to be competitive for lawmakers to pay attention to the voters' desires.

The first premise was met. Over time colonial lawmakers increasingly sought reelection. Between 1696 and 1775, turnover dropped in every assembly save New Jersey's, and the decline was usually impressive. In the most extreme case, turnover in Pennsylvania dropped to a mean of 18 percent in the decade from 1766 to 1775 from a mean of 62 percent in the decade from 1696 to 1705 (Greene 1981). And over half of the "new" members in later decades were actually returning former lawmakers (Tully 1977, 181–82).

Across the colonies a cadre of reelection-seeking members arose. By the middle of the eighteenth century newspapers often took note of incumbents' electoral success (*BPB* 1763; *MDG* 1764b; *SCG* 1754a, 1762d, 1768c). In 1761, for example, Maryland readers learned that in the recent elections 35 of the winners "were of the last Assembly," another 8 "have served before, but were not of the last Assembly," and only 15 had "never served before" (*MDG* 1761). Such results were common. In Boston's annual elections between 1719 and 1775, most of which were contested, incumbents won more than 80 percent of the seats (Warden 1970, 22). Clearly there was a robust incumbent advantage.

It is with the assumption of greater electoral competition that potential problems with the representational hypothesis arise. Many assembly races were uncontested, with only enough candidates named to fill the available number of seats. Indeed, voters did not always expect a contest. Thus one announcement about a Virginia election—"A Writ is order'd to be issued, for Electing a Burgess to represent the College of *William* and *Mary* . . . And we are credibly inform'd, that *Edward Barradall*, Esq; Attorney General of this Colony, will be unanimously elected this Day"—likely did not cause readers to bat an eye (*VG* 1738). Competition for assembly seats started at low levels and increased only episodically (Kolp 1992; Leonard 1954). Broadly contested races were sufficiently unusual that they have merited scholarly attention, as with the heated New York races in 1768 and 1769 (Champagne 1963; Friedman 1965; Leder 1963). Only in Rhode Island did anything like modern political parties develop; elsewhere they were not present to recruit candidates and generate competition (Greene 1979, 40; Main 1973, 5, 11).

The intermittent nature of competitive assembly elections can be demonstrated in several ways. First, during an election within one colony, some contests might be tight while others were not. A 1754 news story stated, "We hear from several Parts in New-Jersey, that there has been lately the greatest Struggles in electing Representatives, in some of the Counties, that ever were known." The report then noted "In Essex and Bergen are both new Members without much Opposition" (*DRNJ*, vol. XIX, vol. III 1897, 382–83). Second, a constituency could be calm in one election and agitated in another. Samuel Sewall recorded in his diary in 1703, "This was the most unanimous Election that I can remember to have seen in Boston" while seventeen years later he wrote, "I went to the choice of Representatives, [and] took notice the people were under a great Ferment" ("Diary of Samuel Sewall," vol. II 1879, 74; vol. III 1882, 257). Consistent with this characterization, figure 5.1 shows the winning vote percentages for the first- and fourth-place finishers in Boston elections between 1717 and 1774. Some contests were competitive while others were not, with no discernible pattern. The same was true in smaller towns. Mendon, Massachusetts, records show that in 1762 "Capt. Phinehas Lovett was chosen Representative by a majority of one vote" while nine years later "Edward Rawson was chosen Representative by 108 votes to 7 scattering" (Metcalf 1880, 293, 313). Third, over an extended career a candidate might enjoy easy victories and close calls or defeats. In Braintree, John Quincy (great-grandfather of John Quincy Adams) had a long and distinguished career in the Massachusetts assembly, serving as speaker from 1729 to 1740. But in the town records characterizations of his victories vary. In 1729 he was "chosen Representative having all the votes except one," in 1730 he was

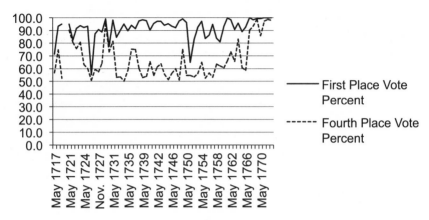

Fig. 5.1. Boston elections for House seats, 1717–74. (Compiled from *RRCB* 1883, 1885a, 1885b, 1886, 1887.)

"chosen Representative, by all the voters present," and in 1731 he was "chosen by a majority of the votes." The next five elections Quincy won unanimously; then there was a series of victories "by a majority of ye vot^e." In 1741 he lost. Quincy was elected several more times over the following two decades, and he lost at least once more (*RTB* 1886).

Given all this, a link between assembly elections and heightened concern with constituent opinions cannot be assumed. Scrutiny of the voting process is necessary to uncover any electoral connection between the represented and the representative. I begin with election mechanics.

Election Mechanics

Assembly elections in Massachusetts were usually held each May. Pennsylvania and Delaware held theirs every October. Semiannual contests in Connecticut and Rhode Island were typically held in May and October in the former and April and August in the latter. In some colonies elections were held everywhere on the same day. In Pennsylvania elections were held on October 1, unless that date fell on a Sunday, in which case they were held the following day. The only exception was the election of Philadelphia City's two members, which occurred the day after the county's representatives were chosen.

In colonies where elections were called irregularly they might occur at any time of the year. Sometimes they conflicted with other scheduled events. In Maryland one year, public notice had to be given that "the FAIR, which was to have been held at Upper Marlborough, on Tuesday the 16th Instant, is put off 'til the Tuesday following, on Account of the Election" (*MDG* 1753b). Setting the day or days for an election typically fell to the sheriff (*CSP* 1910b, 3). That allowed voting within a colony to occur on different days in different constituencies. In 1764 elections in Georgia's 13 constituencies were scheduled on days scattered between October 18 and November 6 (*GG* 1764).

Having elections occur on different days allowed for the possibility of political mischief. An adviser to a New Hampshire governor recommended holding all contests on one day so "there wont be so good an opportunity" for the governor's opponents "to ride from Town to Town" rallying against his candidates (Batinski 1996, 119). A Rhode Island governor persuaded his assembly to schedule elections on the same day, arguing that allowing "the Choice in all the Towns at Different Times . . . gives great Room for Ill Designing Persons to Create Divisions and Make parties amongst the Inhabitants by goeing from Town to Town to be present at each meeting in Order by their Subtill contrivances to get in Such Persons as will suit their Turn's" (*Correspondence of the Colonial Governors* 1902, 37–38).

Scheduling offered opportunities for electoral maneuverings in colonies where voters were entitled to vote everywhere they held sufficient estates. Following a New York contest there were complaints that it "was appointed to be upon the same day in all places . . . whereby the best free-holders who had estates in several Counties, were deprived of giving their votes at several elections" (*DRNY*, vol. IV 1854, 621). A Virginian reported that "the days of Election for Loudoun & Fairfax [counties] happen both the 20th which will weaken Col. Lee's Interest, & it is thought occasioned him to be Drop't" (*LW*, vol. II 1899, 346).

Such intrigues were not imaginary. In June 1768, Thomas Marshall, the sheriff of Fauquier County, Virginia, "declared his Intentions of standing a Candidate at the next Election for the said County, and continued such his Intention until the 23[d] of *August*, when he, as Sheriff, received the Writ of Election, appointed the 18th Day of *September* for holding the same." Marshall served as sheriff until September 2, when his replacement received his commission. Stepping down was necessary so that Marshall could serve as a burgess if elected, which he was. But the third-place finisher challenged the outcome, claiming Marshall had manipulated the schedule to his own advantage. The assembly committee that investigated the complaint found that "M[r] *Marshall*, in appointing the Election for the said County, on the same Day of the *Stafford* Election, with a View to Prevent the Inhabitants of *Stafford* from voting at the *Farquier* Election, acted improperly." It concluded, however, that the number of votes impacted by the mischief was insufficient to overturn the results, thereby allowing Marshall, whose son would become Chief Justice of the United States, to serve (*JHB* 1766–1906, 290–91).

Writs were issued to notify voters of an impending election. In colonies with regular election schedules there was little controversy surrounding them. Indeed, writs were not required in Pennsylvania (*SLP*, vol. II 1896, 212). But where elections were held irregularly they could be a source of trouble. Their absence in early-eighteenth-century North Carolina led the governor to protest that voting "appointed without any writ for it which occasions a great deal of Mobbing and tumults" (*CRNC*, vol. III 1886, 181).

One consideration with writs involved how much notice needed to be given to voters. A lack of adequate warning was a common complaint (*CRNC*, vol. IV 1886, 118; Salley 1898, 253). In New Hampshire in the 1690s, the lieutenant governor informed London officials, "I have been told that in several towns the inhabitants were not warned of the election of Assembly men, and that but a few, malignant to the King's Government, met and chose them." He passed along a letter that alleged, "I hear that not above six met at Exeter and not above twenty at Hampton" because of the lack of proper notice (*CSP* 1905, 92). When a similar situation unfolded in West Jersey, the proprietors complained, "The writs were issued and the elections directed to be made in such haste . . . many of the towns had not any (much less due) notice of the day of the election" (*CSP* 1916a, 688). In this instance, the Council of Trade and Plantations admonished the colony's governor "to be mindful for the future of giving such notice (14 days at least) that all who have a right may have time to repair to the place of election, as they shall see fit" (*CSP* 1916b, 39). The time required between the notice of an election and day on which it took place varied at the margins. At the longer end, New Jersey and Virginia mandated at least 20 days, while New Hampshire specified 15, New York 12, and Georgia 10 (*ANJ* 1776, 69; Bishop 1893, 281; *CLNY*, vol. I 1894, 406; *Miscellaneous Provincial* 1890, 354, 603; *SLV*, vol. III 1823, 236).

Writs were public documents. Virginia's 1655 election law required that sheriffs must "within ten dayes after the receipt of such writs . . . cause the same to be published and by giving notice of the same from house to house by the sheriff or [his] deputy to all persons interested in elections." That process did not work well. Several years later, "WHEREAS frequent complaints are made by the people that they have noe notice of the time appointed for election of Burgesses and by that meanes are deprived of giving their voyces in the election of their owne representatives," the assembly put in place new procedures. Sheriffs were to make copies of their writs with the date of the election noted and to distribute them "to the minister or reader of every parish in their county, who is to read the same to the people two Sundays successively, both in the Church and Chappell." After having done so, the ministers and readers were to attest to that fact, "which attestation shalbe sufficient to discharge the sheriffe from blame." This process was maintained in later laws (*SLV*, vol. I 1809, 411; vol. II 1823, 82; vol. III 1823, 236).

Other colonies put in place similar practices. A 1719 South Carolina act specified that church wardens were to "give publick notice in writing of all and every such writs, two Sundays before the appointed time of election, at the door of each parish church, or at some other publick place." The stated goal of this effort was so "the time and place of election may be better and more fully made known" (*SLSC*, vol. third 1838, 50). In New Jersey, sheriffs were to post writs "at three of the most publick Places in their County, City or Town" (*ANJ* 1776, 69). North Carolina's 1760 election law required each sheriff to "advertise, or cause to be advertised, [writs] at every Church and Chappel, and Court-house within his County, imme- diately after Devine Service, on Three several *Sundays*, successively, next before the Election" (*CAAA* 1764, 200). Not every law was so specific; New York's 1699 measure gave sheriffs six days after receiving a writ to "cause publick notice to be given of ye time & place of Election" (*CLNY*, vol. I 1894, 406). Most officials made an effort to disseminate election informa- tion. In 1737 a Londonderry, New Hampshire, constable wrote to colony officials, "By virtue of the [election] warrant I have posted up S^d warrant as usuall and went to as many of the freeholders Houses as I Could in the time and notified them" (*ERL* 1908, 189).

Delays in receiving writs affected election schedules. A Virginia letter reported, "The Writs for Election being so long on their way that it was ye 4th (our Court Day) before they came to ye Sherifs hands, made it Impos- sible to have ye Election before the 24th as ye Law directed 20 day's between ye time they come to hand & that day [of election]" (*LW*, vol. II 1899, 343). In some cases writs never made it to the appropriate official or there was no officer to receive them, and as a result elections were not conducted ("Deposition of Jireh Bull and Thomas Paine, 1699" 1885, 155–56; *JHB* 1766– 1906, 18–19, 190).

Laws established how long voting was to occur. South Carolina's 1704 statute stated that voting for assembly members "shall not continue longer than two days, and shall begin and be made between the hours of eight and twelve in the forenoon, and the hours of two and six in the afternoon." In 1716 it was loosened, so that voting would "begin at sun rising each day, and end at sun setting," and then three years later it was changed again, to "begin at seven of the clock in the morning and end at seven in the evening." In 1721 the hours were shortened, with voting beginning at nine and ending at four (*SLSC*, vol. second 1837, 250, 684; vol. third 1838, 51, 136). Some elections took longer. In 1761 voting in New York City and County began on a Tuesday and continued through "Friday about Ten o'Clock in the Morning" (*NYG* 1761e). In other places they were shorter. Voting in Massachusetts and Pennsylvania usually took one day.

Poll openings were vulnerable to political manipulation. In a 1769 case, a Virginia sheriff who was partial to a candidate was accused by one of the other candidates of opening the polling too early, before the unhappy candidate's supporters from the farthest reaches of the county had arrived. According to one account, the aggrieved candidate, "stripped, with his Coat and his Waist-coat off, and his Collar unbuttoned," was seen "shaking his Cane over [the sheriff's] Head, saying . . . '*that he would be dammed if he should read the Writ yet.*'" The sheriff responded, "*He would be dammed if he did not.*" Nobody ended up being hit. The assembly sided with the sheriff and charged the upset candidate with obstructing the election (*JHB 1766–1906*, 243–45).

Sometimes polls were left open longer than usual to aid a favored candidate. In 1725 a New Jersey sheriff backing one contender kept "the Poll open for a fortnight" and then adjourned it "without the consent of the other candidate to the edge of the county." According to the governor, the partiality exhibited by the sheriff "was so visible" that the assembly passed a reform bill "to provide a Remedy against the like for the future" (*DRNY*, vol. V 1855, 767).

More common were complaints that election officials truncated voting without good cause. Maryland's assembly voided a Baltimore County election because, "altho' many of the Candidates requested and agreed, that the said Sheriff might adjourn the Election to the next Day, he omitted so to do." The sheriff's decision meant that "many Voters were deprived of an Opportunity of giving their Votes." The same body unanimously overturned a 1768 election in the same county for the same reason: "[T]he Polls were closed . . . when the Sheriff had good Reason to believe that a Number of Persons were on their Way." Again, "the People were prevented from having a full and free Election" (*VPMD* 1752, 11; 1770, 217–18, 228). Decisions about when to open and close the polls had consequences. After it was found that the polls had closed too early in a

1762 Virginia election, the assembly added to the incumbent's totals the votes of two voters who had not arrived in time, thereby giving him the victory (*JHB 1761– 1907*, 89–90).

Elections could be mismanaged at the end of the process as well. In Georgia results were occasionally returned by someone other than the official specified on the writ, resulting in an assembly decision to declare that the "said Election is undue." One contest was overturned because it "appears that there is an Arrasement in the return of the name of the Representative, and of the Date" (*CRSG*, vol. XIII 1907, 21, 25, 26, 86–87). The North Carolina assembly vacated an election because "from the time of issuing the Writs of election to the County of Pasquotank to the day of the election there was no Sheriff in that County." In another county a deputy sheriff ran an election in which the sheriff was returned as one of the winning candidates. That outcome, too, was tossed out (*CRNC*, vol. IX 1890, 459–60, 756, 759). A Maryland election was voided simply because the sheriff failed to submit the required documents (*AM*, vol. XXXIV 1914, 72).

Some incidents were egregious. The North Carolina assembly over-turned an election when it found that the marshal supervising the polling had returned the wrong candidate (*CRNC*, vol. IV 1886, 117). A New York sheriff submitted two separate returns listing different sets of winning candidates. The assembly spent considerable time sorting out the mess (*JVNY* 1766, 658, 678). And the South Carolina assembly found that a church warden had turned in the name of a winner when there was "no such Person in this Province" (*CRSC* 1956, 17).

Voting was conducted at designated locations. Virginia's 1705 election law specified that it was to occur at the "court-house of the county" (*SLV*, vol. III 1823, 239). Pennsylvania's law required elections for the city and county of Philadelphia to be held "at or near the market-place,' while those in Bucks County would take place "upon the court-house ground in the town of Bristol" and in Chester County "at or near the court-house in the town of Chester" (*SLP*, vol. II 1896, 212–13). Delaware specified the courthouse as the election site for each of its counties (*LGD* 1763, 118). South Carolina's law was looser, requiring only that "every election for members of Assembly shall be in some open and publick place" (*SLSC*, vol. second 1837, 250). New York's law was similarly flexible, stipulating that voting was to happen "at ye most public & usuall place of Election" (*CLNY*, vol. I 1894, 406). On occasion, the only space that could accom-modate large numbers of voters was an open expanse. In 1761 New York City and County voters were instructed to assemble "on the Green near the Work-House, in the City of New-York." Space was needed because more than 1,400 voters participated (*NYG* 1761d, 1761e). A few years later "Township of Schenectady" freeholders and freemen were directed to vote at "the Dwelling House of Robert Clench" because they were far fewer in number (*PSWJ*, vol. VI 1928, 585). Small venues were the norm in most New England towns. The 1765 election for the representative from Amherst and Bedford, New Hampshire, was held at "Ensn Daniel Moors barn" (*Diary of Matthew Patten* 1903, 151).

At times additional polling places were established to meet the voters' needs. In 1748 the New York assembly mandated a second polling site in Orange County because "a large Range of Mountains running through the Middle of the Same County" caused voters to find it "very Inconvenient, Troublesome & Expensive" to get to where they were required to go. Many of them "not being able to bear the fatiegue of Crossing the said Mountains [and] have been obliged to Stay home, and thereby were deprived Voting for their Representatives." The assembly later made a similar accommodation for Westchester County voters (*CLNY*, vol. III 1894, 713–15, 847–48).

Deviations from holding elections at the usual place caused problems. When, because of a smallpox outbreak, Spotsylvania County, Virginia, relocated its voting site some distance away from the Fredericksburg courthouse, it was moved to a private home in the countryside. Some freeholders, including a few from outside the county, missed the balloting because of the switch. There was a hint of electoral mischief; an old bridge crossing a river between Fredericksburg and the temporary polling place was removed three days before the election, with a worker telling people it had been done "*To laugh at the* Rappahanock *Electors*" (*JHB*, 1742– 1909, 292–93).

The mechanics of how votes were cast varied. The earliest elections for the Massachusetts assembly were conducted by means of the raising of hands, but by 1635 it was decided they were to be conducted "by pa[per]s" (*RGC*, vol. I 1853, 157). Still, some towns continued "the lifting up of hands" (Sheldon 1879, 146). Paper ballots were common in New England. Connecticut's first election law required voters to "bring the names of such, written in sev[r]rall papers, as they desire to have chosen for that Imployment" (*PRCC* 1850, 23). Paper ballots were mandated in East Jersey, but West Jersey decided that elections would "be not determined by the common and confused way of cry's and voices, but by putting balls into balloting boxes" (*Grants, Concessions* 1758, 155, 405). Voting in Pennsylvania was initially done by ballot in Philadelphia County, but "at upland & in all the Lower

Countyes, by black & white beanses put into a hatt," which, one official argued, was "a balloting in his sense." Shortly thereafter it was decided that "Each County shall hence fforward Elect or give their Suffrages . . . by ye ballat" (*MPCP*, vol. I 1838, 239–40, 282). By 1755 the established practice was that "every one votes as he pleases, and as privately as he pleases, the Election being by written Tickets folded up and put into a Box" (*PAG* 1755). South Carolina mandated that each voter "shall put, into a box, glass, or sheet of paper prepared for that purpose by the . . . church-wardens . . . a piece of paper rolled up, whereon is written the name of the Representatives he votes for, and to which paper the elector shall not be obliged to subscribe his name" (*SLSC*, vol. third 1838, 51). A similar system was used in North Carolina. After giving his name to the sheriff and the appointed inspectors, a voter submitted "a Scroll of Paper, rolled up, with the Name or Names of the Person or Persons he votes for, written therein; which Scroll shall be immediately, by the Sheriff, put into the Box." The box was to be small, "with a Lid or Cover, having a Hole in it, not exceeding Half an Inch in Diameter" (*Acts of Assembly* 1751, 177–78).

A petition contesting a Portsmouth, New Hampshire, election provides an account of voting with ballots: "Pursuant to a precept to us, Wee gave notice to the voters in the usual manner of the time, place & occasion of holding a meeting, which was duly attended; a moderator chosen & then the votes in writing bro't in for a Representative, which were fairly put into a Box standing before the moderator & clerk, by the voters passing by man by man. When all were bro't in, the votes were turned out on a table & counted by the moderator & Clerk" (*DRRT* 1875, 699).

The main alternative to ballot voting was to make one's choice by voice. In 1646 Virginia responded to concerns about the "disorderly and illegal election of Burgesses, by subscribing of hands" by requiring voters to express their choices by "voices; and that no hand writing shall be admitted." A 1705 law went into more detail, specifying that "every freeholder . . . shall appear accordingly, and give his vote." In turn the sheriff was to "appoint such and so many person or persons, as to him shall seem fit, to take in writing, the name of every freeholder who gives his vote, and the person or persons he votes for" (*SLV*, vol. I 1809, 333–34; vol. III 1823, 238–39). Similarly, New York stipulated in its 1699 election act that the sheriff or his deputy was to "truly and Indifferently . . . sett Down ye names of each Elector & ye place of his ffreehold & for whom he shall poll" (*CLNY*, vol. I 1894, 407).

In 1760 North Carolina switched from using written ballots to a system in which "Votes shall be given openly" (*CAAA* 1764, 199). An account of the process under the new rule related, "The voting was done openly and orally. The candidates sat on the magistrates' bench in open court, the sheriff down below to oversee the voting to ascertain how every man voted. The candidates were permitted to acknowledge the vote of his constituents by a nod, and sometimes words of thanks were spoken to those voting for him" (Turner and Bridges 1920, 70–71). Virginia elections were much the same (Syndor 1952, 19–22).

When the outcome appeared obvious, voice-voting elections could be determined simply by the election official evaluating "a view" of those attending, (*ANJ* 1776, 69; *CLNY*, vol. I 1894, 406; Scharf 1886, 110–11; *SLV*, vol. III 1823, 172; Syndor 1952, 19–22). If a poll was requested by a candidate it was usually taken; an election official's failure to grant one could lead to a contest being declared invalid (*AM*, vol. XXVII 1907, 457). But if all involved agreed not to bother, no count was made. This happened with George Washington's election in 1769. In his diary, Washington noted that he "Went to Alexandria, to the Election for Burgesses for Fairfax and was chosen, together with Colo. West, without a Pole, their being no opposition" (*Diaries of George Washington*, vol. I 1925, 344). Even when the voters were polled, not every possible vote might be voiced. Once a contest's outcome became evident, losing candidates often withdrew. Thus, with the two leading candidates having received 268 and 257 votes in a 1750 New York race, the third-place candidate, who had just 53 votes, conceded, and the polling was stopped. An estimated 300 freeholders in attendance had yet to voice their preferences (*NYWJ* 1750).

Departures from legal voting procedures occurred occasionally and were usually treated harshly. In 1776 a Massachusetts representative complained that the first week of the legislative session had been consumed with "controverted elections." He recounted, "We yesterday sent home the Salem members for the irregularity of the proceedings of the town in their choice." Salem's violation was that "the electors voted by kernels of corn and pease" and not with the required paper ballots (*Warren-Adams Letters*, vol. I 1917, 252–53).

Proxy voting was allowed during the early years in some colonies. Elections in parts of New York employed an electoral college variant. Huntington records reveal that in 1691 two men were "chosen by ye towne to goe to Southhamton to joine with the Rest of the Countie in chussing too assembly men." Later, proxy votes were carried to county meetings from both Hempstead and Huntington (*Huntington Town Records* 1888, 92, 131; *Journal of the Legislative Council* 1861, xi; *Records of the Towns of North and South Hempstead* 1896, 409–10; *Second Book of Records* 1877, 286). But such practices disappeared in most colonies. In South Carolina, where norms initially allowed voters "to bring Papers for others & put in their votes for them," a 1704 law held that no "voice or vote" could be given "by proxy, letter, or any other way whatsoever." Instead, it was required that each voter "shall be present in person, or his voice to be taken for none" (Rivers 1856, 407; *SLSC*, vol. second 1837, 250).

Voters were expected to cast votes for as many names as there were seats. According to Maryland's assembly, "[E]very Voter shall, upon such General Election, or other Election for more than one Delegate, give in his Vote for the whole Number to be chosen on that Election, at the Time of his voting at the Poll, or shall be precluded from giving any further Vote during that Election" (*VPMD* 1749, 24). That decision followed earlier ones in Pennsylvania, which had ruled that a ballot containing "more names than by this act is allowed any one elector to vote for, such papers shall be rejected" and that "a Ticket containing a less Number of Names than by Law are directed to be returned, of Representatives for each County" was not "a good Ticket" (*SLP*, vol. II 1896a, 216; *VPPP* 1732, 5). Delaware had a law requiring ballots with "fewer or more Names" than were allowed to be tossed out (*LGD*, vol. I 1763, 122). Both North Carolina and South Carolina mandated that ballots with too many names were to be, in the former's wording, "cast away, as useless and void" (*Collection of all the Public Acts of Assembly* 1752, 178; *SLSC*, vol. second 1837, 684). But there was no unanimity on this point. Poll lists from New York City and County elections in the 1760s show that nontrivial numbers of voters cast votes for fewer than the four candidates allowed (*Copy of the Poll List* 1880a, 1880b, 1880c).

Over time colonists came to grasp the political implications of different voting systems. Problems were alleged with each approach. In the 1730s some New Yorkers began pressing for voting by ballot, arguing that it would "prevent Bribery and Corruption" of the sort found with voice voting (*Many of the Electors* 1739). A 1755 assessment of South Carolina's practices by the Board of Trade argued the opposite, maintaining that ballot voting was "liable to great Fraud and Juggle in the Execution" (Greene 1961, 80).

In the 1760s procedural reforms were contemplated by several colonies. As noted earlier, North Carolina switched to voice voting from the use of ballots, while Georgia's governor thwarted an attempt to make the opposite change (*CAAA* 1764, 199; *CRSG*, vol. 28, part II 1979, 336). A fiery debate on the topic erupted in New York. Arguing for a switch to the use of a secret ballot, one writer asserted that if, "in our method of collecting vote's, every man's suffrage is publicly known, their choice will not be so free as it ought to be, and many will be loath from selfish principles, to vote to the disadvantage of a man with whom they have considerable connections, and whose displeasure, for this, or other reasons they are afraid of" (*NYJ* 1768a). Others took up this theme, claiming, "The Suffrage, as given by the *Ballot*, prevents all Inconveniences that might otherwise attend a Person on the Account of his having voted to the Pleasure or Displeasure of any, Leaving it a Secret with himself whom he votes *for*, or *against*" (*The Ballator* 1768). The secret ballot was even seized on by defenders of the Livingston Manor seat as a mechanism that would assure that it did not function as a pocket borough (*The Case of the Manor* 1769, 3).

Responding to the political pressure, in 1769 the assembly voted by an 18 to 5 margin to allow a bill to be brought in that would allow the switch to ballots (*JVNY* 1770, 47). The subsequent legislation's preamble gave its justification: "[T]he present Mode of taking the Voices of Electors publickly at the Polls, excites Tumult and Disorder, leads the Candidates to Prodigality, and the People to Intemperance, and exposes the Electors to the undue Influence of Terror and Corruption" (*NYG* 1770e). Efforts were made to generate additional public support for the reform. A broadside was produced, which claimed, "It is not in human Power to devise a more effectual Antidote to Corruption, than a Law for Elections by Ballot" (*To the Freeholders, and Freemen of the City and Province of New-York* 1769). Among the reasons another publication listed for supporting "a Balloting Law" were that it would "prevent Tumults, Riots, and Disorders at Elections . . . prevent Men of Property, Power, and Tyranical Dispositions, from prostituting their Wealth and Influence, in giving Weight to their Threats," and "in a great Measure, prevent that Dangerous and Detestable Practice of Bribery and Corruption." Those who might prefer voice voting were assured that the proposed reform would not "prevent any Man, from boldly declaring, at the Time of Polling, the Names of those, for whom he gives his Vote, if he chooses" (*To the Freeholders, and Freemen, of the City and County of New-York* 1770). A large group of supporters who met at the "Liberty Pole" instructed their representatives that "we desire that you use your utmost Endeavours" to get the measure passed (*NYG* 1770a, 1770g).

But opposition to the reform emerged. A broadside "from a Squinter on Public Affairs" took issue with the assertion that ballots were less susceptible to fraud and corruption (*The Mode of Elections* 1769). A group requested that "*independent Freeholders and Freemen* of this City . . . meet at the Merchant's Coffee House . . . to convey their Sentiments respecting this Matter to their Representatives, and to convince them that they are not to be diverted by any Motives whatever, from daring and chusing to speak their

Minds freely and openly; to do which at all Times is their *Birthright* as *Englishmen*, and their Glory as *Americans*" (*To the Independent Freeholders* 1770). The resulting gathering—said to have consisted of "One Thousand and Seven Freeholders and Freemen"—sent representatives a competing set of instructions, encouraging them to "oppose, by all legal Means in your Power, the proposed Alteration." They argued that, rather than reducing corruption, ballots both increased the chances of it and made it more difficult to uncover when it happened, "as both in the Government of *Pennsylvania*, and in the Colony of *Connecticut*, where Elections have constantly been by Ballot, Frauds are greatly and more and more complained of, and the Impossibility of detecting them by any after Scrutiny, has been found to be the greatest Encouragement to their Perpetration" (*NYG* 1770b).

In the end, the opposition's arguments carried the day; an assembly vote to allow the ballot bill to have a second reading failed when the speaker voted against it, breaking a tie (*JVNY* 1770, 66). The New York City and County members, saying that "they would always pay a due Regard to *constitutional* Instructions from a Majority of their Constituents," switched from voting two to one in favor of the measure on its first vote to four to nothing against it on the second vote. (The speaker was a delegation member and only voted the second time.) Given public interest, after rejecting the bill the assembly ordered the clerk to have its text printed in the newspapers (*NYG* 1770e, 1770f). Not everyone had found the debate enlightening. One cynic wrote that he did not "care one farthing which way it may be determined" because "let the Affair be desided as they please, they can never prevent bribery and Corruption in elections" (*PSWJ*, vol. VII 1931, 334). But the battle may have had larger ramifications than anyone at the time realized. The political split foreshadowed the upcoming division on independence: 11 of the 12 supporters of the ballot reform would support the Revolution, while 9 of the 13 opponents would remain loyalists (Bonomi 1971, 277; Lossing 1860, 50).

The argument that having votes publicly identified by voter made resolving contested elections easier was valid. Lawmakers could examine contested votes and know exactly how adding or subtracting them would change an outcome. After assessing the evidence in a disputed 1758 race, the Maryland assembly, finding that "the Petitioner having disqualified the Votes of [eight voters], on the Sitting Member's Poll, and the Sitting Member having added one Vote to his Poll, and the Polls [now] being even," declared the contest void and called for a new election writ to be issued (*MDG* 1759a; *VPMD* 1759, 46). Similarly, the New York assembly calculated that "after having made a state of the votes on both sides, it appearing to the house, that supposing the four objected votes on Mr. Morris's side (which the house has not yet determined upon) to be all good, Mr. De Lancey has a majority of one vote" (*JVNY* 1769, 26). In one contested election the Virginia assembly included a table giving the reported votes for each candidate, the "bad Votes" that were deducted, and the two votes added to one candidate's total because two gentlemen were found "to have voted for the Petitioner, but their Names not entered upon the Poll" (*JHB 1770– 1906*, 252).

At the same time, the downside to voice voting was as its opponents alleged. Being on record as failing to support some prominent person was risky. Candidates took note of those who voted for and against them. Following his 1758 election as a burgess, George Washington was given a "True Copy of the Poll" listing the voters and their votes. The supporter who assembled the list did so to allow him to be a "Compitent Judge of your Friend^s." Washington not only copied the list by hand but also alphabetized the names in the process (*LW*, vol. II 1899, 398, 401).

Standards for determining who was elected differed. A plurality rule was specified in several colonies. In Connecticut those "that have greatest nu[m]ber of papers written for the the[m] shall be deputyes for that Courte" (*PRCC* 1850, 23–24). A 1646 Virginia law stated that no burgess was to be elected "but by plurality of voices," while a 1705 measure credited victory to the candidate who "shall appear to have the most votes" (*SLV*, vol. I 1808, 333–34; vol. III 1823, 239). Pennsylvania's law stipulated that the man "whose name is oftenest mentioned" on the ballots was elected (*SLP*, vol. II 216). North Carolina employed the same approach in its 1760 law, holding "the Person or Persons who shall have the greatest Number of Suffrages, to be duly elected" (*CAAA* 1764, 199).

Majority standards were stipulated in other places. New York established that "in all elections the Majority of votes shall carry itt" (*CLNY*, vol. I 1894, 245). Similarly, New Jersey's law held that representatives "shall be chosen by the Majority of Voices or Votes of the Freeholders of each County" (*ANJ* 1776, 6). Georgia, Massachusetts, and South Carolina also required a majority (*Acts and Resolves* 1869, 11, 89; Bishop 1893, 282; *SLSC*, vol. second 1837, 684–85). An astute observer of Massachusetts politics wrote, "By custom, all elections . . . are determined not by the major vote, but by the majority of voters; because where there are more than two candidates, a person may have a major vote, though not a majority of the voters" (Douglass, vol. I 1755, 491). Accordingly, a 1759 Boston contest required three additional ballots before a fourth candidate achieved a majority (*RRCB* 1886, 22–23).

Sometimes it was not clear what standard was used or if the difference between plurality and majority was understood. Notoriously, a 1730 New Jersey law called in one section for a decision about where to build a county courthouse to be made "by Plurality of Voices" and in another section by a "Majority of Voices" (*ANJ* 1776, 92). Such confusion occasionally occurred. When in 1698 the high sheriff of "Berkly County" in South Carolina summoned "all the free Holders of Berkly and Craven Counties Quallified for Electing members of Assembly to Convene at Charles Town . . . the s^d ffree Holders Did then and there by Majority of Voates Chose, Twenty memb^rs." The actual election results, however, suggest that a plurality rule was employed (*JCH* 1914, 5–6). This appears to have been an ongoing problem in the colony. A 1721 election law explicitly required the use of a "majority of votes" standard (*SLSC*, vol. third 1838, 136). Yet an account of a 1735 special election stated, "On Wednesday, Mr. John Dart Merchant, was elected by a plurality of Votes, Member of the Hon. the House of Commons" (*SCG* 1735).

What happened in the event of a tie? In Georgia, Maryland, New York, and Pennsylvania another election was called to determine the winner (*AM*, vol. XXXVII 1917, 461; *CRSG* vol. XV 1907, 35–36; *GG* 1769; *JVNY* 1728, 25; *PA*, fourth series, vol. III 1900, 308–9). In other places different methods were used. In 1698 South Carolina faced two tied contests; in one the assembly simply picked the winner, and in the other it eliminated one candidate because he had "Executed the precept for Electing members of Assembly for Craven County." He was ordered to "mend his Returne by Raceing his owne name" (*JCH* 1914, 8, 10). When a 1757 contest ended in a three-way tie, the assembly ordered a new election (*JCH* 1996, 18; see also *CRSC* 1952, 80). The method used to break a tie also changed over time in North Carolina. In a 1735 case the assembly chose between the candidates (*CRNC*, vol. IV 1886, 117). A distinctive mechanism was introduced in the 1760 election law: in the event of a tie, "the Sheriff shall have the casting Vote, and in no other case give his Vote" (*CAAA* 1764, 199). A 1705 Virginia election bill provided for the same tie breaker (*SLV*, vol. III 1823, 239). But when a Maryland sheriff cast a tie-breaking vote in a 1745 race the assembly threw out the result (*VPMD* 1745, 34, 42–43).

Deference and Candidate Emergence

More discriminating than the formal qualifications for assembly service discussed in chapter 3 was the norm of deference, a sentiment that assembly service was best left to members of the disinterested economic elite (Kirby 1970; Tully 1977). Because of it one historian observed, "It seems not to have been so much a question of *what* as *who*" (Griffith 1970, 2). Deference meant that, although many white adult males met qualification standards, few of them were thought to be suitable to hold office. As John Adams explained, in Massachusetts voters "must every Year determine who they esteem the better sort. The whole Body of the People, in every Yearly Election, depute a Number of Persons to represent them, and by their suffrages they declare such Persons to be the better sort of People among them" (*John Adams diary 13* 1766, 34).

The "who" clearly mattered, and letters and pamphlets identified traits suitable candidates should have. Many touted the virtues of electing members of the landed elite with whom a voter would be familiar. Thus one writer advised his fellow New Jersey electors, "Chuse not Men whose Abilities, Probity and Fortune, are not well known to you; for when you have chosen them, it will be too late to know them" (*NYG* 1751). A Massachusetts pamphlet focused on the wealthy's likely incorruptibility, posing the question, "Whether the Men of the best Knowledge, Reason and Vertue, as well as Estates, are not more likely to serve us in the General Court, and less liable to be tempted from their Trusts, with Posts of Honour and Profit, than Men of different Characters?" (*A Letter to the Freeholders and Other Inhabitants* 1742, 5). Allusions to this alleged relationship appeared regularly. In New York it was said lawmakers "ought to be Men that have good Estates, *above Bribes*" (*NYWJ* 1737a). Another writer urged voters to select only men "that scorn to give up the *meanest Branch of Property*, to the *largest Bribe* from the Hand of Corruption; but would rather chuse to fall with their *Country*, and the *Comfort* of an *unblemish'd Integrity*" (*A Letter to the Freemen and Freeholders* 1750, 12). A South Carolina "portrait" of a good lawmaker stated that he should be "particularly careful to live within his current income of his own fortune, without which it will be very difficult to preserve his honour." Personal wealth was critical because "the man who is independent, is honest" (*SCG* 1765b). Another benefit conferred by wealth was identified by a writer who urged electors to "chuse those that are Men of Probity, Courage and Ability; and that are both *Spirited* and have *Leisure* to serve their Country" (*English Advice* 1722, 2).

A Massachusetts letter took the importance of a candidate's wealth as self-evident: "A Man of Estate, *ceteris Paribus*, is, for Reasons that are obvious, to be preferr'd to one in low and dependent Circumstances of Life." The writer bemoaned the voters' unfortunate choices: "Strange Absurdity, I confess! that we should commit the publick Interest to those Men with whom we would not trust our private Affairs" (*BEP* 1750). Reservations about the masses were often expressed. A Marylander exclaimed, "[W]hat is very astonishing to me! How many little upstart insignificant Pretenders to the Honour of a Seat in our House of Assembly, do we find in almost every County in our Province! The *Creature* that is able to keep a little Shop . . . or, at most, to judge the Quality of a Leaf of Tobacco, instantly commences Statesman, and esteems his little petty Parts adequate to the great and complex Science of Legislation" (*MDG* 1767). Similar sentiments were registered by a New Hampshirite who cautioned against electing those who "only give their attendance to bear their expences, while they do their own private business," and by a Pennsylvanian who warned against electing "indigent Person[s]" because they might be "under a Temptation to abuse their Trust, to gain their own Ends" (*NHG* 1762; *Some necessary Precautions* 1727).

Some hyped the virtues of merchants. A South Carolina writer recommended a candidate who "has been long practising the Affairs of Commerce" (*SCG* 1741). A Philadelphian advised more generically, "Be sure to have your Eye upon Men of Industry and Improvement: For those that are ingenious, and laborious to propagate the Growth of the Country, will be very tender of weakening or impoverishing it" (*Some necessary Precautions* 1727). That advice later resurfaced in New York (*NYWJ* 1737c).

Attorneys were often singled out as being unqualified because of their profession. A Pennsylvanian counseled against choosing "a crafty popular Lawyer, who by the Wiles or Tricks of his Profession, together with abundance of unintelligible Stuff that he calls Law, hath a knack at making ignorant People gape and stare . . . For which Reason I am also of the Opinion, that you should be very careful how you choose any of that Profession into the Assembly" (*Advice to the Free-holders* 1735, 4–5). A New York pamphlet warned readers "to banish from your minds all thoughts of giving your votes for any lawyers" because "too many of them look upon themselves to have a separate interest from the rest of the community, and hold opinions incompatible with the general welfare" (*A Few Observations* 1768, 6).

Some observers emphasized a candidate's competence. A Massachusetts pamphlet promoted the value of "Men of Knowledge and Skill in public Affairs," arguing that "Knowledge in your Representatives is a necessary Requisite, to judge what Laws are proper to be made, and what Sanctions are proper to enforce them" (*A Letter to the Freeholders and other Inhabitants* 1749, 6). A Bostonian advised, "Let us beware, in our Choice, of Men too young, and unexperienc'd in the Affairs of Government" (*BEP* 1759). A New Yorker argued that "*a deep Knowledge in publick Affairs*" was "absolutely necessary, in at least a great many of the Members" (*NYWJ* 1737a). A pragmatic reason to focus on ability was offered by a Pennsylvanian, who cautioned that "such Men . . . will endeavour in the most decent and honourable Manner, to dispatch the Publick Business, that by shortening our tedious Sessions" (*Advice and Information* 1727, 4).

For many of the same reasons some came to see incumbency as an important qualification. Writing to Portsmouth, New Hampshire, electors, a writer asked, "[H]ave not those who last Represented you served the Public with Fidelity? . . . Is not the Province Law-Book an Evidence both of their Diligence and Skill in the Business of Legislation?" He highlighted the value of experience, arguing against electing nonincumbents because it "will cost you some considerable Expence before they can be in any tolerable Degree acquainted with the State of public Affairs." He concluded, "Law-making requires a minute Knowledge of the Persons and Places represented, their Trade, Interest, and Connections; and is all this to be obtained without Time and Experience, or are the new Members to get the Knowledge of these Things by Inspiration?" (*NHG* 1774c). Previous officeholding was not always thought to be necessary; two Massachusettsans argued, "It matters not whether they are all chosen out of the Number of the *Select-Men* of the several Towns; for it is pretty certain, that every Select-Man is not fit for a *Representative*" (*English Advice* 1722, 2–3). Still, almost all of that colony's representatives had local government experience before being sent to the assembly (Schutz 1997, 22–23).

Finally, in the places where it was allowed, some urged voters not to elect representatives who would concurrently hold other paid governmental positions. In Massachusetts, it was recommended that voters should "by no Means . . . chuse any Persons to serve, that sustain a publick Post in the Government; such as Sheriffs, Military Officers, and the like" because "It is very difficult to find Men of that Resolution and Integrity, who are able to withstand the Snares and Temptations that Places of Honour and Profit subject them to" (*English Advice* 1722, 2). Almost four decades later another colony resident pushed a slightly different theme, saying that "it has been thought highly improper, that those Gentlemen who serve in the *Executive Trust*, should act at all in a *Legislative Capacity* . . . because the many Affairs that necessarily fall under their Cognizance, often-times clash and interfere, when they exercise the different Powers they are invested with" (*BEP* 1759). A New Yorker differentiated among potential dual offices, suggesting, "If the Person you would chuse holds any Office, let it be such an Office as is dependent on the good Will of the People and not any Court Office *During Pleasure*" (*NYWJ* 1738). A Pennsylvania pamphlet gave a practical reason to oppose multiple officeholding, speculating, "May be he that sets up for an Assembly-man is a Magistrate, and therefore this honest plain Man, doth not care to appear against him, lest he should feel the Weight of his Resentment at Court, whenever it is his Misfortune to be dragged thither" (*Advice to the Free-holders* 1735, 4).

Candidate emergence was the most mysterious aspect of colonial elections. There were many contests in which voters made selections without any of their choices making themselves available or even being consulted prior to the voting. After participants in a Norton, Massachusetts, town meeting selected "Cap. Brintinal" to represent them, they sent a delegation to his house to get his answer. His wife informed them that "her husband was Gon to Coneticut . . . & she did not Expect him home tell next tueseday; & If he went farther, as he did Expect when he went from home, not So soon." The town called another meeting and chose someone else (Clark 1859, 281). Because they had not offered themselves, many a representative could credibly claim that "he was not chose of his own seeking" (*CSP* 1910b, 429). The resignations of four Pennsylvania Quakers because of their desire to avoid voting on defense bills could rightfully be couched in language stating that "we who have (without any Solicitation on our Part) been returned as Representatives in this Assembly, request we may be excused" (*VPPP* 1757, 5). And a South Carolina member-elect could legitimately tell his voters, "The unsolicited, and truly Honourable Favour you have conferred upon me . . . is a sufficient Incitement to draw me from that Retirement I had planned for my future Life" (*SCG* 1758).

That candidate nominations, or even the most rudimentary advanced planning, were not a regular feature of assembly elections is demonstrated by the surprising number of those elected who declined the honor. In New Haven, John Miles was elected, "But Capt. Miles Declining the Choice, and giving his Reasons for it the Freemen proceeded to Choose another deputy in his roome and place" (*ATR*, vol. III 1962, 86). In 1737 the first two candidates elected to represent Lancaster, Massachusetts, refused to serve, and only the third person elected agreed to do so (Marvin 1879, 205). The same sequence transpired in Rehoboth (Bliss 1836, 131). All three people elected to the New Hampshire assembly from Hampton in 1717 declined (*LNH*, vol. two 1913, 249). When three men in a row refused in both Norton and Plymouth, Massachusetts, the towns left their posts unfilled (Clark 1859, 281; *RTP* 1903, 54). Getting those elected to agree to serve was a problem throughout the colonies (Allen 1860, 63–64; *ATR* 1919, 137, 139; Currier 1902, 678; *ERTPr*, vol. XIII 1897, 28; Metcalf 1880, 233; Myers 1904, 112–13; Nourse 1894, 414; *PA*, second series, vol. IX 1880, 739, 756; *RTP* 1892,

222, 281, 339; Sanford 1870, 44; *TRS* 1868, 183; *TRT* 1917, 85; *WR* 1900, 162, 213; *WTR* 1882, 47).

Refusals greatly troubled Georgia and South Carolina, which did not compensate members for serving. In the latter, a writer grumbled, "And such hath been the *Unwillingness* of the *Elected* to serve, that not a few, and those some of the fittest Persons in Point of Fortune and Capacity, have *refused* to do it when chosen" (*SCG* 1747–48). The governor communicated the same message to London officials, complaining about "many persons of property and figure declining to attend" (*JBTP*, vol. 8 1931, 289). When a list was compiled of the virtues of a good South Carolina lawmaker, the first was that the member "will ever carefully attend the service of the public in the house, because he knows that the person who is chosen, and does not attend, deserts his post." Difficulties persisted, however. In 1769 a letter writer complained about St. John's Parish "not having one sitting member, in the last assembly, and from the number of gentlemen elected in this, for that parish, who have refused to qualify, *what difficulties* the electors thereof, *in particular*, are put to; to *find* members to represent them." In 1772 another writer pressed South Carolinians to "elect those . . . who will attend" (*SCG* 1765b, 1769b, 1772).

Excuses for not serving were furnished. Othniel Beall wrote to the voters in the three districts that had elected him, "As I am under the highest Obligation for the Favor done me in choosing me for one of your Representatives . . . but as the Situation of my private Affairs at present, will not admit of Serving at this time." He went on to say, "I hope my declining will not give Offence to any of my Friends" (*SCG* 1736c). His was a common justification. In Georgia a member-elect routinely declined by claiming that "his private Concerns wou'd not permit him" to serve (*CRSG*, vol. XIV 1907, 87, 168, 179, 612). Another who refused averred that he was "Elected Contrary to his Inclination" (*CRSG*, vol. XIII 1907, 500). How common were such refusals? In 1749, 9 of the 44 members elected in South Carolina, or just over 20 percent, declined (*SCG* 1749). Such substantial percentages were not unusual (*CRSC* 1951, 13–15, 19, 49, 56, 331; 1952, 31, 32, 44, 74, 81, 82, 156, 204, 239, 292; 1956, 10, 13, 15, 17, 27).

A member-elect might take weeks to decide whether or not he would serve (*SCG* 1754b). Turning down the voters carried some risk. Supporters of a slate of candidates for the Philadelphia city and county seats admitted that the men "have declined accepting our Interest on this Occasion." But they urged, "Choose them therefore, my Countrymen, even against their Inclinations . . . and if, when chosen they should refuse to serve, let them be for ever considered as pusillanimous Men, who either neglect or dare not stand forth to save their oppressed Country" (*Assembly* 1772). An even more forceful approach was taken in Massachusetts. When James Warren, who had represented Plymouth for several terms, announced that "being unable to attend s[ai]d business Constantly Desired the Town would Excuse him from Service as Representative the present year," his request was put as a motion to those attending the meeting, and "it Passed in the Negative Unanimously." The voters again refused to allow him to decline the next year (*RTP* 1903, 213, 228). Sometimes electors accommodated the special needs of those they elected to get them to serve. After the recently widowed James Bishop "declared himselfe as not capable to goe in regard of ye state of his family, haveing noe body to take Care of his Children nor of his busines abroad," those attending the New Haven town meeting assured him that "there would be Care taken for both" (*ATR* 1919, 140).

Some potential candidates made concerted efforts to remove themselves from consideration. One took out an advertisement in a Maryland paper, announcing that, "having been proposed by many worthy Gentlemen . . . to stand as a Candidate at the ensuing Election for a Delegate," he would have to decline "as he is unwilling (in case he should succeed) to be so long from his Family." He asked them to "fix their Choice on some other Gentleman more capable to attend" (*MDG* 1756a). In many cases these candidates would have won had they run (*Papers Read* 1920, 9). But some candidates withdrew when they calculated that they were destined to lose. In 1773, "Mr. *Anthony Stewart* had long declared himself a candidate for the city [of Annapolis]." But his opponent proved more popular, so "on the morning of the election so great was the majority of voters for Mr. *Hammond*, that Mr. *Stewart* thought it prudent to decline" (*MDG* 1773b).

Not every candidate who did run was eager to be elected. One Pennsylvanian confessed in a letter to his father, "For my part, I am not anxious to be in the House. A Seat there would give me much trouble, take up a great deal of my time, and yield no advantage to my family." He ran only because, "as our friends thought it was necessary I should stand for Lancaster, I gave my consent, and am still willing to stand if there is any chance of succeeding" (*Letters and Papers* 1855, 64). Some willingly stepped aside. In 1768 Somerset County, New Jersey, had three candidates for its two seats. Although one was "greatly respected, and . . . was strongly supported, he declined the Assistance of his Friends, and genteely favoured" the other candidates. This was a magnanimous gesture because it appeared that he would have won (*DRNJ*, vol. XXVI, vol. VII 1904, 194–95). Not every defeated candidate felt rejected. The diary of John Rowe, a Boston merchant who ran unsuccessfully for the assembly several times in the

1760s, reveals that he took his losses with equanimity. Indeed, on at least one occasion he agreed to serve on the committee that developed instructions to be given to those who were elected (*Letters and Diary* 1903, 15, 82, 93, 130, 166).

Longtime incumbents risked being reelected even against their wishes. A Maryland delegate who had "been a Representative . . . above Forty Years past" had to "prevail on his Friends to suffer him to rest his remaining Days, at his home, in easy Retirement" (*MDG* 1764a). A Philadelphia representative wrote a letter thanking his voters "for the Mark of your Esteem" signaled by their past support but informing them "as my present Indisposition renders my Attendance at the House impracticable, I beg you will choose some other Person, at the ensuing Election, in my stead" (*PC* 1767). Another incumbent similarly requested, "But as I am now grown old in your service, attended with many infirmities, which, together with the necessary care of my own private affairs, renders my service in that important station any longer very inconvenient to myself; I therefore request you not to put my name in your ticket at the ensuing election" (*Dunlap's Pennsylvania Packet* 1775). But sometimes even when they wished to step down they were not able to do so. Writing to a confidant, a veteran New York lawmaker acknowledged, "But this for a truth I have been tyred of assambley-ship for maeny Years . . . would our frinds could thinck of any other p[er]son in my sted" (Dutchess County Historical Society 1921, 34).

Over the course of the colonial era there was an increase in the number of candidates openly running for the assembly. Sometimes, they let it be publicly known that they were interested in serving. A South Carolina newspaper reported in 1760, "We hear, that *Thomas Shubrick* and *David Deas*, Esqrs, have offered themselves as candidates for *Charles-Town*." The following year, the paper used much the same language to float the name of another candidate (*SCG* 1760e, 1760f, 1761, 1762a). Some declarations were guarded; an enigmatic ad placed in a Virginia paper notified electors, "You are desired not to engage your votes or interest until the day of election, as a Gentleman of undoubted ability intends to declare himself as a candidate on that day, and hopes to succeed" (*VG* 1768).

During the fourth decade of the eighteenth century a transformation in the candidate emergence process took place. Formal announcements of an individual's availability began appearing in newspapers. In 1732 a letter "To the several Worthy Electors of Members of Assembly, *for the Parish* of St. Philip's Charlestown," apprised them that "Your Votes and Interest are humbly desired for *Gab. Manigault*, of *Charlestown*, Merchant, to be your Representative in Assembly." The letter went on to tell when and where the vote was to be held. Voters apparently were comfortable with this new approach because Manigault was elected (*SCG* 1732a, 1732b).

Advertisements declaring a candidacy became more common from that point on (*NM* 1774a). A Rhode Islander made an explicit admission, announcing, "I . . . being proposed as a Candidate . . . take this public Method of soliciting your Votes and Interest at the ensuing Election" (*NM* 1764b). Candidates in New York took to them with particular vigor. The colony's first announcement appeared in 1739, stating, "Whereas a great Number of the Free-holders and Free-Men of the said City, have Agreed and Resolved to choose the following Persons to represent them in General Assembly." After the listing of the four candidates' names, there was an appeal: "Your Votes and Interest are desired for them at the ensuing Election." All four candidates won (*Manual of the Corporation* 1865, 744). Their efforts established a template that was followed in subsequent elections. In 1747 a slate of four incumbents placed a letter in the newspapers offering themselves to the voters of New York City and County, saying, "Your Votes and Interest are Desired at the next ELECTION for REPRESENTATIVES (*NYEP* 1747a; *NYG* 1747f). Again the voters were not taken aback by the open expression of political ambition, and the four incumbents were "*Unanimously* Chosen, and by the *greatest Number of Voters*, that ever appear'd here" (*NYEP* 1747b). Announcements became a regular feature of New York assembly races (*Manual of the Corporation* 1865, 751; *NYG* 1752a, 1761a, 1761b, 1761c, 1768a, 1768b, 1768c; *NYM* 1758, 1761a, 1761b, 1764; *PSWJ*, vol. III 1921, 325).

Candidates also came to be actively recruited (*Assembly* 1772; *Memoirs of the Life* 1942, 213–14; *PSWJ*, vol. III 1921, 325). In 1736 a South Carolina newspaper reported that, immediately following the publication of the election writs, "[W]e hear it was unanimously agreed by a considerable Number of the principal Inhabitants and Electors to put in Nomination for their Members the following [five] Gentlemen." The same story also noted the emergence of another candidate, "A great Number of the principal Inhabitants and Electors of the Parish of St *Philip's Charlestown*, have nominated Mr. *Benjamin Whitaker*." Still, elements of the old norms coexisted, with the article reporting, "Mr. *Whitaker*, by the kind Invitation of his Friends, has been prevailed upon to stand a Candidate at the ensuing Election." The nominations proved important, and Whitaker and four of the five other nominees named won (*SCG* 1736a, 1736b).

Candidate slating systems emerged in several colonies. Evidence of tickets, or organized lists of candidates, first appeared at the end of the seventeenth century. In the 1699 New York assembly elections the governor claimed that "both sides did by a tacit consent name one candidate only, expressing the rest by the word (company), to save time, because there were four candidates of a side whom it would have been tedious to name" (*CSP* 1908, 173). The most developed system evolved in Pennsylvania. There are references by early in the eighteenth century to efforts to recruit assembly candidates to run as part of a ticket (*CBWP*, vol. II 1872, 34, 316–17, 427, 438; "Letters of James Logan to Thomas Penn and Richard Peters" 1911, 274–75).

By 1727 Pennsylvania's use of tickets was acknowledged in passing in that year's election law, where it was declared that "inspectors are hearby authorized and required to administer to every elector or person who presents his ticket for electing representatives to serve in assembly an oath or affirmation" and "the vote or ticket of every person who takes the oath or affirmation shall be put into the box" (*SLP*, vol. IV 1897, 79). During a 1740 dispute with the governor, the assembly confessed that "some of the same religious Persuasion with the Majority of this House, as well as divers Inhabitants of other Persuasions, did meet together, to consider of Persons proper to be chosen for their Representatives, the last Year, as is usually done every Year, may be true" (*VPPP* 1739, 127). In 1765 a pamphlet opened with the statement, "The Election is at hand. Much noise is about *Old Tickets*" (*To the Freeholders and other Electors of Assembly-Men* 1765, 1).

Tickets in Pennsylvania came to involve negotiation and balancing, not just among the slots available for assembly members but also those for other offices (*Letters and Papers* 1855, 221–22, 231; Myers 1904, 296–97; "Notes and Queries" 1898, 386–87). Such efforts could be complicated, as suggested by a 1765 letter from one political activist to another.

> I went lately up to Bucks Court, in order to concert measures for their election, in pursuance of which we have appointed a considerable meeting of the Germans, Baptists and Presbyterians . . . in order to attempt a general confederacy of the three societies in opposition to the ruling party . . . The general committee of our society meet this day, and on Tuesday next shall finally settle our ticket, which is now all fixed but one man . . . I have just received certain advice of a project laid by the Mennonists to turn Mr. Saunders out of your ticket—the only good member you have. I hope it will inspire our people with more industry to keep him in. The only plan I would recommend to you, to run Dr. Kuhn, or some other popular Lutheran or Calvinist, in Webb's place. (*Letters and Papers* 1855, 209–10)

In some cases ticketing decisions were made by means of a vote (*Passages from the Diary*, vol. I 1839–1849, 66). When one group formed a ticket, an opposing group had an incentive to do likewise. During the 1747 election for the two Philadelphia seats, a voter recorded that one side "framed a Ticket for John Ross, and to get it to pass current among the people put Hugh Roberts with him. This being discovered, united us in prosecuting the Old Tickett, and Isreal [Pemberton] & Oswald Peel were chose by a large majority, tho' they got 60 votes for Ross" (Myers 1904, 112–13). Tickets could also be generated on the fly. As the result of a last minute decision to run a slate of candidates for the Philadelphia city and county seats, an announcement asked, "As no Tickets are wrote, to be delivered at the State-House, it is requested, that every Gentleman who approves of the above List, will please to write a few spare Tickets, to furnish his Friends with" (*Assembly* 1772).

Some opposed Pennsylvania's reliance on slates. One pamphlet complained, "To see the vile Abuses of our Rights and Liberties, and how easily the better and more modest of the People give into it. Many of them seem to think and act as if a Set of busy Fellows were appointed by Law to make the Tickets, and the People had only a Right to choose which they liked best" (*A Dialogue* 1725, 30–31). But such arguments did not alter the course of the colony's politics.

While ticketing was most pronounced in Pennsylvania, it also surfaced in a few other places. Given Delaware's ties to Pennsylvania, the appearance of nominating slates there is not surprising. A diary entry by Cesar Rodeney states that he and a friend went to the courthouse, where "many People Met to Conc[l]ude on Sherrifs and Assembly over again the Election" ("Fare Weather" 1962, 65). The 1719 Boston selectmen minutes mention, with regard to the conduct of the upcoming assembly elections, distributing tickets, "as hath been accustomed" (*RRSM* 1885, 51). There are hints that a group organized to control the town's elections emerged around that time (*Peter Oliver's* 1961, 26; Warden 1970, 20–21). By the early 1760s there were intimations of a full candidate slating system. A satirical reference to "the Junto," who "as guardians of the public liberty, hold their *nocturnal* assemblies, and with senatorial wisdom, consult, debate, project, scold, write, drink and smoke, *pro bono publico*," appeared in 1763 (*BEP* 1763). Around that time John Adams committed a similar description of such activities to his diary: "This day learned that the Caucas Clubb meets at certain Times in the Garret of Tom Daws . . . the whole Clubb meets in one Room. There they smoke tobacco till you cannot see from one End of the Garrett to the other. There they drink Phlip I suppose, and there they choose a Moderator, who puts Questions to the Vote regularly, and select Men, Assessors, Collectors, Wardens, Fire Wards, and Representatives are Regularly chosen before they are chosen in the Town" (*John Adams diary 9 1763*, 27). The following year a letter appeared in a newspaper from "The CAUCUS," requesting "your Votes for those Gentlemen who have steadily adhered to *your* Interest in Times past" (*BEP* 1764a). By 1772 several formal caucuses—North End, South End, and a "Caucus in the Middle part of the town"—were operating. That year the North End caucus decided that "this body will use their influence that" four specific candidates "be Representatives for the year ensuing" and they alerted the other caucuses of their decisions. The caucus did the same the following two years. Their efforts always met with victory (Day and Day 1971; Goss 1891, 637–44).

By the end of the colonial era, many assembly candidates were behaving strategically. A potential Virginia entrant "asked the Deponent what Chance he thought he might have amongst the People of his Neighborhood if he should declare himself a Candidate." He was told that "he might have a good Chance," and he subsequently ran (*JHB 1761– 1907*, 271). Some calculations were impressively sophisticated. Another Virginian was told by those recruiting him, "It is possible that the first time you might not be elected, because everyone does not know you . . . Others believe that you intend to introduce popery amongst us, but you have, however, spoken and written very effectively on the equality of the various denominations. These doubts might defeat you in the elections the first time, but this should not discourage you from running for office again" (*Memoirs of the Life* 1942, 214). And potential candidates worked to line up supporters. In 1761 a prominent New York politician received a letter from two men who wanted to run, asking him, "[A]s the gentlemen here in town propose to Set us up for Representatev's for the Citty and County of Albany, and if it's agreeable to you we beg your Interest in wch you'l very much oblige us" (*PSWJ*, vol. III 1921, 324). A century earlier those seeking an assembly seat would have been more circumspect in pursuing their ambitions.

SIX

Campaigns and Voters

Assembly campaigns became progressively less subdued and less mannerly affairs over time. By the eighteenth century their mere approach generated excitement. One Delawarean confided in his diary, "People Very Busey Now about ye Election Being Ney at hand" ("Fare Weather" 1962, 69). A letter to George Washington noted, "Our news here and below—are very triffling—Election of Burgesses take up the whole talk at present" (*LW*, vol. II 1899, 345–46). Enthusiasm often morphed into overheated rhetoric. During an election season, a Pennsylvania commentator cautioned voters that they were "very warm and active at this Time of the Year; Your Feeling is at its greatest Perfection: An Affront now is felt and given in a Minute, which two Months ago, or two Months hence, would take up at least an Hour, and hardly then be perceiv'd" (*AWM* 1729). Such passions caused a relieved Pennsylvanian to remark, "Our election being over, the borough is restored to its former quiet, and the inhabitants have again resumed their senses" (*Letters and Papers* 1855, 232). Apprehensions about assembly races were well grounded. A Virginian stated, "We have had an election of Burgesses . . . in which there hath been . . . promises, threats, spreading scandalous reports among the people of worthy persons, brow-beating at elections, and what not." Concerned about the outcome, he declared, "Pray God deliver us, for great endeavours are used already to gain the Burgesses, and if their House be intirely gained, woe be to us" (*CSP* 1916a, 107–8).

Campaigning

By the eighteenth century, campaigning was a standard part of assembly elections. In 1706 Pennsylvania's secretary reported, "Some of the best of [his] friends did what they could to give the election a better turn, but could not prevail" (*CBWP*, vol. II 1872, 172). In a Delaware race it was said, "At the election for New Castle no man canvassed more for J. Yeates than his late bitter adversary, and by this means he was chosen with the three others" (*CBWP*, vol. II 1872, 327). New York's governor wrote, "I am inform'd that Cheif Justice De Lancey is gone into the country, since the Writts issued personally to influence the People in their elections" (*DRNY*, vol. VI 1855, 578). An informed observer confirmed, "His friends & the Chief Justices who were the men of the best Estates & greatest personal Interest of any in the province used all the force of Money & Interest to carry the Election in his favour. The other party was no less assiduous" (*LPCC*, vol. IX 1937, 353).

An array of people engaged in campaigning. Following a Georgia contest a distressed elector claimed that "on Wednesday last the fourth day of this instant March, Mrs. Heriot Crooke and Mrs. Elizabeth Mossman came in a chair to this deponent's house, and asked him for his vote for Sir Patrick Houstoun to be Member of Assembly for Vernonburgh, and upon his telling them he was pre-engaged, having promised his vote to Mr. Tattnell for Mr. Box, they told him . . . that if the people did not vote for Sir Patrick, they would pay thirteen and sixpence tax for negroes, and would be liable to pay the Governor's salary and all the . . . expenses" (*GG* 1768b). They were not the only women who electioneered. During a "violent" Pennsylvania race, a candidate's wife "mounted her favorite mare, Nelly; a spur, she fastened to her ancle, and away she went, her red cloak flowing to the wind, to scour the county for [her husband]." She was credited with helping him win (*Register of Pennsylvania* 1830, 21; Rupp 1844, 264).

Religious leaders got involved. In the 1760s a North Carolina minister upended the political establishment. According to the reverend's account, "[W]hen the captain of the [local] mob being put into the commission of the peace stood candidate at an election of Burgesses in Edgecombe, wit hall the influence of the Governor's Faction in these parts and had got the huzzah on his side; I painted the scoundrel in his proper colors and overset his election" (Lichtenstein 1910, 17–18). They did not always carry the day. It was reported that the victor of a Woburn, Massachusetts, race won "notwithstanding the diligent & wicked Endeavours of one of the M[iniste]rs of the first Parish, for 3 Weeks past; by evil and false Insinuations, and by being present at the said Meeting, to seduce People" (*BWPB* 1741).

Other local opinion leaders often held sway. John Adams confided in his diary that "an artful man has little else to do but secure the favor of the taverners, in order to secure the suffrages of the rabble that attend these houses, which in many towns within my observation makes a very large, perhaps the largest number of voters" (Adams 1850, 112). Massachusetts tavern keepers were routinely elected to the assembly during the final decades before independence, largely because their vocation kept them in close contact with electors (Conroy 1995, 209–13, 222–23).

Candidates often made appeals on their own behalf. South Carolina's governor complained, "Those who pretend to stand as Members for the ensuing Assembly tell the people that they are against the said petition and for bills because they think that will prevail with the people to choose them" (*CSP* 1936a, 303). A Pennsylvania incumbent reportedly went "from place to place, beating his breast, declaring that he would serve the county to the utmost of his power, if he was chosen" (Jordan 1897, 118). Some campaigned reluctantly. In a letter to his father, one candidate grumbled, "It is a very disagreeable task to appear to solicit for one's self, but if it is necessary, I must submit" (*Letters and Papers* 1855, 62).

A few claimed never to have campaigned. Benjamin Franklin said that during his years in the Pennsylvania assembly he "never did, directly or indirectly solicit any man's vote" (*BEP* 1764c). Such boasts were often empty. A Virginian reported that a candidate was "incessantly employ'd in traversing this County and with indefatigable pains practices every method of making Interest with its Inhabitants for Electing him their Representative in Assembly, [while] his claims to disinterestedness . . . are Trumpeted in the most turgid manner" (*LW*, vol. III 1901, 201). When candidates avoided actively seeking votes, they usually had others working on their behalf. One of George Washington's supporters informed him, "I have done my endeavor to search into the opinions of the people, and cannot perceive your interest on the decline, tho' some try to persuade me to the contrary" (*LW*, vol. II 1899, 349).

Candidates were expected to appear at the polls (*Warren-Adams Letters*, vol. I 1917, 17). Washington received a letter telling him that "your being elected absolutely depends on your presence that day, this is ye Opinion of every thinking friend" (*LW*, vol. II 1899, 344, 346). (A military commitment kept him away, but he still won.) Not all candidates appeared. A Philadelphian admitted, "As my name was in some of the Tickets . . . I did not Chuse to go up to the Courthouse, but was about the town most of the day spreading Tickets for [a candidate for sheriff]" (Myers 1904, 297).

Campaign rhetoric came to play a prominent role. Pennsylvania's secretary protested, "But behold, when the day of a new election was at hand, when to recommend themselves to the people it was necessary to talk big, and sound aloud that useful language (most useful to some purposes) of grievances and oppression, whether real or imaginary, no matter" (*CBWP*, vol. II 1872, 362). Provocative publications became campaign staples and a means by which money influenced outcomes. Virginia's lieutenant governor told London officials about a paper "penn'd (as is credibly reported) by a Member of the Council, and dispersed with great industry through most countys in the Colony to poyson the minds of the populace." Reportedly, it had been written in response to "a rascaly paper [containing] advice to the Freeholders in favour of a Court Party" (*CSP* 1930b, 272–73). Personal interactions mattered. Commenting on a Virginia candidate's lack of interpersonal skills, a pamphlet swore that "he would give a Hundred Pounds could he shake hands with the freeholders, and smile in their faces with as good a grace as Col. Pa——e, that he might be more equally match'd" (*Defence of Injur'd Merit* 1771, 10).

Some campaigns got nasty. A Rhode Island incumbent who thought it "very unkind his being opposed" charged his challenger with being "a man, whose restless ambition refuses to be satisfied with any thing short of the sole direction of the government" (*NM* 1774b). A supporter of a Massachusetts incumbent grumbled about the "incessant detestable Endeavours of an infamous Character who at all Opportunities is essaying to asperse the Characters of worthy Men in a publick Station, and has thereby rendered himself the Scorn and Contempt of all honest Men . . . who have had the Unhappiness of being pester'd and plagued with his ungovernable malicious Tongue" (*BWNL* 1747). In Philadelphia a voter reported that he was approached by backers of one candidate and "they began to inveigh most bitterly against [another candidate] who I found they much feared would be elected Representative for the ensuing Year; & thinking me of their Kidney, they most vilely and falsely Traduced his Character, and earnestly intreated me to use my Interest against him" (*AWM* 1735). When Benjamin Franklin sought reelection in 1764 he was accused of denigrating German voters; his opponents conveniently interpreted his reference to "Palatine *Boors herding* together" as him calling them "a *Herd of Hogs*" (*Letters and Papers of Benjamin Franklin* 1947, 189). Franklin's champions responded by circulating a broadside containing a satirical verse that ridiculed the accusations, saying "*Boar* may be Hogs but *Boor* is Peasant" (*The*

Plot. By Way of a Burlesk 1764). But he lost, reportedly because of an impressive turnout of Germans (Gleason 1961). A campaign against another leading Pennsylvanian cited as a reason to vote against him that "you are said to be so noisy, quarrelsome, and overbearing, that good men are unwilling to serve in the House with you" (*Six Arguments* 1766).

Given such unpleasantness, campaigning did not always meet with public approval. Some took it as a mark against a candidate. A New York essayist argued, "To ask a Man for his Vote, is a Confession in the Candidate, that he is suspicious of his own Merit" (*Independent Reflector* 1753). A New Hampshirite said, "If you see persons dictating to others whom they are to-chuse, or telling some plausible tale, to recommend their friends, can you suppose them disinterested?" (*NHG* 1762). Another railed against "wholly disqualified" men who "not only declare themselves Candidates, but are using every Art and Strategem, to impose themselves on you." In such situations, "it becomes every one's Duty to point out such Disqualifications as make their Election Dangerous to the Liberties of the People, and destructive to the Welfare of the Province" (*NHG* 1774b). A New Yorker reveled in his candidates' success in the face of their opponents' "utmost Efforts . . . in Meetings and Entertainments in all Corners of the County." He proclaimed that "we know our Interest too well to be deceived either by Paper or Parchment" (*NYG* 1752c).

Concerns about campaigning focused on its effect on voters. A letter in a New York newspaper expressed unease that candidates, "by forc'd civilities, high treats and fair promises, often cajole the freeholders and freemen, into a declaration in their favour contrary to their more deliberate sentiments" (*NYJ* 1768a). A Rhode Island tirade on the topic began with "At this Time, when Misrepresentation, Detraction, and every Artifice, is made use of to influence the Minds of the Freemen against the approaching Election" (*Observations and Reflections* 1763, 1). A Massachusetts candidate's supporters complained that he had won "notwithstanding the Endeavours of some disaffected Persons, influenced by Letters, Pamphlets, Treats, and Promises of further Rewards from some contemptible wrong headed Politicians" (*BG* 1751). A Marylander griped, "When I perceive such uncommon arts practised by publick meetings, parading with drums, and publick orations to rouse your passions, and influence your judgments against one of the candidates for the approaching election, I cannot but believe these people are influenced more by the spirit of party than a desire of promoting the publick peace, welfare, and happiness." He protested "for my own part I do not understand the doctrine that now prevails, of speculating in a case of this nature . . . as if we were bartering for a horse" (*MDG* 1773a).

There were those so troubled by electioneering that they sought legal limits on it. A New York broadside suggested, "Every Species of Bribery might be made a Felony,—all Solicitation, and every Art of Seduction punished severely and made infamous" (*To the Freeholders and Freemen of the City and County of New-York* 1768, 1). New Jersey did not go that far, but it did pass a law that forbade slandering candidates "by Assertions or false Reports . . . either in Words or Message or Writing, or in any other Manner." The penalty was a ten-pound fine (*ANJ* 1776, 70). Such reactions show that aggressive electioneering was common and thought to be effective.

Both the public and politicians developed a healthy skepticism toward it. Candidates came to express little confidence in the voters' trustworthiness. One of Washington's political associates warned him that his "own experience has convinced me there is no relying on the promises of the common herd, the promise is too often forgot when the back is turned" (*LW*, vol. II 1899, 349). A report on a contested Virginia election substantiated such notions. It recounted that on "the Day before the Election a large Number of Freeholders came to Mᴿ *Marrable's*, and were genteely entertained; at which Time their Votes were sollicited for by Mᴿ *Marrable* . . . and Mᴿ *Marrable* declared they all promised him their Votes, but only one of them was as good as his Word" (*JHB 1758–* 1908, 83). Along these lines a Rhode Island newspaper published a joke about a barber who shaved two candidates. After receiving a generous tip, he promised each of them his vote. When confronted by the candidate he failed to support in the balloting, the punch line went "Yes, Sir (says the Barber) but the other gentleman was shaved twice" (*PRG* 1768).

Voters harbored doubts about candidates' credibility. A Virginia pamphlet declared, "If a man sollicits you earnestly for your vote, avoid him; self-interest and sordid avarice lurk under his forced smiles, hearty shakes by the hand, and deceitfully enquires about your wife and family" (*Defence of Injur'd Merit* 1771, 10). A Pennsylvanian cautioned electors to choose a candidate "who will deport himself, in November [after the election], agreeable to his Behaviour in September [before the election]" (*AWM* 1729). In a humorous vein, a young New Yorker penned a "Political Bill of Mortality for the month of August, in the year 1750, in a certain quarter of the town near the Bowling-Green" in which he claimed that "roaring against the four [assembly] members" had caused seven to perish, that "Running about for votes" had contributed to the demise of another 14, and that "a letter to the freeholders" had exacted the final toll of 39 (Sedgwick 1833, 65).

Class resentments surfaced, as might be expected given a system built on deference. It was reported of one candidate's wealthy supporter in a New York contest "that he fetch't some Persons of low Rank in his Coach and walk'd on Foot himself. Some Women cry'd out *These are fine Times when Carmen and Chimney Sweepers must ride in Coaches*" (*AWM* 1737). Before another New York election, a writer wryly reflected, "A most friendly intercourse seems establish'd in all parts between gentlemen of estates and their tenants, between the rich and the poor; every gentlemen's table is now free and open to his friends, and he thinks it an honour to receive a visit from the meanest freeholder, nay condescends to shake hands with the dirtiest mechanic in the county" (*NYJ* 1768b). The same theme was pursued with more venom in a Pennsylvania letter to the editor. The writer noted, "A poor man has rarely the honor of speaking to a gentleman on any terms, and never with familiarity but for a few weeks before the election. How many poor men, common men, and mechanics have been made happy within this fortnight by a shake of the hand, a pleasing smile and a little familiar chat with gentlemen, who have not for these seven years past condescended to look at them." He scoffed, "Thus the right of annual elections will ever oblige gentlemen to speak to you once a year" and concluded with a biting rhetorical question: "Do you think ever Mr. J—— would ever speak to you, if it were not for the . . . election?" (*Pennsylvania Evening Post* 1776).

The Importance of Issues

Campaigns did not revolve only around "who" but also around "what," arguably to a greater degree than has been appreciated. Issues were central to many contemporaneous explanations of election outcomes. For instance, in 1699 an ex-council member was alleged by New York's governor to have "rode night and day about the country endeavouring to possess the people that now was the time to get rid of a revenue and set themselves on an equal foot of liberty with the neighbour Colonies." His campaign enjoyed a slogan: "The country people learnt from him a by-word, Now or Never, which was very common among them." A pamphlet "intended to influence the elections of Assembly men with a view to their refusing to continue the King's Revenue" circulated (*CSP* 1908, 172–73, 177).

Issues surfaced in many campaigns. In 1706 Pennsylvania secretary James Logan made clear to William Penn that the election of an assembly that was "the worst that ever I knew in the Province" was the product of several topics that "provoked the people . . . chiefly the Act for altering the money . . . next the tax, and lastly a dissatisfaction at some other things" (*CBWP*, vol. II 1872, 171–72). In a letter to London officials, a Virginia lieutenant governor declared that voters were motivated in the recent election "by what I have yet heard, the business of taking up land is the cheif grievance they have recommended to their Burgesses to get redressed" (*CSP* 1924, 234). New York's governor pinned an election outcome on one issue, writing, "The newly elected members of the Assembly have been the chief opponents of the Auditor's claim" (*CSP* 1936a, 467). Maryland's governor wrote that two incumbents were "rejected at the same Election almost on the same Account. They had both in the preceeding Session vehemently opposed & spoke against the Bills that were brought into the Lower House agst Papists, [and] this was reported much to their Disadvantage in their respective Counties & much lessened their Interest" (*AM*, vol. VI 1888, 302). Another Virginia lieutenant governor wrote to the Council of Trade and Plantations that "if any further proof was necessary of the general inclination of the country, it may be seen in the choice made of new members this session . . . who are all friends to the [tobacco] law" (*CSP* 1939, 126).

Incumbents revised policy positions in response to public opinion. Commenting on the appearance of three laws "relating to the *ringing of hoggs*," a Virginia official declared that the laws, "however triffling in themselves may serve to shew how great an alteration there is in the tempers of the people, since even in my time it was enough to lose a man's election as a Burgess, that he had show'd the least inclination to the ringing of hogs" (*CSP* 1928, 87). Lawmakers became sensitive to such shifts in voters' interests.

Campaigns often revolved around local issues (Kolp 1992, 663). Between 1716 and 1725 contests in Northampton, Massachusetts, were driven by policy disputes over dredging a channel in the Mill River and building a fort (Trumbull 1902, 20, 34–35). The election of a candidate from Pennsylvania's Northampton County was attributed to voters "knowing him to be a Man zealous for Defence" (*A Letter from a Gentleman in Philadelphia* 1757, 1). A Virginia candidate attracted supporters "by Introducing various Commercial Schemes, which are to diffuse Gold and opulency thro' Frederick [County]" (*LW*, vol. III 1901, 202). Another Virginian went "to the lower Meeting House of the Dissenters, to know their Sentiments whether they would submit to the damned Tobacco Law, and desired to know whether they also submit to it; that if they would send him Burgess he would be hanged, or burnt (or Words to that Effect) if he did not get that Part of it, directing a Review of Tobacco, repealed" (*JHB* 1761– 1907, 269). A third Virginia candidate wrote his electors, "This shall be my Obligation to be liable and answerable to you, and all who are my Friends, in the Sum of five

Hundred Pounds, if I do not use the utmost of my Endeavours (in case I should be a Burgess) to divide this our County of *Lunenburg*." The promise helped him win (*JHB 1758–* 1908, 83–84).

Limiting the cost of government was an issue that resonated with voters. Consequently, candidates touted their willingness to squeeze gubernatorial spending requests. Virginia's Lieutenant Governor Spotswood claimed that lawmakers "were resolv'd not to depart from that general maxim of recommending themselves to the people by opposing everything that required expence," adding caustically that "indeed most of the late Burgesses had reason, since that was the only qualification they had to merit the people's choice" (*CSP* 1924, 356). New York's governor complained that "by the popular argument of having saved the Country's money, some have got the Election secured to themselves" and "for soe long as ye Members hold their elections by noe other tenure, but that of saveing ye publick money or stareving the Government, there is nothing to be depended upon from them" (*CSP* 1924, 259; 1925, 97). North Carolina's governor groused that "men of sense who sincerely mean the Publick good are so much afraid of the next Elections that they are obliged to go in with the majority whose Ignorance & want of education makes them obstruct everything for the good of the Country even so much as the Building of Churches or erecting of schools or endeavouring to maintain a direct Trade to Great Britain" (*CRNC*, vol. IV 1886, 178). Maryland's governor said of his assembly, "They always shew greater Backwardness in every last session to do any thing generous, lest it should induce their Electors to reject them when they offer themselves Candidates at the ensuing Election" (*AM*, vol. VI 1888, 56).

Issues could mobilize voters. An account of South Carolina's 1768 contests noted that a large number of "the people called Regulators coming down from the back settlements to vote where it appeared to them they had a right" were spurred by a set of policies they wanted enacted. Among the "many intolerable grievances they had long laboured under" were "*a more equal representation in assembly . . .* an act *for ascertaining and better regulating public officers fees, . . .* and another *for establishing county courts*" (*SCG* 1768c). Issues could also suppress turnout. A New York governor anticipated that several of his preferred candidates would win until "messengers were immediately dispatched through out the Province with the news of M^r De Lancy's being made Lieu^t Governour, which damp'd the inclinations of all my friends, as dreading the exorbitant power & resentment of this man" (*DRNY*, vol. VI 1855, 417).

By the mid-1700s the idea that candidates should be assessed on their issue stances was widely promoted. A Massachusetts pamphlet asserted, "It is the Right and Duty of the Freeholders and Inhabitants of *New-England*, to examine into the Conduct, and to know the Opinions and Intentions, of such as offer themselves . . . for their Representatives" (*An Address to the Freeholders* 1751, 4). And candidate qualifications became fused with issue stances. A Pennsylvanian counseled that voters should, "with one Voice . . . elect such Men as are of well known Ability, and who are not conscientiously principled against enacting Laws for our common Security" (*PAG* 1754).

Campaign appeals began to focus on incumbent records. Sometimes this worked to incumbents' advantage. A 1764 Pennsylvania election pamphlet asked voters "whether you will chuse for Representatives, those honest and firm Freemen who have faithfully served you a great Number of Years; whether you will refuse to be advised by your old Friends, and turn out those zealous Supporters of your Rights and Privileges" (*To the Freeholders and Other Electors* 1764, 1). New York voters were encouraged to support their incumbents because "Consistently, with the Instructions *you* gave, and *their Proceedings thereupon*, you cannot fail to re-elect them for the ensuing Assembly" (*NYJ* 1769d). Another paper announced that "it is not doubted but the same Members who have in a Capital Instance, acted so highly to the Satisfaction of their Constituents . . . will be re-elected" (*NYG* 1769b).

At other times a legislative record was a burden. After noting that the "consideration that such and such a Gentleman has represented us several Years, is vague in itself," a Pennsylvanian asked rhetorically, "Let us reflect what Services has he done?" (*PAG* 1773). When several Philadelphia members failed to back a defense appropriations measure, a supporter was forced to argue weakly on their behalf, "Supposing they were mistaken, should not Charity, or even common Prudence, induce us to conclude they had some rational Grounds for their dissenting from the Majority of the House?" (*To the FREEMEN of PENNSYLVANIA* 1755, 1–2). In the late 1760s an incumbent accused of having "approved of having a tax laid on all stills in the said county of Lancaster" felt compelled to see that a "certificate" attested to by his assembly colleagues was published in the newspaper, stating that "the report aforesaid, and every part thereof, is false, and without the least foundation in truth" (*PC* 1769).

Legislative records were used to put incumbents on the defensive. An effort to dissolve the New York assembly and call for new elections was advocated by one writer, who suggested, "Those who would agree to a Motion of this Nature would have one good Argument at least to satisfy their Constituents, *That they deserve to be re-elected*" (*Ne quid falsi* 1734, 5).

A few years later another New Yorker cited an incumbent's record to suggest that he did not deserve to be returned to office. He asked, "Has he not been an Assembly Man about 13 years? Has he not been Speaker, and consequently at the Head of the Assembly during the greatest Part of that Time? Was not the Country a little before and about the Time that he was first chosen an Assembly Man in a very flourishing Condition? Has not this City ever since been declining in it's Trade Navigation and Ship Building and the Country growing poorer every Year?" (*NYWJ* 1737d). Opposition to a slate of New York incumbents was expressed directly: "Let us seriously consider, without Partiality and Affection, whether it be most for the Interest of the County, to choose the same Men again, who have had their Passions heated with the past Disputes, and their Spirits exasperated and enflamed with their Resentments" (*NYG* 1747–48). Following his defeat, a Maryland incumbent complained to a newspaper about the "ill Treatment I received from Ten Gentlemen a little before the last Election in *Charles County*, by a scandalous Paper being forg'd and industriously publish'd to the Prejudice of my Character." Defending himself, he asserted, "I never Voted, and afterwards come in and said, that I did not understand the Question, and desire the Votes to be expunged that my Conduct might not appear to my Constituents" (*MDG* 1758b).

Assembly Salaries as an Election Issue

Compensation for assembly service became an issue early in the colonial era because there were concerns that there were too few people willing and able to serve without it. As early as 1645, the Massachusetts General Court argued that financial incentives were needed to attract people to serve (*RGC*, vol. II 1853, 101). Initially, Rhode Island's lawmakers received no wages, but attendance proved to be a problem and pay was introduced "ffor the encouragement and ingadging the . . . Deputies to attend the Generall Assemblyes" (*RCRI* 1857, 443). A representational angle was even developed to justify compensation. Each West Jersey representative was to be paid a shilling a day explicitly "that thereby he may be known to be the Servant of the People" (*Grants, Concessions* 1758, 406).

Outside of Georgia and South Carolina, which did not pay their members, the setting of compensation levels bedeviled assemblies. Pay mattered to lawmakers, and they often lobbied for increases (Squire 2012, 32–35). Some looked askance at such behavior. A New York governor jeered that "by Vertue of an Act giving a daily allowance to each Assembly man, it is now become a trade, and brings them in more then most of them can get by their imploymts" (*CSP* 1924, 259). Virginia's lieutenant governor claimed that members, "by their sallary, thought it worth their while to take extraordinary pains to secure their election, while gentlemen of better understandings and more plentifull estates, not tempted with the same desire of gain, despised making their court to the populace by such vile practices, and by that means were disappointed of representing their county" (*CSP* 1928, 318). Lawmakers resented such claims. Pennsylvania representatives argued, "Nor is the Situation of an Assembly-man here so advantageous, as to make it worth his while to use Artifice for procuring a Re-election; for when the Smallness of the Allowance, the Expence of Living, the Time he is absent from his own Affairs, and other Inconveniences are considered, none will suppose he can be a Gainer by serving the Publick in that Station" (*VPPP* 1755, 48).

Massachusetts towns had to cover the cost of their representatives, and many had difficulty keeping their commitments (*Fourth Report of the Record Commissioners* 1880, 89). One community sent a member in 1719, but only raised the funds to pay him in 1723 (Temple 1887, 201). Groton petitioned the assembly "that ther representative might be relesed from atending the Seshone any more" so they would no longer have to pay him. The following year the town sent a member, but it took him 12 years and a threatened lawsuit to get paid, and even then the town had to borrow the money to do so (*Early Records of Groton* 1880, 107; Green 1894, 120–21). Lawsuits to recover pay occurred elsewhere (Trumbull 1898, 408). So did having to scramble for funds: in the late 1680s Springfield had to borrow to pay its representative, between 1640 and 1680 Watertown regularly carried debts to its member, and even as late as 1775 Murrayfield "voted that the representative be paid in work or grain for his own time and horses" (Burt 1899, 199; Copeland 1892, 98; *WR* 1894, 11, 25, 29, 101). When the town of Harvard opted to send a member in 1747, the clerk wrote in the town book, "Chose Mr. Daniel Perce to represent them in ye great and general Court, and I hope those that chose him will pay him" (Nourse 1894, 414).

Given all this, it is no surprise that salaries were controversial. When Barnstable voted to give its member "six shillings ye day for his services . . . Mr John Bacon & Mr Samll Hinkley did manifest yourselfs to be utterly against allowing him that money: and desired to give dissent &c" (*Barnstable Town Records* 1910, 30). Larger communities quibbled too. In 1750 Bostonians voted "by a very great Majority, that the Town do not expect that the Persons chose as Representatives receive any Pay" (*RRCB* 1885b, 176).

Candidates came to understand that campaign promises to take little or no salary had political appeal. Such guarantees troubled Virginia as early as 1661. That year the assembly adopted a measure setting a per diem but noted that "the excessive expenses of the Burgesses causing diverse misunderstandings between them and the people occasioned an injunction to make an agreement with them before their election which may probably cause interested persons to purchase votes by offering to undertake the place at low rates and by that meanes make the place both mercenary and contemptible" (*SLV*, vol. II 1823, 23). The idea that such campaign promises constituted bribery took root in a few other colonies. Both Pennsylvania and Delaware passed measures stipulating that candidates "that shall offer to serve for nothing or less Allowance than the Law prescribes" were to be fined and declared ineligible to serve (*LGD*, vol. I 1763, 119; *SLP*, vol. II 1896, 25, 214). Pennsylvania lawmakers bragged that they "neither bribe nor solicit the Voters," which was half true (*PAG* 1755).

Some argued that such promises were appropriate. Virginia's Lieutenant Governor Spotswood complained that his burgesses had voted to expel two "gentlemen . . . for having the generosity to serve their county for nothing, which they term bribery." The council concurred; "We know neither Law nor Practice either of *England* or *Virginia*, to hinder any Gentleman generously to Offer to Serve his Country gratis, and can't reconsile it, that your House, which Complains So much of the poverty of the Country Should be the first to discourage Such a generous Practice in these Gentlemen, and So frugal to the Publick." But the assembly held firm (*CSP* 1928, 260; *JHB* 1712– 1912, 128, 153, 165, 168).

Where such promises were allowed, salary became a point of bargaining between candidates and electors. In Newcastle, Massachusetts (now Maine), it was decided that before sending a representative voters would first have to "see what agreement the Town will make with him or what Terms they will send him on" (*Early Town Records of Newcastle* 1914, 49). In 1684 Topsfield voters resolved that their representative "shall have but ffivteene shilings pr weeake" and "have a greeed yt a deputy shall goe to ye Generall Court apon ye Conditions above said" (*TRT* 1917, 52). After a Lexington representative remitted his expenses to the town, the voters came to demand such behavior. For the next several years the records included the following statement: "Voted that whosoever Shall be Chosen to Represent ye Town at ye Great & General Court this Year. Shall Return into ye Town Treasurer all ye mony that Shall be made up in ye General Courts List for ye Representative above thre Shillings a Day . . . ye Person Chosen Doth Promise to Return s[ai]d Mony as afor said the Town to proseed to ye Choice of an other" (Hudson 1913, 59–60). Voters in Spencer were so pleased when their member in the early 1720s served without pay that after he left office they thanked him "for his good service as a representative the year past, and whoever should be chosen this year, should be paid the same . . . *and no other*." His replacement agreed (Draper 1841, 20).

Many candidates were willing to serve for little or no pay. In Rhode Island, those protesting a bill setting legislative allowances asserted, "For there is a great dispute in many towns for their deputies; and that there are enough willing to go without pay" (*RCRI* 1861, 19). In 1751 Watertown, Massachusetts, voted that anyone elected representative would have to give the "Money or Wages" earned for his service "to the Town Treasurey for the Use of ye Town." The newly elected member agreed, and the requirement was kept in place for several years (*WR* 1928, 94–95, 109, 127). During the 1740s Cambridge's member rebated his salary to the town, as did Topsfield's member in the 1720s (Frothingham 1845, 257; *TRT* 1917, 317). Raynham's representative in 1768 and 1769 donated the money he earned toward the town's purchase of a property for a new meeting house (Sanford 1870, 44).

Such behavior became customary in New York. The governor told the Council of Trade and Plantations, "Every County of the Province is by some act or other obliged to pay their representatives, but some of them agree before hand to serve for nothing, others make bargains at a rate under what they suppose they are authorized to demand" (*CSP* 1937a, 474). Incumbents often signed "recorded, ample and proper Releases" absolving New York City and County against any future claims for their pay (*MCCNY, 1675–1776*, vol. IV 1905, 333; vol. V 1905, 214, 357; *NYWJ* 1743). In time these promises became implicit; a 1750 letter from the winners thanking the voters noted, "And altho', in the Dispatch you made in the Election, none of you (as has been usual) insisted on our Declaration as your Representatives in General Assembly, to serve you gratis; yet we humbly declare the same" (*NYG* 1750a).

Taking pay was not always politically fatal. In 1751 Boston voters asked their incumbents seeking reelection whether "they had received or intended to receive any Pay for Serving as Representatives the last Year." One told them that "he was determin'd to receive his Pay, and dispose of it as he tho't proper," and two others indicated they would take it as well. All were returned to office (*RRCB* 1885b, 195). During a New York election candidates were asked, "Will you serve this City Gratis in the Station of an Assemblyman if you are Chosen?" Only one of the six candidates failed to agree, yet he won a seat (*BEP* 1739).

Knowing legislative salaries were unpopular, governors occasionally used them as leverage in negotiations. In 1728 Massachusetts' governor admitted that he intended "to continuing sitting with the Assembly till they comply [with his wishes], that the country who pay about a thousand pounds a month to the Council and Representatives by way of wages during their attendance, may feel the inconvenience of their standing out" (*CSP* 1937a, 195). When the assembly reassembled after being prorogued, he told them he hoped, "The long Recess you have had has given you the time to think calmly on the Proceeding, of the last Session, and to know the Mind of the Country upon them." After the session did not produce the outcome the governor desired, he again threatened the members (*JHHR* 1728, 1, 30). In the end, his efforts to squeeze lawmakers failed because the voters rallied to their cause. A Boston meeting noted that the "last session of the General Court was continued to unusual Length," but their members had "behaved themselves as very Loyal Subjects." They voted to pay them (*NEWJ* 1729a).

Though a minority, some voters advised against allowing lawmakers to serve for free. One cautioned, "If such Men buy their Election, 'tis odds but they will pay themselves double" (*BEP* 1759). Another opined, "I think those who are busy to procure themselves to be elected Assembly men, and those who make fulsome Compliments of forgiving their Wages, as well as those who Promise to Serve for Nothing, are equally to be rejected as Bribers and Ill-designing men" (*AWM* 1735). And while constituents appreciated offers to serve for nothing, they did not always back those who made them. After two Elizabeth City County, Virginia, candidates agreed not to take any wages if elected, a voter reportedly "declared, now we have got two Men that will serve us for nothing, which he was glad of, as he found it very difficult to pay his Taxes, but he did not vote for [one of them] at the said Election" (*JHB* 1752– 1909, 361). In 1750 Watertown voters rejected a proposal to deem a representative elected only if "the said Person will Serve the Town Greatis" (*WR* 1928, 74). And a Dorchester voter recorded that, during the 1772 election, "Esq. Holden offered to go representative for nothing, but they would not choose him" (Dorchester Antiquarian and Historical Society 1859, 362).

Treating

Although treating voters with alcohol and other enticements was accepted in England (Dickinson 1995, 44), colonists worried about it. New Jersey's governor complained that candidates he had opposed were elected through "false suggestions, fraudulent conveyances and the rum bottle" (*CSP* 1930a, 68). But provision of such inducements was common practice. Following his second run for the Virginia assembly, George Washington paid bills for 40 gallons of rum punch, 28 gallons of wine, three and a half pints of brandy, 43 gallons of beer and 8 quarts of cider (*LW*, vol. II 1899, 398–99). Alcohol was the usual treat, but other indulgences might also be offered. A letter detailing a New York member's election preparations listed "6 Barrels of Cider" to be "Distrebutd Before ye Day" but also "Beef, Porck & Backin" and "100 loves" of bread (Dutchess County Historical Society 1921, 35).

Treating was the main way money flowed into colonial elections. The assumption was that treats were part of a quid pro quo. A letter written by a prominent Virginian speculated, "Our friend, Mr. Banister, has been very much ingaged ever since the dissolution of the assembly, in swilling the planters with bumbo, and I dare say from the present prospect, will be elected a burgess" (*Bland Papers* 1840, 27). Bumbo was a rum drink, and the implication was that the candidate had curried his electors' favor by plying them with free refreshments. Another case documented the relationship at its basest level. A review of a 1764 Virginia assembly race reported that "on the Day of the Election one *Grubbs*, a Freeholder . . . came to the Court House, and declared he was ready to vote for any one who would give him a Dram: . . . That *Richard Richardson*, who was a Friend to the sitting Member, but without his knowledge, did, at his own Expense, procure a Dram for the said *Grubbs*, who voted for the sitting Member" (*JHB 1761– 1907*, 272).

Documents expressing trepidation about treating were straightforward. A petition to the Maryland assembly asking that the results of a 1751 Baltimore County contest be thrown out detailed the alleged relationship on a large scale. It stated:

> *William Govane*, one of the Gentlemen who stood a candidate . . . in Order to procure himself . . . chosen, after the . . . Notice of the said Election, and some Days before the Time appointed for the said Election, gave, or caused to be given, great Quantities of Rum, Punch, and other strong Liquors, to the People in several Parts of the said County, in Order to secure the Votes of the said People, for himself . . . at the said Election; and when the said People were warmed and intoxicated with strong Liquors, engaged their Promises to vote for him the said *Govane* . . . at the said Election.

Having been thorough in his efforts, it was further alleged that the said *William Govane*, the better to hold the People to their Promises, procured by the Liquor given them as aforesaid, on the Day of the Election procured great Quantities of Rum and Punch, and other strong Liquors to be lodged in the Way of the People to the said Election, and gave the same to the People; and at the Court House, before the Election, and at the taking the Poll, procured so much strong Liquor to be given to the People, that many of them were made drunk, and not capable of giving their Votes with Prudence and Discretion, or agreeably to what they would have done had they been sober.

With all the alcohol involved, the voting did not go smoothly. The sheriff, "finding the People very obstreperous and violent," adjourned the polls several times and closed the courthouse doors for two hours, preventing some from casting a vote.

It was clear what had taken place, and the assembly threw out the results. When the contest was rerun the following month, "there were as many People as ever appeared at any one Election in this Province," but the results did not change. Govane finished tied for first place, taking one of the county's four seats. None of the gentlemen who had petitioned to toss out the first contest finished higher than fifth. And ugliness continued to be part of the process, for reportedly "two Men who got hurt at the late Election . . . are since dead of their Wounds" (*MDG* 1752a, 1752b, 1752c).

In Maryland, certainly, voters were not offended by treating. When four delegates were found to have engaged in it prior to a 1768 election, they were summarily dismissed from the assembly. A special election to fill the vacant seats was held a few weeks later, and three of the four were reelected. The successful candidates did make a concession in the second contest, and the "Gentlemen carefully avoided Treating, both before and during the Election, to prevent the least Colour for a Second Complaint, on that Account." The delegate who lost was dragged down by an unpopular vote against relocating the county seat, not because of his earlier offense. In a curious twist, he later successfully contested the second election because of procedural errors committed by the sheriff. In the third election, he and several of the candidates who had brought the initial treating charges won (*AM*, vol. LXI 1944, xcii; vol. 426 1979, 63–64; *MDG* 1768a, 1768b; *VPMD* 1768, 185; 1770, 218).

Much treating was conducted only after the polling was finished. This was thought to be less offensive to the process. It may also have helped heal divisions. Following the conclusion of a competitive South Carolina race it was reported that "without the least animosity or irregularity, the company partook of a plain and hearty entertainment, that had been provided by some upon whom this assembly will reflect lasting honour." Consumed were "45 bowls of punch" and "45 bottles of wine," while "many loyal, patriotic, and constitutional toasts were drank" (*SCG* 1768b). After two challengers lost to a slate of four incumbents in a fiercely fought New York election, "The *Four* invited the *Two* to Drink a Glass with them . . . and the *Two* accordingly went and drank the Healths of the *Four*, declaring that they doubted not but that their Conduct would be agreeable to their Promises" (*BEP* 1739).

Some celebrations were elaborate. George Washington recorded in his diary that following his 1768 victory he "Stayd all Night to a Ball wch. I had given." It cost him 25 pounds for, among other things, cakes and a fiddler (*Diaries of George Washington*, vol. I 1925, 301). Washington's 1774 postelection soirée for the "Freeholders and Gentlemen of the town" provided "Coffee and Chocolate" and was, according to an English visitor in attendance, "conducted with great harmony" (*Journal of Nicholas Cresswell* 1924, 28). Not all festivities were so genteel. A Virginian wrote that following the conclusion of the voting, he "walked to the courthouse, where the people were most of them drunk" (*Secret Diary of William Byrd* 1941, 218). Some drinking started early. An account of a 1769 Virginia election noted that when the polls opened "there appeared to be Half the Inhabitants of the County collected together, some of whom were intoxicated" (*JHB 1766*– 1906, 244). Misfortune followed the mass consumption of large quantities of alcohol. After the polling closed in a Maryland election, "some Persons being more merry than wise . . . made themselves Sport with Mr. *Vincent Stewart*, one of the Company (who had been a little too free with Liquor), by throwing and tumbling him about, whereby he got very much hurt and bruised." Stewart later died, with the paper calling it "a very melancholy Affair, as he has left a sorrowful Wife and six helpless Children" (*MDG* 1749).

Although treating was common, many denounced it. One writer warned that "he that will *bid high*, and *give the most Drink* to-Day, may chance to be a Person that will sell their *Religion*, and *Liberties*, and *Fortunes* to-Morrow" (*BEP* 1759). Another cautioned, "Persons who are allured to sell their Voices for Rum and Brandy . . . become the supple Tools of Candidates" (*BG* 1766a). A third counseled, "We must not therefore sell our Birthright (and that of our Posterity too) for a Mess of Pottage, a Feast, or a Drinking-Bout" (*NYWJ* 1738). A broadside reasoned that "the same Motives that induced [a candidate] to contribute so generously to multiply Votes, would doubtless prevail with him to concert Schemes, whereby we shall be obliged to reimburse Ten-fold as much" (*A Tooth-Full of Advice* 1768).

A New York essayist who called treating "downright Bribery and Corruption" offered a novel argument for its unseemliness: "Your representatives have, generally, serv'd you gratis: That Time which they might have gainfully employed in their private Business, they have generously devoted to you and their Country; in planning your Laws; consulting your Welfare, and advancing your Happiness. 'Twas, therefore, unreasonable, unmanly, ungrateful, to load them with the additional Expence of popular Festivity, and costly Revels" (*Independent Reflector* 1753). A letter to the editor speculated on a different toll the process took on those who ran: "I am sure there is no Candidate of good sense and delicacy, but must in his hours of serious reflection blush at the low artifices of coaxing, wheedling, treating, &c. which he has us'd in order to obtain the suffrages of the electors" (*NYJ* 1768a).

Some assemblies acted on such objections. By 1725 New Jersey had passed an antitreating law forbidding assembly candidates to "directly or indirectly give, present or allow to any Person having Voice or Vote in such Election, any Money, Meat, Drink, Entertainment or Provision . . . in order to procure or gain Voices or Votes in his Election" (*ANJ* 1776, 70). This was not the first time the colony had attempted to stop treating. Essentially the same provision had been included in the proprietors' 1677 Concessions and Agreements establishing the West Jersey assembly (*Grants, Concessions* 1758, 403). The need to adopt new legislation suggests that the earlier effort failed to stifle the practice.

Grave concerns about the propriety of Rhode Island elections led to legislation. Stirred by a belief "that Bribery and Corruption hath . . . spread itself in this Government, to the great scandal thereof; so that the Election of publick Officers hath been greatly influenced thereby," the assembly passed a bill intended to rectify the problem. The solution adopted was an oath to be sworn by all new freeman "before the Time of his said Voting," testifying that "you have not, nor will not, receive any Money, or other Reward, nor any promise of any Money, or other Thing . . . at the Election of any Officer" (*Acts and Laws, Rhode-Island* 1752, 12, 14). A few years later Connecticut took a similar step. Holding that "Bribery and Corruption is destructive of civil Communities," the assembly adopted what it hoped would be all-encompassing legislation: "That no Person . . . shall give, offer, accept, or receive any Sum or Sums, or any other Matter, or Thing, by way of Gift, Fee, or Reward for giving, or refusing to give any

Vote, or Suffrage for Electing any Member of the General Assembly of this Colony" (*Acts and Laws, Connecticut* 1756, 299). It reflected the colony's political culture. A letter defending its political practices claimed that any notion that taverns would be open and the voters treated was "absolutely false and groundless. Bad as the people in this colony are, such a practice would be deemed infamous and dishonourable." The writer maintained, "I never have heard of any Tavern or Ale Houses being opened or anything like it, upon these occasions, and am moraly certain nothing of that Kind has ever been done," but he did concede, "I have heard indeed in some few Instances, that after the Election is over, and while the Votes are sealing up, in order to be sent into the Assembly, the Deputies newly elected, have called for a Bowl of punch to drink with the constables . . . One Instance even of this Kind however being complained of to the assembly was generally discountenanced by the House, as having too much the Air of Bribery, and the Member concern'd, if I am not mistaken, publickly reprimanded for his conduct" (*CC* 1770).

Elsewhere the efficacy of antitreating efforts was suspect. Following the series of incidents discussed above, Maryland's assembly passed a resolve against treating. It promised that "on any Petition for Treating, this House will not take into Consideration, or regard the Greatness or Smallness of any Treat" and would declare any election void if "in such Election, any Money, Meat, Drink, Entertainment, or Provision, or . . . any Present, Gift, Reward, or Entertainment, or any Promise, Agreement, Obligation, or Engagement, to give, or allow any Money, Meat, Drink, Provision, Present, Reward or Entertainment, whatsoever" was involved. This tough measure passed by only a single vote (*VPMD* 1768, 206–7). It proved ineffective. When in 1771 two members were expelled after having been found "guilty of treating at the late Election," the voters quickly returned both to office (*MDG* 1771b, 1771c; *VPMD* 1771, 14).

Virginia also fell short in its willingness to punish treating. A 1705 law forbade anyone running for the assembly to "directly or indirectly, give, present or allow to any person or persons having a voice or vote in such election, any money, meat, drink, entertainment, or provision . . . in order to be elected." Violators would not be allowed "to serve in the General Assembly" (*SLV*, vol. III 1823, 243). In 1736 a legislative committee charged with examining a contested election reported that the incumbent who won had given "strong Liquors to the People of the said County; once at a Race, and the other Time at a Muster, and did, on the Day of Election, cause strong Liquor to be brought in a Cart, near the Court-house Door, where many People drank thereof, whilst the Polls of the Election were taking." The committee concluded that "the Liquors given . . . at the Race and Muster, and the Liquor brought to the Election, and given whilst the Polls were taking, were given with Design to procure the sitting Member to be elected." The full assembly rejected the recommendation that the member be deemed "not duly elected" (*JHB 1727*– 1910, 370). Roughly two decades later the assembly confronted a case in which, on the invitation of a candidate, "several Freeholders went [to his home] and were there kindly entertained, with Victuals and Drink, but no Solicitations or Threats were then used . . . touching the Election of Burgesses for the said County." The assembly found him not guilty of treating. The following year the assembly allowed another member accused of treating to keep his seat, even though he had paid for the alcohol that had been served at "the Bar at the Ordinary" while the voting was being conducted (*JHB 1752*– 1909, 359–60, 456–57). Such leniency was common (*JHB 1761*– 1907, 270–72).

Many voters were resigned to treating. One Virginian commented, "I think it ought to be considered that gracious Salutations, kind Squeezes by the Hand, Bowls and Glasses, have been so long the high Road to a Seat, that, should any Gentlemen, excited by the most disinterested Views, attempt to strike out a new Path, he must meet with so many Rubs by the Way [that] . . . he finds himself unable to arrive at the Journey's End" (*VG* 1771). And a Rhode Island newspaper reprinted a British "BALLAD on the General Election" poking fun at it. It rhymed in part:

> By flattering and treating,
> At every meeting,
> With the voters they try to prevail;
> No words can describe
> How they promise and bribe,
> Such eloquence never can fail. (*Gentleman's Magazine* 1768; *NM* 1768)

But opposition grew. Most notable was a resolution adopted by Williamsburg, Virginia, electors after they had unanimously reelected a member. They said they were "greatly scandalized at the Practice which has too much prevailed throughout the Country of entertaining the Electors." Turning the tables, they told their representative, "[W]e earnestly request that you will not think of incurring any Expense or Trouble . . . but that you will do us the Honour to partake of an Entertainment which we shall direct to be provided for the Ocasion" (*VG* 1774e). Similar statements appeared elsewhere (*ORTF* 1898, 99; *WTR* 1882, 139). The public's growing reservations led to changes in candidate behavior. In a New York race the winning candidates, "instead of giving Liquor at the Election (which is an old exploded Custom) jointly made a Present of Two Hundred Pounds for the Use of the Poor of this City and County" (*MDG* 1759b). Although more virtuous, such contributions merely shifted the beneficiaries of candidate largesse.

Voter Turnout

Voter interest in assembly elections was sporadic. Evidence of this is provided in figure 6.1, which shows the number of voters participating in Boston's annual assembly elections between 1717 and 1774. The numbers ebb and flow, with high turnout elections often followed by contests in which relatively few voters showed. In 1763, for example, 1,089 voters appeared, but the next year only 449 cast votes. Clearly, interest waxed and waned. It also appears that hotly contested races brought voters with dubious credentials to the polls. Prior to the 1764 balloting, Boston's selectmen announced that "a strict scrutiny [will be] made as to the Qualifications of the Voters," which may have dampened participation (*RRSM* 1889, 64). Various Massachusetts, New York, Pennsylvania, Rhode Island, and Virginia electoral units showed similar swings in turnout (Brown and Brown 1964, 142–43; Dinkin 1977, 144–80; Kolp 1992, 665–69; Newcomb 1995, 228–31; Syndor 1952, 138–40; Tully 1977, 93).

Fiercely contested races mobilized voters. In a 1737 New York election, it was said, "such was the Zeal of each Party, that it's supposed every one that had a right to vote were brought in, some were sent for in Charriots and Chases" (*AWM* 1737). But in the absence of an active campaign voters had to be prodded to participate. During a sermon a Massachusetts minister scolded, "I have heard it much complained of, that Freemens meetings are not attended, not half of them appear upon choice of Deputies in this Town, and other concerns in that nature" (Allen 1679, 7).

Weather played a role in poor turnout. Officials at a South Carolina polling place reported that on the first day of voting no one appeared due to "the day being very rainy" (*CH* 1996, 17). A Norfolk County, Virginia, election was washed out by "very heavy Rains," which "carried away many Bridges over the Runs and Swamps," preventing voters from reaching the polling place (*JHB* 1761– 1907, 18–19). An "uncommon rainy and blustering Day" kept even the Jamestown sheriff from attending an election, causing it to be rescheduled (*JHB* 1766– 1906, 230).

Short notice contributed. The Virginia assembly ascribed the few votes

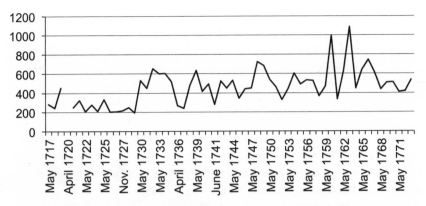

Fig. 6.1. Number of voters in Boston House elections, 1717–74. (Compiled from *RRCB* 1883, 1885a, 1885b, 1886, 1887.)

in one contest to a late change in the election date and to "the Badness of the Weather" (*JHB 1770– 1906*, 195). In January 1769, a New York politician reported that in Albany County the election "was appointed so Suddenly by the Sheriff that it was impossible to Collect the Voters of this extensive County particularly as the roads are so bad & the Rivers impassible" (*Documentary History*, vol. IV 1851, 404). Sometimes weather and work combined to keep people away. A letter discussing an upcoming Virginia election predicted a low turnout because the "late blow in Massanutting & the Harvest will prevent a great many from being down [to the polling]" (*LW*, vol. II 1899, 344). But a Pennsylvania pamphlet ridiculed such excuses: "Let me tell you (my Countrymen) by way of Introduction, that you are very much to blame, for not giving a fuller Attendance at the Election than you sometimes do. Many an honest worthy Candidate hath lost the Day, because forsooth it was Cloudy or Rainy Weather, or a cold Morning, or because there was some trifling Business to be done at Home" (*Advice to the Free-holders 1735*, 3). While appeals to civic duty may not have worked, more concrete inducements could overcome voter reluctance to face bad weather. A Virginia candidate out riding "among the People" the day before the balloting was told that "it was too cold Weather to go so long a Way (it being above 25 Miles) to the Election." So the candidate "told them they should be welcome if they would call at his House in their Way down." Subsequently, "about 10 of them . . . did go to his House the Evening before the Election . . . where they were hospitably entertained" (*JHB 1761– 1907*, 271).

Voter apathy played a role too. In the midst of North Carolina's long apportionment battle, the colony's chief justice lamented that "few of the Electors having come to the last Election by reason a former Election had turned out so ill that they thought it would be to no purpose and therefore were indifferent who were sent" (*CRNC*, vol. IV 1886, 352). Following the 1768 South Carolina elections it was reported, "At St. Helens, no voters attended, consequently, there was no election" (*SCG* 1768d). A malaise forced some Rhode Island town councils to select assembly members (*CSP* 1908, 543). Similar problems surfaced in South Carolina, "Yet, such hath been the *Indifference* or *Neglect* with hath prevailed in that Respect, that Members to represent a Parish have been returned duely elected by *the Votes of the Church-Wardens only*" (*SCG* 1747–1748).

Low turnout was a particular problem in elections called to fill seats that became vacant in the midst of a legislative session. A Massachusetts writer put a conspiratorial spin on it, claiming that if the assembly majority "find any member not for their turn, they purge ye house of him." His replacement then was, "chose by a small number, the rest never having notice. One in our town was chose with but six votes, where the number of freeholders is neer 200" (*CSP* 1913, 436). While there may have been mischief at play in these contests, the real problem was that they took place on an even tighter schedule than regular elections (Bishop 1893, 109–10). Voters were not always able or willing to rearrange their lives so as to participate on short notice.

Deference may have kept people from voting. A Pennsylvania pamphlet suggested, "[M]ay be an honest Country Farmer or Plow-man is afraid to Disoblige a particular Person by giving his Vote against him, when at the same time his Conscience will not allow him to Vote for him, and if he appeared upon the spot, his remaining Neuter would be look'd upon as a Neglect or Contempt" (*Advice to the Free-holders* 1735, 3). And there were efforts to suppress turnout. In Virginia, where freeholders who failed to vote were subject to a nontrivial fine, one candidate promised several gentlemen who supported his opponent that if they "would not come to the Election; and if their Fines were under One Hundred Pounds, he would pay them" (*JHB* 1727– 1910, 426; *SLV*, vol. III 1823, 238).

Given limited participation, organized interests could swing elections. Quakers were viewed as a powerful voting bloc because of their cohesiveness and propensity to participate. A 1701 message to the king signed by 18 inhabitants of West Jersey complained that, "although we exceed the Quakers Parties in numbers, yet by their close contrivances at their pretended monthly, quarterly and yearly religious meetings, they outdo us in elections" (*CSP* 1910b, 364). Such beliefs were widely held. A letter written following New Jersey's reunification asserted, "The state of the Western Division hath always been betwixt the Quakers and others, [for] thô the Quakers are the far less in number, yett they have always had the Government in their hands" (*CSP* 1913, 884). Similar sentiments surfaced in North Carolina, where Quakers were said to be "very diligent at the election of members of the Assembly" (*CRNC*, vol. I 1886, 708). Their success generated a backlash; after several Quakers were elected as Talbot County, Maryland, delegates, a politically damaging report circulated claiming, "Friends should be the occasion of the Leavyes being raised so high." The accusation so unsettled the Quaker community that it created a committee "for ye clearing of Friends and ye Truth" (Tilghman, vol. I 1915, 126).

Voter Intimidation and Election Violence

At times assembly elections generated great passion because much was thought to be at stake. Consequently, some resorted to intimidation to assure their preferred outcome. In 1695 it was alleged that New York's governor had warned incumbents that "if they came to any elections he would shoot them, and thereupon imposed upon the freeholders seamen and soldiers, armed with clubs and bayonets." Another voter said that he could not "enjoy free privilege of election because several soldiers and sailors were to be packed upon the freeholders, and the sailors of H.M.S. Richmond were to be there to deter the people from voting as they liked." A third person professed witnessing voters complaining, "We have not our privileges for there are several sailors and soldiers among you, not freeholders, whom you have clothed in other habits; and besides if we do vote the sailors of the King's ship are ready armed with clubs." Adding insult to injury, he saw "the sailors of the King's ship march with a violin at the head of them, who mocked at the inhabitants who did not vote" (*CSP* 1904, 148, 287–88).

Bullying occurred elsewhere. A Virginia assembly investigation revealed that a tobacco inspector had "solicited the People who brought Tobacco to his Inspection, to vote for [his preferred candidate]" and told those who did not agree that "he would burn their Tobacco." During the same contest an undersheriff "demanded Quit-Rents" from a voter who supported a candidate he opposed (*JHB* 1727– 1910, 274). The North Carolina assembly concluded in one race that the sheriff "was obstructed by Sundry Persons in such a manner that he could not compleat a free and open Election" (*CRNC*, vol. VI 1888, 366). A Georgia grand jury presentment listed as "a very great grievance, That at our publick elections for representatives in this province, arms have been carried, and other threatening and insulting methods made use of, to deter electors from giving their votes freely, especially in the parish of St. Andrew" (*GG* 1768c). A Pennsylvania voter recounted how he "stood amazed at the *Tann'd* Impudence of a Fellow two Years ago, who stood upon the Stairs with Heaps of prepared Tickets; asked to see mine as I was going up; I was not forward to shew it, but being between my Thumb and Fingers, he took it, look'd on't, and then told me it was not the right, would have kept it, and offer'd me another, as it seems he had managed several. With some Trouble I got mine again, but so provoking was the Looby's Conduct, that our Neighbour *Evan* (his Blood being up) asked me, why I did not spit in his Face" (*A Dialogue* 1725, 31).

In response to such incidents, laws were passed making voter intimidation illegal. South Carolina adopted a bill stating, "[I]f any person or persons whatsoever, shall on the day appointed for the election of a member or members of the Commons House of Assembly . . . presume to violate the freedom of the said election by any arrests, menaces, or threats, or endeavor or attempt to overawe, fright, or force any person qualified to vote against his inclination or conscience, or otherwise by bribery obtain any vote," such persons would upon conviction be fined "fifty pounds currant money" and be subject to imprisonment until the sum was paid (*SLSC*, vol. third 1838, 53–54). How effective such measures were in practice is debatable.

Most assembly elections transpired without controversy or conflict. A 1735 Dorchester, Massachusetts, contest was "very peaceably and orderly carried on" (*Boston Weekly News-Letter* 1735). In 1756 Cumberland County, Pennsylvania, reportedly had "never [seen] an Election Carry'd on with so much forwardness and Quietness among the whole as this was" (*PA*, sixth series, vol. XI 1907, 153). A competitive 1768 New Jersey race "was carried on with the greatest coolness and good order: no reflecting nor abusive words were heard during the whole election" (*DRNJ*, vol. XXVI, vol. VII 1904, 208–9). An English visitor observed admiringly that in a 1774 Virginia election, "The Poll was over in about two hours and conducted with great order and regularity" (*Journal of Nicholas Cresswell* 1924, 28). Still, things did not always proceed easily. A Cambridge, Massachusetts, election only got down to voting after "the Select Men had put an End to some tedious *Contests* and lingering *Delays*" (*NEWJ* 1740).

Sometimes the passions generated by competitive races came close to sparking violence. During a heated North Carolina contest, an observer claimed the losing side was "making all the confusion they could in the time of election, and endeavouring to stir up strife and quarrels among the people." He added that, "if Col Pollock (being on a plantation of his that joined on the election field) had not hindered and persuaded the people to keep the peace, [the contest] would have ended in blows" (*CRNC*, vol. I 1886, 696). While investigating a contested election, a South Carolina assembly committee asked if there had been "any Menaces or Threats in Disturbance." The church warden in charge testified that "some Words arose between Mr. Vanderhorst & Mr. Tookerman . . . & at his desire they departed out of the Church" (*JCH* 1996, 17). A 1738 newspaper article lauded the competing upper and lower Burlington County, New Jersey, factions for the "peaceable Manner" in which they conducted a contentious election, specifically commending them for not "using of Canes in a Hostile Manner" (*DRNJ*, vol. XI 1894, 550).

Peacekeeping efforts were not always successful, often because of the mixing of drinking and voting. One candidate supplied voters with alcohol, though with an admonition to "take Care they should not intoxicate themselves, least a Riot might ensue at the Election" (*JHB 1758–* 1908, 83). Such pleas sometimes failed. Usually only fisticuffs ensued. In Calvert County, Maryland, it was reported, "Two of the Electors got into a Fray, and one of them, in the Engagement, bit Part of the other's Nose off" (*MDG* 1754b). On other occasions full-fledged riots broke out. The Augusta County sheriff informed the Virginia assembly that during an election "the People were so tumultuous and riotous, that I could not finish the Poll; for which Reason no Burgesses could be returned for the said County." According to another account of the incident, after being told "The Election is going against us," a supporter on the losing side responded, "It should not, if we cannot carry it one Way, we will have it another: I will put a Stop to the Election" (*JHB 1752–* 1909, 347, 447). During a review of the 1742 Philadelphia election a witness testified that "he saw a Company of Sailors coming toward the Court-House, huzzaing and flourishing their Clubs, who immediately flung Brick-bats among the People, and with their Clubs knocked some of them down." According to another report, a voter who "was not an unactive Spectator of the Riot . . . receiv'd a violent Blow on his Arm, had his Cane struck out of his Hand, and his Foot so bruised, that he was obliged to retire." The sailors at the center of the violence were said to have "appeared much heated with Liquor" (*VPPP* 1743, 30, 33, 76).

A few years later another election riot broke out in Pennsylvania, this time in York County. It was actually a series of violent episodes. The first involved a few men using clubs "in a riotous manner." Later there was "a general fighting among the people, [during which] Several were knock'd down, but at last the Dutch prevailed and came in a body to the Number of

150." At that point the sheriff suspended the election and locked the ballot box. From a window he told the unruly mob that "if they would be easy the Election would be opened by and by, but the people behaved in a tumultuous, disorderly manner, and threatened in the German Language that if their Tickets were not taken in immediately they would break open the Door." After more brickbats resulted in broken windows, the voting was concluded. The assembly accepted the results but admonished the sheriff that he must "take all the Care in his Power for the future to prevent any further Complaint of tumultuous Elections" (*PA*, vol. II 1853, 50–52; *VPPP* 1751, 7–8).

Such violence was so disturbing that the Pennsylvania assembly passed "A Supplement to the Act for Electing Members of Assembly" in response. It was motivated by the "great numbers of disorderly persons, many of whom not being qualified to vote for members of assembly, &c., have mixed themselves among the electors at the time of choosing inspectors, and have by their rude and disorderly behavior disturbed the electors and created strifes and quarrels, to the great danger and disquiet of the peaceable people there met together and in delay of said election" (*SLP*, vol. IV, 1897, 331)." Over the following years the assembly devoted considerable time to tweaking rules to allow elections to proceed smoothly (*SLP*, vol. IV, 1897, 331–36, 375–81; vol. V, 1898 16–22, 153–58, 195–96, 465–66).

Their efforts met with only partial success. In fact the threat of violence came to be viewed as a political tool. An instructive guide written by a political operative of Irish heritage gave the following advice in advance of the 1765 assembly elections.

As soon as your ticket is agreed on, let it be spread through the country, that your party intend to come well armed to the election, and that you intend, if there's the least partiality in either sheriff, inspectors, or managers of the election, that you will thrash the sheriff, every inspector, Quaker and Mennonist to a jelly; and further, I would report it, that not a Mennonist nor German should be admitted to give in a ticket without being sworn that he is naturalized and worth £50, and that he has not voted already; and further, that if you discovered any person attempting to give in a vote without being naturalized, or voting twice, you would that moment deliver him up to the mob to chastise him. Let this report be industriously spread before the election, which will certainly keep great numbers of the Mennonists at home. I would at the same time have all our friends warned to put on a bold face, to be every man provided with a shillelah, as if determined to put their threats in execution, though at the same time let them be solemnly charged to keep the greatest order and peace. (*Letters and Papers* 1855, 211–12)

Voting Irregularities

Claims of voting irregularities surfaced in the aftermath of many contests. Sheriffs were at the center of the process in most colonies outside New England—South Carolina, where church wardens managed the voting during most of the colonial era, was an exception (*SLSC*, vol. second 1837, 684)—and consequently they were well positioned to cause mischief if they chose. They were not supposed to participate; when one did in a Virginia race the assembly struck his vote from the poll (*JHB 1770–* 1906, 252). Sometimes it is not clear whether their ineptitude or their deceitfulness triggered complaints (*CVSP*, vol. I 1875, 142). In tossing out an election because a required voter oath had not been administered, the North Carolina assembly concluded "it appearing that the Sheriff had only misconstrued the Law so was not guilty of any partiality" (*CRNC*, vol. IV 1886, 653). The alleged misbehavior was not always thought sufficiently grievous to invalidate an election (*JVNY* 1737, 32).

But many sheriffs were charged with nefarious acts. Claiming that "the frequent false returns of sherriffs upon writts for election of burgesses, have caused great disturbances and endangered much the peace of his majesty and quiett of his subjects," the Virginia assembly passed a 1676 measure imposing a significant fine on any sheriff found to have submitted erroneous results (*SLV*, vol. II 1823, 356–57). In 1698 New York's new governor, Lord Bellomont, told London officials that he considered the sheriffs appointed by his predecessor "to be the scum of people, tailors and other scandalous persons, who, notwithstanding my proclamations against illegality at elections have contrary to their oath and duty made corrupt and false returns of members" (*CSP* 1905, 280–81). He replaced them, and in turn his political opponents accused the new officeholders of similar behavior in the next election, alleging, "The Sheriffs performed the business they were appointed for by admitting some for freeholders who were not so, and rejecting others who were really so, as they voted for or against their party, and by appointing Inspectors of the poll who upon any complaint of unfair dealing gave this general answer, 'If you are aggrieved, complain to my Lord Bellomont'" (*CSP* 1910a, 116; *Remonstrance* 1698). In

1699 the assembly passed legislation regulating voting because in its view "of late ye Election of ye Representatives to Serve in Assembly . . . have been mannaged with great ourage tumult & Deceit" (*CLNY*, vol. I 1894, 405). Still, just two years later the lieutenant governor then in command had to issue a proclamation requiring "all Sheriffs, Justices of the Peace, Free holders" and others to be "very Circumspect and Observing of the Laws made for the due and fair Elections of Members to be Returned on the next Assembly" so that "the said Elections [would] be permitted with all Freedom and Fairness imaginable" (*A Proclamation* 1701).

Comparable problems occurred across the colonies. Several South Carolina representatives, along with many voters, protested the conduct of Colleton County elections in 1701, citing abuses by the sheriff, who was, at that point in time, in charge of the process. The petitioners claimed that "at the said Election, many threat'nings, many intreaties & other unjustifiable actions were made use of, & illegal and unqualified votes given in to the Sheriff, & by him receiv'ed & returned." Specifically, "the votes of very many unqualify'd Aliens were taken & enter'd . . . [and] a great number of Servants & poor & indigent persons voted promiscuously with their Masters & Creditors, as also several free Negroes were receiv'd, & taken for as good Electors as the best Freeholders in the Province." They listed violations elsewhere, claiming that "at this last Election, Jews, Strangers, Sailors, Servants, Negroes, & almost every *French* Man in *Craven* & *Berkly* County came down to elect, & their Votes were taken, & the Persons by them voted for were returned by the Sheriff, to the manifest wrong & prejudice of other Candidates" (Rivers 1856, 455, 459).

One New Jersey sheriff was said to have contributed directly to voter fraud. According to an account, "There appeared in the field on the Scotch interest but 42 persons (and a great part of them came from New York and Long Island) who were qualify'd to vote. Whereas on behalf of the Country there appeared betwixt 3[00] and 400 men qualify'd . . . yet the Scotch having by a false representation to H[is] E[xcellency] prevailed with him to appoint one of their number to be made High Sheriff, he did, contrary to all law, reason justice or president, return the choice of the 42 electors against the choice of more than 300." In effecting this chicanery, "First, by delay of time, they thought to tire out the Country by detaining them so long in a place where there was not any accomodation for such a number of people, at that time of the year, several hundreds of substantial housekeepers being forced to lye out of doors in the bitter weather . . . [and] when that would not do, he multiply'd tricks upon tricks, till at last barefaced, he made the return contrary to the choice of the Country" (*CSP* 1913, 884).

Maryland's assembly tossed out a 1719 election because "the Sherriff has been very partiall and remiss in his Duty" (*AM*, vol. XXXIII 1913, 386–87). Several decades later the assembly deemed a St. Mary's County contest to be "wholly null and void" because of the sheriff's antics. Not only did he fail to give proper notice of the election, but he "did behave with great Partiality, by endeavoring to deter and hinder, by Threats and Menaces, some of the Freeholders and other Voters of the said County from their Freedom of Voting." He also, "by offering a Reward to another Person, did induce him, and terrify them, into giving their Votes for the four Candidates by him the said Sheriff afterwards returned for the said County, as Delegates" (*VPMD* 1749, 29). At times assemblies had to remind election officials to run them properly. After Maryland lawmakers concluded that a Cecil County contest "was not a free Election," they emphasized that "every Voter in this Province hath a Right to name and give in his Vote, upon every General Election" (*VPMD* 1749, 24).

Other officials might also misbehave. When Annapolis's mayor ran for the Maryland assembly, a complaint was made that he "sat and Acted as Mayor during the whole Time of the said Election and did not withdraw himself from the Bench on any Controversy about the Qualification of the Electors but objected in his Seat to the Qualifications of such as Offered to vote against him." The assembly overturned the outcome (*AM*, vol. LIX 1942, 136, 152–53). South Carolina's reliance on church wardens did not allow it to escape mismanagement claims. A charge was leveled in a 1773 contest, stating, "That many undue practices were allowed by the Church Wardens during the Election to obtain a Majority of votes for Mr Gaillard. That several persons were refused the liberty of Voting for your Petitioner on the first day of Election, and on the second were, offered their Votes, provided they would vote for Mr Gaillard" (Salley 1898, 253).

Contentions that ineligible voters participated were widespread. It was claimed that "Three Hundred unnaturalized *Dutchmen* . . . armed with clubs" had voted in a disputed Philadelphia contest (*VPPP* 1743, 76). A petition from 17 North Carolinians protested that "when a new General Assembly was to be chosen . . . the Election was managed with very great partiality and Injustice, and all sorts of people, even servants, Negroes, Aliens, Jews and Common sailors were admitted to vote in Elections" (*CRNC*, vol. I 1886, 639). An observer of another North Carolina contest claimed that the losing side "were only sixty five, counting several that were but boys and otherwise unqualified" (*CRNC*, vol. I 1886, 696). In a third North Carolina election, complaints were made that a candidate had "procured several Foreigners not naturalized and other persons not qualified to vote for him and they were accordingly poll^d by the Sheriff" (*CRNC*, vol. IV 1886, 495). There were accusations of underage voting in Massachusetts (Brown 1955, 40). A petition contesting a Georgia election focused on two allegedly unqualified voters, "Viz^t William Johnson and John Jones the pretensions of the former being only that of A Verbal purchase of Fifty Acres of Land and the Latter being a free Negro" (*CRSG*, vol. XIII 1907, 561–62). A complaint about a South Carolina contest charged that "many Persons under Age, some who had no property in the Parish, and several Mulatoes were allowed to Vote" (Salley 1898, 253). Virginia also wrestled with race; in 1756 the assembly tossed out the votes of two men who each had a white parent but were "of dark Complexion" (*JHB 1752–* 1909, 360).

Doubts about freeholder status were raised. In 1768 the New York assembly rejected two votes because each voter had acquired his freehold just days prior to the election. At the same time, it accepted the vote of another suspect voter, finding the value of his freehold sufficient (*JVNY* 1769, 24–25). In 1756 the Virginia assembly found a "good right to vote" for one contested voter because he "hath paid Quit-Rents for [his land] eight or ten years past, and sold Timber from off the same," but found "no Right to vote" for a second contested voter because, while he claimed title to land through his wife, he "has never been in Possession thereof." A third voter was determined to have to had "no Right to vote for Burgesses" because, although he "possessed of Eighty-six Acres of Land in said County," the dwelling on it was "much out of Repair, most Part of the Weather-Boards being off and Part of the Shingles, and Sills rotten . . . [also] the said Land hath not been tended, nor hath any Person resided thereon for several Years" (*JHB 1752–* 1909, 359–60). Religion and citizenship could also be at issue. A 1771 petition contesting a Maryland election claimed some voters, "on Account of their religious Tenets had refused to take the Oaths required by Law" and that "a Number of Voters (foreign Protestants) did not produce Certificates of their Naturalization" (*MDG* 1771c).

Ballot stuffing was alleged (Drake 1878, 262). Following a Cambridge, Massachusetts, election, "Samuel Smith was charged with putting in two votes in the first voting for Representative." The accused "made oath that he put in but one vote for Representative" (Paige 1877, 127). Pennsylvania was not always vigilant on this score. During a review of a 1748 Bucks County race, the assembly learned that "a Number of Tickets, which did not appear folded up like those deliver'd in by the Electors, but much rumpled, were taken up from off the Floor, by the Coroner, and put among the remaining genuine Tickets." Although the disputed ballots altered the election's outcome, it was not overturned (*VPPP* 1749, 5, 8–11).

In 1715 Rhode Island revamped its voting process because of "the great abuse and clandestine proceedings and irregular practice, as they are credibly informed, [that] hath been acted by sundry loose and fractious freemen of said colony, in putting or delivering into the hat sometimes two, three or more votes for one officer, at the general elections." The assembly passed a measure requiring "that every freeman admitted to vote, shall write his name at length on the back side of his vote, and all proxy votes shall have the same." Votes lacking a signature would "not be esteemed of any value." But having one's name publicly identified with one's vote proved unpopular. Within a few months the assembly learned that the requirement "hath given great dissatisfaction and uneasiness to many of the good people of this colony." The members voted to abolish it and directed town officials to devise local procedures to prevent fraud. Proxy votes, however, still had to be signed (*RCRI* 1859, 195–96, 207–8).

There were efforts to fraudulently qualify voters. In 1736 the Virginia assembly passed a resolution stating, that "making Leases of small and inconsiderable Parcels of Land, in order to create a Right of voting at Elections, for Burgesses to serve in the General Assembly, is a fraudulent Practice, contrary to Law, and tending to destroy the Rights of the true Freeholders" (*JHB 1727*– 1910, 283). Enforcement proved problematic. In a 1762 case, the burgesses determined that a man who owned "Half of a Lot" in Elizabeth City had "purchased a small tight framed House, of the Dimensions of 10 feet by 8, and had the same removed and placed on his said Ground, on Purpose (as he acknowledged) to qualify him to vote at the Election." They decided he "had a good Right to vote for Burgesses at the said Election" (*JHB 1761*– 1907, 87–88).

At times fraud and violence were interwoven. During a Lancaster County, Pennsylvania, election, "the People pressed and crouded in a Body to deliver their Tickets, which some presented to the Inspectors at the Ends of cloven Sticks." An analysis held that "the Election was carried on in so tumultuous a Manner that no regular List could be taken of the Voters Names." As a consequence, votes were "given in by Persons under Age" and "many of the Voters voted repeatedly, some three, four, five, and some ten Times." Most troubling was the claim that "the Number of Voters did not exceed a Thousand, tho' the Tickets found in the Box were more than Two Thousand Three Hundred." The assembly upheld the election results but reprimanded the sheriff for procedural violations (*VPPP* 1750, 15, 23, 34–35).

New England elections were not immune to irregularities (Bell 1888, 77–78; *DRRT* 1875, 242–43, 562–63). A 1730 account of Massachusetts elections observed that votes "are made by a town meeting, and they [are] governd by a Moderator for that day, from whom there is no appeal." During one Boston town meeting, "Doctor Cook was Moderator, and also one of the candidates, he refused some votes and scrutinized others well qualifyed, but passed all who voted against Mr. Craddock" (*CSP* 1937b, 133). And elections could be far from sedate. A 1768 complaint in Salem charged that "great disorder usually exists here on Election days by negroes assembling together, beating drums, using powder and having guns and swords" (Felt 1827, 471).

Voter Behavior

Political elites cared about voter decision making. A letter to a Virginia newspaper even hinted at a paradox of voting argument: "[S]ay not I am but one; my single Vote can be but of little Consequence, let me give it to whom I will. Should each One follow your Example, pray tell me what Sort of a Representative would you send?" (*VG* 1771). But there is little direct testimony about how electors arrived at their choices. One Pennsylvania voter admitted that he participated with growing reluctance: "I go to *Elections*, because I think it my Duty, but confess my self almost tired of it" (*A Dialogue* 1725, 30). Another Pennsylvanian committed to his diary, "Being our Annual Election the Old Assembly Men were rechose . . . For my part, I thought the last Six had been in long Enough, & therefore Voted for [six others] in their room" (Myers 1904, 112). Some voters were persuadable at the polls. A Virginian recorded, "[W]e went to the courthouse where the freeholders were met to choose burgesses. After a great deal of persuading the choice fell on Colonel Eppes and Sam Harwood, notwithstanding Mr. Parker thought he should have carried it. But Colonel Hill used his endeavors to make the people vote for Colonel Eppes and he had it by one vote" (*Secret Diary of William Byrd* 1941, 217–18).

There are indications that voters behaved in a self-interested manner. Virginia's Lieutenant Governor Spotswood offered one such assessment: "[F]or the mobb of this countrey having tryed their strength in the late election, and finding themselves able to carry whom they please, have generally chosen representatives of their own class" (*CSP* 1926, 70). Those on the losing end of the 1698 New York elections made a similar claim, finding, "Three hundred and sixty-eight of the electors who returned the four Dutch members for the City and County of New York pay less to the public taxes than 29 of the electors who voted against them. The whole body of that faction pay scarce 1/5th part of the public assessment and scarce 1/50th of the revenue from Customs" (*CSP* 1910a, 117). Voters apparently acted in familiar ways.

Gubernatorial Influence

Governors tried to influence elections. A New York politician provided a roundabout admission, writing in the 1730s that "never was an Election more free from any Attempt of Influence from a Governor, than the last" (*LPCC*, vol. IX, 1937, 242). An inventory of the ways in which a Virginia governor could attempt to bend elections to his will highlighted the power of patronage: "Having the nomination of all the militia officers he has a great stroke in the election of Burgesses, as also by the nomination of the Justices and the Sheriff." Such positions generated large sums of money for their holders and could be leveraged: "The Sheriff's place being granted anew every year, there is a constant temptation to a great many pretenders to manage the election of Burgesses in the Governor's interest" (*CSP* 1904, 650). Before one election the James City County sheriff was told that if the governor's preferred candidate did not win, "he should never expect any favour." Greater pressure was exerted elsewhere, "At Surry Election tho' Major Tho. Swan were chosen unanimously, Major Allen did, in the Governor's name, forbid the Sheriff, at his perill, to return him" (*CSP* 1916a, 107). Clerkships were deployed in comparable fashion (*CSP* 1936b, 91). It was said that Lieutenant Governor Spotswood took full advantage: "Commissions flew about to every fellow that could make two or three votes . . . He gave the power to his friends to make a discreet use of [them]. And indeed never fouler play was by men, than at most of our elections" (Wertenbaker 1958, 172). New York executives behaved similarly (*LPCC*, vol. IX 1937, 352).

But governors found voters obstinate and being a gubernatorial supporter was often used against candidates (*NYWJ* 1733a). In 1709 Maryland's governor admitted that after dissolving the assembly he "issued new writts of election . . . hoping the severall Countys would take better care who they sent to represent them, but contrary to expectation found the most of the persons, return'd to the last convention, appear as Delegates of this Assembly" (*CSP* 1922, 195, 250). A Massachusetts governor griped, "The common people of this Province are so perverse, that when I remove any person from the [assembly-elected] Council, for not behaving himself with duty towards H[is] M[ajesty] or His orders, or for treating me . . .

ill, that he becomes their favourite, and is chose a Representative, where he acts as much as in his power, the same part that he did when in Council" (*CSP* 1933, 45). Attempting to steer an election, a New Hampshire governor asked his friends to "exert & bestir" themselves on his behalf. But his hopes were dashed. An adviser reported, "The Discontented have Succeeded in their Choice almost to a Man" leaving the new assembly beholden to "Envy malice & hate and all the other Attributes of Satan" (Batinski 1996, 110).

Governors were aware of their limited influence, and many made realistic assessments when timing elections. Lieutenant Governor Spotswood informed London officials while he hoped "that this unaccountable behaviour of the late Assembly will in all probability give a new turn to the humours of the people, and make them choose for their next Representatives persons of more disinterrested principles: but I shall first be well assured of that disposition before I call another Assembly" (*CSP* 1924, 356). Several decades later another Virginia lieutenant governor reached a comparable judgment: "I intend the Assembly shal meet for that purpose in May, unless I find the Members fall in with the tempers of the basest of the people" (*CSP* 1939, 98). New Jersey's governor admitted that, given his problems with lawmakers, he had "noe hopes that I can think of for any remedy here, for, as to ye calling of a new Assembly, I shall either have all the same Members, or such others who will returne with greater fury" (*CSP* 1924, 483). A New York governor acknowledged, "It did not appear to me that it would avail anything by dissolving the Assembly, as we do not know of one member, that supports the resolution, who would not be returned again, upon a fresh election, but of the few that oppose it, some would be obliged to give place to others of opposite interests" (*DRNY*, vol. VIII 1857, 265). A newly arrived Georgia governor related that his predecessor's secretary "had the insolence to insinuate to me that if I had any design of dissolving the Assembly the consequences I might expect from such a step would be defeated inasmuch as he had taken measures to have the same men rechosen." He admitted, "I am in hopes I shall be able to effect my designs by gentler methods" (*CRSG*, vol. 28, part I 1976, 13).

The influence of governors was weak even in races in which they had a direct stake in the outcome. In 1748 the Massachusetts assembly expelled James Allen of Boston because he had "uttered certain Expressions grossly reflecting on his Excellency the Governour." A town meeting was held four days later to fill the vacancy, and Allen was returned with 73 percent of the vote (*JHHR* 1748, 91, 93, 117–18; *RRCB* 1885b, 153). Such rebuffs were common. In 1750 four New York City incumbents were unanimously reelected, "notwithstanding the false and malignant Aspersions of some of our late ministerial Scribblers" (*NYG* 1750b).

Ethnic Politics

Although it was discussed in sinister tones, ethnic politics was a staple of colonial elections. Ethnic groups were said to have engaged in bloc voting to swing elections. New Jersey's governor, for example, credited "the sur-prize of an inundation of Swedes" for the victory of one of his opponents (*CSP* 1928, 188). Ethnic politics were played with vigor in Pennsylvania. Appeals were directed to German voters, and campaign materials were printed in their language (*An die Freyhalter der Stadt und County* 1764; "Two Addresses of Conrad Weiser" 1899). One politician's letter discussed the need to balance a ticket's appeal "by putting in two Germans, to draw such a party of them as will turn the scale in our favor." Mentioning another possible candidate, he went on to say, "It would be equally agreeable, if Mr. Ross came in place of any of the Irish, but as their interest must be much stronger than his, it would be imprudent to offend them by rejecting one of their proposing" (*Letters and Papers* 1855, 205).

Incorporating ethnic groups into electoral politics met resistance. The inclusion of the two German candidates in Pennsylvania drew unfavor-able comment in New York. A letter to a public figure there noted that by putting them on the ticket "they have opend a door to the Germans into the Assembly," which might prove to be "a plant that will take a deep Root overspread the Province & last in all appearance as long as the Prov-ince itself" (*PSWJ*, vol. IV 1925, 564). Yet, in the 1769 New York election campaign, appeals were printed in German (*NYG* 1769c). Still, during that colony's battle over voting reforms the following year, a broadside oppos-ing the use of ballots demurred, "The Germans, who are very numerous in [Pennsylvania's] Government, as well as this [one], being of foreign Birth and Education, are in general so unacquainted with our Language, that they are incapable of knowing whose Name is inserted in the Ticket they deliver; and are thereby frequently the Means of electing Persons, whom they detest in their Hearts" (*The Mode of Elections* 1769).

Ethnic appeals occasionally lapsed into farce. New York's governor mentioned during the 1699 elections one faction that was "an artifice to draw all the English to vote for their friends, called themselves the English Party." This was "very ridiculous" because "three of the four candidates they set up were as mere Dutch as any are in this town. Alderman Wenham was the only Englishman of 'em; the other three were Johannes van Kipp, Rip van Dam, and Jacobus van Courtlandt. The names speak Dutch and the men can scarce speak English" (*CSP* 1908, 173).

Contemporary Assessments of Elections and Representation

Contemporary observers took incumbent reelections as evidence that the public approved of their policy stances. A letter published on a controversial Maryland fees bill noted that proposals to increase charges were "contrary to the Sentiments of the late Lower House, which seem to be approved in the new Choice of the old Members at the late Election" (*MDG* 1771a). In another letter, three Maryland delegates justified their position on a divisive issue by noting, "But the people, the ultimate and conclusive *judges* of the propriety of the conduct of their *representatives*, have approved their conduct by *two several re-elections*" (*MDG* 1773h). Following the 1769 South Carolina contests, it was reported, "The inhabitants of Charles-Town have testified their approbation of the conduct of their former Members, by re-choosing them all, at the General Election" (*SCG* 1769a). Electors in Rehoboth, Massachusetts, told their representative, "It is evident from the repeated suffrages of the freeholders and other inhabitants of this town, that your late conduct in the General Assembly of this Province has met with a favourable reception" (Bliss 1836, 143). Incumbents interpreted reelection as affirmation of their policy positions. A South Carolina member thanked his voters for "this public and repeated Testimony of your Approbation of my conduct in Assembly" (*SCG* 1760d). Following his reelection a few years later, he told them, "Your favourable acceptance of my endeavours, so kindly evinced by my being re-chosen at the late election, will ever be remembered by me with the most grateful acknowledgments" (*SCG* 1762b).

Uncontested races were seen as a sign of voter approval. In one election, Haverhill, Massachusetts, voters "thought the Public Interest would be best served by sending their former Representative again, and accordingly last Tuesday unanimously made choice of Richard Saltonstall, Esq; to represent them in the General Court the Year ensuing" (*BEP* 1767). When four New York City and County incumbents were reelected without opposition it was seen as "the most ample Testimonial, of the Sentiments of our Citizens, of the Conduct of the late General Assembly" (*NYEP* 1747b). Several years later, following another unanimous reelection, "the People expressed the most ardent Affection for their former Representatives, by three of those popular and triumphant *Huzzas* . . . From which we may fairly infer, that the Conduct of these Gentlemen is universally approv'd of by their Constituents" (*NYG* 1750b). The unanimous reelection of two Virginia members demonstrated that the electors were "sensible that their late representatives had discharged their duty to their country" (*VG* 1774g).

Incumbents traded on such assessments. A Rhode Island deputy seeking election to the council promoted his candidacy by pointing to the fact that Newport voters had made "unanimous Choice of him to the office of a Deputy for several Years past" (*NM* 1764a). By the same token, incumbent defeats were ascribed to a failure to follow voter preferences. When one Massachusetts incumbent lost, a writer commented, "This it is hoped may be a warning to Representatives rather to act the sentiments of their Constituents" (*BEP* 1769b).

It may be that assembly elections were often uncompetitive because incumbents became so adept at their representational activities that voters saw no need to seek alternatives. Thus uncontested reelections reflected strategic calculations on the part of potential challengers, who opted out of races "where there could be no hope of success" (Tully 1977, 40). There is speculation that constituent satisfaction with assembly performance increased over the decades, dampening competitive fires (Bonomi 1966, 446–47; Greene 1981, 456). But there were changes in what representation was thought to entail that may have contributed to an increase in lawmaker attention to constituent preferences. Those developments will be examined in the next chapter.

Epilogue: The 1733 Westchester and 1768 and 1769 New York City and County Elections

No single election is representative of all that took place during the colonial era. Most that we know about in any detail were either challenged before the assembly or held during a time of political strife, both of which circumstances might leave us with a skewed impression. Fortunately, the most thorough account of an assembly election we have happens to be of an uncontroversial 1733 Westchester, New York, race (*NYWJ* 1733b). Without a detailed newspaper report it would have been forgotten. But the report documents many behaviors discussed in this chapter.

The contest was characterized as "being an Election of great Expectation, and where in the Court and Country's Interest was exerted (as is said) to the Utmost." As required, the county's "High Sheriff" had "by Papers affixed to the Church of *East-Chester*, and other Publick Places, given Notice of the Day and Place of Election." Unfortunately, whether through incompetence or duplicity, he failed to include the time of day the election would be held. The omission "made the Electors on the Side of [one candidate] verry suspicious that some Fraud was intended." Thus, "about 50 of them kept Watch upon and about, the Green at *Eastchester* (the place of Election) from 12 o'Clock the Night before, 'til the Morning of that Day" (*NYWJ* 1733b).

Some voters had to travel many miles to reach the polling site. They were "beginning to move on Sunday Afternoon and Evening, so as to be at *New-Rochell*, by Midnight." A festival-like atmosphere prevailed along the way, with voters having entertainment and food provided for them in the communities through which they passed. Because there was insufficient room to accommodate all of them in New Rochelle, "a large Fire was made in the Street, by which they sat 'til Day-Light." They were later joined by about "70 Horse of the Electors of the lower Part of the County." Together they "then proceeded towards the Place of Election in the following Order, *viz.* First rode two Trumpeters and 3 Violines; next 4 of the principal Freeholders, one of which carried a Banner, on one Side of which was affixed in gold Capitals, KING GEORGE, and on the Other, in like golden Capitals LIBERTY & LAW" (*NYWJ* 1733b). Such pomp was typical (e.g., *AWM* 1737).

Following the fanfare came one of the candidates and his supporters, "above 300 Horse of the principal Freeholders of the County . . . a greater Number than had ever appear'd for one Man since the Settlement of the County." The other candidate appeared a while later, accompanied by several county officials and "about 170 Horse of the Freeholders and Friends." His supporters shouted, "*No Land-Tax*" while the first candidate's backers countered with "no *Excise*," indicating that these issues mattered to the voters. The sheriff arrived within an hour. With the voters gathered on "the Green" it was determined that while one candidate appeared to enjoy a clear majority that "a Poll must be had." It took two hours to get "Benches, Chairs, and Tables" assembled so the votes could be taken (*NYWJ* 1733b).

As the contest progressed, challenges were registered against the votes cast by 38 Quakers who had refused to take an oath attesting to their voting qualifications but had instead offered to affirm their status, something the law allowed. But the sheriff refused to record their votes, despite the fact that they were "Men of known and visible Estates." The polling then continued with only occasional dispute. It concluded "About Eleven o'Clock that Night." Fortunately, the result was clear. The first candidate won by a vote of 231 to 151, and the unrecorded Quaker votes would only have added to the winner's total. At the conclusion, "the whole Body of Electors, waited on their new Representative to his Lod[g]ings, with Trumpets sounding, and Violins playing" (*NYWJ* 1733b).

Arguably, the most intense colonial era campaigns were the 1768 and 1769 New York elections. Driven by a struggle for political control between two leading families, the De Lanceys and the Livingstons, the clash was so heated that the lieutenant governor told London officials "the City of New York is now divided into two parties, which violently oppose each other" (*DRNY*, vol. VIII 1857, 146). Voters were deluged with unprecedented newspaper coverage of the campaigns, as well as a large number of pamphlets and broadsides (e.g., "New York Broadsides, 1762–1779" 1899, 23–27). The volume of published material provides us with a good picture of how these races were conducted.

Candidate occupation was employed as an important cue in the 1768 campaign. The Livingston faction touted the virtues of merchants in contrast to the vices of attorneys. A letter in a newspaper launched an attack along these lines, claiming, "As a Maritime City, our chief Dependence is upon Trade, for which Reason Merchants (who are well acquainted with the commercial Interest of the Colony) are the properest Persons to represent us in the Assembly; not Lawyers, whose sole Study it is, not to increase the Wealth of the State, but to divide the Gain of the industrious Merchant and Mechanick, if possible among themselves" (*NYJ* 1768c). Other appeals circulated on the backs of playing cards. One said, "[I]t's requested that no Man will vote for a Lawyer, unless he prefers the Craft of the Law, to the Business of the Merchants, and the Welfare of their Friends" (*MERCHANTS'-HALL* 1768). Another calling for "No Lawyer in the Assembly" held that "it is Trade and not Law supports our families" (*A Card* 1768). A third offered antilawyer doggerel, a snippet of which read, "Beware my good Friends of the Wolf's griping Paw, And the Man who will rob, under sanction of Law" (*A Word of Advice* 1768).

Backers of the De Lancey faction rallied to the legal profession's defense. One queried, "Why are we quarrelling about the immaterial circumstance, whether he be a *Merchant* or a *Lawyer* . . . that represents us? . . . Is the point, once settled that a candidate has superior abilities, extensive knowlege, a thorough acquaintance with the constitution, and approved integrity, what other qualification can we ask for or desire?" (*NYG* 1768d). The merits of merchants were drawn into question. One pamphlet asserted, "But of merchants in general thus much may be fairly said, that all their services done to the community, is by their search after private gain, and it is their accidental advantage to have that coincide with public interest" (*The Occasionalist* 1768, 4). Among the mocking assertions circulated in a broadside was a purported oath: "I believe that none but Merchants are proper to represent this City, and that every Cockfighter, Horseracer, and Whoremonger, is in the Politicks of the present Day, a Merchant, this is to say, is not a Lawyer" (*A Political Creed* 1768).

The 1768 election failed to settle the conflict between the families, and the losing side maneuvered the resulting assembly to dissolve itself. The resulting 1769 elections were framed by questions about the way the candidate slates were composed. And religious differences became a wedge issue (*To the Freeholders and Freemen of the City and County of New-York, in Communion* 1769; *To the Freeholders and Freemen, of the City and County of New-York. The Querist, No. II* 1769; *Observations on the Reasons* 1769; Van Schaack 1842, 10).

An attempt was made at the beginning of the campaign to assemble a coalition ticket: "In order to avoid a heated Election for Representatives in the next General Assembly, it is proposed by several Committees of the different Non-Episcopal Denominations in this City, that they do appoint two of the Members for the City and County of New-York, and that the Episcopalians do appoint [the] other Two; and that both Parties do vote for the Four so to be appointed; And that if any Fifth or other Person, do set up for a Representative, both Parties do vote and use their Interest against him" (*To the Freeholders and Freemen of the City and County of New-York* 1769a). The effort foundered when one side claimed, "They found it to be the general Sense of their Constituents, that the Four late Members should be re-chosen; and that therefore they conceived it would have been highly improper and ungrateful in Them to consent to any other Junction" (*New-York, January 6th, 1769* 1769).

As a result, two competing candidate slates were assembled (*New-York, January 9, 1769* 1769; *NYJ* 1769a). One included Philip Livingston (*To the Freeholders and Freemen of the City and County of New-York* 1769a; *New-York, January 4, 1769* 1769). His presence proved controversial because supporters of the opposing De Lancey ticket alleged that during a public meeting "We the Subscribers were present, and did hear, Philip Livingston, Esq. declare, That he did decline serving as a Member, for this City and County . . . and, after so declining, he did return his Public Thanks to the Gentlemen present" (*City of New-York, ss.* 1769). Livingston had to issue a statement saying he had intended to run on the proposed alliance ticket, and when it fell apart, he decided that he "could not join with either

Party." But he changed his mind when "many People declared they would vote for me, whether I offered myself as a candidate or not," adding that "as I had declined, I had not the least Expectation of being elected; but if I was elected, I should think it my Duty to serve" (*NYG* 1769a).

With his decision the two slates began to aggressively solicit votes (*To the Freeholders and Freemen, of the City and County of New-York* 1769b). One observer wrote to a friend that it was "the Strongest Election ever known all in uproar & Confusion" (*PSWJ*, vol. VI 1928, 586). Only a few appeals were positive. The Livingston ticket proposed the adoption of a series of clean election agreements, among them, "That no treating or open Houses shall be directly or indirectly made Use of by either Party, or their Friends or Agents, . . . That no bad Votes, among which the non-resident Freemen are reckoned, shall be attempted to be introduced by either Party" and "That no Colours, Drums, or Instruments of Musick, or Badges of Distinction, shall be carried about the City" (*To the Freehold-ers and Freemen of the City and County of New-York* 1769c). Several issues were raised, most notably an excise tax, trade, the opening of assembly debates to the public, and the dissolution of the previous assembly (*An Address to the Freeholders of Dutchess County* 1769; *The Examiner, No. II* 1769; *As a Scandalous Paper* 1769).

But most appeals fell on the negative side. De Lancey backers accused a Livingston supporter of saying in private that his candidate was "a snake in the grass," that he had "near worne out a pair of shoes . . . in getting him in a member at the last election," and that "he would wear out a whole, or two pair, at another election to keep him out" (*NYJ* 1769b). A candidate on the De Lancey slate was accused of having had a man imprisoned for fail-ing to pay a debt he did not owe (*To the Freeholders and Freemen of the City of New-York* 1769). That candidate responded with a broadside defending his actions and a newspaper advertisement providing depositions attesting that he "has long been a most uncommon Instance of Charity and Benevo-lence" (*Mr. Jauncey* 1769; *NYJ* 1769e). The same candidate then had brib-ery charges leveled against him (*An Address to the Freeholders of Dutchess County* 1769). His defenders responded with another broadside endors-ing him, claiming that he "makes use of no undue Influence to procure Votes; nor would do a dirty Action to gain a Seat in the House." Drawing a contrast to their candidate's virtues, they then charged a member of the Livingston slate with being "much impaired by Debauchery and Excess" because he "dances with, and *kisses (filthy Beast!)* those of his own Sex" (*A Contrast* 1769).

Given the charged atmosphere, vote fraud was a concern. A broadside circulated announcing that to keep "the conducting of Elections free from Corruption on the one Hand, and Threats and Terror on the other," a procedure would be formulated to allow those who witnessed such events "to give the proper Intelligence by leaving an Account thereof with the Printer" (*NYG* 1769d; *A Seasonable Advertisement* 1769). Some De Lancey operatives were accused of attempting to bribe a leading Livingston follower to abandon one of the candidates on that ticket. Specifically, it was alleged the voter was told "if he voted against Mr. *Scott*, that the Board of Commerce would give him the Inspection of all the Flour they shipp'd; and that if the ensuing Assembly did not appoint him sole Inspector, they the Board of Commerce would; but if he voted for Mr. *Scott*, they would not employ him at all" (*Liberty* 1769). The alleged bribe giver admitted that he had visited the voter in question but only to inform him "that most of the Members of the Chamber of Commerce, were in the opposite Interest to Mr. Scott, and therefore if he voted for him, I was afraid they would give their Business to some other Person" (*An Advertisement having appeared* 1769). There were hints of possible voter intimidation as well. Prior to the election, Peter Livingston, the representative from Livingston Manor, wrote to another representative, bragging, "But there is a great deal in good management of the votes. Our people are in high spirits, and if there is not fair play shown there will be bloodshed, as we have by far the best part of the Bruisers on our side, who are determined to use force if they use any foul play" (Lossing 1860, 236).

Voters took note of all this. As the election drew near, a student wrote to a friend, "Party spirit runs high, (as Coke says of ambition,) it rideth without reins." In a letter to his father, he wrote, "I inclose you some papers that have appeared on the occasion of the election. Numberless others were handed about, but of little merit." He then confessed, "It is surprising while trifles can be turned to the greatest advantage in elections, and be made to captivate the passions of the vulgar." Ethnic politics also entered his account, for "the Germans were like firebrands . . . These gentlemen have also made themselves remarkable by a song in the German language, the chorus of which is: 'Measter Cruger, Delancey / Measter Walton and Jauncey.' 'Twas droll to see some of the first gentlemen in town joining in singing this song" (Van Schaack 1842, 8, 11–12). A local merchant who was a strong partisan evinced the furies the campaign unleashed, blasting the opposition in a letter: "Damn them All—a pack of hipocritical, Cheating, Lying, canting, illdesigning Scoundrells" (*PSWJ*, vol. VI 1928, 575).

Election Day brought a resounding victory for the De Lancey slate.

A newspaper reported, "The four Candidates, who had the Majority of Voices in their Favour . . . were attended from the City-Hall, by a vast concourse of People, with Music playing, and Colours displayed; in this Manner they proceeded down the Broad-Way, and through the main Street to the Coffee-House, being repeatedly saluted with loud Huzzas." The account concluded, "After closing the Pole, the four Gentlemen elected, generously gave £200, for the Benefit of the Poor of this City, which was accordingly distributed" (*NYJ* 1769f).

SEVEN

Expectations for the Representative's Role

In England, representatives were initially to behave as delegates, acting as attorneys promoting and protecting their clients' interests (Bailyn 1967, 162–63; Huntington 1966, 389). Thus a late-sixteenth-century discourse on politics observed, in regard to Parliament, that "everie Englishman is entended to bee there present, either in person or by procuration and attornies" (Smith [1583] 1906, 49). Members "were preoccupied with local and special interests" (Beer 1957, 615).

By the time the colonies were established the parent country's notion of representation was changing. Members of Parliament started seeing themselves as trustees (Dickinson 2007, 29–30). One early-eighteenth-century assessment concluded, "Though a Representative is chosen by some *one County, City* or *Town*, and is particularly obliged to consult the Interest of it; yet it must be admitted that he is a Representative of the *People in general*; that the *House of Commons* are the Trustees for the whole Kingdom." Thus, "[T]he Interest of a *particular County, City, or Borough* is not to be preferr'd to the *common Good of the Kingdom in general*" (D'Anvers, vol. X 1737, 186–87). Speaker Onslow offered a similar take: "Every Member, as soon as he is chosen, becomes a representative of the whole body of the Commons, without any distinction of the place from whence he is sent to Parliament" (*Precedents of Proceedings*, vol. II 1818, 76). Members took this perspective to heart; one of them reminded his colleagues that "after we have taken our seats in this House we ought, every one of us, to look upon ourselves as one of the representatives of the whole body of the Commons of England, ought not to have any particular bias for the county, city or borough we represent" (*Cobbett's Parliamentary History*, vol. IX 1811, 450).

Both Bailyn (1967) and Huntington (1966) argue it was the earlier Tudor notion of delegate representation that took root in the American colonies, allowing them to diverge from the trustee perspective that became dominant in England. But as the discussion in chapter 2 suggests, the reality of colonial notions of representation was more complicated. The New England colonies were created with a clear delegate orientation, which they maintained. In the other colonies a trustee perspective initially held but was later displaced. How delegate behavior came to prevail in the colonies when it was being rejected in the parent country is the focus of this chapter.

What They Were Called and How They Were Treated

With the emergence of representative assemblies came two small questions to be answered: what should those elected to serve in them be called and how should they be treated? During the colonial era seven different titles were applied to lawmakers: assemblyman, burgess, committee, delegate, deputy, representative, and trustee. The first label was *burgess*, which appeared in the opening sentence of the 1619 Virginia assembly's journal. The Virginia Company actually considered each electoral unit a borough and each voter a burgess, but the name quickly came to be applied only to assembly members (*JHB 1619–* 1915, xxvii, 3). Although it was used at times elsewhere, notably in North Carolina, it never became dominant outside Virginia.

The most archaic appellation was *committee*. Used in the sense of "one who is committed," it was applied to lawmakers in the early New England colonies but disappeared from use around 1650 (*PRCC* 1850, 9; *RCNP* 1861, 6, 11, 31; *RCRI* 1856, 147). The least common name was *trustee*. It was mentioned only fleetingly by the West Jersey proprietors when they held that one proprietor or freeholder was to be elected from each district "to be Deputies, Trustees or Representatives" (*Grants, Concessions* 1758, 405).

Delegate was used occasionally in many colonies but only became customary in Maryland. *Assemblyman* most often surfaced in reference to New York lawmakers (e.g., *NYWJ* 1737d). Although Pennsylvania and New Jersey members usually called themselves *representatives*, on occasion they employed *assembly-men* (*Journal and Votes* 1872, 107; *VPPP* 1755, 48). Across the colonies, *representative* gained currency only around the end of the seventeenth century, timing consistent with etymology of the word in relation to Parliament (Pitkin 1967, 241–52). *Deputy* was the term most often applied throughout the colonial era. Indeed, it was used in Rhode Island until the 1790s (Denison 1878, 158–59; Perry 1886, 117–18; Tucker 1877, 58).

No differences of substance were read into the various titles. Indeed, the names were interchangeable. A 1675 Maryland assembly journal entry began, "It is this day ordered by the Bu[rgesses], Dep^tys or Delegates of this Province" (*AM*, vol. II 1884, 441). Early Boston records listed those "chosen for Deputyes or Committees" (*SRRC* 1881, 10, 11, 20, 55). A 1684 election return submitted by the Chester County, Pennsylvania, sheriff referred to "Delegates & Representatives." Almost three-quarters of a century later a return submitted by the Bucks County sheriff referred to "Representatives or Delegates" (*PA*, vol. I 1852, 86; sixth series, vol. XI 1907, 89). While *representative* was the most common term used in Pennsylvania, members elected from Philadelphia City were called burgesses both in common parlance—in his autobiography Benjamin Franklin wrote that Philadelphians "elected me a burgess to represent them in the Assembly"—and in the assembly's journals (*AWM* 1734; Franklin 1921, 120; Myers 1904, 112–13; *VPPP* 1738, 3; 1739, 3). The 1752 Plymouth, Massachusetts, records show that the town voted against sending "two representatives"; instead it chose "one Assemblyman" (*RTP* 1903, 41). Documents from the first New Jersey assembly refer to members as "Burgesses or Deputies" (*Grants, Concessions* 1758, 80). A 1705 New York assembly measure called members "Representative or Deputy" (*CLNY*, vol. I 1894, 584–85).

Even when the title was formally changed from deputy to representative, as it was in Massachusetts between 1689 and 1692, nothing should be made of it. Election writs still called on towns to "Elect and Depute one or more Persons to Represent them in a Great and General Court" (*BEP* 1738; *RRSM* 1887, 15; *WR* 1900, 104, 113, 119). Towns used both titles. During the quarter century in which the Dorchester records were kept by the same clerk, they show that in some years the town chose a deputy and in others a representative (*Annals of the Town of Dorchester*, vol. two 1846, 41–68). The same was true elsewhere. According to a history of Wethersfield, Connecticut, "In 1698, the term 'representative,' as a synonym for 'deputy' was first used; but dropped the next year; and thereafter until 1708, the office was usually called *deputy*. After that date, both terms were used" (Stiles 1904, 184).

The lack of a uniform title may have resulted from the less than exalted social status assembly service accorded a member. While being elected marked a man as a member of the elite, it did not mean he was venerated. In Boston the title "Mister" was applied to only a few men who held society's highest posts, and assembly members did not automatically qualify (Scudder 1880, 487). The early records of Watertown, Massachusetts, refer one of their representatives simply as "bro[ther]" (*WR* 1894, 59).

Furthermore, assembly members were not always treated respectfully. A drunken Maryland merchant, "to the disturbance of the whole howse in their quiett & rest," blistered the colony's lawmakers with a series of slurs, calling them, among other things, "a Turdy shitten assembly" and "a Company of pittifull Rogues, & puppyes" (*AM*, vol. II 1884, 55–56). And not only inebriated constituents hurled such abuse. A complaint lodged against Maryland's governor alleged, "While at Common Prayer, at the beginning of the Litany, he called Captain Thomas Waughop, member of Assembly, rogue and rascal, and kicked him out of the church" (*CSP* 1905, 246). Assembly members were even the butt of voters' jokes. After one Chelmsford, Massachusetts, representative was chosen it was suggested that a committee accompany him to Boston to make sure he found the State House. On another occasion, a voter moved that a newly elected member be instructed not to tell anyone what town he represented (Waters 1917, 455).

More disturbingly, representatives were occasionally the targets of physical violence. Several South Carolina lawmakers charged that during a controversy over an early-eighteenth-century elections bill several of their colleagues "were assaulted & set upon in the open Street, without any provocation or affront by them given or offered." One had a sword drawn on him, "the point held at the said [member's] belly." Another was taken to an assailant's ship, where "reviling & threat'ning of him as they drag'd him along; and having gotten him on board . . . they sometimes told him they would carry him to *Jamaica*, & at other times threatn'd to hang him or leave him on some remote Island" (Rivers 1856, 457–58). Virginia's journal records that in 1715 "one *John Bolling* of the County of *Henrico* hath Assaulted beaten and very much wounded Mr *Richard Corke* [*Cocke*] a Member of this House" (*JHB 1712– 1912*, 125). Pennsylvania's assembly sent its governor a message complaining that "some Dissatisfied Persons . . . have of late taken the Liberty of Menace, and Threaten . . . some of the Members of this House" (*JVPA* 1729, 31). Even a whole chamber could be endangered. During a period of civil unrest, the New Jersey assembly learned that a "Number of Evil-minded Men" who had just forcibly liberated a comrade from the Hunterdon County jail "did then give out certain threatening Expressions of their Intentions of coming to this town in a great Body" to intimidate lawmakers into not holding them criminally responsible for their actions. The assembly passed a resolution "to Discourage such large Numbers of Persons coming down to this Place." Lawmakers pleaded that any lobbying "ought to be done in a decent Manner, by a small Number of others in their Behalf" (*Votes of the General Assembly* 1747 (November), 36–38).

Representatives were expected to behave properly. A Delawarean admonished, "Is it fit that the Speaker of an Assembly . . . & a professed Orator of no small Reputation should thus descend to the language of men of the meanest Rank & lowest breeding" (*Some Records of Sussex County* 1909, 192). The more respectable members of society were not, however, always good judges of who their fellow voters might find acceptable. One of George Washington's friends wrote, "Our Election comes on next Monday, cannot say who will be our Burgesses tho' expect B. Grymes will be one altho' every Man of any tolerable understanding I believe will be against him" (*LW*, vol. III 1901, 363). The writer correctly predicted Grymes' victory. A letter to another prominent Virginian offered a harsher assessment of a particular candidate: "Last Wednesday, Robert Wade, Junr. And Nathaniel T—— were (by a great majority) elected representatives for this county, but I expect we shall have another election, as I am certain Mr. T—— will not be allow'd to take a seat in the house, where none but gentlemen of character ought to be admitted" (*Bland Papers* 1840, 12). This prediction proved wrong, and Nathaniel Terry served many years in the assembly.

Representation and the Frequency of Assemblies and Elections

Assemblies and elections occurred at different intervals across the colonies. In the case of Virginia, the periods changed appreciably over the course of the colony's history. As noted in chapter 2, the original intent was that an assembly "should be helde yearly once," an expectation that was later reiterated ("Instructions to Berkeley, 1642" 1895, 281–82; *JHB 1619–* 1915, 36; *SLV*, vol. I 1809, 231). The early records are sparse, but it appears assemblies met almost every year between 1629 and 1656 (*Colonial Virginia Register* 1902, 55–76; "Virginia in 1636-'8" 1903, 263). In contrast, although Parliament was directed to meet annually, by the seventeenth century that notion had long been ignored and it did not meet at all between 1629 and 1640 (Tasewell-Langmead 1946, 176–77).

The 1656 assembly broke precedent by remaining in session for longer than one year. In 1659 the assembly passed a measure specifying biennial sessions, in effect confirming the new schedule (Miller 1907, 47; *SLV*, vol. I 1809, 517). The assembly that met in 1661, however, continued in session through adjournments and prorogations until 1676. Known as the "Long Assembly," it was dominated by the governor. A grievance filed by Charles City County in 1676 makes the extended session's consequences clear: "[W]e have of late feared . . . that our s^d representatives . . . have been over-swayed by the power and prevalency of the s^d [Governor] S^r Wm. Berkeley and his councell (divers instances of which wee conceive might be given, and have neglected our grievances made knowne to them)" ("Charles City County Grievances" 1895, 141–42). Representatives rendered unaccount-able to the voters due to the lack of elections came to view the governor and his officials as their constituents (Wertenbaker 1914, 135–37).

Unhappiness with the Long Assembly helped fuel Bacon's Rebel-lion. A James City lawyer wrote that "the rabble rise, exclameing ag't the p'ceedeings of the Assembly and seeme weary of it, in y^t itt was of 14 y'rs continuance" ("Bacon's Rebellion" 1893, 170). In response to the revolt, the Long Assembly was adjourned and writs were issued for a new assem-bly. Royal instructions issued in 1677 told the governor, "You shalbe noe more obliged to call an assembly once every yeare, but only once every two yeares," returning matters to the prior status quo (*SLV*, vol. II 1823, 424). There was popular support for the decision; Gloucester and Surry coun-ties had registered qualms about "too frequent Assemblyes and the high Charges of Burgesses of Assembly." Still, there was an expectation that the newly called assembly would be more responsive to constituent concerns than the Long Assembly had been. Following the election Isle of Wight voters declared that "wee all expect redress from this [new] Assembly" ("Causes of Discontent in Virginia, 1676" 1894, 168, 170–71; 1895b, 380).

The assembly met at least once every two years for most of the rest of the seventeenth century. An assessment of the colony's governance writ-ten around 1697 for the Board of Trade by John Locke and James Blair recommended that the governor "call an Assembly once a Year" because there was no mechanism through which to get "to Know the true State of the Country, or to try the fitness of a Governour to manage the people like that of frequent Assemblies" (Kammen 1966, 164–65). But no action was ever taken on the suggestion.

Early in the eighteenth century there were extended intervals between assemblies, which met with pushback. A bill requiring triennial assem-blies passed in 1715. This time span was in keeping with three trien-nial acts passed in the previous century to govern Parliament (Randall

1916). But the Crown rejected Virginia's measure because its prerogative to call assemblies would have been "Clipt" (*JHB 1712– 1912*, 156, 159, 160, 167). Extended assemblies continued. The one begun in 1727 lasted until 1734, and the following one opened in 1736 and stayed on until 1740. Motivated by a belief that "frequent new assemblies tend greatly to the happiness and good government of this colony," in 1762 the assembly passed a measure holding that "henceforth a general assembly shall be holden once in three years at the least." Another provision in the bill stated that no assembly, including the current one, could last "longer than for seven years at the furthest," a time period that conformed to the one under which the Parliament had operated since 1716 (Lease 1950; Randall 1916). Again the bill did not meet with the Crown's approval (*SLV*, vol. VII 1820, 517–18, 530). Assemblies during the remaining colonial years lasted from two to four years.

The situation in several of the northern colonies was remarkably different. Connecticut and Rhode Island held elections followed by new assemblies on a regular schedule every six months. In 1733 Rhode Island's governor prevailed on his assembly to switch to annual elections because he thought twice yearly contests amplified divisions among the voters. But assembly members quickly changed their minds, and the colony reverted to semiannual contests for the rest of the colonial era, largely because people considered them a charter privilege to be defended (*Acts and Laws, Rhode-Island* 1745, 171, 255; *Correspondence of the Colonial Governors* 1902, 37–38; Douglas, vol. II 1755, 86; Potter 1842, 7; *RCRI* 1859, 484). Elections were held annually in Delaware, Massachusetts, and Pennsylvania. The schedules in all five of these colonies were dictated by their charters and afforded them considerable political independence, much to the chagrin of those who promoted the Crown's powers. New York's governor, for example, complained to a London official, "The Government [of Connecticut] is a republic . . . and no friends to monarchs" (*CSP* 1903, 169). Regular and frequent elections provided these colonies with a buffer against royal intrusion into their politics.

The other colonies generally had irregular elections, although the histories behind them varied. In 1694 South Carolina's lawmakers passed a measure "for preventing of inconveniencies happening by long intermission of general assemblies." It specified annual meetings and held that no assembly could sit longer than three years. A 1721 law confirmed the commitment to triennial assemblies while also holding that no intermission could last longer than six months (*SLSC*, vol. second 1837, 79–80; vol. third 1838, 140). When in 1724 the governor seized on a possible security threat to the colony to push the assembly to extend its session, the members refused, telling him, "[W]e did not at yor pressing instances Revive the Assembly for a longer time than limitted by Law which We could neither justifie to yor Selves or to our Electors unless a Sufficient reason had occurr'd for that purpose" (*JCH* 1944, 42–44, 46–47).

In 1745 the Commons House of Assembly passed an act requiring annual assemblies (*SLSC* vol. third 1838, 657). This schedule proved unpopular with voters; the governor told the Board of Trade that "at the last election there were four returns made by the parish officers only, there being no elector, occasioned by their not caring to give themselves the trouble of attending elections so frequently" (*JBTP*, vol. 8 1931, 289). Concluding that annual elections were "very inconvenient," the assembly passed a bill mandating biennial elections (*SLSC* vol. third 1838, 692). London officials subsequently rejected both the annual and biennial measures, effectively reinstating the triennial law (*APC*, vol. IV 1911 49–50; *JBTP*, vol. 8 1931, 335). It continued in effect for the rest of the colonial era, although there were complaints that it was a "Wrong Practice" (Greene 1961, 76–77, 80–81). Georgia's assembly admired its neighbor's triennial elections and agitated for a similar law. Its governor told London officials, "It would be happy for us if South Carolina was at a greater distance as our people are incessantly urging & aiming at the priviledges enjoyed there" (*CRSG*, vol. 28, part I 1976, 193).

For some years North Carolina operated with two-year elections. A 1715 act specifying biennial meetings maintained that "the frequent sitting of Assemblies is a principal safeguard of their peoples Priviledges." But several governors found this schedule counterproductive. One cautioned that "the time of an Assemblies continuance being So Short causes Several well meaning Members to be Timorous fearing they should not be chosen again." Another offered a more encompassing reservation: "The greatest objection is that there must be a new election every two years which is too short a time to settle a Country which has been so long in confusion." In 1737 London officials disallowed the biennial election law because it encroached on the Crown's powers. By the middle of the eighteenth century the colony experienced gaps of five and six years between elections. The assembly unsuccessfully pressed for the adoption of a law mandating triennial assemblies (*APC*, vol. III 1910, 568; *CRNC* vol. II 1886, 213–16; vol. III 1886, 207, 453; vol. IV 1886, 177–78; vol. VII 1890, 903, 936, vol. IX 1890, 412, 457, 529, 530, 540, 713, 714, 744, 752, 855, 899).

In colonies where elections were called irregularly, the public and politicians pushed for them to be held more often. The Crown spurned the efforts of New Jersey's representatives to enact triennial elections in 1731 (*APC*, vol. III 1910, 333–34). But they persisted in arguing that frequent elections would allow them to better understand their voters' preferences. In 1757 members implored their governor, "It is now nigh three Years since the Present House of Assembly was Chosen A Variety of Unprecendented Troubles has introduced a Large & unprecedented Expence. The Part We have acted has been in Consequence of the Sentiments & Applications of our Constituents[.]Whether they are willing to Continue the Expence will be best Known by a new Choice, and it is but reasonable at a Time of Such Encreasing Danger, that their Sentiments shou'd be Known in the most effectual Manner." Lawmakers went on to say, "[A] Triennial Election has been Expected and wou'd be very acceptable to us" (*DRNJ*, vol. XVII, vol. V 1892, 94–95).

Agitation on this issue was greatest in New York. A 1734 pamphlet declared, "We want a Law *for more frequent elections, triennial at least*," because they were "one of the best Methods to preserve Liberty" (*Ne quid falsi* 1734, 1). A letter to the editor the same year argued that "the long sitting of this Assembly is dissagreable to the Generality of the People" (*NYWJ* 1734a). Such sentiments festered, and by 1737 another writer proclaimed, "The long Continuance of past Assemblies, we have look'd upon to be one of our great Grievances." Lawmakers were urged to "use their utmost Endeavours to procure an Act, to enable you to choose your Representatives, either once every Year, or at least once every three Years" (*NYWJ* 1737a). The assembly took up the cause, sending a message to the lieutenant governor suggesting that "for the Safety of the People," elections should be frequent because "No Government can be safe without proper Checks upon those entrusted with Power" (*To the Honourable GEORGE CLARK* 1737, 1). After a triennial bill passed, the lieutenant governor provided the Lords of Trade with a judicious assessment of it. He reported that the colony was unhappy with "the long continuance of their Assemblies," believing they had led to disabling "party heats animossities and divisions." He noted that members and their constituents "look upon frequent Assemblys, as the best and surest protection of their liberties and properties, [for] tis to the laws subsisting in the other Colonys . . . for frequent Elections, that they ascribe the happyness of those people, the increase of their Trade and the peopleing their Countrys." Officials in London rejected the measure because it impinged on the Crown's right "of calling and continuing the Assembly of this Colony." A few years later a new measure was passed holding that the colony's assemblies could "have continuance for Seven years & no longer," matching the interval under which Parliament operated (*APC*, vol. III 1910, 617; *CLNY*, vol. II 1894, 951–52; vol. III 1894, 295–96; *DRNY*, vol. VI 1855, 112, 130, 135–36).

Curiously, while London officials regularly asserted the Crown's prerogatives over the holding of elections in colonies where they were not dictated by charter provisions, New Hampshire escaped their attention. That colony passed a triennial act in 1728, and it was never overturned (*LNH*, vol. second, 1913 402–3). There is no explanation for the discrepancy in treatment (Labaree 1930, 212).

Frequent elections became widely peddled because it was reasoned that they enhanced representation. Samuel Adams explained to a friend that in Massachusetts "our House of Representatives are annually elective. Thus far they are accountable to the People, as they are lyable, for Misbehavior, to be discarded" (*Warren-Adams Letters* 1917, 196). It was also thought that they kept lawmakers honest. A Pennsylvania assembly speaker said, "It is our great Happiness, that, instead of triennial Assemblies, a Privilege which several other Colonies have long endeavoured to obtain, but in vain; Ours are *annual*, and for that Reason, as well as others, less liable to be practiced upon or corrupted either with Money or Presents" (*VPPP* 1738, 59). Other positive outcomes were ascribed to the colony's election schedule: "And as they are to be chosen annually, the common People whose Votes are so frequently necessary in Elections, are generally better treated by their Superiors on that Account. Besides as Assembly-men may so soon be chang'd and mix'd again among the People, it is scarce worth the Proprietaries while to bribe them with an Office, nor worth theirs to accept of it, to oppress their Constituents with unnecessary heavy Taxes, or other burthensome Laws, since a Post may fail while the Burthens continue, and they come in to bear their Share of them" (*NYM* 1756). Pennsylvania was the rare province where a governor (who also served Delaware) concurred with such sentiments, saying, "Amongst the many valueable Privileges derived to this Colony . . . that of annual Elections is none of the least, whereby frequent Opportunities are given to the Legislature of inspecting & regulating our Publick Affairs" (*MPCP*, vol. III 1840, 391).

Other unelected executives took a contrary view. A Maryland governor argued that frequent elections kept better qualified candidates from running, contending that "few Gent[s] will submit so frequently to the inconveniences that such as canvass for Seats in the House must necessarily subject themselves to . . . [and] there would be no want I apprehend of Gent[n] to appear as Candidates if the Drudgery of Electioneering was to return less frequently" (*AM*, vol. VI 1888, 68). A Massachusetts governor thought yearly elections brought assembly members too close to their voters, saying,

"Representatives, who by being annually elected are render'd extremely dependent upon the Humour of their Constituents." He recommended triennial elections because members "endeavor to distinguish themselves by their Opposition [to the executive], and moving some popular Points in order to recommend themselves to their Constituents, and secure their Elections for the ensuing Year, which . . . is wholly owing to the frequency of their Elections" (*Correspondence of William Shirley* 1912, 88–89, 473).

In spite of elite opposition, the idea that more frequent elections were preferable became conventional wisdom among the colonists. In 1774 a New Hampshire writer demanded "that we may have annual, instead of triennial Assemblies, which are certainly more beneficial to the People for many obvious Reasons" (*NHG* 1774a). The colonists wanted representatives to be tightly tied to their constituents.

Consulting Constituents

As discussed in chapter 2, in some colonies lawmakers were initially charged with pursuing the greater good while in others they were directed to follow their constituents' preferences. The second approach dominated in New England. Perhaps the most compelling evidence of deference to the constituency was the initial design of the Rhode Island legislative process. It mandated what we would characterize as a "bottom-up" system. Legislative proposals were to originate at the local level: "The Towne where it is propounded shall agitate and fully discuss the matter in their Towne Meeting and conclude by Vote." Any measure that passed would then be distributed to the other towns for their consideration. Legislation that passed in "the Major parte of the Colonie" would go into effect "till the next Generall Assembly . . . and there to be considered, whether any longer to stand yea or no." A few years later this process was simplified, with the assembly being allowed to enact laws, but towns were to be notified of all that passed and given an opportunity to veto them if "the major parte of the people in each towne" wished to do so (*RCRI*, vol. I 1856, 148–49, 229, 401, 429).

Plymouth instituted a "top-down" process that placed a high priority on consultation. The procedure "provided that the lawes they doe enact shalbee propounded one Court to bee considered of till the next and then to bee confeirmed if they shalbee approved of except the case require p[r]sent confeirmation" (*RCNP* 1861, 91). Under most circumstances representatives had to bring bills they were considering back to their constituents for review before they could be passed into law.

Although it was not mandated, a similar process emerged in Massachusetts. In 1641, the assembly required that an electoral reform bill "should bee p[ro]pounded to the ffreemen of the countrey, that, by their advise & consent, some order may bee established at the next Generall Court." Accordingly, "The deputies are to carry the coppey hearof to the sev^rall towns, & make returnes at the next Court, what the minds of the freemen are hearin, that the Court may [pro]cede accordingly." Another proposal was "to bee carryed by the deputies to the freemen of every towne, & their answere returned to the next session of this Court." The session's final record stated that "the bodye of la[w]es formerly sent forth amonge the freemen . . . was voted to stand in force" (*RGC*, vol. I 1853, 333–34, 340, 346, *WJ*, vol. II 1908, 49).

Outside New England similar procedures were never instituted. But assemblies did take breaks to allow members to confer with voters on important legislation. There was English precedent for doing so, with the medieval Parliament having allowed members to have "a conference with their countries" before voting on significant policies (*Cobbett's Parliamentary History*, vol. VIII 1811, 1300–1301). In the colonies such pauses served two purposes. First, they permitted lawmakers to ascertain constituent opinion. During a battle over a 1773 tobacco inspection bill, the Maryland assembly broke "to consult their Constituents on the present distressed Circumstances of the Province" (*AM*, vol. LXIV 1947, 38). The Pennsylvania assembly adjourned in 1709 so that "as many Members thereof as have Opportunity, may advise with as many of the principal Inhabitants of this Province . . . and acquaint the House with the Inclinations of the said Inhabitants at their next Meeting" (*VPPP*, vol. the Second 1753, 35). A few decades later they requested of the governor, "In the mean time, as it is a Matter of considerable Importance, [that] we may have the opportunity of knowing more generally the Minds of our Constituents; and it will give such of them, as shall think it fit, an Opportunity of applying to us" (*VPPP* 1741, 17). The New Jersey assembly petitioned its governor, "What further remains to be considered . . . we hope your Excellency will permit us to consult our Constituents upon" (*VPNJ* 1744, 10).

Executives played this angle too. When New York's governor prorogued the assembly in 1749, he scolded, "I therefore think that I cannot, at this Time, more effectually show the Concern I have for the People of this Province, than by giving you Time, cooly to consult with your Constituents, on the Consequences your Proceedings may have" (*JVNY* 1766, 258). But such gambits usually failed to work. In 1739 New York's lieutenant governor admitted that on a tax measure his assembly members "remained inflexible and seemed resolved to run all risques rather than give into it, they knew the Country were unanimous in the same sentiments and from thence they were assured of their elections." He "prorogued them for a few days hoping they might some how or other change their minds, but this had no effect" (*DRNY*, vol. VI 1855, 150).

Second, breaks gave lawmakers a chance to slow the policy-making process and, in turn, deploy their constituents as a shield against the governor and his policy preferences. During a debate over who should cover the costs incurred by a 1765 Boston riot, Massachusetts representatives informed their governor "that it was a business of too much importance to transact without consulting their constituents." The governor ridiculed the lawmakers' intentions, writing to London officials, "As the necessity of consulting their constituents had been made the pretense for postponing the business, the members in general found themselves obligated actually to consult their constituents in form." These consultations "produced a number of instructions against paying the money out of the treasury." The governor, who favored paying compensation, bemoaned the fact that many representatives "were obligated to come fettered with instructions to act against it." In the end, he conceded that "the bad weight of the instructions could not be got over," and his position lost (*A Collection* 1777, 114–15).

Even when special consultation mechanisms were not instituted, assembly members came to place great value on their constituents' views. Occasionally this surfaced in the context of specific issues. One Connecticut community's deputies "Proposed to the Town's serious consideration of that weighty affair respecting our Honored Governor which was debated in the General Court in October last and desired the town serious to consider it and send in their mind to the Court" (Steiner 1897, 143). Rhode Island's assembly once asked its towns to engage in "Searious consideration of Some way for the Raising of moneys for sending an Agent for England" and to communicate a response through their deputies by the beginning of the next session (*ERTPo* 1901, 203–4).

Assemblies began to tout their tight connections to the voters. During a spat with their upper house, members of the New Hampshire assembly bragged that they "find themselves under a necessity of Differing in opinion from the Hon[ble] Council, which they conceive arises from their more intimate knowledge of the minds of their constituents, their concerns & connections than the Council can be Reasonably supposed to have" (*DRNH*, vol. VII 1873, 135). During a similar confrontation the Maryland assembly reminded its council that "since you must own we more immediately represent the People than your Honble Board you must allow us to know more of their Oppressions and we offer the properest Remedies we can to relieve them" (*AM*, vol. XXIX 1909, 188–89). Broad assertions of harmony between representatives and the represented were common. In response to a gubernatorial address, the North Carolina assembly members declared, "Permit us, Sir, to say, that we shall always look upon the Interest of our Constituents as our most indispensible Duty" (*Journal of the House of Assembly* 1755, 7). Members of South Carolina's assembly avowed, "It must be the Conduct of the present Assembly that shall demonstrate to their Constituents how much they have their Welfare at Heart, and how sensible they are of the Obligations they are under, from the important Trust reposed in them" (*SCG* 1736d). Delaware's representatives asserted that they were "zealous for the Happiness of [their] Constituents" (*VPDE* 1770, 29).

There are indications that lawmakers understood that such sentiments helped them pander to their voters. A longtime Virginia burgess wrote in a letter to his brother just before an election—a missive we can assume was meant to be widely shared—"I shall always act to the utmost of my capacity, for the good of my electors, whose interest and my own, in great measure, are inseparable" (*Bland Papers* 1840, 4). A South Carolina representative assured his constituents, "And you may continue in the firmest perswasion that I shall have too scrupulous a Regard for your good Opinion, to forfeit it, either by a Supiness or Servility of Conduct." Another South Carolinian promised, "If my vote will not be of service to *preserve* your privileges, I will never *assume* to myself the right (that my conscience tells me you can never have given me) that of voting for the giving any one of them *up*" (*SCG* 1758, 1763b).

Sometimes the need to consider constituent interests was put bluntly by the voters themselves. A leading New York politician admitted that incumbents "Phillip Schyler & Hanse Hansen were Sett up by the people of Albany, so I sent for them, & told them if thy would do their best for the good of the Country We would not Sett up any body against them now but if thy would not do good now for the Country, We would Sett up others next time." A few years later that same activist wrote to another representative, "I readily gave you the Assistance of my family at the late Election that you Might be the better enabled to exert yourself in the defence of the [the member's electoral unit]" (*PSWJ*, vol. I 1921, 293–94; vol. VII 1931, 1028). During a New York assembly debate, a member offered his colleagues a colorful warning about the realities of their relationship with their constituents, saying, "The places of Honour they now enjoy are but like a fine laced Livery coat of which the vain Lacquey may be stript at the pleasure of his proud Master & may be kikt out of Doors naked" (*LPCC*, vol. VIII 1937, 239).

Given all this, it is no surprise that representatives took constituent consultations seriously and largely followed voters' preferences. When a New Hampshire governor tried to persuade his assembly to adopt measures to fund the government, he complained to his superiors in London that "they all went to advise with [their constituents], and then absolutely refused to pass the enclosed and other good Bills" (*CSP* 1898, 575–76). A desire to consult one's electors was pervasive. A Massachusetts speaker said, "The Representatives thought it proper to acquaint their principalls of these difficultys by printing the notes . . . that so they might for the future have directions in an affair of so great importance" (*CSP* 1936a, 211). And there is evidence that consultation swayed members. Pennsylvania's James Logan recorded that during an accidental meeting with two representatives, "they informed me that they found, since they had last parted, the masters [of servants] intirely disapprov'd of their measures [which would allow servants to leave for military service]." The lawmakers reversed their earlier positions because of what they had heard from their voters (*PA*, second series, vol. VII 1890, 238). A New York governor confessed that he could not get members to follow his lead on an important matter because following consultations "they were under a necessity of persisting, for fear of their constituents, who, as I have said . . . are engaged warmly in the dispute" (*DRNY*, vol. VIII 1857, 265).

Outside New England legislators felt cross-pressured, on the one hand being asked to work for the common good while on the other hand needing to be sensitive to their constituents' preferences. But pressure to give greater weight to the latter came to prevail. In the mid-1740s, a successful candidate for the North Carolina assembly asked his voters, "Are [members] not thus appointed, by each several County, in the Province, to give due Attendance at the General Assembly, there to appear, as Eyes for the Commonality, as Ears for the Commonality, and as Mouths for the Commonality" (Borden 1746, 2–3). If a lawmaker was not cognizant of this relationship, others would point it out. When a potential challenger canvassed for support, one of George Washington's friends advised him, "I'm persuaded that the cause of his opposition will by shewing your watchfull care for whatever might affect your Constituents, promote in place of diminishing your Interest with them" (*LW*, vol. III 1901, 202–3).

Instructions

Instructions were explicit directions given to representatives by constituents to guide their actions. They were first employed in England early in the seventeenth century, behavior consistent with the Tudor conception of members acting as their constituents' attorneys (Porritt 1903, 263–64). But over that century instructions evolved to be used to communicate voter concerns rather than to dictate member behavior (Kelly 1984, 170–71; Sutherland 1968, 1005–7). The notion that instructions should guide lawmakers came to be disparaged. The Scottish philosopher David Hume worried that requiring members to follow instructions "would introduce a total alteration in our government, and would soon reduce it to a pure republic" (Hume, vol. I 1760, 52). Speaker Onslow held, "Instructions . . . from particular constituents to their own Members, are or can be only of information, advice, and recommendation . . . but are not absolutely binding upon votes (*Precedents of Proceedings*, vol. II 1818, 76). Not everyone approved of this development. One reformer lamented, "In *England* our members do not hold themselves responsible to their *constituents*, but to the *house*." With envy he noted, "The People of *New England* keep up the right of instructing their members" (Burgh 1774, 204–5). There are indications that a spurt of instructions issued in Great Britain in the final decades of the eighteenth century was motivated by lessons drawn from the colonies (Veitch 1913, 43).

It was the original notion of instructions as directives that took root in the colonies. It first surfaced in a 1640 Plymouth Colony act requiring assembly members to call town meetings to inform voters about General Court actions and "to receive instruc[ti]ons for any other busines they would have donne" (Colegrove 1920, 414; *RCNP* 1861, 36). The earliest instructions issued appear in the 1647 Providence, Rhode Island, town records (*ERTP*, vol. XV 1899, 9–10).

The use of instructions varied across the colonies. As shown in table 7.1, they were common in New England; were infrequent in the mid-Atlantic colonies; and, outside of occasional appearances in Virginia, were almost never found in the southern colonies. The data aggregated in table 7.1 (and listed by case in appendix A) should be interpreted guardedly. Instructions were culled from town and county records and histories; newspapers; and, less commonly, legislative journals and colony records. There were instructions issued that were not recorded in any of those places. A New Hampshire resident, for example, wrote in his diary, "I was chose one of the Commitee to prepare instructions" for a newly elected member, but we do not have any evidence of them (*Diary of Matthew Patten* 1903, 338). We know some instructions were issued orally, as in New Haven, where "nothing was Concluded upon that account, onely some Verball instructions left with ye deputies to be proposed to ye sd Assembly" (*ATR* 1919, 143). It is also likely that instructions appeared in records that have been lost or exist in records that, in the case of town histories, historians chose not to mention. Consequently, these data are not exhaustive. But they give us a sense of where and when instructions were issued, the sorts of topics they covered, and how they were perceived by those who issued them and those who received them.

The first question to address is why instructions were more common in New England than elsewhere. Several reasons can be advanced. First, New England lawmakers were always closely tied to those they represented. If a member was to vote as if the full town were present, then instructions were an obvious mechanism to achieve that goal. Second, these colonies apportioned seats on the basis of towns, and those towns operated with town meetings, which were ideal vehicles for canvassing constituent opinion and conveying it to representatives. They created perfect conditions in which a delegate orientation could flourish (McCrone and Kuklinski 1979, 280).

That, then, raises the question of why instructions were issued more frequently in Massachusetts than elsewhere in New England. Part of the answer may be that there are more and better town records in Massachusetts and far more town histories were written, and thus more instructions were recorded. But it also seems clear that there was an expectation that they would be issued in Massachusetts. A 1722 pamphlet pleaded, "We hope that you will give Instructions to your Representatives" (*English Advice* 1722, 3). A broadside advised the colony's voters to "Choose therefore honest Freemen, who when they have been your Representatives, have followed your Instructions" (*Letter to the Freeholders and other Inhabitants* 1739, 11). On the other side of the relationship, Massachusetts lawmakers actively solicited constituent guidance. During a debate over a 1731 tax measure it was decided to ask towns to hold meetings so that "the several Members of this House may have their Advice and Instructions" (*Extract from the Journal* 1731, 14). Although according to Pole (1966, 72) instructions were rare in Massachusetts prior to 1740, they were actually a regular feature of the colony's political life from the mid-1600s on.

There also was a structural difference between Massachusetts and the other colonies that may help account for the discrepancy. Connecticut and Rhode Island voters did not need to give instructions as often because their

TABLE 7.1. Breadth and Focus of Instructions Issued to Assembly Representatives

Colony	Number of Electoral Units Issuing	Number of Instruction Sets Issued	1764 and Earlier		1765		1766 and Later	
			Instructions Focused on Local Issues	Instructions Focused on Colony Issues	Instructions Focused on Local Issues	Instructions Focused on Colony Issues	Instructions Focused on Local Issues	Instructions Focused on Colony Issues
New England								
Connecticut	13	42	27	1		4	2	8
Massachusetts	116	437ᵃ	101	64	1	56	6	195
New Hampshire	4	5	1			1		3
New Haven	0							
Plymouth	3	13	6	7				
Rhode Island	13	25	3	3		3	5	11
Mid-Atlantic								
Delaware	0							
Maryland	4	6	1	4		1		
New Jersey	6	7	2					5
New York	7	15	4			1		10
Pennsylvania	3	5	1	2				2
South Atlantic								
Georgia	0							
North Carolina	1	1						1
South Carolina	0							
Virginia	30	36	2	3			13	31
Total	200	592	148	84	1	66	13	266

Source: See appendix A.

ᵃThere were 14 instruction sets with unrecorded subjects in Massachusetts. They are included in the number reported here.

members served six-month terms. As lawmakers were elected just before each legislative session, voters in those colonies could already keep them on a short leash. Indeed, the fact that instructions were issued at all in Connecticut is noteworthy because Daniels's (1979, 130) authoritative study of that colony's towns suggests otherwise. Massachusetts representatives were elected for a full year, and voters may have felt a need to provide them with specific guidance on matters of importance.

What, then, of New Hampshire and New Haven, the outliers among the New England colonies? Their histories were different. As noted in chapter 2, unlike their neighbors, both were established with trustee orientations. New Haven's members "were invested wth full power to act in all things, according to the nature of that Trust." Toward the end of the colony's brief existence they were given the "power to consult of & determine all such matte[r]s as concerne ye publick welfare of this Colony" (*ATR* 1917, 212, 240, 484). Once it fell under Connecticut's control, and with it a different orientation, the town of New Haven issued instructions, as documented in appendix A. This indicates a turn toward a delegate model. New Hampshire was unusual in the region because its elections were held triennially. Thus, its voters could not easily anticipate what issues were to be tackled by lawmakers serving over a longer time period. Instructions were apt to be of less utility.

Structural reasons also account for the lack of instructions outside New England. Representation was mostly organized around counties rather than towns, and elections typically were irregular. Early in the histories of some parts of New Jersey and New York, town meetings were used to instruct representatives (*Huntington Town Records* 1888, 92, 131; *RTN*, 90, 94, 111–12). But such behavior fell out of fashion as apportionment schemes were fixed on counties. Without constituent meetings and a direct tie to the representative, issuing instructions was more difficult to do, especially when there was little tradition supporting it.

This is not to say that instructions were completely unknown. As shown in table 7.1, there is evidence that they were issued, albeit on rare occasions, in Maryland, New Jersey, New York, North Carolina, Pennsylvania, and Virginia. Some of the early use of instructions in those places was likely cultural. Newark, New Jersey, for example, was settled by people from Connecticut, and early in its history town meetings were held and instructions issued to its deputies (Atkinson 1878, 8; *RTN* 1864, 90, 94, 112). The later use of instructions may have been a learned fad. As more newspapers circulated in the mid-eighteenth century, voters in the mid-Atlantic and southern colonies were alerted to New Englanders' use of instructions.

During the Stamp Act crises the *South-Carolina Gazette* (1765c) reproduced the instructions issued by Providence and the *Georgia Gazette* (1765) published Boston's instructions. The *Maryland Gazette* (1765a, 1765b) reprinted instructions promulgated by Providence and Newport. The Providence instructions were published just four days before the freemen of Maryland's Anne Arundel County approved directives to their delegates, suggesting that the former may have influenced the latter's decision to pursue the locally uncommon form of guidance. The bulk of Virginia's use of instructions came in the last moments of the colonial era and was likely inspired by those issued in Massachusetts.

Where instructions were rare, there was resistance to their employment. In Philadelphia a detailed set of instructions claimed to be "generally signed by the Freemen" was issued in 1768 by an unofficial group. This effort was characterized as a push "by a *majority* of the most *sober, wealthy*, and *loyal freeholders* of the city and county . . . that, from this *time* forth *for-ever-more, town-meetings* (in imitation of . . . *Boston*) shall be held to instruct our *dignified servants*." But they generated a backlash, with one detractor asserting that public meetings to issue instructions "are *unknown* to the *constitution* of *Pennsylvania*" and that their supporters "will meet with great *opposition* from the lovers of 'TRANQUILITY;' for this *dignified servant*, the immediate object of your resentment, and more obnoxious to *us republicans*, than all the *impositions* laid on the colonies" (*PC* 1768a, 1768b). A 1766 effort by Orange County, North Carolina, voters to arrange "a Conference on Publick affairs with our representatives" was snubbed by their intended targets. Those who wanted to use the forum to issue instructions reported, "And whereas at the said meeting none of [their representatives] appeared tho' we think properly acquainted with our appointment and request yet as the thing is somewhat new in the County though practiced in older Governments they might not have duly considered the reasonableness of our request." Of course even the mere threat of instructions may have produced the desired effect on the behavior of lawmakers. In any event, in 1773 Orange County electors issued extensive instructions to their representatives (*CRNC*, vol. VII 1890, 251–52; vol. IX 1890, 669–706).

Interestingly, the rhetoric of instructions was employed in colonies where instructions were rarely dispensed. A 1683 letter to its proprietor by the Maryland assembly asserted that the freeholders "have given instruccon to their severall delegates to pray and make provision That they be restored to their former freedome of choosing & Electing the Accustomed number of Dep^ties for each County To be the Representative body of this province" (*AM*, vol. VII 1889, 407). Representatives wrote that when a popular law was rejected by South Carolina's governor in 1701, "several of the Members, jealous of their Privileges, & being so ordered by those that sent them, left the House" (Rivers 1856, 457). In Maryland in 1773 two delegates defended their policy positions by publishing a letter that ended with the declaration, "With pleasure, we comply with the instructions of our constituents." At the same time, when another set of delegates suggested that they, too, were acting on the directions of their constituents, more than 100 of them signed a letter to "publickly disclaim and disavow our having directly, or indirectly, given you any such instructions" (*MDG* 1773c, 1773e, 1773f).

Even in colonies where instructions were not issued often or at all, members still sought guidance from their voters on controversial issues. In 1763 a South Carolina representative published a letter to his constituents regarding a dispute with the governor over a contested election, saying, "[I]f I have the satisfaction of your approving my reasons, I may be rendered more firm in opposing such a step; or, that you would be obliging enough to point out my errors, that I may have the pleasure of uniting my own conviction with the desire I have of acting agreeable to your sentiments" (*SCG* 1763a). And voters expressed similar thoughts. A letter from "A Tradesman" in South Carolina issued a call to "directly *instruct* our Representatives" (*SCG* 1765a). In Maryland "An Elector" asked fellow voters "whether it would not be proper to instruct our representatives" to pursue a particular policy directive (*MDG* 1773i). And a New Yorker stated that "it behoves the Constituents of the several Members of our Assembly throughout the Province, and in particular of this City, to advise their Representatives" (*NYG* 1749). The idea that representatives could be guided to vote the way their constituents want them to was widely held.

The Practice of Instructions

Where they were issued routinely, instructions were written by an appointed committee—in one instance the elected member may have drawn them up (Bailey 1880, 290)—and then approved at a town meeting. They would usually be drafted the same day as the election, although sometimes several days or a week or two might be devoted to negotiating details. The committee drafting the instructions was composed of leading community figures, often including losing candidates (*Letters and Diary* 1903, 131, 147, 166; *RRCB* 1883, 156; *RTB* 1886, 257). In the final years before the Revolution, unofficial committees or caucuses took the lead in drafting instructions in colonies outside New England (Goss 1891, 640, 644; *Montresor Journals* 1882, 340; *NYM* 1765; *PC* 1768).

Town meetings took the content of their instructions seriously. When too few freeholders were left by the time instructions were drafted, the meeting would be adjourned to another date when, presumably, attendance would be higher (*RRCB* 1885a, 143). The care with which instructions were considered is suggested by Boston records, which show that the ten directives issued in 1721 were "Several times Read over and each of them voted to be Instructions to the Representatives at the Genneral Court at their approaching Sessions" (*RRCB* 1883, 155). On another occasion the town voted that the proposed instructions "be Considered of Paragraph by Paragraph" (*RRCB* 1885b, 60). When new information was obtained or circumstances changed, towns revised or reversed their instructions (Corey 1899, 724; Willard 1826, 49). Marblehead once told its representative that "if any important matter relating to this dispute [with Parliament] shall be agitated in the house which our instructions do not relate to, that you make the earliest communication of them to your constituents and receive their advice thereon" (Roads 1880, 102). Instructions were often thought important enough to be printed for the public, although sometimes those in attendance voted against doing so because of the cost (*RRCB* 1883, 158; 1886, 157, 230; 1887, 2; *RRSM* 1889, 67; Waters 1917, 198).

Once in a while towns decided against issuing instructions. In 1760 a Boston committee appointed to consider instructions regarding a provincial agent appointment concluded that "it would be premature for the Town" to do so. In 1771 a town meeting rejected a proposal to give instructions, and the following year the records show that the "Committee [could not] Agree upon any set of Instructions" regarding salaries for judges (*RRCB* 1886, 36; 1887, 54, 88). Many towns decided to forgo instructions (Chamberlain 1908, 377; Currier 1896, 515; Daniels 1892, 126; Felt 1834, 128, 129; *Records of the Town of Hanover* 1905, 9, 17; *RTP* 1903, 255; *Town of Weston* 1893, 119; Waters 1917, 152–53; *WTR* 1882, 142).

When instructions were issued they tended to follow a template. They usually began with an endorsement of the representative and a justification for their issuance. For instance, Boston's 1765 instructions began, "You being chose by the Freeholders and Inhabitants of the Town of Boston to Represent them in the General Assembly the ensuing Year, affords you the strongest Testimony of that Confidence which they place in your Integrity and Capacity—By this choice they have delegated to you the power of acting in the Publick Concerns in general as your own prudence shall direct you, always reserving to themselves the Constitutional Right of expressing their Mind and giving you such Instruction upon particular Matters, as they at any Time shall Judge proper" (*RRCB* 1886, 120).

The policy content contained in instructions changed over time, as table 7.1 documents. Prior to 1765, they were more likely to be focused on matters of local concern than on colonywide issues. In 1693, for example, the town of Mendon told its representative, "You shall take effectual care to represent to the General Court the great wrong we doe Conceive is done to us by the County Commissioners" (Metcalf 1880, 119). Instructions often centered on transportation matters such as roads, bridges and ferries. Town and county boundaries were also of interest. In 1693 Ipswich directed its member to ask the assembly to divide its county; in 1736 the town issued instructions to oppose any such effort (Felt 1834, 63).

A pronounced shift toward colonywide concerns occurred with the Stamp Act. Colonists thought it dramatically altered their relationship with Great Britain, and representatives were directed to vigorously oppose it. It was said that in Massachusetts "most every Member of the Honorable House of Representatives have received Instructions from their Constituents" on the matter (*Boston News-Letter* 1765). From that point on, the majority of instructions were focused on issues of colonywide interest. Local topics receded in importance.

Typically, instructions were specific and detailed. Occasionally they were directed toward small matters. A 1773 Boston town meeting appointed a committee that included John Adams to "make draught of a Bill for regulating Lamps &ᶜ. which draft they are desired to hand into the Representatives of this Town as soon as possible" (*RRCB* 1887, 136). Smaller towns would sometimes issue instructions simply to follow Boston's lead (Babson 1860, 359; Griffith 1913, 92; Morse 1856, 329; Nash 1885, 58). Sometimes a decision was made to leave matters to the representatives. At a 1733 Boston town meeting it was asked, "Whether or no the Representatives of this Town in the Affair of the Supply of the Treasury be left to use their best Judgment and Discression notwithstanding the Instructions given them in May Last." The question was sufficiently divisive that those at the meeting were first asked if they wanted to vote using a written ballot to decide it, which they declined to do. They then voted 153 "yeas" to 87 "Nays" to leave the issue to their members (*RRCB* 1885a, 52). Decisions to defer were not unusual (Benedict and Tracy 1878, 84; Chamberlain 1908, 418; Frothingham 1845, 274; Jameson 1886, 53; Metcalf 1880, 301; Trumbull 1902, 323).

Instructions were often adopted with little dissent. When Boston meeting participants were asked, "Whether You do Give it as an Instruction to the Representatives of this Town, That they shall, to the utmost of their power and Skill, Oppose all Motions or Endeavours, for the Settling A Salary on the Governour for the time being?" their answer was unequivocal: "It Pass'd in the Affirmative Unanimously" (*RRCB* 1885a, 86–87). But sometimes a community would be so divided that coming to an agreement proved difficult. When in 1772 a smallpox epidemic broke out in Rhode Island and the use of inoculations to combat it was debated, a Newport resident noted that during discussions about the directions to give to their representatives, "It is remarkable that the Town is so nearly divided that in five different Votes there has been a difference of but six or seven Votes." In the end, the town decided that the matter was "best to be left with the Deputies Discretion . . . [and] a vote thus put was carried by a small Majority" (*Literary Diary of Ezra Styles* 1901, 298). Proposed instructions were rarely rejected, as Boston voters did in 1745 with directives regarding a planned lottery (*RRCB* 1885b, 75).

Local officials sometimes made requests that were less formal than instructions (*ATR* 1919, 320; Frothingham 1845, 159). Boston's selectmen routinely asked the town's representatives to bring particular matters to the assembly's attention. In many instances members reported back on legislative responses (*RRSM*, 1884, 22–23, 108, 151, 207, 217; 1889, 222).

Representatives and Instructions

Representatives relied on instructions where they were regularly issued. When "some of Guilford" petitioned the Connecticut assembly to be allowed to pay for a minister, their deputies, "pleading the towne had not impowered them to act in this matter," persuaded their colleagues to delay the matter until the next session. In the interim, it was decided to "appoynt the deputies of Guilford to give theire towne notice thereof" so that the community could determine what it wanted the assembly to do (*PRCC* 1868, 144–45). Lawmakers often sought direction. The Ipswich records show that on one important matter "The deputies [were] desiring to know the town's mind" (Felt 1834, 123). Boston's records note, "The Representatives of the Town having expressed their Desire of being Instructed by their Constituents relative to the expediency of a Repeal or amendment of the Bankrupt Act," it was then decided "that the Selectmen be desired to warn a Meeting of the Inhabitants that the Sense of the Town may be taken respecting this Matter" (*RRCB* 1886, 174). Many representatives made such appeals (*RTP* 1903, 178; Tilden 1887, 153; Waters 1917, 191).

Voters expected their instructions to be followed. In a pamphlet published just before the 1751 Massachusetts elections, a writer asked his fellow electors "how can they be truly represented by one, who acts contrary to the Mind and Instructions of his Constituents?" (*An Address to the Freeholders* 1751, 4). Along the same lines a broadside asserted that "at the same Time it is most certainly the Duty of those who are appointed by the Body of People to act for them and plead their Cause, to adhere closely to the Interest of their Constituents" (*To The Printer* 1739). Such assumptions were expressed in New York as well: "That *Instructions* to our Representatives, are not only very proper and constitutional;—But that our Representatives are indispensably oblig'd to comply with them" (*NYJ* 1769c).

This was a widely held view and often stated boldly (*BEP* 1764b; Worthington 1827, 64). In one set of directives Rutland voters insisted that, "inasmuch as you accept the office of our Representative, we expect you will make our Instructions the rule of your conduct in said office" (Reed 1836, 60–61). Worcester advised its representative to "adhear to these our Instructions (and ye Spirit of them) as you Regard our Friendship & would avoid our Just Resentment" (*WTR* 1882, 140). Pittsfield was similarly frank, noting that "it is the expectation of this town, that you strictly adhere to these our instructions, as you value [your constituents'] regard or resentment" (Smith 1869, 185–86). Sometimes pressure was expressed more subtly. Embedded in a set of instructions given to Boston's representatives was the statement, "We have given you Gentlemen our full sentiments touching this important concern, because you ought not to be at any loss how to conduct yourself herein conformable to the Judgment of your Constituents" (*RRCB* 1887, 30).

Lawmakers were reluctant to act contrary to instructions. In 1768 a keen observer of the New York assembly wrote in his journal that on a controversial matter on which constituent guidance had been given, "It appeared to [representative] Colo. Schuyler that the House in the Main were desirous to take no Notice of the Matter of the Instructions but yet that if a Motion was made they would join in it for Fear of the Populace" (*Historical Memoirs* 1956, 48). A Connecticut representative recorded in his diary that on a bill "so many of ye freemen had instructed yr. Deputies to yt. Purpose &c finally twas thot best to take a vote whether it sho'd be admitted & a great Majority admitted it" (*Journal Kept by William Williams* 1975, 45). Voters expected compliance even when they knew they were asking their member to change his vote (Chase 1861, 368). Only rarely did members ignore instructions, typically only because circumstances had changed (Dorchester Antiquarian and Historical Society 1859, 435–36).

Acquiescence made political sense. One member issued his voters a formal reply, saying, "I also accept your Instructions with that pleasure that every Loyal Subject and good Citizen should feel" (Stearns 1906, 72). There were obvious reasons to adopt such a stance. In its 1772 instructions Rochester warned that "if our representative . . . has or shall hereafter basely Desert the Cause of Liberty for the Sake of being promoted to a post of Honour or profit or for any other Mean View to Self Intrust shall be looked upon as an Enemy to his Country & be treated with that Neglect & Contempt that he Justly Deserves." The member who got that message lost the following year (Leonard 1907, 127).

Incumbents who failed to hew to voters' preferences often paid a price. Take the case of Morris Morris, a Pennsylvania representative from Philadelphia County who failed to be reelected in 1728. When the assembly voted not to hold a special election to fill a seat vacated by another Philadelphia County delegation member, Morris refused to join with his city and county colleagues in breaking quorum to protest the decision (*JVPA* 1728, 12–16). Following his defeat, Morris issued a pamphlet defending his actions, writing, [A]ltho' it has been expected by some in *Philadelphia*, that have been very Active of late in Elections, that those they voted for, should take their Instructions from them, how to act in the Assembly: Yet . . . I never came under such Agreement with them, but thought that when I was chosen, I was at Liberty to follow the Dictates of my own Conscience and Understanding" (*Morris Morris' Reasons* 1728, 1).

A pamphlet credited to "Timothy Telltruth" provided a rejoinder to Morris. It chided him for going "exceedingly out of the Way, in saying thou had'st no Regard to the Inclination of those who elected thee; and has't by this shewn thy self to be a very unfit Person for thy Country's Service. Thou may'st believe what thou pleasest, in the Sincerity and Knowledge of those Men by whom thou ar't now directed; but I assure thee, for my own Part, I shall never think the *Legislative Authority* safe, in the Hands of such as do not act chiefly for the Interest of the People who entrusted them; And who does thou think can be better Judges of the People's Interest, than themselves?" (*To Morris Morris* 1728, 2). Voters knew their answer.

Morris was not the only lawmaker to fall victim to voters' unhappiness that their preferences had been disregarded. When Boston incumbent Thomas Hutchinson told his constituents that he would ignore their instructions to back paper money legislation, there was an uproar. "Mr Balston, a vociferous man, called out 'Choose another Represent^e, Mr Moderator;' but this was not seconded." Hutchinson kept his seat at that point. But after he "publickly and zealously opposed the measures in the house" he lost the following election (*Diary and Letters* 1884, 50).

Perhaps the best summation of the degree to which instructions came to be thought to tie their recipients to a specific course of action was offered by Daniel Dulany the Younger, a prominent figure in mid-eighteenth-century Maryland politics. Dulany held, "It would, now, be an unfashionable Doctrine, whatever the ancient Opinion might be, to affirm that the Constituent can bind his Representative by Instructions; but tho' the obligatory Force of these Instructions is not insisted upon, yet their persuasive Influence, in most Cases, may be; for a Representative, who should act against the explicit Recommendation of his Constituents, would most deservedly forfeit their Regard and all Pretension to their future Confidence" (Dulany 1765, 3). That disregarding instructions would put a representative in political peril was obvious to a politician even in Maryland, a colony where such directives were rarely issued.

The lesson was learned on a larger scale as well. Assemblies began to defend their decisions by citing voters' preferences. Responding to their governor, Massachusetts lawmakers asked, "Whether your Excellency can reasonably expect that the house of representatives should be active in bringing a grievous burthen upon their constituents? Such a conduct in us would be to oppose the sentiments of the people whom we represent, and the declared instruction of most of them" (*JHHR* 1765/1766, 135). Such attitudes were prevalent even where instructions were unusual. Maryland delegates rejected their governor's tax increase bid, pleading that their opposition should be "ascribed to the real Motive of our Conduct, a prudent Care of, and Regard to, the Interests of our Constituents" (*VPMD* 1753/1754, 73). Defending their opposition to the governor, Pennsylvania representatives coolly commented, "If our Constituents disapprove our Conduct, a few Days will give them an Opportunity of changing us by a new Election." They then took a swipe at the appointed executive, adding, "and could the Governor be as soon and as easily changed, *Pennsylvania* would, we apprehend, deserve much less the Character he gives it, of *an unfortunate Country*" (*VPPP* 1755, 176).

Thus a responsiveness theme gained currency. In a campaign letter, a Bostonian argued against an incumbent "who lately refused to follow the Instructions of his Constituents" in favor of a colleague "who honestly endeavoured to answer the Intentions of their Constituents" (*To the Freeholders of the Town of Boston* 1760, 1). More generally, a Philadelphian urged voters to make their preferences known to their assembly members: "If you don't ask, how shou'd they know what you want? If you do Petition, you'd at least discover your Friends from your Enemies, and see who are, and who are not, fit to be your Representatives, and the next Election prefer them accordingly" (*AWM* 1733b).

The notion even worked its way into popular culture. *The Candidates* was a play written in 1770 by Robert Munford, a sitting Virginia burgess. It is said to be America's first satirical comedy (Hubbell and Adair 1948). In it Mr. Wou'dbe, an incumbent seeking reelection, fears he will lose to his opponents: Sir John Toddy, the local lush; Mr. Strutabout, an arrogant planter; and Mr. Smallhopes, a gentleman more interested in horses than humans. The prospect that any of the challengers might win leads the county's other incumbent and most distinguished person, Mr. Worthy, to agree to seek reelection with Wou'dbe, and the two are swept back into office. Most tellingly, as Mr. Wou'dbe contemplates what he must do to win reelection, he objects, "Must I again be subject to the humours of a fickle croud? Must I again resign my reason, and be nought but what each voter pleases?" (Munford 1798).

Recall of Members

There is little evidence that colonial lawmakers could be recalled if voters were unhappy with their behavior in office. The 1629 Massachusetts charter hinted at such a power, establishing a process through which officers could "be removed from his or their severall offices before or places before the saide generall day of elec[ti]on" (*RGC*, vol. I 1853, 12). But it does not appear that it was applied to assembly members. A 1644 effort by Gloucester voters to replace their representative after a "falleinge out betweene ye church & him" was rejected by the assembly, which asserted a right to determine its membership (*RGC*, vol. III 1854, 3). There is a reference to two Connecticut deputies being "stripped of their offices by their fellow-townsmen" in the middle of a 1687 legislative session (Schenck 1889, 237–38). And on the Revolution's eve Weston, Massachusetts, voters removed their representative because he was a Tory (Lamson 1913, 73). Beyond these few examples, there are no indications of recalls. Once a representative was elected he could serve his full term, even if his constituents became disenchanted with him.

Burkean before Burke

Well before Edmund Burke articulated the difference between delegates and trustees colonial lawmakers struggled with the philosophical question of what the role of an elected representative should be, particularly in places where there was a predilection to favor the larger colony interests over those of one's constituents. In a 1736 speech accepting the Virginia speakership, John Randolph advised his colleagues, "We must consider ourselves chosen by all the People; sent hither to represent them." He then cautioned:

> And surely, a Desire of pleasing some, and the Fear of offending others; Views to little Advantages and Interests; adhering too fondly to ill-grounded Conceits; the Prejudices of Opinions too hastily taken up; and Affectation to Popularity; Private Animosities or Personal Resentments; which have often too much to do in Popular Assemblies, and sometimes put a Bias upon Mens Judgments, can upon no Occasion, turn us aside in the Prosecution of this important Duty, from what shall appear to be the true Interest of the People; Tho' it may be often impossible to conform to their Sentiments, since, when we come to consider and compare them, we shall find them so various and irreconcileable. (*JHB 1727– 1910*, 240)

Perhaps the most thoughtful contemplation of the Burkean dilemma was by Landon Carter, another Virginia burgess. Writing in his diary in the 1750s, Carter noted that he and his colleagues had confronted this quandary during a debate on a measure to regulate the growing of tobacco ("the Bill for a Stint Law"). The bill in question was prompted by "A Petition of sundry Inhabitants of the County of *Westmoreland*, praying that the Number of Tobacco Plants may be reduced, and that this House will ascertain how many Plants every Person employed in making Tobacco may be allowed to tend" (*JHB 1752– 1909*, 214). As Carter framed it, "[T]he question was Whether a Representative was obliged to follow the directions of his Constituents against his own Reason and Conscience or to be Governed by his Conscience."

In his view, on one side were "the favourers of Popularity," who held, "The Arguments for implicit obedience were that the first institution of a Representative was for the avoiding the Confusion of a Multitude in assembly. He, therefore, was to Collect the sentiments of his Constituents and whatever that Majority willed ought to be the rule of his Vote." On the other side—where Carter placed himself—were "The Admirers of Reason and Liberty of Conscience," who asserted that "where the matter related particularly to the interest of the Constituents alone, there implicit obedience ought to Govern, but, where it was to affect the whole Community, Reason and Good Conscience should direct." This was necessary, "for it must be absurd to Suppose one part of the Community could be apprized of the good of the whole without Consulting the whole. For that Part, therefore, to order an implicit vote must be absurd and the Representative acting accordingly could only augment the Absurdity because he must suppose his people so perverse as not to be moved by Reasons ever so good that might be advanced by other parts of the Community" (*DCLC* 1965, 116–17).

Representatives outside New England articulated similar predicaments. Those in North Carolina informed their governor of their desire to "persue such Measures as the real Interests of our Country and the Sentiments of Honour dictate, which must at the same time render us acceptable to our Constituents and gain us the Applause of our own Merits" (*CRNC*, vol. VII 1890, 64). In a message to its governor, the Maryland assembly observed that "as your Excellency has professed the Welfare of the Province to be the Object of your Attention and Care, and propos'd the Attainment of that End, for which we are instructed by our Constituents, and to which all our Views shall be unalterably directed" (*MDG* 1753a). Delaware lawmakers told their executive, "[W]e have nothing more at Heart, than the true Interest of the People we represent, which we apprehend to be so interwoven, and so much the same with the Governor's, that we do not think we can effectually serve the one, without a due regard to the other" (*AWM* 1720). The response of the South Carolina assembly to a gubernatorial request for military funding noted, "We feel ourselves *bound* by the strongest Obligations, *to strengthen Your Hands* for Action, to *co-operate* with You in *every* salutary Measure, and, as far as the Circumstances of our Constituents will reasonably admit" (*SCG* 1757). When Georgia's governor negotiated several Indian treaties, the representatives' response was to caution him that they would have to determine "how far they can [go in support of them] consistent with the Duty they owe to their Constituents." The governor scoffed that he did "not conceive it Possible that any Gentleman can 'consistent with his Duty to his Constituents' have the least objection" (*CRSG*, vol. XV 1907, 60, 63). But, if their constituents had concerns, so did their representatives.

Some opinion leaders continued to promote a trustee orientation. Among the virtues of the good lawmaker on a South Carolina list was that he "never gives any vote towards the passing of any law, or resolution, which he does not in his conscience believe to be for the benefit of his country" (*SCG* 1765b). A New Hampshirite urged electors to "keep in view the *good of the whole community*; Remember you are all members of one family, or (to bring it closer) of one body" (*NHG* 1762). Even in Massachusetts a published letter asserted that "those Gentlemen who are impower'd to consult and act for the Good of their Country, and do, or ought to make it their principal, if not only Business, are more capable of judging what Steps are proper to attain that End, than such as from a Design of making themselves popular" (*A Letter from a Gentleman to his Friend* 1754, 1). Another advocated for those "who will act, not like Slaves, as they are bid, but as Representatives, who make the Good of the People the Object of their Views" (*A Letter to the Freeholders and other Inhabitants* 1749, 8). So Burgess Carter was not alone in his beliefs.

But even those who wanted to promote a trustee approach found themselves calling for delegate behavior. In identifying the characteristics of an ideal representative, a Portsmouth, New Hampshire, writer observed that a member should "Secondly, . . . promote by every Means, the real Interest of the Province; And Thirdly . . . encrease the Trade of this Town in particular, and procure its greatest Prosperity" (*NHG* 1774b). Among the questions posed to New York City and County assembly candidates was "Will you do the best you can for the Benefit of the Colony in general, and of this City in particular, and promote the Interest, Trade and Commerce thereof?" (*Many of the Electors* 1739). Lawmakers found themselves trapped in this representational dilemma. Writing about a budget bill, a New Jersey representative observed, "[W]e are very oddly situated; while we are blamed by our Constituents for our Compliance in going *so far*, we are censured on the other Hand, by the Governor for not having proceeded *farther*" (*A Letter to B. G.* 1739).

There was sporadic opposition to the idea that representatives were to be held accountable for representing their constituents' views, again even in Massachusetts. During a heated Salem town meeting, it was reported that one "honorable Gentleman . . . insisted that we had no right to approve or disapprove of our Representatives; for said he, if they are to be call'd to an account for any part of their conduct in the G[eneral] Ass[embl]y it does intirely destroy the freedom of that House." But the retort to that claim was devastating: "[I]f our Representatives (creatures of our own making) were to pass a vote that all their constituents should be slaves to them, we had no right to disapprove of it" (*BEP* 1768a). The colony's representational priorities were captured in the town of Shirley's instructions: "Finally, your constituents expect, that on all occasions, you will view their interest as closely connected with your own, and at all times endeavor to promote it, and also the interest of the Province generally" (Chandler 1883, 115).

By the mid-eighteenth century, Burgess Carter and others who shared his trustee preference were in the minority. As a New Yorker summed up the prevailing view, "The Matter is now reduced to this single Question, Whether the Representative shall prefer his own Judgement to that of all (or what in political Estimation ever amounts to the same Thing, the Majority of) his Constituents? And most singularly arrogant and self-confident indeed must we suppose that Man to be, who conceives himself wiser than the whole Body of the People." He concluded with an extreme take on the power of constituent directions: "By their particular subsequent Instructions, [the voters] have now so far revoked . . . their general original Delegation . . . and consequently the Representative is, from that Moment . . . no more than the Mouth, Vehicle, or Conduit by which they chuse to deliver *their* and not *his* Sense, to the House" (*NYG* 1770c). The Maryland assembly acknowledged this reality, asserting in 1762, "It is a Maxim in Politics, almost universally adopted, that the Representative is justified by the Instructions of his Constituent, in acting even against his own Judgment" (*VPMD* 1762, 118).

Information about Assembly Actions

Accountability hinges on the represented knowing the actions of the representative. This need was facilitated early on with assemblies requiring that the public be notified of the laws they passed. Initially this was done by having them read before a public meeting. In 1640 Plymouth adopted an act requiring town meetings to be held during which representatives were "to acquaint them with what is [pro]pounded or enacted at the [General] Court" (*RCNP* 1861, 36). A 1650 Rhode Island law mandated that any laws passed "shall be returned [to the towns] within six dayes after the breaking up or adjournment of that Assemblie; and then within three dayes after, the chiefe officer of the Towne shall call the Towne to the hearing of the lawes so made" (*RCRI*, vol. I 1856, 229). The Providence records show numerous instances in which "This day was read the Gennerall Assemblys actes" (*ERTP*, vol. III 1893, 151, 157, 160, 201). That same year Massachusetts approved a measure requiring that within two months after the end of each session a copy of laws passed was to be sent to every community "to be audibly read in a publicke towne meetinge" (*RGC*, vol. III 1854, 204). Connecticut had a similar requirement; the 1687 New Haven meeting records show, "The Orders of the Generall Court of the 30th of March last were red." Given that there were two legislative sessions each year, such readings were frequent (*ATR* 1962, 35, 50, 52, 65, 69, 70, 118, 204, 275). In New

York around 1700 the notification process took a shortcut. According to the governor, "The publication of an Act of New York is after this manner. At the close of the Session of General Assembly, a Bell is rung to give notice that the Governor, Councill and Assembly do resort to the publick Town Hall of the City, where all Acts of Assembly that pass'd that Session are publickly read in open Court, and this is understood to be the publication to all the inhabitants of the Province" (*CSP* 1910b, 9–10). This procedure was not unusual. After passing a 1709 bill "regulating the Rates of Money" the Pennsylvania assembly ordered two of its members to "go to the Mayor of the City of *Philadelphia*, and acquaint him, that the Assembly desires him to order the Bell to be rung forthwith; and that himself, with the Aldermen, and Constables, do attend forthwith in the Market-place at the Publication of a Law forthwith to be published there" (*VPPP*, vol. the Second 1753, 27–28).

Members took the need to keep their constituents informed seriously, even at their own political peril. After Connecticut adopted a law governing religion, a Norwich minister reported to his congregation the first part of the legislation, giving preference to his denomination, but he failed to disclose the second part, which protected the rights of religious dissenters. The town's deputies then "rose in their seats and laid the whole act before the people." The minister had enough political pull to persuade the assembly to censure them for their actions (Caulkins 1874, 285).

The public pressed assemblies to open their proceedings. In the 1760s a New York pamphlet encouraged voters to make assembly candidates promise "that galleries, or seats, shall be erected in the assembly room, in order that the inhabitants who have leisure and inclination, may have free access, and attend to hear the debates of the house." Doing so would ensure that "the public may, from time to time, be well informed what bills are preparing, or before the house" so "that if any of them should be thought to be improper, oppressive, or inconvenient . . . they may have an opportunity to petition and remonstrate against them, before they are passed into laws" (*A Few Observations* 1768, 5). It was also said that open doors would afford an opportunity of "seeing with our own eyes, and hearing with our own ears, in what manner those act, whom we have entrusted with our most valuable interests" (*An Address to the Freeholders of Dutchess County* 1769).

Most efforts to pry open assemblies succeeded. Prior to the 1766 Massachusetts assembly session, Cambridge's representative was instructed to "endeavor to get a vote passed in the House, that a gallery be provided where as many persons as conveniently can, may be admitted to hear their debates." Again the rationale was to "give an opportunity to any person who desires it of seeing that nothing is passed by that assembly that is not of real benefit, and of advantage to their constituents" (Paige 1877, 140). The effort succeeded, and it was ordered that "the Debates of this House be open; and that a Gallery be erected on the Westerly Side of this Room for the Accommodation of such Persons as shall be inclined to attend the same." It was also agreed that every person attending had to be introduced by a member (*JHHR* 1766, 35, 74). New Jersey's assembly opened its doors in 1769, overturning "a Custom of long standing" in response to "the Sentiments of the People of this Province" (*VPNJ* 1769, 5–6).

Some assemblies resisted having the public watch them in action. In 1764 a group of Philadelphians petitioned the Pennsylvania assembly to open its deliberations. A committee that included Benjamin Franklin was appointed to "examine the Journals of the House of Commons, and report the Usage and Practice thereof . . . and to enquire likewise what the Practice is in the other *American* colonies." It subsequently reported, "With Regard to the Practice in the Colonies, we have not been able to obtain perfect information concerning all of them; but we understand, that in the Provinces of *Maryland* and *Virginia* the Assembly Doors are left open . . . but that in the neighboring Provinces of *New-Jersey* and *New-York* the Practice is, as hitherto it has been in this Province, to keep the Doors shut" (*VPPP* 1764, 54, 57–58). The assembly opted to keep its doors closed, and it eventually proved to be the lone holdout; in 1773 a visitor observed, "Their debates are not public, which is said now to be the case of only this house of commons throughout the continent" (Quincy 1915–16, 476).

There were two reservations about open doors. The first involved decorum. When in 1768 the New York assembly contemplated opening its sessions in response to the public pressure noted above, the proposal it considered came with stringent conditions. As in Massachusetts, a member would have to introduce each visitor, but in New York it was also proposed that each lawmaker could introduce no more than one person at a time. Those in attendance were to "behave orderly and quietly, and that none presume to speak or whisper." Ominously, "If any member shall desire the house to be cleared, the house be cleared immediately." Even this measure proved too generous, and it lost by a single vote (*JVNY* 1769a, 12). A majority only agreed to open the doors the next year after it became obvious that it was "one of the most popular Motions that could be made" (*An Address to the Freeholders of Dutchess County* 1769; *Historical Memoirs* 1956, 60–61; *JVNY* 1770, 25). The second reservation was a fear that members would play to their audience. During the growing tension between Great Britain and the colonies, Massachusetts governor Thomas Hutchinson alluded to this when he wrote to a London official that, with regard to the colonists' beliefs about their economic leverage on the parent country, "In this Colony all this is openly asserted in the House of Representatives, for the sake of the people in the Gallery" (*Diary and Letters* 1884, 116).

Assemblies started printing their journals, as well as compilations of the laws they passed, which greatly increased the information available to voters (Olson 1992, 562–64; Surrency 1965). New York was the first to publish its journal. In early 1695 the governor denied the assembly's initial request to have its journal printed, noting that "it never was asked before." After that assembly was dissolved, the next one again asked the governor "to order the Printer to print the daily Votes of this House at the Publick Charge," which this time he was "very willing" to do. Only enough copies were printed for assembly and council members and the governor to get one (Hasse 1903; *Journal of the House of Representatives for his Majestie's Province of New-York* 1695, 5).

Most of the other colonies followed suit but only slowly and for different reasons. In 1707 New Jersey's assembly passed a motion that "the proceedings of this house shall be printed, if a Printer can be got to do it." It was not until 1711 that William Bradford, who published New York's journal, agreed to print New Jersey's too (*Journal and Votes of the House of Representatives* 1872, 103; *JVNJ* 1711, 35). In 1715 Massachusetts representatives moved to "Unanimously Agree and Conclude to Print their Journal of the present Sessions." They did so to defend themselves against their governor, who had publicly justified his decision to prorogue the body by claiming that "the Houses were distempered" and "they had done little or nothing for the good of the Province." The assembly designated "the Representatives of Boston to take care that the same might be Seasonably done; and the Clerk to prepare a Copy accordingly" (*Journals of the House of Representatives of Massachusetts* 1919, 44–45).

In 1711 the Pennsylvania assembly voted down a motion "that any Person in this Province may have Transcripts or Copies of all or any the Votes or Resolves of this House . . . they paying for the same" (*VPPP*, vol. the Second 1753, 78). A little over a decade later there was a change of heart. The printer Andrew Bradford—son of the New York and New Jersey printer—was ordered to appear before the House, where he "was demanded by the Speaker for what Consideration he would print the Votes of this Assembly." Bradford agreed to charge 25 shillings per sheet and deliver 50 copies (*PA*, eighth series, vol. II 1931, 1394). Within two weeks Bradford advertised for sale "*A Journal of the Votes and Proceedings of the*

Honorable House of Representatives of the Province of Pennsylvania, who are now sitting" (*AWM* 1722).

The idea of publishing Maryland's journal was first broached in 1706, but nothing developed from the suggestion. Serious consideration only occurred more than 15 years later and only after a battle between the two legislative houses. Although there is a passing reference in the records to "Several printed Copys of the Address and the Resolves of the Lower house in October Assembly 1722 being produced," there is no evidence today of such a publication. Instead, it appears that the idea was first pursued with a 1725 printing—in Philadelphia by Andrew Bradford—of an unofficial version of the proceedings that was "Collected from the Journals, and Published by Order of the Lower-House." In "An Epistolar Preface to the *Maryland* Readers" the case was made for its printing, most likely by Thomas Bordley, a leading delegate: "The publick Parliamentary Proceedings of *Maryland* have commonly been so little known to the Inhabitants of that Province, that they have scarce had any Opportunity of Judging whether they were Served or Prejudiced by their Representatives." With the arrival in the colony of printer William Parks the following year, the assembly proposed that he publish the session laws, the "Journalls Votes Speeches and other debates and Resolves that may happen in each Session," and a compendium of all of the colony's laws. The council agreed to the printing of the laws but added, "[W]e think the printing [of] the Journalls and other proceedings an unnecessary Charge to the publick, and therefore cannot agree to it." Despite the council's objections, the assembly forged ahead: "Notwithstanding . . . It is Resolved that such of the debates and proceedings of the last Session of Assembly as relate to the Government or Judicature of this Province or other materiall publick Affairs thereof be printed at the Charge of the Publick." A printed journal soon appeared (*AM*, vol. XXVI 1906, 576–77; vol. XXXV 1915, 102, 149, 451–52, 455, 475–76, 484–85; *The Charter of Maryland* 1725, iii; *Votes and Resolves* 1728; Wroth 1922, 56–57).

Parks's arrival in Annapolis appears to have motivated the Virginia assembly to pursue him to print its journal. The notion was first discussed in 1727, but it took until 1732 for the assembly to give him leave "to print the Votes and Proceedings of this House." Parks then submitted a petition, "praying that the House will establish such a Salary for Printing the Laws, Proclamations, and Journals of Assembly, for Public Use," at a level that would allow him to stay in business. The burgesses agreed to pay Parks 120 pounds a year to print various government documents, among them "the

Journal of this House, every Session; and to deliver a Copy of each of them, to every Member" (*JHB* 1727– 1910, 25, 121, 138, 141).

An assembly's desire for a published journal often had to wait for a printer to set up shop in the colony. After years of discussion, in 1747 North Carolina finally hired a printer, James Davis, who had been trained by William Parks. In 1749 Davis printed the assembly's journal, the first book produced in the colony (*CRNC*, vol. IV 1886, 976–78, 995; *Journal of the House of Burgesses* 1749; Thornton 1944). In some colonies a printer was not always available or willing. In 1745 the New Hampshire assembly appointed a committee to "print and publish the Whole or any Part of the Journals of this House," and a volume was produced for that session. But four years later the assembly was forced to allow that "any Person or persons Disposed to print the Journals of ye General Assemblys or any parts of them have Liberty so to Do." Apparently, there were no takers; another printed journal did not appear for several years (*Journal of the General Assembly* 1762; *Journal of the House of Representatives of the Province of New-Hampshire* 1745, 38; *LNH*, vol. three 1915, 42). Finally, not every assembly had full journals printed. Starting in 1747, the Rhode Island assembly opted to have a "Printer residing or dwelling in *Newport*, upon the best Terms he can" publish the acts and resolves passed each session. These volumes constituted a sketch of the assembly's decisions (*At the General Assembly* 1747, 3).

Printed journals were distributed to members and government officials. They were also offered for purchase by the public. Rhode Island made such a commercial arrangement explicit, allowing that the printer "shall have Liberty to make as many more Copies as he or she shall think fit, and dispose of the same for his or her private Profit or Advantage" (*At the General Assembly* 1747, 3). Advertisements for printed journals appeared in a number of colonies, most simply announcing their availability (*NYWJ* 1737b; *North-Carolina Magazine* 1764; *PAG* 1748). An advertisement for volumes "Just published, and sold by B. Franklin" listed the 1746 Pennsylvania journal below "POOR RICHARD's ALMANACK" and "The POCKET ALMANACK" (*PAG* 1746). A Maryland notice offered options, saying that for those wishing information about lawmakers' activities, "The Votes and Proceedings of the present Assembly are now in the Press, and designed to be publish'd twice a Week, if possible, during the Session." Those who did not want them "as they are publish'd" could get them "all together at the End of the Session" (*MDG* 1745).

Government officials and some in the general public placed great value on printed journals. A letter written by one prominent New Yorker to

another began with the admission, "I was very much surprised on perus-
ing the Votes of Assembly which the printer lately sent me" (*LPCC*, vol.
VIII 1937, 310). A Philadelphia broadside assessing "the present State of
Affairs of this Province" footnoted the assembly journal (*To the FREEMEN
of PENNSYLVANIA* 1755, 1). When journals failed to appear in a timely
manner their absence was met with suspicion. In 1733 Andrew Bradford
had to publish an announcement, stating, "Whereas great Complaint is
made among the people in *New-Jersey*, for want of the Acts of Assembly
which were passed at *Burlington* the last sitting of the Assembly, and many
blame *Andrew Bradford*, supposing it his neglect in their not being Printed."
It went on to claim that "the said Acts are not come to the Hands" of either
Bradford or his father, William Bradford in New York, and "therefore their
not being Printed cannot be our Neglect" (*AWM* 1733a). North Carolina's
printer was fined by the assembly for not expeditiously sending copies of
the journals to members and county officials. A decade later the colony's
governor castigated him for "His negligence in not Printing the . . . Journals . . . nor dispersing them in proper numbers for the use of the Province"
(*CRNC*, vol. IV 1886, 1340–41, 1344–45; vol. VI 1888, 1200).

Because it met behind closed doors, Pennsylvania's assembly was vulnerable to conspiracy theories about its actions. When in the wake of a
budget controversy publication of its journal was delayed, charges of a
cover-up flew. One pamphlet asked, "If all was fair, why were not their
Minutes published immediately after their last Adjournment? Why is the
Publication artfully deferr'd till they have taken their Measures for getting
themselves re-elected?" (*To the Free-Holders* 1742, 2). The journal's printer,
Benjamin Franklin, took out a newspaper advertisement defending both
himself and the institution: "I think I owe this Justice to that Honourable
House, as to declare, that I have had the Minutes in my Hands for Publi-
cation ever since the Adjournment; that I receiv'd no Directions from the
House to delay it, nor the least Intimation from any Member, that such
Delay would be agreeable; that no Person has been refus'd a Sight of them,
and that the sole Cause of the Delay was my Desire of first finishing the
Body of Laws, the Minutes being very little enquired after" (*PAG* 1742).
His response failed to satisfy skeptics (*The Letter to the Free-Holders* 1743;
"Two Addresses of Conrad Weiser" 1899, 516).

Printed legislative journals became so conventional that by 1768 Connecticut's failure to produce them garnered public condemnation. A letter
titled "To the Freemen of the Colony of Connecticut" encouraged voters
"at your next meetings for election of representatives, to give them special
instructions that they publish a *journal* of their proceedings of the General

Assembly, and that the same be lodged in the town clerk's office, in each town in this colony, for the inspection of the freemen." The author noted that "publishing a Journal of the proceedings of the assemblies, is practised by every province on the continent, where galleries are not provided for persons to be present, and hear the debates and proceedings of their assemblies." He promoted the value of publishing roll call votes, pointing to "A journal of the house of representatives of the province of N. York, I have now lying before me, which contains the names of the voters on each side [of] the question, in all resolves which their constituents would be desirous to know." His conclusion harkened back to early arguments in favor of publishing journals: "Whereas being an elective government, we stand in more need of such knowledge, and information" (*CC* 1768).

Another information source was newspapers. Over the colonial era they became widespread, providing people with news about the actions of their government (Leder 1966; Merritt 1963). Stories largely focused on election results, constituent instructions, disputes between the governor and assembly, and laws passed. Given the colonies' high literacy rates (Grubb 1990), representatives became aware that many of their legislative actions might become public.

Papers reported roll call votes as early as the 1720s (*New-England Courant* 1726; *NEWJ* 1729b). A few journals included them starting in the 1730s. Though rare, they helped voters judge their members' decisions; New York voters requested that their lawmakers have them printed, so "we may see who have best discharged their Duty" (*Many of the Electors* 1739). When Pennsylvania roll calls were published, a writer noted, "Therein we find some Grievances happily redressed, which entitles those distinguished Gentlemen to the highest Esteem" (*PAG* 1773). Where votes were not published, interested observers sometimes attempted to reconstruct them so as to know who to reward or punish at the polls (*A Letter to the Freeholders and Qualified Voters* 1749). A counterargument surfaced claiming that published roll calls would discourage members from acting as trustees in favor of delegate behavior. One facetious analysis contended that in the absence of published votes members "may assume to themselves a Power of making use of their own Reason . . . and what is as bad, or worse, of acting upon Principles of Honour and Conscience, and hope to escape without giving an Account to the People of such their pernicious Conduct." Printing them would force members to "give up their own Reason and Conscience to Ours, or if they will be obstinate, and refuse to do so just a thing, they will be pointed out to Us in Print, and then the Lord have Mercy upon them, for We shall not" (*An Unanswerable Answer* 1739, 3).

Assemblies began to order that important legislation be published in the newspapers. In 1760 the South Carolina assembly required the texts of a smallpox bill and a grain exportation measure to be printed (*SCG* 1760a, 1760b). Several years later the Pennsylvania assembly ordered that "*An Act to prohibit the Selling of Guns, Gunpowder, or other Warlike Stores, to the Indians* ... be immediately printed in the public News-Papers, both *English* and *Dutch*" (*VPPP* 1764, 9). Controversial measures that were being considered or had failed to pass were also published. During a Virginia debate over a tobacco bill the measure "was ordered to be printed for the Perusal and Consideration of the Inhabitants" (*DCLC* 1965, 117). The Maryland assembly asked "Mr. Jonas Green ... [to] print the said Bills in one or more of his Weekly News-Papers." He did so, noting that the first measure "did not pass into a Law" and the second "was put off for the Consideration of the next Session of Assembly." A few years later a bitter dispute between the assembly and council prompted an order to have printed not only the bill in question but also "the Amendments proposed by the Lower House ... and the Messages that have passed [between the houses]." Another dispute between the houses led to the publication of their exchanges over a controversial bill to regulate attorney fees (*MDG* 1750c, 1750d, 1750e, 1758a, 1770; *VPMD* 1750, 43–44). By printing the texts of bills, amendments, and messages, the papers gave voters an opportunity to make their own assessments. Such efforts had the desired effect. After the New York assembly postponed consideration of a bill to divide Albany County, it voted that a copy of it should be "inserted in, or annexed to the public News-Papers." Subsequently, a prominent colonist wrote to a leading politician, "I have never heard any thing of this till the publication in the prints by order of the house which made it known to all the Inhabitants" (*JVNY* 1769b, 59; *PSWJ*, vol. VII 1931, 20).

Assemblies were not equally energetic about getting information out to the public. When consideration of an acrimonious Rhode Island measure was put off until the following session, it was resolved that "any of the Members of the General Assembly, or any other Persons, may take out from the Clerk of this House, Copies of this Bill, and if they think proper, to put the same in the public prints, at their own Expence." Later that year "A Countryman" prevailed on the *Providence Gazette* to print a divisive money act, arguing that "the Proceedings of the Legislature of this Colony is what every Inhabitant had a Right to know" (*PRG* 1763a, 1763b). Not every attempt to make more information public succeeded. Pennsylvania lawmakers rejected a 1740s effort by Bucks County voters to have roll call votes printed in the assembly journal so that "their Constituents may be acquainted with their Conduct" (*VPPP* 1745, 26).

Moreover, at times government officials actively sought to stifle public discourse. During a 1747 quarrel with the New York assembly over a remonstrance it had written, the governor issued an order to the colony printer expressly forbidding him to "re-print or otherwise publish the said Paper." In response lawmakers voted unanimously, "That it is the undoubted Right of the People of this Colony, to know the Proceedings of their Representatives in General Assembly; and any Attempt to obstruct or prevent their Proceedings being printed and published, is a Violation of the Rights and Liberties of the People of this Colony." A few weeks later the assembly escalated the dispute by ordering the printer "to reprint our humble Remonstrance to his Excellency, and that he deliver ten Copies to each Member of the House; that our Constituents may know, that it is our firm Resolution to preserve the *Liberty of the Press*, and to communicate our Proceedings to them, that they may judge of our Conduct" (*NYG* 1747a, 1747b, 1747c, 1747d, 1747e). Yet several years later the assembly reprimanded a New York newspaper publisher for the unauthorized printing of a controversial section of the Crown's instructions to the new governor (Ford 1902, 5–7; *JVNY*, vol. II 1766, 358–59; *NYM* 1753). In this instance there is a hint that the punishment was "a sham" and that the publisher only got in trouble because he had reproduced the instruction's full language rather than just its substance as the assembly had wished (Smith 1829, 165). More troubling, when a Virginia burgess tried to present the assembly's side in a controversial policy dispute with the governor, he was unable to persuade local printers to publish his letter. Instead he had to turn to the *Maryland Gazette* (1754a), where his dispatch began by protesting, "When you are informed that the Press in this Colony, either through particular Inclination, or some other cogent Bias . . . is, in many Instances, shut against us; you will, I am persuaded, readily excuse my Desire of transmitting, by your Paper, a Matter to the Consideration of every impartial Reader."

By the mid-eighteenth century the essential role printing and the press played in representative government was acknowledged. A pamphlet writer observed, "The *Liberty of the Press* was never struck at by the People: They always esteem it one of their greatest Blessings, as being the *Means* of conveying public Intelligence, so that *they* may come to the Knowledge of what *their Delegates* are about" (Agrippa 1751, 4). Thus over time more demands were made on the legislature, and lawmakers knew that the public would be informed about their responses to those demands. The change in the way lawmakers responded is the focus of chapter 8.

EIGHT

Representation in the Colonial Legislative Process

Over time colonial lawmakers came to defer to the wishes of their constituents. Much of the evidence supporting this assertion is anecdotal. Most voting in the assemblies was conducted by means of some form of tellers. Recorded votes were rare, except in the later years in three assemblies, and most legislative journals reveal much about procedure but little about debates. To understand how lawmakers reached decisions we often have to rely on personal journals, such as the one kept by William Williams, a Connecticut representative. According to his account, a 1757 New Haven justice of the peace nomination was initially blocked because some members complained about the candidate "having been very frequently Drunk." But the nomination was confirmed after other "Members were examined respecg. sd. Rept. & declared it to be Common in N[ew] H[aven] & ye Neighboring Towns" (*Journal Kept by William Williams* 1975, 25). In this instance, deference was accorded to community standards and voter preferences over the representatives' personal judgments regarding the larger colony's good.

The idea that lawmakers were to be responsive to their constituents took hold early in New England, for all the reasons that have been discussed. Thus we find in Winthrop's journal an entry noting that in one 1643 controversy "the deputies stood only upon this, that their towns were not satisfied in the cause (which by the way shows plainly the democratical spirit which acts our deputies)" (*WJ*, vol. II 1908, 118). Concerns that lawmakers outside New England were beginning to put the voters' interest ahead of the larger good surfaced by the early eighteenth century. It was a pet peeve of Virginia's Lieutenant Governor Spotswood. In a 1710 message to London officials, he chided voters for advocating "dividing old and erecting new parishes," lamenting that "the People in their elections have oftener considered the disposition of the Burgesses to such particular designs, than their qualifications for promoting the publick interest." He harped on this theme again five years later, saying of the burgesses that "some of them have so little shame as publickly to declare, that if in Assembly anything should be proposed, which they judged might be disagreeable to their Constituents, they would oppose it, tho they knew in their consciences that it would be for the good of the country." He was similarly scathing in his private correspondence, denigrating members "who, for fear of not being chosen again, dare in Assembly do nothing that may be disrelished out of the House by ye Comon People" (*CSP* 1924, 234; 1928, 318; *OLAS*, vol. II 1885, 124).

Spotswood even blistered the burgesses in person, telling them that "the Giddy Resolves of the illiterate Vulgar in their Drunken Conventions you hold for the most Sacred Dictates to your proceedings . . . [and] all your proceedings have been calculated to Answer the Notions of the ignorant Populace; And if you can Excuse your Selves to them, you matter not how you Stand before God, your Prince, and all Judicious men, or before any others to whom, you think, you owe not your Elections." In this instance, he went too far. When apprised of his comments, the Council of Trade and Plantations scolded him, writing that "thô the Assembly was compos'd of mean ignorant people, and thô they did not comply with what you might reasonably expect from them, yet we are apprehensive that such a speech, so full of sharp expressions may not only incense them but even their electors to such a degree as may require a considerable time before the people are brought to temper again." Spotswood responded that he would "resign my own opinion to be govern'd by that of yor. Lordps. Board," but he assured them, "The people of the best consideration, who knew the characters and behaviour of the late Burgesses are far from being displeased with my treatment of them" (*CSP* 1930a, 102, 282–83; *JHB* 1712– 1912, 167, 170).

Similar sentiments were expressed by a North Carolina governor, who claimed that in his colony "men of sense who sincerely mean the Publick good are so much afraid of the next Elections that they are obliged to go in with the majority whose Ignorance & want of education makes them obstruct everything for the good of the Country" (*CRNC*, vol. IV 1886,

178). A Maryland governor contended that "many of the Members find themselves under a necessity in order to keep fair Weather with their Constituents to Vote differently from what they would willingly do" (*AM*, vol. IX 1890, 525).

Some lawmakers concurred. Writing about a bill he opposed to provide government money for "killing Crows and Squirrels," a Virginia burgess noted of his colleagues that "some voted to Please their Constituents and others, particularly the Townsmen of Northfolk, voted for it by a Perswasion that grain would grow cheaper by it." Even more troubling was the reaction to another measure when it was brought up for a vote: "[T]he Worthy Members for it so bent upon pleasing their Constituents that is was remarkable to hear them without doors exclaiming against yet plum for it on every motion within" (*DCLC* 1965, 74, 119). A South Carolina lawmaker recorded that on one bill a colleague "countenanced it with his voice at the Second reading, but as if his conscience & his Interest were at variance he would vote on neither side at the third, but retired when the question was going to be put" (*Papers of Henry Laurens* 1974, 382).

Lawmakers and Representational Activities

What we consider direct representational activities—lawmakers' efforts meant specifically to advance the parochial interests of their constituents— surfaced early in Massachusetts. In the 1640s, "Att the request of the towne of Hampton, by their deputie," the assembly granted the community the right to hold a Thursday market (*RGC*, vol. III 1854, 395). In 1660 Springfield's records noted with regard to a critical boundary question, "But the deputy is gott as much in all these respects as [the General] Co^rte may be inclined unto" (Burt 1898, 285). A few years later, "In ans^r to the motion of the deputyes of Portsmouth, the Court judgeth it meete to order, that the bounds betweene Portsmouth & Hampton, as to their tounships, be determined & settled" (*RGC*, vol. IV—Part II 1854, 530). In 1685, "In ans^r to a motion made in behalfe of the toune of Newbery by [Deputy] Richd Bartlet, Mr John Woodbridge is hereby appointed & authorized to administer oathe, & joyne persons in marriage there who shall desier it" (*RGC*, vol. V 1854, 483).

Such district-directed behavior became common throughout the colonies (Caulkins 1860, 166–67; *Records of the Town of Jamaica* 1914, 166; Tompkins, 1903, 31–32; Tucker 1877, 28; Turner and Bridges 1920, 66). There are even hints that lawmakers began to invent problems for the assemblies to solve for their own electoral advantage. This possibility was raised by Lieutenant Governor Spotswood, who scolded the burgesses, "Your Design, in labouring first to procure Grievances, and afterwards to Vindicate them, appears plainly enough, when you made a long train of them Serve in a formidable manner to introduce a most unrighteous Bill" (*JHB 1712– 1912*, 167).

Efforts to promote and protect local interests grew routine. In 1724 the Connecticut assembly passed a bill, "Upon the motion of the Representatives of the several towns in the northeast part of this government, viz: Norwich, Windham, Canterbury, Plainfield, Pomfrett and Kellingsly, That all goats that are or may be within the said townships shall have liberty to go at large." They were free to roam from mid-September to mid-April, and their owners were "not be judged damage feasant" unless their animals were found "in winter corn sufficiently fenced." A single winter's experience with this policy was enough for one of the instigating communities. In the assembly's next session, the journal reveals, "The Representatives of Norwich having laid before this Court, that the act respecting goats, in October last, is very grievous to their town." Their concerns were accommodated, and the court granted "liberty to said town of Norwich to except themselves out of said act, if they see cause," which the town quickly did (Caulkins 1874, 296; *PRCC* 1872, 491, 544).

In the late 1740s, the Pennsylvania assembly had to balance competing local interests. It received "A Petition from a Number of Inhabitants of *Chester* County, setting forth the Mischief done to the Corn by the great Encrease of Squirrels, and praying that an Act may be made to encourage the Killing of them." A similar petition was submitted by Bucks County residents. The assembly speedily passed "An Act to Encourage the Killing of Squirrels within This Province." Motivated by concerns that the rodents "greatly damnify the farmers and others by destroying their wheat, Indian corn, and other grain," the law required counties to pay three pence for each squirrel killed within their jurisdiction (except for those killed by Indians), as evidenced by the submission of their heads or scalps.

After only one year the act encountered a backlash. The Assembly Committee on Aggrievances, acting at the behest of its Philadelphia City and County, Lancaster County, and York County members, reported that "the late Law upon Squirrel Scalps, is a very great Grievance" because "the Expences thereby arising, are likely to prove so large." It recommended repeal. Support for this position was provided by a York County petition complaining that "the Expence of paying Threepence *per* head for every Squirrel kill'd . . . will vastly exceed the Damage done by those Creatures."

The county preferred to spend its limited revenues on "all the necessary publick Buildings" it needed to construct. Opposition to the repeal effort surfaced in petitions from Bucks and Chester counties, each of which argued that the act was a success, with "very few Squirrels now appearing in the Province." They cautioned that if it were repealed the squirrels would "in a few Years encrease again to prodigious Numbers." Unrepresented inhabitants on the colony's western fringe then weighed in on the side of repeal for a novel reason: "That the Bounty given for Squirrels Scalps, hath taken off all the Jobbers and hired Men from Labour, to the great Damage and Disappointment of the Farmers." Given competing interests, lawmakers did what they could to assuage them all. They amended the act by cutting the bounty in half, a settlement that held through the rest of the colonial era (*SLP*, vol. V 1898, 68–70, 97–98; *VPPP* 1749, 16, 18, 26, 29, 32, 35; 1750, 16, 24, 32, 36, 41, 44, 50).

Local concerns even commandeered lawmakers' positions on matters of colonywide import. In the mid-1740s parts of New Jersey were wracked with riots over land titles. Centered mostly in Essex County, these were serious civil disturbances involving "the gathering together of great Numbers of people Armed: Assaulting and wounding Sheriffs and other Officers: Breaking open County Gaols: and Rescuing and Releasing prisoners, Legally Committed." In October 1745 the governor called on the assembly to pass legislation "to prevent the Like for the future." By May 1746 a bill *"for preventing Tumults and Riotous Assemblies"* was brought to a vote. It failed, with 16 votes against and only 6 in favor. Many lawmakers opposed it, arguing that existing laws were sufficient to handle the crisis. Both Essex County representatives, one of whom was allegedly a supporter of the rioters, voted against it. Immediately thereafter a motion was made, asking "whether the said Bill be printed for the Perusal of the Publick or not?" It passed on a close vote, 12 to 10, with all its backers opposing the legislation. The failed bill's text subsequently appeared in the assembly journal.

Over the following year the colony's slide into chaos continued, and the governor continued pressing for a legislative response. Members were pressured by the rioters, who submitted petitions expounding on their grievances. Petitions opposed to the rioters also came in, among them one from "a great Number of the Inhabitants" of Morris and Somerset counties where landed families claimed to be in "great Terror and Fear of their lives." Torn between constituents on both sides, the only action the assembly could agree to take was to appoint a joint committee with the council to consider "Ways and Means for suppressing the Riots and present Disorders in this Colony, and make Report to the House." Finally, facing growing violence and a warning about the possibility of a mob descending on the assembly itself, in early 1748 *"An Act for the suppressing and preventing of Riots, Tumult and other Disorders within this Colony"* was passed with only two dissenting votes. Both Essex representatives were in favor. But within two days the assembly also passed, without a recorded vote, *"An Act to pardon the Persons guilty of the Insurrections, Riots, Tumults and other Disorders, raised and committed in this Province."* Representatives responded to the crisis, albeit slowly, in a way that minimized alienating competing constituencies (*ANJ* 1776, 171; *DRNJ*, vol. VI 1882, 323–51, 397–418; *Votes of the General Assembly* 1747 (May), 40–41; *Votes of the General Assembly* 1747 (November), 36–38, 99, 102; *VPNJ August 1746* 1746, 6–10; *VPNJ 1745–6* 1746, 38–40; *VPNJ May 1746* 1746, 22–23).

Explanations for an Increase in Constituent Influence

Over time the assemblies experienced a swelling of their legislative agendas. Problems such as defense, Indian relations, and transportation, which had been resolved at the local government level in earlier years, required colonywide solutions in later years (Olson 1992). The colonies also became increasingly complex polities. Population growth in some was explosive. Between 1700 and 1760 Pennsylvania's population increased to 183,703 from 17,950, South Carolina's to 94,074 from 5,704, and Virginia's to 339,726 from 58,560 (*Historical Abstract of the United States*, part 2 1975, table Z 1–19). At the same time their economies expanded and diversified. Agriculture was the dominant sector, but industries arose that manufactured a range of products traded worldwide. Ships built in New England came to constitute about a third of the British fleet, and by time of the Revolution the colonies accounted for 14 percent of the world's pig iron production (Main and Main 1999, 121; McAllister 1989, 247–48). Thus, as time passed, there were more people and more interests, which combined to generate more demands on the assemblies.

Many of these demands were made directly. Assembly agendas were packed with propositions, which were requests for legislation from local governmental entities, and petitions, which were vehicles utilized by individuals or groups to call for legislative action on particular problems (Olson 1992). Lawmakers often responded to these concerns by introducing bills (Bailey 1979, 59–60; Haight 1984; Tully 1977, 188–89). In Delaware in 1720, Cesar Rodeney wrote in his diary, "Money Being Very Scarce people are Sending petitions to ye Assembly to Make paper money." An entry the following month noted, "[Y]e Assembly mett and the only Law yt. they made wass 12 thousand pounds of paper Money" ("Fare Weather" 1962, 69–70).

Constituent pressure is demonstrated by two 1740s measures the Virginia assembly pursued with regard to the town of Port Royal. Port Royal was incorporated in Caroline County in 1744. The following year the county submitted a proposition making two requests: to establish a free ferry to connect Port Royal with Colonel Turner's property and to outlaw the building of wooden chimneys in the new town. The assembly rejected the ferry request but found the idea that wooden chimneys should be prohibited "reasonable." The latter decision was to be expected because communities regularly requested such legislation to reduce fire hazards. Accordingly, the assembly ordered one of Caroline County's burgesses to "prepare and bring in a Bill, pursuant to the Resolution for preventing the building [of] Wooden Chimnies in the Town of *Port-Royal*." Shortly thereafter, the assembly directed that the measure also incorporate "a Clause or Clauses, to prevent Hogs and Sheep from running at large in *New-Town*, in the *County of Princess-Anne*." Again, communities frequently demanded laws to contain livestock. Following parliamentary procedure, the bill was formally read twice. After the second reading it was referred to the assembly's Committee on Propositions and Grievances. The committee was asked to further amend the measure to also prohibit the building of wooden chimneys in the towns of Newcastle and Suffolk and to allow all three of the communities mentioned to tear down existing wooden chimneys. The committee was also told to incorporate language permitting Newcastle to host two fairs a year. The assembly passed the now omnibus measure following its third reading (*JHB 1742–* 1909, 171–72, 175, 181, 183, 185, 190, 192; *SLV*, vol. V 1819, 287–92).

The preambles to the act's sections make clear their intended appeal to constituent concerns.

- Whereas the inhabitants of the several towns of Port Royal, in the county of Caroline, Newcastle, in the county of Hanover, and Suffolk in the county of Nansemond, are in great danger of having their houses and effects burnt and consumed, by reason of many wooden chimnies
- And whereas it is represented, that a great number of hogs are raised, and suffered to go at large, in Newtown, in the county of Princess Anne, and the said town of Newcastle, to the great prejudice of the inhabitants thereof

· And whereas allowing fairs to be kept in the said town of New-
castle, will be very commodious to the inhabitants of that part of
this colony. (*SLV*, vol. V 1819, 387–88)

A few years later a "Petition of the Inhabitants of *Port-Royal*" was entered in
opposition to a "Proposition from the County of *Essex*, for Erecting a Public Warehouse for the Inspection of Tobacco." Port Royal residents argued
that the proposed warehouse would be inconvenient for them to use and
a financial threat to their own facility, which they claimed was "sufficient
to contain all the Tobacco inspected there." The petition was referred to
the Committee on Propositions and Grievances, on which one of Caroline County's burgesses sat. After reviewing the petition, the committee
found it "reasonable," thereby ending the threat of another warehouse
being approved (*JHB 1742– 1909*, 280, 307). In a clash of local interests,
Port Royal's residents were able to win because of the efforts of a well-
placed representative. Such behavior on the part of assembly members was
expected (McCleskey 2012, 48–50).

Data on petitions show that their use increased significantly over the
course of the 1700s (Bailey 1979, 62; Batinski 1987, 7; Harlow 1917, 19;
Leonard 1948, 376–80; Longmore 1995, 428; Olson 1992, 556–58; Purvis
1986, 179). Their impact on the legislative process grew as well. Approxi-
mately half of all colonial laws passed during the eighteenth century origi-
nated as petitions (Bailey 1979, 64; Olson 1992, 556; Purvis 1986, 178;
Tully 1977, 99).

Documenting the Growing Pull of Local Interests

There are several reasons why we would anticipate that over time colonial
lawmakers were driven to think more of their own constituencies at the
expense of larger colony interests. First, turnover decreased, and in order
to get reelected members had to take actions to please the voters back
home, if only to prevent any challengers from emerging in future elections.
Second, the colonies became more socially and economically complex. As
populations diversified, conflicts inevitably surfaced, creating competing
interests that had to be attended to. Finally, policy agendas expanded, with
lawmakers being asked to pursue local angles on a host of issues.

One way to demonstrate the growing pull of local interests on the
behavior of legislators is to examine the laws they passed. As electoral
incentives for lawmakers to pass parochial legislation increased, we should

expect the number and proportion of local bills passed to reflect that reality. To test this hypothesis, I coded all the laws passed by five assemblies from 1700 to 1769 to determine the proportion of them that were targeted at specific electoral units as opposed to applying colonywide. Thus I determined whether a law applied to the entire colony (e.g., "An Act to prevent infectious Distempers being brought into this Colony and to hinder the Spreading thereof"), applied to several specific electoral units (e.g., "An Act to prevent the destruction of Deer by Blood Hounds or Beagles in the Counties of Albany, Ulster and Orange"), applied to a single electoral unit (e.g., "An Act to Raise a Sum not Exceeding Fifty Pounds for finishing of the Court House and Goal in Dutchess County and defraying Such Charges as are already laid out and Expended towards the Building the Same"), or applied to a specific named individual or individuals (e.g., "An Act for Naturalizing the Several Persons therein mentioned") (*CLNY*, vol. III 1894, 941–42, 1071–73, 1075–77; vol. IV 1894, 976).

The five assemblies for which data were collected are New Hampshire, New Jersey, New York, Pennsylvania, and South Carolina. Each was established a few decades prior to 1700, allowing time for assemblies to pass any colonywide legislation required by a new polity before the beginning of the period for which data were gathered. They represent the full geographic range of the colonies. Their assemblies met and passed legislation regularly, unlike those in Delaware and North Carolina, which passed bills sporadically (*Acts of Assembly* 1751; and *Laws of the State of Delaware*, vol. I 1797). Finally, as noted in chapter 2, trustee representational orientations were set for all of them at their creation, so there is no confusion on this score to muddy any findings.

The results of this analysis are reported in table 8.1, which aggregates the laws passed by each colony by decade. As organizations the assemblies evolved independently; consequently, the manner in which they produced legislation also differed (Squire 2012). New York and South Carolina passed more acts than did the others, in part because their measures often incorporated sunset provisions requiring them to regularly revisit even insignificant policies. New Hampshire passed acts, but unlike the others it also made laws through concurrent votes and resolves. Pennsylvania tended to write large bills rather than splitting matters into many smaller ones. Thus the legislative process in each assembly was distinct.

In general, the assemblies passed far more legislation in the 1760s than during the century's first decade. But the relationship is uneven. The number of laws passed in South Carolina ebbed and flowed at the margin, but stayed relatively constant. New Hampshire, New Jersey, New York, and

TABLE 8.1. Total Legislative Acts and Acts Targeted to a Specific Electoral Unit or Several Electoral Units, 1700–1769, by Decade

	New Hampshire		New Jersey		New York		Pennsylvania		South Carolina	
Decade	Total Number of Acts[a]	Total Targeted Acts (percent)	Total Number of Acts	Total Targeted Acts (percent)	Total Number of Acts	Total Targeted Acts (percent)	Total Number of Acts	Total Targeted Acts (percent)	Total Number of Acts	Total Targeted Acts (percent)
1700–1709	74	6 (8)	21	1 (5)	130	41 (32)	167	7 (4)	118	25 (21)
1710–19	194	30 (15)	89	19 (21)	171	45 (26)	72	12 (17)	130	30 (23)
1720–29	88	21 (24)	30	1 (3)	158	62 (39)	67	14 (21)	107	29 (27)
1730–39	42	11 (26)	34	3 (9)	151	65 (43)	46	5 (11)	139	62 (45)
1740–49	107	32 (30)	65	17 (26)	181	74 (41)	26	5 (19)	106	32 (30)
1750–59	111	25 (23)	79	15 (19)	236	87 (37)	72	11 (15)	115	57 (50)
1760–69	144	51 (35)	203	86 (42)	310	162 (52)	150	72 (48)	102	47 (46)

Source: CLNY, vol. II 1894; vol. III 1894; vol. IV 1894; vol. V 1894; *Index of Colonial and State Laws of New Jersey Between the Years of 1603 and 1903 Inclusive* 1905; *LNH*, vol. one, 1904; vol. two, 1913; vol. three, 1915; *SLP*, vol. II 1896; vol. III 1896; vol. IV 1897; vol. V 1898; vol. VI 1899; vol. VII 1900; *SLSC*, vol. second 1837; vol. third 1838; vol. fourth 1838. [a]New Hampshire also enacted laws using concurrent votes and resolves. They are added to the number of acts reported here. Missing legislative journals may account for the reduction in the number of laws passed by means of concurrent votes and resolves in the 1730s, deflating the numbers reported here.

Pennsylvania witnessed dramatic increases in legislation in the final decade. Interestingly, most of the colonies experienced a spurt of lawmaking in the second decade examined, followed by two decades with fewer laws passed.

The relationship of particular interest is the change in the number and proportion of local laws. As hypothesized, in each assembly laws targeted at specific electoral units grew more prominent. At the beginning of the eighteenth century, local laws accounted for little of the legislation passed in New Hampshire, New Jersey, and Pennsylvania. They were comparatively more prominent in New York and South Carolina. But in each assembly the number and proportion of locally targeted laws increased, with the highest number and proportion found in the 1760s in all but South Carolina. Thus the assemblies' behavior is consistent with the notion that over time lawmakers became more likely to see their representational responsibilities as linked to the interests of their constituents rather than the colony at large.

Member Voting Behavior

Explaining how and why individual assembly members voted is a challenge because, as noted earlier, direct information is limited. The most common assertion, however, comes as no surprise. Representatives routinely pointed to their constituents' preferences to explain their votes, a claim that contemporary observers supported. New York's governor attributed the "long and considerable arrear of H. M. Quitt-rents in this Province" to "that too great caution . . . not to displease Assembly men, who, with their friends (of which number are all those that do but vote for their elections) are" (*CSP* 1937a, 392). In a row with voters over legislative pay, the Virginia assembly prefaced a bill with a statement: "WHEREAS, the excessive expenses of the Burgesses causing diverse misunderstandings between them and the people." This was followed the next year with a mea culpa: "WHEREAS the immoderate expences of the burgesses causing diverse heart burnings between them and the people." When the public uproar failed to subside, members voted to cut their pay because it was "complained of as greiveous and burthensome to the people" (*SLV*, vol. II 1823, 23, 106, 398–99). And, as we might expect, impending elections affected behavior. A Maryland governor stated, "I must attribute in great measure the Obstinacy that has appeared in the Lower House of Assembly . . . to the near approach of another Election which . . . has no little influence on the Conduct of such Representatives as for the most part compose our present [Assembly]" (*AM*, vol. VI, 1888, 70).

There were familiar reasons why members occasionally voted contrary to their voters' wishes. Self-interest sometimes played a role. An observer of a Maryland battle over lawyer fees claimed, "The county court lawyers voted for the bill, because, if carried into a law, it would increase their fees; but the provincial court lawyers voted against it, on a similar motive, because it would lessen their business" (*MDG* 1773d).

Contemporary commentaries suggested that religion influenced the way members approached some issues. In a 1692 assessment of Maryland delegates' likely vote on a controversial religious rights bill—perhaps the earliest interest group vote count—religious affiliation was seen as determinative. The Anglican who compiled the list said of the Dorchester delegation, "Dr. Jacob Lockerman and Mr. Ennalls are Good Moderate men. Vestrymen and wish well ye church." Undecided was "Mr. Hicks an humdrum fellows knows not what he is for himself." Labeled opposed was "Mr. Cambel of ye kirk of Scotland" (Jones 1902, 51). Across the colonies complaints were lodged that religion swayed the behavior of some members. New Hampshire's governor lamented that "no obedience" to his preferred policies could be expected "if the Assembly and other men in public trust consist of Congregated Church members" (*CSP* 1898, 576). Maryland's governor expressed concern about Catholic influence, claiming they "have such an ascendant over severall in this Province that thereby they are alsoe enabled to gaine many voices in ye General Assembly, who as well as others here are made sencible that such as favour Popery are likelyest to be ye kindlyest dealt by in grants of land" (*CSP* 1916a, 264). Perhaps the strongest fears were voiced about Quakers. In 1708 New Jersey's governor told London officials, "I am of the opinion that as long as the Queen is pleased to allow the Quakers to sit in the Assembly, they never will settle a Revenue, nor a Millitia" (*CSP* 1922, 15).

Governors had much at stake in assembly decisions; consequently, they had every reason to try to influence members. Being on good personal terms with representatives was helpful, although not all governors were adept at it. A Virginian complained about his governor's "penurious way of . . . publick treats," although he conceded, "Of late he had usually treated the Assembly four times a week except once, and commonly sends drink to several of their chambers." Another colony resident maintained that "all means were used to gain the House. The Burgesses were treated very high and closetted one by one, and those days [the governor] did not treat, he eat with them at the Ordinary" (*CSP* 1916a, 103, 105).

As suggested in chapter 3, governors were often in a position to use patronage to entice assembly members to do their bidding. Virginia lieutenant governor Spotswood admitted as much in a letter to London officials, bragging that he had "clear'd the way for a Gov'r towards carrying any reasonable point in the House of Burgesses, for he will have in his disposal about forty Agencys, which one with another are likely to yield nigh 250 Pounds P[er] ann[um] each." He disclosed, "[M]y intentions are . . . principally to gratify with a Place all the members of the Assembly who were for the bill [he supported]" (*OLAS*, vol. II 1885, 49). Such behavior was expected. A quarter century later a prominent colonist complained that another lieutenant governor "will not have the least Influence, with our Assembly, if he can't make Friends by the skillful distribution, of the Few Places, that have always been in his Gift." Adroit use of patronage was vital because "All other Acts of Persuasion are empty and vain" ("Letters of the Byrd Family" 1929, 30).

Patronage was exploited everywhere. When one Massachusetts governor took office in 1731, 25 percent of the assembly members held appointed positions. Within a few years 60 percent did (Bushman 1985, 77). A pamphlet remarked on the governor's "Friends and Dependants in the *House*" (*Account of the Rise* 1744, 16). A Georgia governor was similarly proactive. After taking over, his successor marveled that, as a means of gaining leverage, "11 of the 19 [assembly] Members have been distinguished by such places of honor & trusts as this Government affords" (*CRSG*, vol. 28, part I 1976, 13). Advice given to Maryland's governor by the colony's proprietor offers the baldest statement of intent behind such use of patronage.

> There are 58 Members of that [lower] House . . . Now the buissiness is to find Baits for 30 of these; which number is a clear Majority . . . To answer therefore this purpose, I would appropriate the 14 Sheriffs places, which will undoubtedly secure 14 Members & may by good Management of their Comissions secure double that number . . . There are 14 Farmers of his Lordships Quit-Rents, 14 Deputy Comiss[rs] and 14 Deputy Surveyours; all these places are considerable to the Middling sort of people, of whom the Lower House is composed, & might gain a great Majority of that House by being properly applyed amongst them. (*AM*, vol. XIV 1895, 3–4)

But such labors proved futile when a governor's agenda ran afoul of voters' preferences. A professor visiting America in 1748 observed that in New York, "The colony has sometimes had a governor, whose quarrels with the inhabitants, have induced their representatives . . . through a spirit of revenge, to oppose indifferently every thing he proposed" (Kalm 1770,

260). Governors were aware of their limited ability to influence representatives. Writing to South Carolina's governor, a Virginia lieutenant governor conceded that his legislative proposals, "wou'd have no Weight with my Assembly, as they are too headstrong to be under any Direct'n but from their own Opinions and Arguments." He made the same point in a missive to Maryland's governor, writing, "I am convinc'd if a Gov'r of this Dom'n sh'd direct the Assembly either in regard to raising Men or Money, [it] w'd be the infallible way of being disappointed of both, for they depend greatly on their own Notions and Judgm't" (*Official Records of Robert Dinwiddie*, vol. I 1883, 128, 145). In a private moment Maryland's governor carped, "[T]he Assembly of this Province as well as that of a Neighbouring one seems to take pleasure in shewing their Constituents that they are determined to pay no Regard to any Recommendation that comes from a Superior." He later offered a global appraisal, observing about patronage that "a great Influence hath at times been gained in the British House of Commons by such means is certain but it cannot be thence inferred that the same might be easily done here" (*AM*, vol. IX 1890, 10–11, 429). Governors did not have the number of enticing positions at their disposal that the Crown enjoyed (Bailyn 1968, 72–80; Purvis 1986, 124–25; Zemsky 1971, 52–54).

Pork-barreling happened. Some cases must be inferred. In 1686 Virginia's governor reported that on a ports and wharves measure "the Burgesses agreed, as their journal shows, excepting that they wished there to be one port in each county, whereas it was limited by the Council and myself to two in a river" (*CSP* 1899, 150). A few years later similar charges were leveled against the process through which new towns were established. An observer commented that "every man desires the town to be by his own door, and every Burgess setting up one for his own county, they have commonly contrived a town for every county" (*CSP* 1904, 644). Because almost all burgesses were elected by county, it makes sense that they would prefer to see ports, wharves, and new towns distributed in an equitable fashion, allowing each to claim credit with his constituents.

Other pork-barreling claims were more direct. Rhode Islanders protesting a 1761 bill "granting . . . money, out of the general treasury, for the re-building Weybosset Bridge, in the town of Providence," did so "by reason there being but thirty-five members now present, and fourteen of that number belonging to the county of Providence, we think they have a great advantage of voting money to their own county" (*RCRI* 1861, 294). New York's governor complained about his lawmakers' defense spending, writing, "In the fortifications they have every where employed Men intirely ignorant of the art, who have no more pretence to knowledge than the meanest Plowman, and have squandered away large sums of money with no other view than can appear, but in being usefull to Relations, or to such Persons as they thought could serve them in future Elections" (*DRNY*, vol. VI 1855, 462). Similar contentions were made about the patronage lawmakers controlled. A New Yorker wrote, "Every Body knows the assembly have generally in their view to secure their next Election by this means, and therefore pay little Regard to the other qualifications of the persons" (*PSWJ*, vol. I 1921, 417).

Sophisticated observers understood that organized interests influenced member behavior. A matter-of-fact admission was offered by a New York governor, who wrote to London officials, "If there had been such a body of the inhabitants averse to the passing of those Acts, 'tis a wonder they petitioned not the General Assembly against them, while they were passing, which is always done where a body of people look upon themselves like to be hurt by a Bill depending before the Assembly" (*CSP* 1910b, 2–3). Lawmakers became attentive to the preferences of organized groups. In 1709 a Pennsylvania member told the assembly that he "and divers other Members of this House, had, this Morning, a private Conference, with . . . the People called *Quakers*, upon the Subject Matter of the Governor's Speech" (*VPPP*, vol. the Second 1753, 35). Commenting on the politics surrounding a retail businesses bill, New York's governor stated, "The shopkeepers of New York are for it, the generality of others against it" (*CSP* 1928, 242). Lobbying was common. In 1768 a New Yorker wrote in his journal, "[T]his Morning I was informed the Merchants were in a body to attend the Assembly" to inquire about an important policy matter (*Historical Memoirs* 1956, 46).

Organized interests knew that lobbying could move lawmakers. Unhappy with a New York assembly vote, a "Son of Liberty" publicly urged those who agreed with him to "assemble in the fields" and then "go in a body to your members, and insist on their joining the minority, to oppose the bill" (*Documentary History*, vol. III 1850, 320). Such pressure was productive. Another New Yorker noted that on one bill "[Representative] Thomas was Not for it on the Com[mittee] but having been visited by the Sons of Liberty as they stile themselves he now moved to have it rejected" (*Historical Memoirs* 1956, 47). On a land tax proposal a legislative participant noted, "The Assembly seem'd at first well enclin'd to it for not many of them had any Interest to Oppose it. . . . But this good Design was prevented by the Art of some leading men who were chiefly concerned in those large Tracts" (*LPCC*, vol. VIII 1937, 166). An assessment of the Massachusetts assembly led an analyst to claim, "Any well-disposed person without doors may submissively offer advice or proposals, even after a bill is enacted, because acts are frequently explained or altered by subsequent acts for the publick good" (Douglass, vol. I 1755, 509).

A 1738 battle in the Pennsylvania assembly demonstrated the power of organized interests. Lawmakers received a petition from "a great Number of the Inhabitants of *Philadelphia* County" complaining about the "great Annoyance arising from Slaughter-Houses, Tann-Yards, Skinners Lime-Pits, &c." The petitioners requested, "for the Convenience and Reputation of the City, and the Health of the Inhabitants," that no new such facilities be allowed and existing ones be relocated. Tanners in Philadelphia immediately responded with their own petition, requesting time to formulate a detailed response and, in the meantime, promising not to establish any new facilities. Within a few months, the assembly received another petition from Philadelphia residents, this time "praying" that "the Tanners may not be obliged to leave the City, but laid under such Regulations and Restrictions, as may effectually remove the Mischiefs complained of." Within a few days the assembly approved a proposal from the tanners imposing new regulations on the way they conducted their businesses but not requiring them to move (*VPPP* 1738, 43, 46, 54, 56–57).

Occasionally governors complained that the residents of the town where the assembly met influenced members. In 1728 Massachusetts' governor adjourned a session in Boston, where the assembly normally met, and reconvened it in Salem. His reason was that Bostonians were "continually endeavouring to pervert the minds of the Members that come from the Country, who it is to be hoped will not be so much tampered with in the Country and particularly at Salem." Lawmakers denied the allegation. They complained to the king that the assembly had been relocated "upon a pretence that the people in Boston influenced the representatives against settling a sallary." They swore, "[W]e acted freely therein, and that the same reasons that prevailed with us at Boston, would go with, and influence us everywhere" (*CSP* 1937a, 225, 312–13; *JHHR* 1728, 105, 109–10). But two decades later another Massachusetts governor railed about the "Experience of the bad Influence, which the mobbish factious Spirit of the Town of Boston . . . have ever had upon the other Towns in the government and upon their own Members" (*Correspondence of William Shirley*, vol. I 1912, 474).

Constituents and Their Representatives

What happened when members knowingly fell out of step with their constituents? A New Jersey assembly speaker resigned his seat after he voted against what he knew to be the preference of a majority of his constituents. In a letter to colleagues, he confided, "But as at present there appears a great Dissatisfaction at my Conduct, that has spread even among some of my Constituents, whom I have served many Years in General Assembly, to the Utmost of my Abilities; I beg Leave of the House, to resign my Seat in it; whereby my Constituents may have an Opportunity of sending another Person in my Room, who may act more agreable to their present Sentiments" (*VPNJ* 1765, 4). A Maryland delegate opted not to seek reelection after he followed his conscience on a critical issue. He told his constituents, "'Tis true, that just before our election, I was desired by several to 'alter my opinion,' and 'declare against the proclamation,' and that in consequence thereof, I might most assuredly depend on the country's continuance of the honour of a seat in the house of assembly to me; but surely my countrymen, who proffered me these terms, did not well consider the nature and import of them; Could I have prevailed on myself to *forswear*, and *sacrifice* to *popularity*, the clear *conviction* of my own mind, in relation to the tendency of the *proclamation*, my seat might have been secured by jumping in with the majority, and going with the current" (*MDG* 1773g). When lawmakers realized that they were not doing what their constituents wanted, they often stepped down. Such behavior is consistent with a shift to a delegate orientation.

Sometimes when representatives acted contrary to their constituents' preferences, they were only publicly scolded. In 1768 a "large Number, more than one Hundred Petitioners," asked the Haverhill, Massachusetts, selectmen to call a meeting to repudiate their representative's vote on a controversial measure (*BEP* 1768b). Similarly, "a large number of the inhabitants" of Salem petitioned for a special meeting "to let the public know that the minds of the people in this place were not similar with those of their Representatives." That session was characterized as "the fullest meeting perhaps ever known in this place," indicating an engaged electorate (*BEP* 1768a).

On rare occasions, incumbents persuaded voters to change their views. In 1734 almost 80 constituents of a New York lawmaker wrote a public letter thanking him for his "Conduct in the last Session of Assembly." Only one voter declined to join them. Many of those who signed "had opposed" the representative's election, and "every one of them (with the former single Exception) laid aside their private Resentments to shew their publick gratitude." They credited the member's actions with having "indeared you to your Constituents" (*NYWJ* 1734b, 1734c).

Thus voters were not always displeased. Newark records show that in 1699, "The Town gave unto their Representatives their Thanks, for not consenting to the passing of an Act, entitled, an Act for redressing a force of our Neighbour Province" (*RTN* 1864, 113). A published South Carolina letter extolled "a measure acknowledged by their constituents in general, laudable and praise-worthy" (*SCG* 1759). A Boston meeting "Voted, unanimously, that the Representatives of the Town having already made humble application to his Excellency the Governor . . . the Town do approve of their Conduct therein" (*RRCB* 1886, 223). In 1747 Talbot County, Maryland, residents directed their delegates to support a law preventing the export of "trashy" or poor quality tobacco. When three of their four delegates helped pass the measure, it was reported that "on the return home of their Representatives, and hearing that the [tobacco] Inspection Law had Passed, they made great Rejoicing, and fired many Cannon, most of which were wadded with Trash Tobacco" (*MDG* 1747a, 1747b). Voters in Chester County, Pennsylvania, sent a message to the assembly, stating that "the Petitioners are highly sensible of the Zeal and Diligence of this House for the Interest and Welfare of their Constituents." At the same time, they warned them that "should any Consideration whatsoever, but the immediate Preservation of the Lives of the Inhabitants, influence their Proceedings in this Session of Assembly, they will by no Means answer the Expectations of their Constituents, who elected them to be the Guardians of their Lives as well as of their Fortunes" (*VPPP* 1756, 11).

Did Representatives Represent Their Constituents' Policy Preferences?

To this point, the claim that representatives came to represent the interests of their constituents has been documented through an accumulation of anecdotes and contemporary observations consistent with members acting as delegates. There are two more systematic ways to assess the degree to which assembly members represented their voters' interests. The first involves a specific issue in Massachusetts, one for which we have a direct indication of public opinion by town. In 1754 the governor, needing revenue to support a military expedition, asked the assembly to devise a new system "relating to the levying [of] Taxes in the most just and equitable Manner." Lawmakers decided that an excise tax "should be paid on all spirituous Liquors expended within this Province" (*JHHR* 1754, 14). The existing alcohol tax was paid by the poor, who purchased liquor by the glass at taverns, while the wealthy escaped paying by buying their own barrels. The proposed tax would generate more revenue by taxing the wealthy's alcohol consumption and in doing so would make the overall system fairer.

The excise bill moved quickly through the legislative process. Within days the assembly passed on a rare roll call vote "An Act for granting to His Majesty an Excise upon Wines and Spirits distilled, sold by Retail, or consumed within this Province, and upon Limes, Lemons and Oranges." The bill's margin of victory was overwhelming: 52 "yeas" to 17 "nays." But to the assembly's dismay, the council, whose consent was required, speedily "non-concur'd" with the measure. Appealing that decision, the representatives highlighted the bill's rationale: "The House, to prevent Polls and Estates from being over-burthened, projected and passed to be enacted, a salutary Excise Bill, whereby all that consumed spirituous Liquors, the Rich as well as the Poor; those who consumed them for Luxury, as well as those who consumed the same for Necessity, might pay an Excise." They added that should the measure not be approved, "the Treasury is in Danger of remaining empty." The council subsequently reversed its decision and endorsed the measure (*JHHR* 1754, 38, 40, 43–44).

But the political drama was just beginning. The act was controversial because it required citizens to keep track of their alcohol consumption if their families consumed more than 30 gallons annually, and they could be forced to legally swear that their records were true. There was also a regional dimension: the tax would fall more heavily on those in the coastal areas while inland agricultural communities would only be lightly touched.

Sizing up the politics, the governor chose to protect his own reputation by declining to sign the bill (Zemsky 1971, 277). He told the assembly, "Upon the whole, *Gentlemen*, I think the least you can do in Justice to your Constituents upon this Occasion, will be to pursue the Method frequently us'd by the General Assembly in Cases of the like Nature, by ordering the Bill to be printed; that your Constituents may be fully acquainted with the Contents of it during the Recess of the Court, and your selves informed of the general Sentiments of the Country concerning a Matter of this Importance, and Difficulty, which so nearly touches the natural Rights of every individual Member in his private Family" (*JHHR* 1754, 45–47). Newspapers reprinted the message (*BG* 1754a).

The assembly responded to the governor's decision in two ways. The action that received more attention was an order to inform the public about the act. It stipulated that "the several Members of this House be directed to lay before the Select-Men of their respective Towns, that Part of the Excise-Bill which relates to the private Consumption of Wines and Spirits distill'd, and to acquaint them it is the Desire of this House that they call their several Towns together, that this House may know the Minds of their Constituents with Regard to said Bill" (*JHHR* 1754, 48). That order, too, was reprinted in the papers (*BEP* 1754).

Less noticed was the assembly's second action, a negative vote on "*Whether the Excise-Bill in the usual Form should be continued for any longer Term?*" (*JHHR* 1754, 48). The decision not to revive the old excise law was key because, although the assembly occasionally ignored the rule, accepted parliamentary procedure dictated that once a bill was determined during a session it could not be reconsidered (Hutchinson 1767, 438–39; Squire 2012, 58). This meant that some new measure would have to be enacted to keep revenue flowing into the treasury.

The excise bill's passage and veto unleashed a political furor. One member had to take to the floor to get his colleagues to vote that during the debate on the act he "did not say any Thing reflecting on the Merchants, or on any other Persons." Word on the street had him making a politically explosive attack, declaring that "the Merchants as a Sett of Men . . . had no Regard to the Good of their Country, and that no Regard ought to be given to any Thing they said" (*JHHR* 1754, 48). But it was the publication of *The Monster of Monsters* that most inflamed assembly members. *Monster* was America's first political satire (Olson 2001). Today it reads as a sophomoric stab at commentary: the "MONSTER of the most hideous Form" was the excise tax bill, while the representatives were lampooned as "a large Assembly of *Matrons*" (*Monster of Monsters* 1754, 1, 4). In righteous indignation, the assembly voted that *Monster* was "a false scandalous Libel, reflecting upon the Proceedings of this House in general, and on many worthy Members in particular." They ordered that "the said Pamphlet be burnt by the Hands of the common Hangman below the Court-House in King-Street, *Boston*." In an uglier step they sent for the alleged printer—it was probably not published by him but by his brother—and his apprentices. The printer was briefly imprisoned over the affair (*JHHR* 1754, 63, 67, 72).

More consequential than *Monsters* were the numerous pamphlets published in support of and opposition to the bill, making it arguably the first American political controversy fueled by mass media (Boyer 1964). As the following excerpts show, almost all these publications encouraged people to convey their opinions to lawmakers.

As the Honourable House of Representatives has published part of the *Excise Bill*, on Purpose that the Minds of the Inhabitants of the Province concerning it may be known; it is supposed that they expect and desire such Persons as do not like the Bill, to let them know their Thoughts about it with freedom. (*A PLEA for the Poor and Distressed* 1754, 14)

This Bill is therefore now expressly submitted to publick Examination, and every Member of the Community . . . has a Right to deliver his Sentiments upon it without Doors, with the same Freedom, as the Members of the General Court may make use of within Doors. (*Some Observations on the Bill* 1754, 2)

I take it the Design of the General Assembly in committing this Bill to public Examination, was, that they might have the Satisfaction of knowing the Minds of their Constituents, and of hearing what Gentlemen had to say, for, or against it. (*The Good of the Community* 1754, 31)

The governor received praise for his actions (*RRCB* 1885b, 260). One pamphlet gushed, "In Consequence of the Bill's being published, every Man now, thank the Governor for it, will have an Opportunity to see with his own Eyes, how near he has been to Slavery, and to judge for himself, whether he will consent to wear a Yoke for the future" (*Freedom the First Blessing* 1754, 6).

Most of the pamphlets articulated arguments in opposition to the act and asserted that public opinion was on their side. One published just after the council rejected the measure declared that decision reflected "the VOICE OF THE PEOPLE" (*The Voice of the People* 1754, 8). Another stated, "There never was an Affair that related to the Public, which while it was depending, has been more universally the Subject of Censure, than the Bill for an Excise" (*Freedom the First Blessing* 1754, 1). The opponents expected the weight of public opinion would force members who initially supported the measure to reverse course. As one put it, "It is therefore to be presumed, that as there is so much Time for mature Consideration, those very Gentlemen who have been in Favour of the Bill, will upon Adjournment of the Court, drop all favourable Thoughts of it; and agree upon some other Method of collecting these Duties, that shall not be liable to the Objections against this Bill" (*Some Observations on the Bill* 1754, 12).

Reports on the town meetings held to discuss the measure seemed to confirm the opponents' impressions: Boston, Dorchester, Kittery, Medford, Newbury and Weymouth opposed it, while only Cambridge was supportive (*BG* 1754b, 1754c, 1754d; *BPB* 1754). Boston's meeting "Voted unanimously, that the Thanks of the Town be and hereby is given to the Gentlemen the Representatives of the Town for the strenuous Opposition they made to said Bill, and that they be desired still to Use their utmost Endeavours to prevent the said Bills from being pass'd into a Law" (*RRCB* 1885b, 260). The assembly, however, forged ahead. It voted not to consider "the Returns from the several Towns respecting the Excise Bill which pass'd the two Houses last Sitting" and after deliberation, ordered a committee to "bring in a Bill laying an Excise on all Spirits distilled." By the end of the year, "after a large Debate," the representatives passed on an unrecorded vote a lightly revised act (*JHHR* 1754, 60–62, 101, 112, 160). While members' votes were hidden from public view, the decision itself was not. The assembly ordered an advertisement announcing the act to be "Printed, and sent to the Clerks of the several Towns and Districts within this Province, who are hearby directed to Post up the same, in some public Place" (*Advertisement. Province of the Massachusetts-Bay* 1754).

As might be expected, the act's resurrection generated more controversy. Opponents dismissed its amendments. One scoffed, "Some Persons would indeed make us believe, that this is a New B[i]ll, in which all that was exceptionable in the former, is amended: If these Folks are serious in what they say, I pity their Understandings" (*The Relapse* 1754, 1). Another called them "some circumstantial Alterations" (*The Eclipse* 1754, 1).

The opponents' real anger was directed at the process employed to pass the revised version. One noted with distain, "The People themselves exprest their Abhorrence of the B[i]ll, when it was submitted to them— They deprecated it,—They instructed their R[epresentative]s to oppose it." This writer offered a sophisticated analysis: "Some may indeed dispute whether a single R[epresentativ]e who acts for the Publick, is oblig'd to follow the Instructions of his own single Town: But will any one assert, that the H[ous]e have a Right to act contrary to the united Voice of the whole C[ommu]nity which they repr[ese]nt, in a Affair that concerns all; and that has been formally submitted to the Judgment of the People" (*The Eclipse* 1754, 4, 5). Another observed that "a great Majority of the Towns thro' the Province solemnly condemned it, and instructed their Representatives to oppose it . . . No one suspected, that the Representatives of a Free People would dare to act contrary to the declar'd Sense of their Constituents, in an Affair which concern'd their Purses, and which had been formally submitted to their Judgement." He then protested that the members had "not only refused to be bound by your Instructions, but even to hear them read" (*The Review* 1754, 2–3). This last decision on the assembly's part grated on opponents. One expressed bewilderment: "For when His Excellency requir'd that this Bill should be submitted to the Judgment of the People, and when the Inhabitants of every Town through the Province had been convened in order to examine and act upon it, their Rep[resen]tat[ive]s never thought it worth While to pay even so small a Regard to the Decision of the Constituents, as to enquire what it was" (*The Relapse* 1754, 3). Opponents promised to seek retribution at the next election, one writing, "But I hope my Countrymen will consider how much they have been deluded and abus'd in Times past, and will very carefully inquire into the Conduct of the last House, before they proceed to make Choice of those who are to compose the next" (*The Review* 1754, 1).

The act's supporters were fewer but more dispassionate in their defense of it and the assembly. They painted a different picture of the process. One noted, "Some Towns voted upon it, others did not, acquiesing in the Conduct of their Representatives; knowing them to be the best Judges of the Arguments for and against the Bill: This was the Case with many Towns: Those Towns that did meet, & determine upon the Bill, many of them were pleased with the Spirit of it, and expressed their Desires that it might be preserved, with a few Amendments" (*BG* 1754e). Such interpretations suggest uncertainty as to the voters' true preferences.

There is enough information on the record to judge whether the opponents or the supporters had the stronger argument. More important, we can use the available data to assess whether members represented their constituents' preferences. As shown in table 8.2, we can compare how members voted on the first excise bill with the positions their towns later took on it. There are two important observations. First, consistent with the opponents' claim, far more towns took positions opposing the excise act than took positions supporting it. But, as one astute observer noted, the largest number of towns failed to take any stance. In at least six towns voters either explicitly opted to avoid taking a position or failed to take a position even though the measure was on their agenda. Not all the communities that avoided a position had sent representatives to the assembly, but in eleven of them their member had not recorded a position when the measure first passed.

Second, the evidence suggests a high degree of congruence between the positions initially adopted by the members and those subsequently taken by their voters in town meetings. The Braintree representatives split on the measure, with one voting in favor and the other voting against. Town opinion was also divided. An August meeting backed the bill by a single vote. A month later the town reversed that decision (*RTB* 1886, 335–38). Setting aside Braintree, only the Newton representative failed to support the bill when his voters back home later would, so 21 of his colleagues correctly anticipated their voters' preferences. Lawmakers from towns that opposed the act were not as accurate. But the 12 who opposed the measure constituted by far the largest part of the original nays.

The votes of the members from the towns that later failed to take a position were skewed in favor of the bill, 11 ayes to 3 nays. This is significant because it suggests that the final unrecorded vote to pass the measure could well have accurately reflected public opinion, contrary to the claims of excise opponents. Combining the votes in favor of the act from the representatives of the towns that later supported it with those from towns that failed to take a position on it, plus the possible participation of other members who had not voted the first time, it is conceivable that it enjoyed sufficient support to pass with only a few, if any, members from the towns that opposed it acting contrary to their instructions.

This supposition is consistent with the results of the next election. We cannot know which members sought reelection; we only know the identity of those who were returned. Moreover, towns could opt to send fewer or no representatives. Thus, as shown in table 8.3, we can only determine whether a member in the 1754 session was returned in the 1755 assembly or was replaced by a new member; whether the town did not send a representative; or, in the case of Braintree, whether the town sent one member rather than its former two. The results reveal remarkable consistency. Lawmakers who voted for the act from towns that subsequently supported the bill were returned at essentially the same rate as those who voted in favor initially but represented towns that later came out in opposition. Voters

TABLE 8.2. Initial Member Floor Vote and Subsequent Town Position on the 1754 Massachusetts Excise Bill

Representative(s)' Position on First Vote	Town Later Supported Bill	Town Later Opposed Bill	Town Split (Braintree)	Town Later Took No Position
Voted for	21	19	1	11
Voted against	1	12	1	3
Failed to vote	8	24[a]		11
Town not represented during session		2		50

Source: See appendix B; *JHHR* 1754, 38.

[a]Boston had two representatives who failed to vote, one of whom was the speaker. Salem and Danvers also had a representative who failed to vote.

throughout Massachusetts apparently enjoyed similar levels of content-ment with their representatives.

The second type of data that can be used to assess how closely assembly members hewed to their constituents' preferences is roll call votes in the chambers that recorded them. Maryland began logging roll call votes in 1732. The first roll call recorded was, appropriately, on the question "That on each Vote of this House, the Names of the Persons that vote for and against any Question or Bill, be incerted in the Journal, in Order for print-ing?" The measure passed on a 30 to 18 vote, demonstrating that the idea did not enjoy universal support (*VPMD* 1732, 4). Several years later New Jersey and New York began to record votes on some of their decisions. Pennsylvania used roll call votes sparingly, with multiple votes recorded only during the 1753 and 1764 sessions. Massachusetts rarely recorded votes, with a total of 22 roll calls between 1725 and 1765. Although there were roll call votes in most of these bodies after 1765, this analysis focuses largely on those recorded before then to avoid any contamination caused by the rise of revolutionary politics and "hurrah" votes.

These data shed light on representation by revealing how cohesively town or county delegations voted. Except for the occasional special elec-tion to fill a vacant seat, delegation members were elected at the same time

TABLE 8.3. Return and Replacement Rates of 1754 Massachusetts Representatives in the 1755 Elections, by Member Excise Vote and Town Position

Initial Member Vote	Subsequent Town Position	Number of Members	Outcome for Members in 1755 (%)		
			Returned	Replaced	Town Not Represented
In favor	In favor	21	10 (47.6)	9 (42.9)	2 (9.5)
In favor	Opposed	19	10 (52.6)	6 (31.6)	3 (15.8)
Opposed	In favor	1	1 (100)		
Opposed	Opposed	13	7 (53.8)	5 (38.5)	2 (15.4)
In favor	No position	12	4 (33.3)	3 (25.0)	5 (41.7)
Opposed	No position	3	1 (33.3)	1 (33.3)	1 (33.3)
Member did not vote		39	20 (51.3)	14 (35.6)	5 (12.8)
All members		109	52 (47.7)	39 (35.8)	18 (16.5)

Source: Data from appendix B, *JHHR* 1754, 38; 1755, 4.

by the same voters. If delegations voted together on most issues, we can infer that they were representing the preferences of the people who elected them. Alternative explanations for delegation cohesion can, of course, be advanced. In a catty assessment of how Maryland delegates might vote on a religion bill, an analyst said of the Somerset County delegation, "Major Wm. Whitington always accounted a Jacobite. Mr. Walter Lane & Mr. Samuel Collins are silly drunken fellows, easily persuaded by Whitington" (Jones 1902, 51). A satirical account of New York politics made a similar observation, suggesting that the leader of one county delegation so dominated the other members that they proved "themselves plain *Yea* and *Nay* Members; that they were so intirely under [the leader's] Direction, that they were observed to watch his Motions, when they should say *Yea*, and when *Nay*" (*NYG* 1752b). So delegation leaders may have persuaded their colleagues to follow their lead. But we would assume any delegation that routinely voted contrary to its constituents wishes would be unlikely to stay in office.

How these data might be analyzed to provide insight into representation is not obvious. I opted to calculate how many delegation members agreed on each roll call vote, aggregated across each legislative session. Only multimember delegations could be analyzed and only when more than one member participated in a vote. The critical requirement is to establish the level at which agreement between the voting behavior of delegation members and their voters might be inferred to have occurred. In the data examined, delegation sizes range from two members, the most common size, to eight, found only in some Pennsylvania delegations. Where only two delegation members voted, the calculation and its interpretation are straightforward; members could disagree on all votes, producing an agreement score of 0 percent, or they could vote alike on all roll calls, producing an agreement score of 100 percent or any score in between. Difficulties come with larger delegations. Where only three members voted (there are no three-member delegations in the data, but often in four-member delegations only three members participated), and assuming a binary vote choice (always the case, except in New Jersey, where a few votes offered three options and in one case four options), at least two members will always vote in agreement. That would set 67 percent as the minimum agreement score. Where four members served in a delegation, three voting in agreement would suggest 75 percent as the standard for representation. It is that last threshold that I adopt. Where delegation members voted together 75 percent of the time or more I infer that they were voting consistently with the preferences of their constituents. Members agreeing at a lower rate would suggest that they differed on the issues or, perhaps, that their constituents had no consensus preference.

Analysis of delegations in Maryland reveals a high rate of agreement across the six legislative sessions for which data were gathered. As table 8.4 reveals, almost 89 percent of the delegations met or surpassed the 75 percent threshold, while 51 percent met or surpassed the 85 percent threshold. Only the two-member Annapolis city delegation shows much dissention, with its votes in the 1745 session agreeing less than 6 percent of the time. Interestingly, Robert Gordon held one of the Annapolis seats during all six sessions, and the other seat was held by six different individuals. Clearly, Gordon agreed far more often with some of his local colleagues than he did with others. All the Annapolis delegation members, however, appear to have been well regarded by their constituents because they all held local and provincial offices following their assembly service (*AM*, vol. 426 1979, 146–47, 246, 285–88, 327, 367, 801).

Vote agreement scores for the New Jersey assembly sessions examined were similar to those found in Maryland. As can be seen in table 8.5, all the delegations had two members. These delegations surpassed the 75 percent

TABLE 8.4. Roll Call Vote Agreement Scores by Constituency Delegation, Maryland, 1732–1748

		Delegation Roll Call Vote Agreement Scores by Session (%)					
Constituency	Number of Seats	1732–34 (36 vhotes)	1734–37 (46 votes)	1739–41 (56 votes)	1742–44 (43 votes)	1745 (36 votes)	1746–48 (72 votes)
Annapolis (city)	2	*66.7*	*59.0*	**90.7**	**90.0**	*5.7*	**95.5**
Anne-Arundel	4	**81.9**	**79.9**	**87.6**	**88.5**	**95.0**	**92.9**
Baltimore	4	**83.6**	**88.9**	**96.6**	**75.6**	**84.8**	**79.5**
Calvert	4	**86.9**	**91.7**	**92.9**	**90.2**	**99.3**	**92.4**
Cecil	4	**86.4**	**88.2**	**88.4**	**90.2**	**83.3**	*74.5*
Charles	4	**78.7**	**81.7**	**78.0**	**86.1**	**80.9**	**75.8**
Dorchester	4	**80.5**	**80.3**	*71.6*	**88.8**	**83.0**	**76.8**
Kent	4	**85.0**	**90.8**	*64.9*	**76.0**	**86.3**	**82.1**
Prince George's	4	**91.3**	**89.3**	**95.3**	**86.9**	**96.1**	**83.2**
Queen Anne's	4	**75.7**	*74.3*	**87.8**	**80.8**	**89.9**	**81.1**
Somerset	4	**75.2**	**86.7**	**76.6**	**94.6**	**94.9**	**98.9**
St. Mary's	4	*67.8*	**82.1**	**88.2**	**85.0**	**81.1**	**93.7**
Talbot	4	**79.0**	**79.0**	**85.2**	**88.3**	**83.3**	*60.0*
Worcester[a]	4				**94.0**	**93.0**	**86.5**
Delegations scoring 75 percent or higher		72 (88.9%)					
Delegations scoring 85 percent or higher		41 (50.6%)					
Delegations scoring 95 percent or higher		7 (8.6%)					

Source: AM, vol. XXXIX 1919; vol. XL 1921; *VPMD*, 1732, 1733, 1735, 1740, 1745, 1746, 1747, 1748.

Note: Entries in bold met or surpassed 75 percent threshold. Entries in italics failed to meet 75 percent threshold.

[a]Worcester representatives began participating in the middle of the 1742–44 session.

TABLE 8.5. Roll Call Vote Agreement Scores by Constituency Delegation, New Jersey, 1738–1760

		Delegation Roll Call Vote Agreement Scores by Session (%)						
Constituency	Number of Seats	1738-39 (19 votes)	1740-41 (20 votes)	1744 (26 votes)	1745 (11 votes)	1746-48 (34 votes)	1751-54 (29 votes)	1754-60 (95 votes)
Bergen	2	73.7	76.5	100.0	88.9	54.5	89.3	75.0
Burlington	2	78.6	89.5	100.0	90.0	59.1	84.6	86.8
Burlington (city)	2	94.4	83.3	87.5	100.0	96.4	100.0[b]	67.9
Cape May	2	57.9	100.0	50.0	100.0	86.4	92.9	87.5
Essex	2	66.7	65.0	80.0	85.7	84.8	95.2	86.7
Gloucester	2	88.9	92.3	77.8	100.0	57.9	80.8	42.9
Hunterdon	2	100.0	82.4					
Hunterdon, Morris	2			76.0	88.9	33.3	25.0	
Hunterdon, Morris, Sussex	2							77.5
Middlesex	2	93.8	100.0	88.0	60.0	72.2	77.8	41.1[b]
Monmouth	2	76.5	78.9	96.0	100.0	88.9[b]	82.1	100.0[b]
Perth Amboy (city)	2	100.0	—[a]	—[a]	—[a]	100.0[b]	94.4	93.9
Salem	2	47.4	68.8	90.5	88.9	86.7		
Salem, Cumberland	2						82.1	76.9
Somerset	2	93.8	50.0	90.0	55.6	90.0	91.7	88.9

Delegations scoring 75 percent or higher   62 (76.5%)
Delegations scoring 85 percent or higher   44 (54.3%)
Delegations scoring 95 percent or higher   16 (19.8%)

Source: *VPNJ* 1738, 1740, 1741, 1744, 1745 (April), 1745 (September), 1746 (February 1745–46), 1746 (May), 1748, 1749, 1750, 1751 (January), 1751 (May), 1752, 1754 (April), 1754 (October), 1755 (February), 1755 (April), 1755 (July), 1755 (December), 1756 (March), 1756 (May), 1757 (March), 1757 (May), 1757 (August), 1757 (October), 1758 (March), 1758 (July), 1759, 1760 (March), 1760 (October); *Votes of the General Assembly* 1747 (May), 1747 (November).

Note: Entries in bold met or surpassed 75 percent threshold. Entries in italics failed to meet 75 percent threshold.

[a] One delegation member served as speaker and did not vote.

[b] During most of the 1746–48 session a Monmouth delegation member served as speaker and never voted. A Perth Amboy delegation member finished the session and never voted. During the 1751–54 session a Burlington City delegation member served as speaker and seldom voted. During most of the 1754–60 session a Monmouth delegation member served as speaker and seldom voted. A Middlesex delegation member served as speaker toward the end of the session and voted once.

agreement threshold 77 percent of the time and the 95 percent threshold almost 20 percent of the time. Some delegations enjoyed high levels of agreement across all seven sessions, while others experienced less cohesion. When Hunterdon County elected its own representatives, they voted together most of the time. When Hunterdon shared representatives with Morris County, agreement levels slipped. In the final session examined, those two counties were joined by Sussex County and the agreement score rebounded, but not to the levels the delegation had enjoyed when it was elected solely by Hunterdon voters.

Agreement scores in New York were less impressive than those in Maryland or New Jersey. During the three sessions in which roll call votes were recorded, shown in table 8.6, only half the multimember delegations surpassed the 75 percent threshold. There were two constituencies—New York and Suffolk—that regularly voted together, while the others were inconsistent. To further investigate the colony's roll call voting behavior, I examined the large number of votes recorded during the 1769–75 assembly, the session following the second heated election discussed in chapter 6. If cohesive voting were to be found in New York, it should have been during this period. But, as can be seen in table 8.7, the vote agreement scores were

TABLE 8.6. Roll Call Vote Agreement Scores by Multimember Constituency Delegation, New York, 1737–1745

| | | Delegation Roll Call Vote Agreement Scores by Session (%) | | |
| | Number of | 1737–38 | 1739–43 | 1743–45 |
Constituency	Seats	(37 votes)	(35 votes)	(27 votes)
Albany	2	*63.6*	**96.8**	**88.2**
Dutchess	2	**94.4**	*71.4*	*68.2*
King's	2	**88.6**	*53.3*	*65.4*
New York	4	**82.4**	**97.5**	**78.4**
Orange	2	*72.0*	*63.3*	*73.7*
Queens	2	*45.7*	**100.0**	**86.4**
Richmond	2	**75.7**	*51.7*	**87.5**
Suffolk	2	**94.7**	**100.0**	**93.3**
Ulster	2	*29.7*	**88.2**	*47.4*
Westchester	2	*50.0*	*69.6*	*43.5*
Delegations scoring 75 percent or higher		15 (50.0%)		
Delegations scoring 85 percent or higher		12 (40.0%)		
Delegations scoring 95 percent or higher		3 (10.0%)		

Source: JVNY 1737, 1738, 1739 (March), 1739 (August), 1740, 1741 (April), 1741 (September), 1743; *VPNY* 1744 (April), 1744 (July), 1745.

Note: Entries in bold met or surpassed 75 percent threshold. Entries in italics failed to meet 75 percent threshold.

TABLE 8.7. Roll Call Vote Agreement Scores by Multimember Constituency, New York, 1769–1775

Constituency	Number of Seats	Roll Call Vote Agreement Scores (216 votes)	Number of Roll Calls with Multiple Delegation Votes Cast
Albany	2	*62.4*	109
Cumberland	2	**95.7**	69
Dutchess	2	**86.8**	91
King's	2	**77.6**	165
New York	4	**95.1**	215
Orange	2	*72.3*	173
Queens	2	*48.2*	164
Richmond	2	**86.8**	129
Suffolk	2	*45.4*	141
Tryon	2	**100.0**	11
Ulster	2	**84.9**	166
Westchester	2	*46.2*	130
Delegations scoring 75 percent or higher		7 (58.3)	
Delegations scoring 85 percent or higher		5 (41.7)	
Delegations scoring 95 percent or higher		3 (25.0)	

Source: JVNY 1769 (April), 1769 (November), 1770, 1771, 1772, 1773, 1774, 1775.
Note: Entries in bold met or surpassed 75 percent threshold. Entries in italics failed to meet 75 percent threshold.

TABLE 8.8. Roll Call Vote Agreement Scores by Multimember Constituency Delegation, Pennsylvania, 1753 and 1764

Multimember Constituency	Number of Seats	Roll Call Vote Agreement Scores 1753 (%) (12 votes)	Roll Call Vote Agreement Scores 1764 (%) (7 votes)
Bucks	8	**75.0**	**95.9**
Chester	8	**87.0**	**98.0**
Cumberland	2	**100.0**	**100.0**
Lancaster	4	*54.8*	*60.0*
Philadelphia	8	**76.8**	*60.0*
Philadelphia (city)	2	*33.3*	**100.0**
York	2	**91.7**	**75.0**
Delegations scoring 75 percent or higher		10 (71.4%)	
Delegations scoring 85 percent or higher		7 (50.0%)	
Delegations scoring 95 percent or higher		5 (35.7%)	

Source: VPPP 1754, 46, 48, 49, 55, 56, 71–73; 1764, 11, 13–15.
Note: Entries in bold met or surpassed 75 percent threshold. Entries in italics failed to meet 75 percent threshold.

TABLE 8.9. Multimember Constituency Delegation Vote Agreement in the Massachusetts House, 1725–1765

Constituency																						Roll Call Votes
	1725	1740	1741	1751	1751	1751	1753	1753	1753	1754	1754	1754	1754	1754	1755	1755	1757	1758	1762	1764	1764	1765
Boston	N	Y	Y	N	N	Y	N	Y	Y	Y	Y	Y	N	N	N	Y	Y	Y	Y	Y	Y	Y
	N	Y	Y	N	N	Y	N	Y	Y	Y	Y	Y	N	N	N	Y	Y	Y	Y	Y	Y	Y
	N	Y	Y	N	N	Y	N	Y	Y	Y	Y	Y	N	N	N	Y	Y	N	Y	Y	N	N
	N	Y	Y	N	N	Y	N	Y	Y	Y	Y	Y	N	N	N	Y	Y	N	N	N	N	N
Salem	Y			N	N															Y	Y	Y
	Y			N	N															Y	Y	Y
Ipswich		N	N	N	N																	
		N	N	N	N																	
Newbury							N	N	N	Y	Y	N					Y	Y	Y	N	Y	
							N	N	N	Y	Y	N					N	Y	Y	Y	Y	
Cambridge							N	N	N	Y	Y	Y								Y	N	
							N	N	N	Y	Y	Y								Y	N	
Taunton							Y	Y	Y	N	N											
							Y	Y	Y	N	N											
Braintree										Y	N	N	N									
										N	Y	Y	Y									
Salem and Danvers																	Y					
																	N					
Total Yea votes	48	19	37	42	33	31	36	71	53	41	23	52	41	48	60	39	33	34	43	37	41	42
Total Nay votes	32	58	59	28	46	28	26	13	25	44	42	17	37	31	29	12	48	38	50	40	32	41
Delegation votes											51 Delegation votes, 38 unanimous (75%)											

Source: JHHR 1725, 109–10; 1739, 244–45; 1740, 46–47, 186–87; 1750, 195, 224; 1751, 46; 1753, 18, 88, 152–53, 260; 1754, 38, 152–53, 182; 1755, 59–60, 116; 1756, 375; 1757, 186–87; 1758, 97; 1761, 319–20; 1763, 255–57; 1764, 206.

Note: The date listed is the year in which the vote took place. A 1756 roll call vote did not have any multimember delegation votes.

[a] Delegation member served as speaker and did not vote. The speaker did not vote in one 1753 roll call.

only marginally higher than in the earlier assemblies and lower than those found in Maryland and New Jersey. Overall, these data provide more evidence that colonial New Yorkers were "a fractious people" (Bonomi 1971).

Fewer votes were recorded in Pennsylvania than in Maryland, New Jersey, or New York. During the 1753 and 1764 sessions, delegation agreement scores were comparable to those in New Jersey, as shown in table 8.8. Large delegations from Bucks and Chester counties almost always agreed, as did the smaller York delegation. Lancaster representatives usually split. The Pennsylvania city and county delegations varied in their cohesion, with Benjamin Franklin being the source of much of the disagreement in them. In the 1753 session, Franklin served as a Philadelphia burgess and regularly differed with his city colleague. Most of the 1764 votes revolved around the appointment of Franklin as the colony's London agent. The county delegates split on the question while the city burgesses unanimously opposed him.

The Massachusetts assembly recorded votes infrequently, and in only few sessions was more than one tallied. Moreover, there were few multimember delegations, and on some roll calls no more than one delegation member voted. But examination of the 22 recorded votes from 1725 to 1765 provides further support for the idea that colonial representatives represented their constituents' views. Most of the votes presented in table 8.9 were reasonably close, meaning that there were clearly opposing sides. Yet there was substantial delegation cohesion; of the 51 delegation votes, 75 percent were unanimous. Representatives from Cambridge and Taunton always voted alike, and Newbury's delegation only split once. Salem's members voted together; the only division came when the town shared representation with Danvers. Even Boston's four members voted together more often than they disagreed.

The data presented in tables 8.4 through 8.9 document that during the decades before independence, multimember delegations in the assemblies that recorded roll calls usually voted together. It seems reasonable to infer that because members of these delegations were elected at the same time by the same people they voted alike in keeping with their constituents' preferences. Had these members been more concerned with representing some notion of the larger good, we would have expected less uniformity in their voting. Taken together with the anecdotal evidence and the Massachusetts excise vote, it appears that colonial lawmakers strove to represent their constituents' preferences, documenting the growing dominance of delegate behavior.

NINE

Colonial Representatives and the Enduring Dilemma of Representation

Representative institutions did not arrive in America prepackaged, with set expectations for the role of either the representative or the represented. Save for New York, it took a relatively short period of time for a representative assembly to emerge in each of the colonies. Yet in each the process unfolded differently, and in none did it transpire in a smooth, uninterrupted fashion. As a result the assemblies that emerged were not modeled on Parliament. Rather, they were practical institutions devised to solve current, local governing problems. The colonists did, however, inherit the notion that as English subjects they enjoyed a right to representation. But the distinctive history of each colony allowed contrasting approaches to representation to take root.

Each colony devised rules governing who could vote for the assembly and who could serve in it. These rules mimicked those used in England, although they differed in some details and in the manner in which they were implemented. While both sets of standards were tightened over time, most white male colonists 21 years and older were entitled to vote, and many of them were eligible to serve under the formal qualifications. This was a marked difference from the situation in England, where a far smaller percentage of males were eligible to vote and only an elite few were allowed to serve. The contrast in outcomes was a product of the more generous economic context in which the colonists lived, one that allowed them to more easily meet voting and service qualification standards. The fact that a substantial proportion of the white male colonists could participate and serve planted the seeds that blossomed into American mass democracy in the nineteenth century.

Assembly seats were apportioned using different schemes in different colonies, but, as in England, with few exceptions they were organized around geographic units. The particular schemes adopted had significant implications for representation. Colonies in New England apportioned on the basis of towns. The meetings used to govern these communities proved to be the perfect vehicles for instructing their representatives. The other colonies generally apportioned on the basis of counties or parishes, electoral units that were less amenable to the exercise of direct control over legislator behavior. Thus apportionment reinforced a delegate orientation in New England while initially facilitating trustee orientations elsewhere.

Among the more visible changes that took place during the colonial era were those involving assembly elections. Seats became politically valuable as assemblies assumed significant policy-making powers. Although election schedules and voting mechanics varied across the colonies, two significant developments came to be found in most of them. First, the process of candidate emergence evolved to become more open and less mysterious. Second, although contested races were episodic, they became more intense. Candidates campaigned, election information was printed and distributed, and voters were mobilized. Indeed, by the end of the colonial era assembly campaigns had a familiar appearance to modern eyes. The rise of candidate-identification mechanisms and aggressive campaigns focused on personalities and issues presaged the rowdy mass politics associated with the Jacksonian era.

Expectations about representational roles evolved as well. The changing landscape had little impact in New England, where a preference for delegate behavior was only strengthened. The dramatic shift took place in the other colonies, where trustee-oriented representatives were pressured to adopt a more delegate-oriented approach. What prompted this development was an interaction between the changing interests of those elected to office and the changing interests of those electing them. Lawmakers came to want to stay in office, and because of that they were motivated to become attuned to the concerns of their voters. Their constituents came to make more policy demands of their local representatives, in large part because more complicated and heterogeneous polities generated more problems for lawmakers to solve. From a Burkean perspective, whereas representatives initially were directed to give greater concern to the larger public good, they were later given incentives to direct attention to their constituents' issue preferences. Publication of legislative journals and other related materials magnified the pressure on lawmakers to do their voters' bidding by giving their constituents information about their actions in the assembly.

The weight of the evidence on colonial lawmaker behavior is consistent with the claim that delegate-type behavior became the norm. Representatives even outside New England came to pursue district-centered actions and focus on providing particularized policies benefiting their constituents. Beyond anecdotes, this is more systematically demonstrated by the increase in legislation targeted at specific constituencies and by the marked voting cohesion of multimember delegations in several assemblies. The strong ties between the representatives and the represented are also demonstrated by the analysis of the Massachusetts excise battle of 1754. Delegate behavior on the part of assembly members may not have become universal, but by the end of the colonial era it was demonstrably dominant. This development was not driven by a desire to replicate Tudor era representational norms. Rather it was a pragmatic response to emerging political realities.

But the tension between the idea of working for the greater good and the lure of rewards for seeking localized benefits was never resolved. Indeed, it continues to haunt the relationship between lawmakers and constituents. The fundamentals of the relationship between the representative and the represented are the same today as they were on the eve of the Revolution. That is not to say that nothing has changed. Current lawmakers operate in a different political environment. They must compete in party primaries to gain nomination, which means a smaller party constituency may be more important to them than their larger general election constituency. And most of the electoral units that members of Congress and the state legislatures represent are many times larger and more heterogeneous than those their colonial counterparts represented. Thus the relationships they have with their electors are more distant and less personal. Finally, other structural variations come into play: term limits and multimember districts promote trustee behavior, while smaller districts and single-member districts lend themselves to a delegate orientation. Consequently, current representational incentive structures are complicated and behavioral incentives are confused.

So it comes as little surprise that lawmakers today are still torn over their roles. On the one hand, when asked what orientation they espouse, far more see themselves as trustees than as delegates (Cooper and Richardson 2006, 183; Jewell 1982, 111–12; Walhke et al. 1962, 281). On the other hand, they also profess reverence for and adherence to their constituents' opinions (Patterson, Hedlund, and Boynton 1975, 139–42; Rosenthal 2004, 42–44). To further complicate matters, representational orientations suffer from instability, with lawmakers changing their perspectives over time (Price 1985). And they alter their roles on an issue-by-issue basis, today being more likely to vote their constituents' preferences on taxes and gambling policies while voting their consciences on issues such as abortion and the death penalty (Rosenthal 2004, 47–48).

In the end, lawmakers still grapple with the fundamental dilemma that bedeviled their colonial predecessors. Most operate as politicos between the two extremes. But, as one Idaho lawmaker reflected during a wrenching debate over capital punishment, "It's one of the great questions of political thought: 'Do you vote your conscience or do you vote your district?' By the way, it's unanswerable" (Squire and Moncrief 2015, 171). Actually, the question is answerable, but, as the colonial experience shows, the answer depends on the political structures under which lawmakers operate and the incentives given them. At different times and in different places, representatives will reach different conclusions. But the prevailing political pressures will usually push them toward delegate behavior.

Appendix A

Instructions to Representatives

Electoral Unit	Year	Subject(s)	Source
Connecticut			
Colchester	1725	County boundaries	*ERC* (1864, 29)
Colchester	1726	Town boundaries	*ERC* (1864, 31)
Colchester	1727 (Apr.)	Town boundaries	*ERC* (1864, 33)
Colchester	1727 (Oct.)	Town boundaries	*ERC* (1864, 33)
Danbury	1770	Colony taxes	*MS* (1770)
Guilford	1772	Main town road	Steiner (1897, 213)
Guilford	1773	Western lands	Steiner (1897, 146–47)
Hartford	1716	New Haven Collegiate School	"Hartford Town Votes" (1897, 323)
Hartford	1765	Stamp Act	*CC* (1765a)
Lebanon	1768	Great Britain relations, imports	*NLG* (1768)
Middletown	1714	Town boundaries	*History of Middlesex County* (1884, 135)
Middletown	1775	Colonial congress, militia, trade restrictions	*Connecticut Gazette* (1775)
New Haven	1665	Mr. Leete's summons	*ATR* (1919, 139)
New Haven	1666	County rate	*ATR* (1919, 194)
New Haven	1668	Town boundaries	*ATR* (1919, 230)
New Haven	1673	Town boundaries	*ATR* (1919, 310)
New Haven	1674	Town agreements	*ATR* (1919, 318)
New Haven	1682	Indian complaints	*ATR* (1919, 419)
New Haven	1693	Wallingford Bridge agreement	*ATR* (1962, 102)
New Haven	1694	Magistrate salaries	*ATR* (1962, 109)
New Haven	1707	Thomas Goodsell lawsuit	*ATR* (1962, 265)
New Haven	1715	West farms petition	*ATR* (1962, 381)
New Haven	1716	East farms petition	*ATR* (1962, 387)
New Haven	1732 (Apr.)	Pine Bridge	*ATR* (1962, 591)

Electoral Unit	Year	Subject(s)	Source
New Haven	1732 (Sept.)	Pine Bridge	*ATR* (1962, 591)
New Haven	1765	Stamp Act	*CC* (1765b)
New London	1713	Town expenses	Caulkins (1860, 430)
New London	1722	Grammar school	Caulkins (1860, 399)
New London	1765	Stamp Act	*BPB* (1765d)
Norwich	1765	Stamp Act	*NLG* (1765)
Norwich	1769	Constitutional rights, colonial relations, manufacturing, lobbying, ungranted lands, petitions publication	*NLG* (1769)
Norwalk	1664	Town boundaries	*AHRN* (1865, 50)
Norwalk	1668	Town boundaries	*AHRN* (1865, 54)
Wallingford	1712	Town copper mines	Beach (1912, 55)
Wallingford	1775	Town boundaries	Davis (1870, 410)
Windham	1727	Land grant	Larned (1874, 270)
Windham	1733	Manor annexation	Larned (1874, 353)
Windham	1766	Judicial process, sheriffs regulation, court clerks, king's attorneys, multiple officeholding, debt recovery, commerce, husbandry, industry, legislative proceedings transparency, charter privileges	*NLG* (1766)
Windham	1768	Manufacturers, colonial congress	*BEP* (1769a)
Woodbury	1751	New county	Cothren (1854, 153)
Woodbury	1752	County boundary	Cothren (1854, 154)
Woodbury	1774	Shipley speech	Cothren (1854, 175)

Maryland

Electoral Unit	Year	Subject(s)	Source
Anne-Arundel County	1765	Charter privileges, colonial congress, Stamp Act	*MDG* (1765c)
Prince George's County	1754	Anti-Catholic laws	*PAG* (1754b)
Somerset County (130 freeholders)	1755	Bill of supply	*MDG* (1755a)
Talbot County	1747	Tobacco law	*MDG* (1747a)
Talbot County	1750	Inspection law	*MDG* (1750a)
Talbot County	1757	Acadians	*MDG* (1757)

Massachusetts

Electoral Unit	Year	Subject(s)	Source
Abington	1766	Boston riot	Hobart (1839, 135)
Amesbury	1726	County boundaries	Merrill (1880, 185)
Amesbury	1734	Free school	Merrill (1880, 195)
Amesbury	1735	County boundaries	Merrill (1880, 198)
Amesbury	1761	Courts relocation	Merrill (1880, 231)
Amesbury	1766	Boston riots	*BG* (1766b)
Andover	1728	Tax abatement	*ATMR* (1961, 5150)
Andover	1735	County boundaries	*ATMR* (1961, 5161–62)
Andover	1765	Stamp Act	*ATMR* (1961, 5203–4, 5205)

Andover	1766	Boston riot	*ATMR* (1961, 5208)
Andover	1773	British government	*ATMR* (1961, 5228–29)
Attleborough	1766	Boston riot	Daggett (1894, 119)
Attleborough	1774	Provincial congress	*PRG* (1774)
Barnstable	1655	Indian boundary	*Barnstable Town Records* (1910, 4)
Barnstable	1773	Great Britain relations	*Barnstable Town Records* (1910, 44)
Barnstable	1774	Charter privileges, provincial congress	Palfrey (1840, 52–54)
Bellingham	1774	Great Britain relations	Partridge (1919, 125)
Berwick	1772	Superior court judges	*History of York County* (1880, 296)
Berwick	1774	Charter privileges, provincial congress	*History of York County* (1880, 297)
Beverly	1765 (Sept.)	Great Britain relations, riots	*BPB* (1765a)
Beverly	1765 (Oct.)	Jury trials, government spending	*History of Essex County*, vol. I (1888, 699)
Beverly	1769	Constitutional measures	*History of Essex County*, vol. I (1888, 699)
Beverly	1772	Charter privileges	*History of Essex County*, vol. I (1888, 699)
Beverly	1773	Judicial salaries	*EG* (1773e)
Beverly	1774	Charter privileges, provincial congress	*EG* (1774)
Billerica	1731	Charter privileges	Hazan (1883, 226)
Billerica	1766	Stamp Act	Hazan (1883, 226)
Bolton	1773	Charter privileges	*MS* (1773d)
Boston	1653		*SRRC* (1881, 114)
Boston	1661		*SRRC* (1881, 159)
Boston	1662		*RRCB* (1881, 6)
Boston	1663	Town concernments	*RRCB* (1881, 15, 17)
Boston	1664		*RRCB* (1881, 20)
Boston	1665	Privileges, number of representatives, town officers, weights and measures, brick standards	*RRCB* (1881, 26)
Boston	1669		*RRCB* (1881, 48)
Boston	1677	Peace efforts, justice system, charter, number of representatives, weights and measures, brick standards, debt laws	*RRCB* (1881, 110)
Boston	1679	Peace efforts, justice system, charter, number of representatives, weights and measures, brick standards, debt laws, town planning, currency, militia, pewter and silver standards, ecclesiastical laws	*RRCB* (1881, 133–34)
Boston	1681	Number of representatives	*RRCB* (1881, 142)
Boston	1683	Legal code, candle standards, butter standards, wheat price notifications	*RRCB* (1881, 160)
Boston	1685		*RRCB* (1881, 177)
Boston	1698		*RRCB* (1881, 228)
Boston	1700		*RRCB* (1881, 241)
Boston	1701	Tithing law	*RRCB* (1883, 5–6)

Electoral Unit	Year	Subject(s)	Source
Boston	1702	Tax abatement, powder houses (selectmen request)	*RRCB* (1884, 22–23)
Boston	1711	Land use plan (selectmen request)	*RRCB* (1884, 151)
Boston	1714 (June)	Provincial loan (selectmen request)	*RRCB* (1884, 207)
Boston	1714 (Nov.)	Welfare (selectmen request)	*RRCB* (1884, 217)
Boston	1715		*RRCB* (1883, 112)
Boston	1716 (Mar.)	Communicable diseases	*RRCB* (1883, 119)
Boston	1716 (June)	Town clock	*RRCB* (1883, 122)
Boston	1717	Cord wood sealers	*RRCB* (1883, 131)
Boston	1719	Common good	*RRCB* (1883, 139)
Boston	1720	Charles River bridge	*RRCB* (1883, 145)
Boston	1721 (Mar.)	Taxes	*RRCB* (1883, 152)
Boston	1721 (May)	Civil rights, economic development, public land logging, militia, river navigation, agent payment, riot measures, charter, public health, public lands	*RRCB* (1883, 154–55)
Boston	1721 (Aug.)	May instructions, plague law, charter privileges, Indian policy, poverty, council dispute, French silks	*RRCB* (1883, 156–57)
Boston	1722	Previous year's instructions, smallpox vaccinations	*RRCB* (1883, 166–67)
Boston	1723	Regulation of Negroes and mulattoes	*RRCB* (1883, 175)
Boston	1724	Tithing men	*RRCB* (1883, 185)
Boston	1725	Tithing laws	*RRCB* (1883, 192)
Boston	1726	Gambling	*RRCB* (1883, 200)
Boston	1727	County boundary	*RRCB* (1883, 213)
Boston	1728	Wharf	*RRCB* (1883, 223)
Boston	1729	Civil rights and properties, governor salary	*RRCB* (1885a, 8)
Boston	1731	Charter privileges, governor salary	*RRCB* (1885a, 23–24)
Boston	1732	Charter privileges, governor salary, taxes, public lands	*RRCB* (1885a, 32–34)
Boston	1733 (May)	Charter privileges, governor salary, taxes, public lands	*RRCB* (1885a, 42–44)
Boston	1733 (Sept.)	Representatives' discretion on treasury supply	*RRCB* (1885a, 52)
Boston	1734 (May)	Governor salary, militia fines	*RRCB* (1885a, 86–87)
Boston	1734 (June)	Militia fines	*RRCB* (1885a, 91)
Boston	1736	Charter privileges, taxes, treasury audit	*RRCB* (1885a, 146–47)
Boston	1738 (May)	Trade, taxes, public currency	*RRCB* (1885a, 197–201)

Boston	1738 (Nov.)	Rumney Marsh	*RRCB* (1885, 208)
Boston	1739 (May)	Trade, taxes, paper currency	*RRCB* (1885a, 225–29)
Boston	1739 (Sept.)	Coastal defenses	*RRCB* (1885a, 232–33)
Boston	1740	Grain measurement	*RRCB* (1885a, 251)
Boston	1741	Representatives' pay	*RRCB* (1885a, 275)
Boston	1742	Grain monopolies	*RRCB* (1885a, 304)
Boston	1743	Cart regulations	*RRCB* (1885b, 11)
Boston	1744	Taxes	*RRCB* (1885b, 58–60)
Boston	1745 (Apr.)	Assessors	*RRCB* (1885b, 71)
Boston	1745 (May)	Lottery (*rejected*)	*RRCB* (1885b, 74–75)
Boston	1746	Sherriff's behavior	*RRCB* (1885b, 71)
Boston	1747	Grain millers' behavior	*RRCB* (1885b, 117)
Boston	1748	Scavengers	*RRCB* (1885b, 140)
Boston	1751 (Mar.)	Firewards	*RRCB* (1885b, 188)
Boston	1751 (June)	Assessments	*RRCB* (1885b, 203)
Boston	1752	By-laws revisions, firewards	*RRCB* (1885b, 206–7)
Boston	1753	Assessments	*RRCB* (1885b, 238–41)
Boston	1754 (May)	Chimneys, cadets, estate valuations	*RRCB* (1885b, 258)
Boston	1754 (Aug.)	Excise bill	*RRCB* (1885b, 260)
Boston	1755 (Jan.)	United colonial government	*RRCB* (1885b, 266)
Boston	1755 (May)	Excise tax, farmers' taxes, contractors as representatives, tax burden, charter privileges	*RRCB* (1885b, 277–78)
Boston	1756	Powder house	*RRCB* (1885b, 290)
Boston	1760	Colony agent, taxes	*RRCB* (1886, 36–37)
Boston	1763 (Mar.)	Firewards, market forestalling	*RRCB* (1886, 83, 86)
Boston	1763 (Oct.)	Wharfs	*RRCB* (1886, 100)
Boston	1764	Charter privileges, multiple officeholding, excise taxes, judicial support, garrison expenses, trade, taxation without representation, smallpox expenses and prevention	*RRCB* (1886, 119–22)
Boston	1765 (May)	Building codes, gravel digging, smallpox prevention	*RRCB* (1886, 148–49)
Boston	1765 (Sept.)	Stamp Act	*RRCB* (1886, 155–57)
Boston	1765 (Dec.)	Assembly prorogation	*RRCB* (1886, 161)
Boston	1766 (Jan.)	Justice administration, Stamp Act	*RRCB* (1886, 161–62)

Electoral Unit	Year	Subject(s)	Source
Boston	1766 (May)	Bankrupt Act, appropriations, executive salaries, slavery, trade, defense expenditures, Great Britain relations	*RRCB* (1886, 181–84)
Boston	1766 (Oct.)	Boston riot	*RRCB* (1886, 187–88)
Boston	1766 (Dec.)	Compensation Act	*RRCB* (1886, 194–95)
Boston	1767 (Mar.)	Slavery	*RRCB* (1886, 200)
Boston	1767 (Dec.)	Government debt, trade, alcohol consumption, Great Britain relations	*RRCB* (1886, 227–30)
Boston	1768 (May)	Excise tax on spirituous liquors	*RRCB* (1886, 252)
Boston	1768 (June)	Great Britain relations, ship seizures	*RRCB* (1886, 257–59)
Boston	1769	Parliamentary debate rights, quartering of troops, taxes, ships and cargoes confiscation	*RRCB* (1886, 285–89)
Boston	1770	Great Britain relations, assembly session location	*RRCB* (1887, 26–32)
Boston	1772	Great Britain relations,	*RRCB* (1887, 83–86)
Boston	1773 (May 5)	Great Britain relations	*RRCB* (1887, 131–34)
Boston	1773 (May 11)	Lamp legislation	*RRCB* (1887, 136)
Boston	1773 (May 14)	Revenue to pay provincial agent	*RRCB* (1887, 141)
Boston	1774	Provincial congress	*RRCB* (1887, 191–92)
Boxford	1689	Charter privileges	Perley (1880, 105)
Boxford	1765	Stamp Act, government spending	Perley (1880, 202–4)
Bradford	1689	Taxation and representation	Kingsbury (1883, 89)
Bradford	1773	Great Britain relations	Kingsbury (1883, 100)
Braintree	1717		*RTB* (1886, 92)
Braintree	1739	Fishing regulations	*RTB* (1886, 220)
Braintree	1748	Fishing regulations	*RTB* (1886, 286)
Braintree	1757	Military conscription	*RTB* (1886, 356)
Braintree	1765	Stamp Act	*RTB* (1886, 404–6)
Braintree	1767	Boston riot	*RTB* (1886, 413)
Braintree	1769	Charter privileges, governor's behavior, military in province, provincial agent, judicial process	*RTB* (1886, 424), *EG* (1769b)
Braintree	1773	Fasting and prayer day	*RTB* (1886, 440)
Braintree	1774		*RTB* (1886, 448)
Brimfield	1731	Charter privileges	*History of Western Massachusetts*, vol. II, part III (1855, 17)

Brimfield	1759	Town boundaries	*History of the Connecticut Valley*, vol. II (1879, 1018)
Brookline	1739	School farm land	*MRBR* (1875, 150)
Brookline	1769	Charter privileges, taxes	*Boston Weekly News-Letter* (1769)
Brookline	1772	Charter privileges	*History of Norfolk County* (1884, 847–48)
Brookline	1773		*MRBR* (1875, 241–42)
Brookline	1774	Charter privileges, provincial congress	*MRBR* (1875, 248–49)
Brunswick	1754	Town taxing power	Wheeler and Wheeler (1878, 116–17)
Cambridge	1701	Medford River mill	*RTC* (1901, 338)
Cambridge	1765	Stamp Act	*BEP* (1765b)
Cambridge	1766	Boston riot, separation of powers, assembly public gallery	Paige (1877, 139–40)
Cambridge	1769	Charter privileges, provincial budget	*EG* (1769a)
Cambridge	1772	Great Britain relations	Paige (1877, 144–45)
Cambridge	1774	Mandamus Council	*History of Middlesex County*, vol. I (1880, 342)
Charlestown	1720	Charles River bridge	Frothingham (1845, 249)
Charlestown	1754	Excise bill	Frothingham (1845, 263)
Charlestown	1765	Stamp Act	Frothingham (1845, 272–73)
Charlestown	1766	Boston riot	*MAG* (1766)
Charlestown	1772	Judicial salaries, Great Britain relations	*MAG* (1772)
Chelmsford	1697	Provincial assessment	Waters (1917, 137)
Chelmsford	1729	Town boundaries	Allen (1820, 44)
Chelmsford	1754	Town boundaries	Allen (1820, 50)
Chelmsford	1765	Stamp Act	Waters (1917, 191)
Chelmsford	1766	Boston riot	Waters (1917, 192)
Chelmsford	1773	Great Britain relations	Waters (1917, 194–97)
Chelmsford	1774 (May)	Great Britain relations	Allen (1820, 57–58)
Chelmsford	1774 (Sept.)	Charter privileges, provincial congress	Allen (1820, 61), Waters (1917, 207)
Chelsea	1766	Stamp Act	Chamberlain (1908, 418)
Chilmark	1693	Town boundaries	Banks (1911, 272)
Concord	1765	Stamp Act	*History of Middlesex County*, vol. I (1880, 385)
Concord	1773	Judicial salaries	*MS* (1773g)
Danvers	1765 (Oct.)	Stamp Act	Hanson (1848, 69–71)
Danvers	1765 (Dec.)	Stamp Act	Hanson (1848, 71–73)
Danvers	1772	Charter privileges	Hanson (1848, 75–78)
Danvers	1773	Charter privileges, judicial salaries	*EG* (1773d)
Danvers	1774	Charter privileges, provincial congress	Hanson (1848, 80)
Dedham	1700	Town boundaries	*ERTD* (1899, 273)
Dedham	1732	County boundaries	Worthington (1827, 27)
Dedham	1735	County boundaries	Worthington (1827, 28)
Dedham	1765	Stamp Act	Worthington (1827, 30, 64)
Dedham	1766	Boston riot	Worthington (1827, 31, 64–65)

Electoral Unit	Year	Subject(s)	Source
Dedham	1768	Liquor excise tax	Worthington (1827, 32)
Dedham	1773	Charter privileges, judicial salaries	*MS* (1773b)
Deerfield	1763	County boundary	Sheldon (1895, 577)
Dighton	1728	Charter privileges	*History of Bristol County*, vol. I (1883, 222)
Dighton	1733	School land	*History of Bristol County*, vol. I (1883, 222)
Dighton	1774	Charter privileges, provincial congress	*History of Bristol County*, vol. I (1883, 226)
Dorchester	1727	Grammar school land	Dorchester Antiquarian and Historical Society (1859, 435–36)
Dorchester	1765	Stamp Act	Orcutt (1893, 124)
Dorchester	1772	Charter privileges	Orcutt (1893, 126)
Dorchester	1774	Liberties, provincial congress	Orcutt (1893, 130)
Dover	1658	Charter privileges	*Historical Memoranda* (1900, 50, 144, 146)
Dover	1660	County court, charter privileges, town officer oath	*Historical Memoranda* (1900, 342)
Dover	1663	Portsmouth, county court schedule	Wadleigh (1913, 58)
Dover	1665	Charter privileges, county court schedule	*Historical Memoranda* (1900, 70)
Dover	1666	Charter privileges, crown support.	*Historical Memoranda* (1900, 94)
Dover	1667	Charter privileges, fortifications	*Historical Memoranda* (1900, 96)
Duxbury	1734	Town boundaries	*CORTD* (1893, 244)
Duxbury	1751	Cattle on beach	*CORTD* (1893, 306)
Duxbury	1762	Duxborough North End petition	*CORTD* (1893, 328)
Duxbury	1765	Stamp Act	*CORTD* (1893, 333–34)
Duxbury	1768	Alcohol excise tax	*CORTD* (1893, 339)
Eastham	1773	Great Britain relations	Pratt (1844, 74)
Falmouth	1765	Stamp Act	*History of Cumberland Co.* (1880, 52)
Falmouth	1773	Great Britain relations	Willis (1865, 493)
Falmouth	1774 (May)	Tea reimbursement	Willis (1865, 498)
Falmouth	1774 (Sept.)	Provincial congress	Freeman (1821, 24–25)
Framingham	1721	Land grant	Barry (1847, 47)
Framingham	1765	Stamp Act	Barry (1847, 89–90)
Framingham	1774	Great Britain relations	Barry (1847, 91)
Freetown	1774	Tea Party reparations	Nichols (1902, 17–18)
Gloucester	1754	Excise bill	Babson (1860, 344)
Gloucester	1765	Stamp Act	Babson (1860, 353–54)
Gloucester	1769	Follow Boston's lead	Babson (1860, 359)
Gloucester	1772	Great Britain relations, judicial salaries	*MS* (1773a)
Gorham	1774	Charter privileges, provincial congress	Pierce (1862, 119–20)
Great Barrington	1770	Town boundaries	Taylor (1882, 221–22)
Groton, Shirley, and Pepperell	1765	Stamp Act, taxes, Boston riot	Chandler (1883, 115)
Groton, Shirley, and Pepperell	1773 (Apr.)	Judicial salaries	*BG* (1773a)

Groton, Shirley, and Pepperell	1773 (July)	Charter privileges	Butler (1848, 331–32)
Hadley	1709	Town boundaries	Judd (1863, 196)
Hadley	1772	Charter privileges	*History of Western Massachusetts*, vol. II, part III (1855, 220)
Hanover	1754	Excise bill	Barry (1853, 170)
Hampton	1655	Weekly market	Dow (1893, 50), *RGC* (1854b, 244)
Hardwick	1754	Fine remittance	Paige (1883, 48)
Hardwick	1763	County boundary	Paige (1883, 49)
Hardwick	1766 (Aug.)	Boston riot	Paige (1883, 65)
Hardwick	1766 (Nov.)	Boston riot	Paige (1883, 66)
Hardwick	1773	Charter privileges	Paige (1883, 70–72)
Hardwick	1774	Charter privileges, provincial congress	Paige (1883, 88–89)
Haverhill	1765	Stamp Act	Chase (1861, 363–64)
Haverhill	1770	Assembly meeting location, laws expiration	*BEP* (1770)
Harvard	1773	Charter privileges	*BG* (1773e)
Hingham	1666	Relations with England	Lincoln (1827, 82)
Hingham	1773	Great Britain relations, judicial salaries	Lincoln (1827, 98–99)
Holliston	1769	Follow Boston's instructions	Morse (1856, 329)
Ipswich	1682	Land rights	Felt (1834, 127)
Ipswich	1693	County boundaries	Felt (1834, 63)
Ipswich	1695	Charter privileges	Felt (1834, 123)
Ipswich	1736	County boundaries	Felt (1834, 63)
Ipswich	1755 (Jan.)	Union of colonies	Felt (1834, 128)
Ipswich	1755 (Oct.)	Great Britain relations	Felt (1834, 128)
Ipswich	1765	Charter privileges	*BPB* (1765c)
Ipswich	1766	Boston riot	*History of Essex County*, vol. I (1888, 640)
Ipswich	1772	Judicial salaries, provincial agent	*EG* (1773a)
Ipswich	1774	Charter privileges, provincial congress	Crowell (1868, 202)
Kingston	1766	Boston riot	*History of Plymouth County*, vol. I (1884, 262)
Kittery	1765	Stamp Act	Stackpole (1903, 233)
Lancaster	1728	County boundary	Marvin (1879, 191); Willard (1826, 49)
Lancaster	1731	Governor's salary	Willard (1826, 48–49)
Lancaster	1754	United colonies plans	Willard (1826, 50)
Lancaster	1766	Boston riots	Marvin (1879, 269)
Lancaster	1773	Great Britain relations	Willard (1826, 51)
Lancaster	1774	Tea compensation	Willard (1826, 52)
Leicester, Spencer, Paxton	1765	Stamp Act	Washburn (1860, 280, 434–38)

Electoral Unit	Year	Subject(s)	Source
Leicester, Spencer, Paxton	1773 (Jan.)	Boston support, Great Britain relations	*MS* (1773e)
Leicester, Spencer, Paxton	1773 (May)	Slave trade	Washburn (1860, 280, 442–43)
Leicester, Spencer, Paxton	1773 (Dec.)	Great Britain relations	Washburn (1860, 439–42)
Leicester, Spencer, Paxton	1774 (May)	Boston port	Washburn (1860, 444–45)
Leicester, Spencer, Paxton	1774 (Sept.)	Charter privileges, provincial congress	Washburn (1860, 450–51)
Lexington	1765	Stamp Act, charter privileges	Hudson (1913, 69–72)
Lexington	1772	Great Britain relations	Hudson (1913, 77–81)
Lexington	1774	Great Britain relations	Hudson (1913, 84–85)
Lunenburg	1754	Unimproved land tax	*ERTL* (1896, 166)
Lunenburg, Fitchburgh	1774	Riots, charter privileges, treating, provincial congress	*ORTF* (1898, 99–100)
Lynn	1766	Boston riot	Lewis (1829, 168)
Lynn	1773	Great Britain relations	*MS* (1773f)
Malden	1765	Stamp Act	Corey (1899, 723)
Malden	1766 (Oct.)	Boston riot	Corey (1899, 724)
Malden	1766 (Dec.)	Boston riot (reconsidered)	Corey (1899, 724)
Malden	1769	Charter privileges, provincial budget	Corey (1899, 726)
Malden	1773	Judicial salaries, humiliation day	Corey (1899, 731–32)
Malden	1774 (Aug.)	Immorality suppression of, humiliation day	Corey (1899, 732–33)
Malden	1774 (Sept.)	Charter privileges, provincial congress	Corey (1899, 738–39)
Marblehead	1754	Excise bill	Roads (1880, 63)
Marblehead	1765	Stamp Act, taxes	*BEP* (1765b)
Marblehead	1769	Great Britain relations	*History of Essex County*, vol. II (1888, 1080), Roads (1880, 80–81)
Marblehead	1774	Port bill, charter privileges	Roads (1880, 99–102)
Marlborough	1773 (Jan.)	Great Britain relations	Hudson (1862, 148–50)
Marlborough	1773 (Sept.)	Charter privileges	Hudson (1862, 152)
Marlborough	1774	Charter privileges	*History of Middlesex County*, vol. III (1890, 822)
Marshfield	1765	Stamp Act, Boston riot	Richards (1901, 100–101)
Marshfield	1774 (Jan.)	Tea party	*MAG* (1774)
Marshfield	1774 (Sept.)	Provincial congress	Richards (1901, 104)

Medfield	1765	Stamp Act, provincial budget	Tilden (1887, 151–52)
Medfield	1766	Boston riot	Tilden (1887, 153)
Medfield	1767	Foreign imports, local manufacturers	*MAG* (1767; 1768)
Medfield	1773	Rights and liberties, slave trade	*MAG* (1773b)
Medfield	1774	Charter privileges	Tilden (1887, 162–63)
Medford	1712	Local ministry financial support	Brooks (1855, 211)
Medford	1732	Charter privileges	Brooks (1855, 105)
Medford	1765	Stamp Act	*MAG* (1765)
Medford	1772	Judicial salaries, Great Britain relations	*MAG* (1773a)
Medway	1765	Stamp Act, Boston riot	Jameson (1886, 52–53)
Medway	1766 (May)	Boston riot	Jameson (1886, 53)
Medway	1766 (Nov.)	Boston riot	Jameson (1886, 53)
Medway	1773	Constitutional rights	*BEP* (1773b)
Medway	1774	Provincial congress	Jameson (1886, 55)
Mendon	1692	County tax assessments, Nipmuck River bridge, county commissioners assessment	Metcalf (1880, 119–20, 125)
Mendon	1765	Stamp Act	Metcalf (1880, 298)
Mendon	1766 (Aug.)	Boston riot	Metcalf (1880, 301)
Mendon	1766 (Sept.)	Boston riot (reconsidered)	Metcalf (1880, 301)
Mendon	1766 (Oct.)	Boston riot (reconsidered again)	Metcalf (1880, 301–2)
Mendon	1773	Judicial salaries, standing armies, quartering of troops, dockyard law, iron manufacturing, wool transportation	*BG* (1773b)
Middleborough	1765	Stamp Act	Weston 1906 (106–7)
Middleborough	1774	Charter privileges, provincial congress	Weston (1906, 110–11)
Milton	1765	Stamp Act, Boston riot, militia	Teele (1887, 419–20)
Milton	1766	Boston riot	*History of Norfolk County* (1884, 746)
Milton	1773	Great Britain relations, judicial salaries	Teele (1887, 420–21)
Needham	1766	Boston riot	Clarke (1912, 186)
Newbury	1685	Representative's attendance	Currier (1902, 679)
Newbury	1765	Stamp Act	Coffin (1845, 230)
Newbury	1774	Charter privileges	Coffin (1845, 244)
Newburyport	1765	Stamp Act, riots	*BPB* (1765b)
Newburyport	1766	Boston riot	*BG* (1766b)
Newburyport	1773	Great Britain relations, town name	Cushing (1826, 7); Currier (1906, 34)
Newburyport	1774	Charter privileges, provincial congress	Currier (1906, 535–37)
New Cambridge	1689	Freemen qualifications	Smith (1880, 51)
Newton	1765	Stamp Act, provincial budget	Smith (1880, 318–19); Jackson (1854, 177–78)
Newton	1766	Boston riot	Jackson (1854, 178)

Electoral Unit	Year	Subject(s)	Source
Newton	1773	Judicial salaries	*BEP* (1773a)
Newton	1774		Jackson (1854, 183, 396)
Northampton	1770	County court sessions	Trumbull (1902, 331)
Northampton	1773	Pascommuck incorporation	Trumbull (1902, 334–35)
Norton	1765	Stamp Act, riots	*BEP* (1765f)
Oakham	1765	Stamp Act	*History of Worcester County*, vol. II (1889, 1087)
Peabody	1765 (Oct.)	Stamp Act	*History of Essex County*, vol. II (1888, 1008)
Peabody	1765 (Dec.)	Stamp Act	*History of Essex County*, vol. II (1888, 1008)
Peabody	1772	Union of provinces, charter privileges, government salaries	*History of Essex County*, vol. II (1888, 1009)
Peabody	1774	Charter privileges, provincial congress	*History of Essex County*, vol. II (1888, 1009)
Pembroke	1740	Charter privileges	*History of Plymouth County*, vol. I (1884, 238)
Pembroke	1765	Stamp Act, provincial budget	*BEP* (1765e)
Pembroke	1772	Great Britain relations, charter privileges, judicial salaries	*History of Plymouth County*, vol. I (1884, 238–39)
Petersham	1773	Great Britain relations	*EG* (1773b)
Pittsfield	1774	Tea Party	Smith (1869, 184–86)
Plymouth	1754	Excise bill	*RTP* (1903, 63)
Plymouth	1765	Stamp Act, provincial budget	*RTP* (1903, 164–67)
Plymouth	1766	Boston riot	*RTP* (1903, 181–82)
Plymouth	1768	Spirituous liquor excise tax	*RTP* (1903, 200)
Plymouth	1772	Supreme Court judges	*RTP* (1903, 266)
Plymouth	1774	Charter privileges, provincial congress	*RTP* (1903, 293)
Plympton	1765	Follow Boston's lead	Griffith (1913, 92)
Plympton	1774	Charter privileges	Griffith (1913, 95)
Princeton	1774	Charter privileges, provincial congress	Hannaford (1853, 37–38)
Reading	1765	Stamp Act	*History of Middlesex County*, vol. II (1880, 276)
Reading	1773	Judicial salaries, Great Britain relations	*History of Middlesex County*, vol. II (1880, 277)
Rehoboth	1773	Charter privileges	*Providence Gazette* (1773a)
Rochester	1772	Tory sentiments	Leonard (1907, 127)
Rochester	1773	Great Britain relations, taxes, gubernatorial salary, Supreme Court judges	*History of Plymouth County*, vol. I (1884, 330–31)
Rochester	1774	Charter privileges	Leonard (1907, 128)
Rowley	1765	Stamp Act, riots	*BEP* (1765c)
Rowley	1772	Judicial salaries	*Providence Gazette* (1772)
Rowley	1773	Great Britain relations	*EG* (1773c)
Roxbury	1688	Colony government	Ellis (1847, 78)
Roxbury	1765	Stamp Act	Drake (1878, 20–21)
Roxbury	1769	Great Britain relations, quartering of troops, judicial process, provincial budget, manufactures	*BPB* (1769)

Roxbury	1772	Judicial salaries	*MS* (1772)
Rumford	1740	Town be in Massachusetts	*CTR* (1894, 55)
Rutland	1765	Stamp Act	Reed (1836, 60)
Rutland	1773	Great Britain relations	Reed (1836, 60–61)
Salem	1663	Freemen qualifications	*TRS* (1913, 37)
Salem	1685		*TRS* (1934, 135–36)
Salem	1686	Assembly participation	*TRS* (1934, 162)
Salem	1720	Provincial budget, Charles River bridge	Felt (1827, 370)
Salem	1735	Fisheries decay, trade policies	Felt (1827, 410)
Salem	1738	Ministers and marriage policies	Felt (1827, 415)
Salem	1765	Stamp Act, riots	*BEP* (1765d)
Salem	1769	Troop conduct, revenue law	*Standard History of Essex County* (1878, 366)
Salem	1773	Slave trade	*EG* (1773f)
Salisbury	1772	Charter privileges	*Standard History of Essex County* (1878, 406)
Salisbury	1774	Great Britain relations	*History of Essex County*, vol. II (1888, 1453)
Sandwich	1717	Wolf fence	*History of Barnstable County* (1890, 326)
Sandwich	1773 (Mar.)	Great Britain relations	*MS* (1773h)
Sandwich	1773 (May)	Slavery	*History of Barnstable County* (1890, 287)
Scituate	1768	Alcohol excise tax	Deane (1831, 108)
Sheffield	1773	New York encroachment, judicial salaries	*History of Western Massachusetts*, vol. II-Part III (1855, 583)
Sherburne	1742	French prisoners	Bliss (1896, 185)
Shrewsbury	1772	Charter privileges	Ward (1826, 30)
Southborough	1765	Stamp Act	*History of Worcester County*, vol. II (1879, 293)
Springfield	1677	Settlement of accounts	Burt (1899, 131)
Springfield	1694	Election procedures	Burt (1899, 334)
Springfield	1697	County courts	Burt (1899, 348)
Springfield	1702	Town ministry land	Burt (1899, 362–63)
Springfield	1708	County courts	Burt (1899, 380)
Springfield	1729	Town land control	Burt (1899, 447)
Springfield	1774	Boston instructions	Booth (1904, 290)
Stoughton	1766	Boston riot	Huntoon (1893, 331–32)
Stoughton	1773	Charter privileges	Huntoon (1893, 333–34)
Stoughton	1774	Charter privileges, provincial congress	Huntoon (1893, 344)
Stow	1766	Taxes, government expenditures	*History of Middlesex County*, vol. II (1880, 355)
Sturbridge	1765	Stamp Act	*History of Worcester County*, vol. II (1879, 357)
Sturbridge	1766	Boston riot	*History of Worcester County*, vol. II (1879, 357–58)
Sudbury	1734	School farm land grant	Hudson (1889, 308)
Sudbury	1765	Stamp Act	Hudson (1889, 359)
Sudbury	1773	Charter privileges	Hudson (1889, 361)

Electoral Unit	Year	Subject(s)	Source
Suffield	1721	Town boundaries	Sheldon (1879, 206)
Sutton	1731	Provincial budget	Benedict and Tracy (1878, 44)
Sutton	1766	Boston riot	Benedict and Tracy (1878, 84)
Sutton	1773	Charter privileges, judicial salaries	Benedict and Tracy (1878, 89); Town of Millbury (1915, 39)
Topsfield	1698	Town boundaries	*TRT* (1917, 100a)
Topsfield	1699	Town boundaries	*TRT* (1917, 100d)
Topsfield	1731	Ipswich River fish	*TRT* (1917, 340)
Topsfield	1766	Boston riot	*TRT* (1920, 248–49)
Townsend	1773	Great Britain relations	*BG* (1773c)
Walpole	1773	Charter privileges, judicial salaries	Doggett (1930, 9–10)
Walpole	1774	Charter privileges, provincial congress	Lewis (1905, 110)
Waltham	1774	Provincial congress	*History of Middlesex County*, vol. III (1890, 711)
Watertown	1731	Charles River bridge	*WR* (1904, 54)
Watertown	1734	Charles River bridge, grammar schools	*WR* (1904, 111)
Watertown	1735	Unappropriated lands	*WR* (1904, 135)
Watertown	1738	Charles River fish, effective laws, workhouse	*WR* (1904, 179)
Watertown	1739 (May)	Timber slit work	*WR* (1904, 194)
Watertown	1739 (Dec.)	Charles River bridge	*WR* (1904, 299)
Watertown	1747	Unappropriated lands, bridge costs	*WR* (1928, 19–20)
Watertown	1749	Unappropriated lands, bridge costs	*WR* (1928, 70)
Watertown	1752	Charles River bridge costs	*WR* (1928, 110)
Watertown	1767	Follow Boston's lead	*WR* (1928, 337–38)
Wenham	1734	Land grant	Allen (1860, 111)
Wenham	1755	Union of colonies	Allen (1860, 65–66)
Wenham	1774	Provincial congress	*Standard History of Essex County* (1878, 418)
Westborough	1765	Stamp Act	DeForest (1891, 152)
Westborough	1773	Judicial salaries	*BG* (1773d)
Westford	1765	Stamp Act	Hodgman (1883, 87–89)
Westford	1773	Judicial salaries	Hodgman (1883, 91–92)
Weston	1766	Boston riot	*Town of Weston* (1893, 127)
Weymouth	1722	Town boundaries	*History of Weymouth* (1923, 547–48)
Weymouth	1765	Stamp Act, provincial budget	Nash (1885, 56, 296–99)
Weymouth	1766	Boston riot	Nash (1885, 56)
Weymouth	1773	Charter privileges	*History of Weymouth* (1923, 574)
Weymouth	1774	Follow Boston's instructions	Nash (1885, 58)
Woburn	1672	County bridges	Sewall (1868, 130)
Woburn	1766	Boston riot	*History of Middlesex County*, vol. II (1880, 538)
Woburn	1773	Judicial salaries	*MS* (1773i)
Woodstock	1721	Town meetinghouse costs	Ammidown, vol. I (1874)
Woodstock	1728	Gubernatorial salary	Larned (1874, 365–66)
Worcester	1743	Town boundaries	*ERTWo* (1880, 43)

Worcester	1754	Excise tax	*WTR* (1882, 18)
Worcester	1765	Stamp Act	*WTR* (1882, 129)
Worcester	1766	Council elections, roll call votes, fee table, multiple officeholding, excise taxes, grammar schools, elections corruption, representative's attendance	*WTR* (1882, 138–40)
Worcester	1767	Great Britain relations, slavery, fee table, grammar schools, militia, press liberty	*WTR* (1882, 148–50)
Worcester	1768	County court relocation	*WTR* (1882, 157)
Worcester	1772	Town boundaries	*WTR* (1882, 196)
Worcester	1774 (May)	Boston port, charter privileges, union of colonies, Peter Oliver impeachment	*WTR* (1882, 225–27)
Worcester	1774 (Oct.)	Slavery, charter privileges, provincial congress	*WTR* (1882, 241–42)
Wrentham	1766	Boston riot, Pitt statue	Warner (1890, 56), *History of Norfolk County* (1884, 649)
Wrentham	1766 (Nov.)	Boston riot (reconsidered)	*History of Norfolk County* (1884, 649)
Wrentham	1773	Charter privileges, judicial salaries	*BEP* (1773c)
York	1773	Charter privileges	*MS* (1773c)

New Hampshire

Exeter	1770	Produce, manufacturers, imports, tea consumption	*NHG* (1770)
Portsmouth	1765	Stamp Act	*NHG* (1765)
Portsmouth	1768	Great Britain relations	*EG* (1768a)
Plymouth	1775	Great Britain relations	*NHG* (1775)
Rumford	1745	Town security	*CTR* (1894, 78)

New Jersey

Burlington County	1774	Eastern treasurer, excise laws, money bill	*DRNJ* (1886, 417–18)
Essex County	1774	Colonial congress	*NYJ* (1774)
Hunterdon County	1771	Quartering of troops	*DRNJ* (1886, 269–73)
Middlesex County	1769	Colonial relations, provincial spending, lawsuits, small claims suits, illegal writs, laws revision, paper currency, taxes	*DRNJ* (1904, 531–33)
Newark	1683	Town's good	*RTN* (1864, 90)
Newark	1684	Horses in woods	*RTN* (1864, 94)
Somerset County	1774	Congress delegates	"Somerset Patriotism" (1916, 244)

New York

Brattleborough	1773	Poverty, taxing unimproved lands, elections, dissenting meetinghouses	*Annals of Brattleboro*, vol. I (1921, 74–75)
Dutchess County	1774	Great Britain relations	Hasbrouck (1909, 94)
New York	1704	City retail regulations	*MCCNY*, vol. II (1905, 262–63)

Electoral Unit	Year	Subject(s)	Source
New York	1717	New York to Nassau ferry	*MCCNY,* vol. III (1905, 150)
New York	1730	City Hall repair	*MCCNY,* vol. IV (1905, 24)
New York	1735	City tax	*MCCNY,* vol. IV (1905, 285–86)
New York City and County ("about Twelve Hundred Freemen and Freeholders")	1765	Stamp Act, jury trials right	*NYM* (1765)
New York City and County ("Considerable number of respectable inhabitants")	1766	Pitt statue	*NYM* (1766)
New York City and County (unofficial committee)	1768	Quartering of troops, Boston letter	*EG* (1768b)
New York City and County (unofficial committee)	1769		*NYG* (1770a)
New York City and County (unofficial committee)	1770	Ballot vote opposition	*NYG* (1770b)
Orange County ("great Number of Freeholders")	1769	Petition to king, sheriff's behavior	*NYG* (1769f)
Queen's County (general meeting)	1769	Five Pound Act, taxes	*NYG* (1769e); *NYJ* (1769g)
Suffolk County (general meeting)	1769	Freedom and budget	*NYG* (1769e)
Westchester County ("282 Freeholders")	1769	Taxes	*NYG* (1770d)

North Carolina

Orange County	1773	Taxes, debt, Courts of Justice, Courts of Oyer, indemnification law, sheriffs law	*CRNC,* vol. IX (1890, 699–706)

Pennsylvania

Philadelphia	1706	Necessary and good of the city	*MCCP* (1847, 43)
Philadelphia	1722	Flour fraud	*MCCP* (1847, 225–26)

Philadelphia City and County (unofficial committee)	1768	Taxes	PC (1768)
Philadelphia City and County (unofficial committee)	1772	Assembly transparency, Excise Act, leather stamping act, Mud-Island fortification, Loan-Office	*Pennsylvania Packet* (1772)
Sussex County	1688	Council election	VPPP (1752, 44)

Plymouth

Duxbury	1686	County courts, military discipline	Winsor (1849, 109)
Plymouth	1682	Indians assembling	RTP (1889, 170)
Plymouth	1683	Harmon plea	RTP (1889, 173)
Rehoboth	1672	Town good	Bliss (1836, 71)
Rehoboth	1689	Town lands	Bliss (1836, 124–25)
Rehoboth	1692	General town good	Bliss (1836, 71)
Scituate	1665	Appointment of official, courts	Deane (1831, 100–101)
Scituate	1673	Deputy qualifications	Deane (1831, 103)
Scituate	1677	War profits	Deane (1831, 129)
Scituate	1680	Local land inheritance	Deane (1831, 261)
Scituate	1681	Parish boundaries	Deane (1831, 36)
Scituate	1685	Court procedures, treasurer accounts	Deane (1831, 101–2)
Scituate	1686	Laws revision, courts, land taxes, militia training, tax appeals, ancient liberties	Deane (1831, 103–104)

Rhode Island

Barrington	1770	Town boundaries	Bicknell (1898, 412)
Barrington	1774	Boston port bill	Bicknell (1898, 328–29)
Coventry	1773	G. Rome letter	PRG (1773c)
East Providence	1773	Great Britain relations	*History of Providence County* (1891, 148–49)
Hopkinton	1772	Town highway repair	RCRI (1862, 193)
Johnston	1773	G. Rome letter	PRG (1773b)
Little-Compton	1765	Stamp Act	NM (1765)
Middletown	1768	Political parties reconciliation	Arnold (1876, 29)
Middletown	1774	Smallpox vaccination	*History of Newport County* (1888, 779)
Newport	1741	Town boundaries	Arnold (1876, 17)
Newport	1766	Town tax assessment	RCRI (1861, 481–82)
Newport	1765	Court of Admiralty, Stamp Act	Arnold (1860, 259), BEP (1765a)
Newport	1770	Town market house lottery	RCRI (1862, 19)
Newport	1772 (Aug.)	Smallpox inoculations	Dexter (1901, 271)
Newport	1772 (Oct.)	Smallpox inoculations (reversed)	Dexter (1901, 298)
New Shoreham	1773	Harbor	RCRI (1862, 208–10)
Portsmouth	1680	Assessments	ERTPo (1901, 203)
Providence	1647	Assembly proceedings	ERTPr (1899, 9)
Providence	1679	Courts	ERTPr (1895, 47)
Providence	1708	Town rate	ERTPr (1896, 123)
Providence	1765	Stamp Act	PRG (1765)

Electoral Unit	Year	Subject(s)	Source
Providence	1774 (May)	Slave trade	*NM* (1774d)
Providence	1774 (Aug.)	Boston relief	*Connecticut Gazette* (1774)
Warwick	1663	Courts	*ERTWa* (1926, 140)
Westerly	1774	Liberties	*NM* (1774c)

Virginia

Electoral Unit	Year	Subject(s)	Source
Accomack County	1697 (Apr.)	Dog dollar value	*CVSP* (1875, 52)
Accomack County	1697 (Oct.)	Currency value, wolf population	*CVSP* (1875, 53–54)
Accomack County	1766	Paper currency, treasurer	*VG* (1766a)
Albemarle County	1774	Great Britain relations, imports, Boston support	*VG* (1774j)
Augusta County	1769	Great Britain relations	*VG* (1769b)
Brunswick County (Justices of the peace)	1751	Quarterly court bill	McCleskey (2012, 51)
Buckingham County	1774	Taxation, Boston support, manufactories	*VG* (1774j)
Caroline County	1774	Great Britain relations, taxation, Boston support, colonial congress, imports, tea consumption, Africa trade	*VG* (1774g)
Chesterfield County	1774	Lawmaking powers, taxation, Boston support, imports, luxury items, trade	*VG* (1774h)
Culpepper County	1774	Taxation, Boston support, imports, luxury items, livestock, slave trade	*VG* (1774f)
Dinwiddie County	1774	Great Britain relations, Boston support	*VG* (1774h)
Dunmore County	1774	Adopt Frederick County votes	*VG* (1774j)
Elizabeth City County	1774	Taxation, importation, exportation, price gouging, Boston support, colonial congress	*VG* (1774i)
Essex County	1774	Great Britain relations, imports, exports, civil trials, tea consumption, Boston support, price gouging,	*VG* (1774h)
Fairfax County	1774	Great Britain relations, taxation, Boston support, imports, lumber exports, trade	*VG* (1774j)
Fauquier County	1769	Taxation	*VG* (1769a)
Fauquier County	1774	Representation, tea consumption, Boston support	*VG* (1774j)

Gloucester County	1774	King's rights, Boston support, tea consumption, imports, tobacco exports	*VG* (1774i)
Hanover	1774	Colonial congress, slave trade	*VG* (1774i)
Henrico County	1774	Great Britain relations, colonial congress, imports, Boston support	*VG* (1774i)
Isle of Wight County	1774	Great Britain relations, Boston support, tea consumption, trade	*VG* (1774i)
James City County	1766	Multiple officeholding, speaker's compensation, treasurer's office	*VG* (1766b)
James City County	1774	Imports, exports	*VG* (1774f)
New Kent County	1774	Rights and privileges, Boston support, colonial congress	*VG* (1774h)
Norfolk County and Borough	1774	Imports, exports, colonial congress, Boston support	*VG* (1774f)
Northampton County	1652	Taxes; magistrates, governor, tobacco tax collection	Tyler (1893, 191)
Northampton County	1676	County boundary, vestry elections, predators act, tithables list, tax relief powers, county records, taverns, courts, sheriffs	"Causes of Discontent in Virginia, 1676" (1895a, 289–92)
Prince George County	1774	Colonial congress, trade	*VG* (1774c)
Princess Anne County	1774	Freedoms, taxation, imports, livestock, farming, Boston support	*VG* (1774j)
Richmond County	1774 (Apr.)	St. Asoph's sermon	*VG* (1774a)
Richmond County	1774 (June)	Taxation, Boston support, imports, exports, tea consumption, colonial congress	*VG* (1774d)
Spotsylvania County	1774	Great Britain relations, Boston support, trade	*VG* (1774d)
Stafford County	1774	Taxation, Great Britain relations, trade, courts of justice	*VG* (1774i)
Surry County	1774	Taxation, Boston support, slaves importation	*VG* (1774h)
Westmoreland County	1774	Taxation, Boston support, imports, exports, debt recovery, tea consumption	*VG* (1774b)
York County	1774	Taxation, tea, Boston support, murder bill, imports, prayer day	*VG* (1774h)

Appendix B

Initial Floor Vote and Town Position on the 1754 Massachusetts Excise Bill

Town Later Supported Bill			Town Later Opposed Bill			Town Later Took No Position		
Town	Votes in Favor	Votes Opposed	Town	Votes in Favor	Votes Opposed	Town	Votes in Favor	Votes Opposed
Braintree (Aug.)	*1*	*1*	Boston		2	Needham		1
Medfield	1		Roxbury	1		Medway	1	
Rowley	1		Dorchester	1		Chelsea		
Bradford	1		Milton	1		Brookline		
Boxford	1		Braintree (Sept.)	1	1	Hull		
Cambridge	2		Weymouth	1		Bellingham		
Watertown			Hingham	1		Walpole		
Concord, Carlisle			Dedham	1		Lynn[a]	1	
Woburn	1		Stoughton			Topsfield[b]	1	
Reading[c]	1		Wrentham			Wenham	1	
Newton		1	Salem, Danvers		1	Middleton		
Sudbury			Ipswich			Manchester		
Groton			Newbury	2		Littleton		
Billerica	1		Marblehead		1	Westford[a]	1	
Framingham	1		Andover			Lincoln[b]		
Malden	1		Beverly			Lexington		
Weston	1		Salisbury		1	Townsend		
Waltham	1		Haverhill			Sherburne		
Westfield	1		Gloucester	1		Holliston		
Lancaster	1		Amesbury	1		Hopkinton		
Brookfield			Charlestown		1	Stow		
Sutton	1		Marlborough	1		Dracut		
Bolton	1		Chelmsford			Dunstable		
Sturbridge	1		Medford		1	Stoneham[a]		

Town	Votes in Favor	Votes Opposed	Town	Votes in Favor	Votes Opposed	Town	Votes in Favor	Votes Opposed
	Town Later Supported Bill			Town Later Opposed Bill			Town Later Took No Position	
Pembroke			Hadley, South Hadley	1		Nottingham		
Plympton	1		Worcester			Bedford		
Middleborough	1		Leicester, Spencer			Tewksbury		
Abington	1		Lunenburg	1		Acton		
Barnstable			Shrewsbury			Springfield		
			Oxford			Hatfield		
			Mendon	1		Deerfield, Greenfield		
			Uxbridge			Sunderland, Montague, New-Salem	1	
			Plymouth		1	Brimfield		
			Scituate	1		Sheffield	1	
			Marshfield			Suffield		
			Hanover			Enfield		
			Kingston		1	Northfield		
			Rochester			Somers		
			Eastham			Blanford		
			Dartmouth	1		Winchester		
			Rehoboth	1		Pelham		
			Attleborough	1		Greenwich		
			Swanzey			Rutland, Rutland District	1	
			Freetown			Southborough		
			York		1	Harvard		
			Kittery		1	Woodstock		
			Berwick			Dudley		
			Falmouth			Grafton		
			Scarborough			Western		
			North Yarmouth			Duxbury[c]		1
			Brunswick		1	Bridgewater	1	
			Sherburne			Halifax		
						Wareham		
						Sandwich		
						Harwich		
						Yarmouth		
						Falmouth		
						Chatham		
						Truro		
						Taunton	1	
						Dartmouth		
						Dighton		
						Easton		

Town Later Supported Bill			Town Later Opposed Bill			Town Later Took No Position		
Town	Votes in Favor	Votes Opposed	Town	Votes in Favor	Votes Opposed	Town	Votes in Favor	Votes Opposed
						Raynham		
						Berkley		
						Wells		1
						Biddeford	1	
						George-Town		
						Arundel		
						Edgartown		
						Chilmark		
						Tisbury		

Source: The presence of a representative during the session and the June 13, 1754 roll call vote on the initial excise tax were taken from *JHHR* 1754, 4, 38. Town meetings outcomes were taken from *ATMR 1709–May 21, 1776* 1961, 5183-2; Babson 1860, 344; *Barnstable Town Records* 1910, 39–40; Barry 1847, 48; Barry 1853, 170; *BG* 1754b, 1754c, 1754d; *BPB* 1754; Brooks 1855, 109; Coffin 1845, 221; *Collections of the Maine Historical Society*, vol. III 1853, 187–88; Corey 1899, 688; Cuddihy 2009, 814–28; Daniels 1892, 224; Drake 1880, 413; *ERTL* 1896, 166; Felt 1827, 444; Felt 1834, 128; Frothingham 1845, 263; Marvin 1879, 266–67; Merrill 1880, 219–20; Paige 1883, 48; *RTB* 1886, 335–38; *RTP*, vol. III 1903, 63; *RCCB* 1885b, 260–61; Roads 1880, 63; Temple 1887, 202; *Town of Weston* 1893, 38; *TRT*, vol. II 1920, 125; Washburn 1860, 65–66; *WR* 1928, 147; and *WTR* 1882, 18.

Note: Towns in bold had at least one member present during the legislative session.

[a]Town voted to abstain on taking excise bill position.

[b]Town meeting had the excise bill on its agenda but recorded no position.

[c]Zemsky (1971, 278) reports that Duxbury and Reading opposed the bill. I accept Cuddihy's (2009, 818, 822) contrary reading of the records in question.

References

I. GOVERNMENT DOCUMENTS AND PUBLICATIONS

Abridgement and Collection of the Acts of Assembly of the Province of Maryland, at Present in Force. 1759. Philadelphia: William Bradford.

Acts and Laws, of His Majesties Colony of Connecticut in New-England. 1702. Boston: Bartholomew Green and John Allen.

Acts and Laws, of His Majesty's Colony of Rhode-Island, and Providence-Plantations, in America. 1730. Newport: James Franklin.

Acts and Laws, of His Majesty's Colony of Rhode-Island, and Providence-Plantations, in America. 1745. Newport: Widow Franklin.

Acts and Laws of His Majesty's Colony of Rhode-Island, and Providence-Plantations, in New-England, in America. 1752. Newport: J. Franklin.

Acts and Laws Passed by the General Court or Assembly of His Majesty's English Colony of Connecticut in New England in America. 1756. New London: Timothy Green.

Acts and Laws, Passed by the Great and General Court or Assembly of His Majesty's Province of the Massachusetts-Bay, in New-England. 1752. Boston: S. Kneeland and T. Green.

Acts and Laws, Passed by the Great and General Court or Assembly of Their Majesties Province of the Massachusetts-Bay, in New-England. 1692. Boston: Benjamin Harris.

Acts and Laws, Passed by the Great and General Court or Assembly of Their Majesties Province of the Massachusetts-Bay, in New-England, Convened and Held at Boston, the Eight Day of November, 1693. 1693. Boston: Bartholomew Green.

Acts and Resolves, Public and Private, of the Province of the Massachusetts Bay: to which are Prefixed the Charters of the Province, vol. I. 1869. Boston: Wright & Potter Printing Co.

Acts and Resolves, Public and Private, of the Province of the Massachusetts Bay: to which are Prefixed the Charters of the Province, vol. VII. 1892. Boston: Wright & Potter Printing Co.

Acts of Assembly, of the Province of North Carolina: Now in Force and Use. 1751. New Bern: James Davis.

Acts of the General Assembly of the Province of New Jersey, from the Surrender of the Government to Queen ANNE, on the 17th Day of April, in the Year of our Lord 1702, to the 14th Day of January 1776. 1776. Burlington: Isaac Collins.

Acts of the Privy Council of England, Colonial Series, Vol. III, *A. D. 1720–1745.* 1910. Hereford: His Majesty's Stationary Office.

Acts of the Privy Council of England, Colonial Series, Vol. IV, *A. D. 1745–1766.* 1911. London: His Majesty's Stationary Office.

Acts Passed by the General Assembly of Her Majestys colony of New-Jersey, in January, 1709. 1710. New York: William Bradford.

Ancient Historical Records of Norwalk, Conn.: with a Plan of the Ancient Settlement, and of the Town in 1847. 1865. Norwalk: Andrew Selleck.

Ancient Town Records, vol. I. *New Haven Town Records, 1649–1662.* 1917. New Haven: Tuttle, Morehouse & Taylor Company.

Ancient Town Records, vol. II. *New Haven Town Records, 1662–1684.* 1919. New Haven: Tuttle, Morehouse & Taylor Company.

Ancient Town Records, vol. III. *New Haven Town Records, 1684–1769.* 1962. New Haven: New Haven Colony Historical Society.

Andover Massachusetts Town Meeting Records 1709–May 21, 1776. 1961. North Andover: North Andover Historical Society.

Annals of Brattleboro, 1681–1895, vol. I. 1921. Brattleboro: E. L. Hildreth & Co.

Annals of the Town of Dorchester, vol. two. 1846. Boston: David Clapp, Jr.

Anno regni Georgii II, Regis Magnae Britanniae, Franciae & Hiberniae, vicessimo. 1754. New Bern: James Davis.

Archives of Maryland, vol. I, *Proceedings and Acts of the General Assembly of Maryland, January 1637/8–September 1664.* 1883. Baltimore: Maryland Historical Society.

Archives of Maryland, vol. II, *Proceedings and Acts of the General Assembly of Maryland, April 1666–June 1676.* 1884. Baltimore: Maryland Historical Society.

Archives of Maryland, vol. III, *Proceedings the Council of Maryland, 1636–1667.* 1885. Baltimore: Maryland Historical Society.

Archives of Maryland, vol. V, *Proceedings the Council of Maryland, 1667–1687/8.* 1887. Baltimore: Maryland Historical Society.

Archives of Maryland, vol. VI, *Correspondence of Governor Horatio Sharpe,* vol. I. 1888. Baltimore: Maryland Historical Society.

Archives of Maryland, vol. VII, *Proceedings and Acts of the General Assembly of Maryland, October 1678–November 1683.* 1889. Baltimore: Maryland Historical Society.

Archives of Maryland, vol. VIII, *Proceedings the Council of Maryland, 1687/8–1693.* 1890. Baltimore: Maryland Historical Society.

Archives of Maryland, vol. IX, *Correspondence of Governor Horatio Sharpe,* vol. II. 1890. Baltimore: Maryland Historical Society.

Archives of Maryland, vol. XIII, *Proceedings and Acts of the General Assembly of Maryland, April, 1684–June 1692.* 1894. Baltimore: Maryland Historical Society.

Archives of Maryland, vol. XIV, *Correspondence of Governor Horatio Sharpe,* vol. III. 1895. Baltimore: Maryland Historical Society.

Archives of Maryland, vol. XV, *Proceedings the Council of Maryland, 1671–1681.* 1896. Baltimore: Maryland Historical Society.

Archives of Maryland, vol. XVII, *Proceedings the Council of Maryland, 1681–1686/6.* 1898. Baltimore: Maryland Historical Society.

Archives of Maryland, vol. XXIV, *Proceedings and Acts of the General Assembly of Maryland, April 16, 1700–May 3, 1704.* 1904. Baltimore: Maryland Historical Society.

Archives of Maryland, vol. XXVI, *Proceedings and Acts of the General Assembly of Maryland, September, 1704–April, 1706.* 1906. Baltimore: Maryland Historical Society.

Archives of Maryland, vol. XXVII, *Proceedings and Acts of the General Assembly of Maryland, March, 1707–November, 1710.* 1907. Baltimore: Maryland Historical Society.

Archives of Maryland, vol. XXIX, *Proceedings and Acts of the General Assembly of Maryland, Oct. 25, 1711–Oct. 9, 1714.* 1909. Baltimore: Maryland Historical Society.

Archives of Maryland, vol. XXXIII, *Proceedings and Acts of the General Assembly of Maryland, May, 1717–April, 1720.* 1913. Baltimore: Maryland Historical Society.

Archives of Maryland, vol. XXXIV, *Proceedings and Acts of the General Assembly of Maryland, October, 1720–October, 1723.* 1914. Baltimore: Maryland Historical Society.

Archives of Maryland, vol. XXXV, *Proceedings and Acts of the General Assembly of Maryland, October, 1724–July, 1726.* 1915. Baltimore: Maryland Historical Society.

Archives of Maryland, vol. XXXVII, *Proceedings and Acts of the General Assembly of Maryland, May, 1730–August, 1732.* 1917. Baltimore: Maryland Historical Society.

Archives of Maryland, vol. XXXIX, *Proceedings and Acts of the General Assembly of Maryland, 1733–1736.* 1919. Baltimore: Maryland Historical Society.

Archives of Maryland, vol. XL, *Proceedings and Acts of the General Assembly of Maryland, 1737–1740.* 1921. Baltimore: Maryland Historical Society.

Archives of Maryland, vol. LIX, *Proceedings and Acts of the General Assembly of Maryland, 1764–1765.* 1942. Baltimore: Maryland Historical Society.

Archives of Maryland, vol. LXI, *Proceedings and Acts of the General Assembly of Maryland, 1766–1768.* 1944. Baltimore: Maryland Historical Society.

Archives of Maryland, vol. LXIII, *Proceedings and Acts of the General Assembly of Maryland, 1771-June-July, 1773.* 1946. Baltimore: Maryland Historical Society.

Archives of Maryland, vol. LXIV, *Proceedings and Acts of the General Assembly of Maryland, October 1773 to April 1774.* 1947. Baltimore: Maryland Historical Society.

Archives of Maryland, vol. 426, *A Biographical Directory of the Maryland Legislature, 1635–1789.* 1979. Baltimore: Johns Hopkins University Press.

Archives of Maryland, vol. 748, *Chancery Court (Chancery Record), 1671–1712.* 2008. Annapolis: Maryland State Archives.

Barnstable Town Records. 1910. Yarmouth: C. W. Swift.

Calendar of State Papers, Colonial Series, 1574–1660. 1860. London: Longman, Green, Longman, & Roberts.

Calendar of State Papers, Colonial Series, America and West Indies, 1661–1668. 1880. London: Longman & Co.

Calendar of State Papers, Colonial Series, America and West Indies, 1669–1674. 1889. London: Her Majesty's Stationery Office.

Calendar of State Papers, Colonial Series, America and West Indies, 1675–1676, Also Addenda, 1574–1674. 1893. London: Her Majesty's Stationery Office.

Calendar of State Papers, Colonial Series, America and West Indies, 1677–1680. 1896. London: Her Majesty's Stationery Office.

Calendar of State Papers, Colonial Series, America and West Indies, 1681–1685. 1898. London: Her Majesty's Stationery Office.

Calendar of State Papers, Colonial Series, America and West Indies, 1685–1688. 1899. London: Her Majesty's Stationery Office.

Calendar of State Papers, Colonial Series, America and West Indies, 1689–1692. 1901. London: His Majesty's Stationery Office.

Calendar of State Papers, Colonial Series, America and West Indies, January 1693–14 May, 1696. 1903. London: His Majesty's Stationery Office.

Calendar of State Papers, Colonial Series, America and West Indies, 15 May, 1696–31 October, 1697. 1904. London: His Majesty's Stationery Office.

Calendar of State Papers, Colonial Series, America and West Indies, 27 October, 1697–31 December, 1698. 1905. London: His Majesty's Stationery Office.

Calendar of State Papers, Colonial Series, America and West Indies, 1699. 1908. London: His Majesty's Stationery Office.

Calendar of State Papers, Colonial Series, America and West Indies, 1700. 1910a. London: His Majesty's Stationery Office.

Calendar of State Papers, Colonial Series, America and West Indies, 1701. 1910b. London: His Majesty's Stationery Office.

Calendar of State Papers, Colonial Series, America and West Indies, Jan.–Dec. 1, 1702. 1912. London: His Majesty's Stationery Office.

Calendar of State Papers, Colonial Series, America and West Indies, Dec. 1, 1702–1703. 1913. London: His Majesty's Stationery Office.

Calendar of State Papers, Colonial Series, America and West Indies, 1704–1705. 1916a. London: His Majesty's Stationery Office.

Calendar of State Papers, Colonial Series, America and West Indies, 1706–1708, June. 1916b. London: His Majesty's Stationery Office.

Calendar of State Papers, Colonial Series, America and West Indies, June, 1708–1709. 1922. London: His Majesty's Stationery Office.

Calendar of State Papers, Colonial Series, America and West Indies, 1710–June, 1711. 1924. London: His Majesty's Stationery Office.

Calendar of State Papers, Colonial Series, America and West Indies, July, 1711–June, 1712. 1925. London: His Majesty's Stationery Office.

Calendar of State Papers, Colonial Series, America and West Indies, July, 1712–July, 1714. 1926. London: His Majesty's Stationery Office.

Calendar of State Papers, Colonial Series, America and West Indies, August, 1714–December, 1715. 1928. London: His Majesty's Stationery Office.

Calendar of State Papers, Colonial Series, America and West Indies, Jan. 1716–July, 1717. 1930a. London: His Majesty's Stationery Office.

Calendar of State Papers, Colonial Series, America and West Indies, August 1717–Dec. 1718. 1930b. London: His Majesty's Stationery Office.

Calendar of State Papers, Colonial Series, America and West Indies, March, 1720 to December, 1721. 1933. London: His Majesty's Stationery Office.

Calendar of State Papers, Colonial Series, America and West Indies 1722–1723. 1934. London: His Majesty's Stationery Office.

Calendar of State Papers, Colonial Series, America and West Indies 1724–1725. 1936a. London: His Majesty's Stationery Office.

Calendar of State Papers, Colonial Series, America and West Indies 1726–1727. 1936b. London: His Majesty's Stationery Office.

Calendar of State Papers, Colonial Series, America and West Indies 1728–1729. 1937a. London: His Majesty's Stationery Office.

Calendar of State Papers, Colonial Series, America and West Indies 1730. 1937b. London: His Majesty's Stationery Office.

Calendar of State Papers, Colonial Series, America and West Indies 1732. 1939. London: His Majesty's Stationery Office.

Calendar of Virginia State Papers and Other Manuscripts, 1652–1781, vol. 1. 1875. Richmond: Superintendent of Public Printing.

The Calvert Papers, number one. 1889. Baltimore: John Murphy & Co.

The Charter Granted by their Majesties King William and Queen Mary, to the Inhabitants of the Province of the Massachusetts-Bay, in New-England. 1692. Boston: Benjamin Harris.

The Charter of Maryland, together with The Proceedings and Debates of the Upper and Lower Houses of Assembly in Maryland, In the Years 1722, 1723, and 1724. 1725. Philadelphia: Andrew Bradford.

A Collection of All the Acts of Assembly, of the Province of North Carolina, in Force and Use, Since the Revisal of the LAWS in the Year 1751. 1764. New Bern: James Davis.

A Collection of All the Public Acts of Assembly, of the Province of North-Carolina. 1752: New Bern: James Davis.

Colonial Laws of New York from the Year 1664 to the Revolution, vol. I. 1894. Albany, NY: James B. Lyon.

Colonial Laws of New York from the Year 1664 to the Revolution, vol. II. 1894. Albany, NY: James B. Lyon.

Colonial Laws of New York from the Year 1664 to the Revolution, vol. III. 1894. Albany, NY: James B. Lyon.

Colonial Laws of New York from the Year 1664 to the Revolution, vol. IV. 1894. Albany: James B. Lyon.

Colonial Laws of New York from the Year 1664 to the Revolution, vol. V. 1894. Albany: James B. Lyon.

Colonial Records of North Carolina, vol. I—1662 to 1712. 1886. Raleigh: P. M. Hale.

Colonial Records of North Carolina, vol. II—1713 to 1728. 1886. Raleigh: P. M. Hale.

Colonial Records of North Carolina, vol. III—1728 to 1734. 1886. Raleigh: P. M. Hale.

Colonial Records of North Carolina, vol. IV—1734 to 1752. 1886. Raleigh: P. M. Hale.

Colonial Records of North Carolina, vol. V—1752 to 1759. 1887. Raleigh: Josephus Daniels.

Colonial Records of North Carolina, vol. VI—1759 to 1765. 1888. Raleigh: Josephus Daniels.

Colonial Records of North Carolina, vol. VII—1765 to 1768. 1890. Raleigh: Josephus Daniels.

Colonial Records of North Carolina, vol. IX—1771 to 1775. 1890. Raleigh: Josephus Daniels.

Colonial Records of South Carolina, the Journal of the Commons House of Assembly, November 10, 1736–June 7, 1739. 1951. Columbia: Historical Commission of South Carolina.

Colonial Records of South Carolina, the Journal of the Commons House of Assembly, September 12, 1739–March 26, 1741. 1952. Columbia: Historical Commission of South Carolina.

Colonial Records of South Carolina, the Journal of the Commons House of Assembly, September 10, 1745–June 17, 1746. 1956. Columbia: South Carolina Archives Department.

Colonial Records of the State of Georgia, vol. II. 1904. Atlanta: Franklin Printing and Publishing Company.

Colonial Records of the State of Georgia, vol. XIII. 1907. Atlanta: Franklin-Turner Company.

Colonial Records of the State of Georgia, vol. XIV. 1907. Atlanta: Franklin-Turner Company.

Colonial Records of the State of Georgia, vol. XV. 1907. Atlanta: Franklin-Turner Company.

Colonial Records of the State of Georgia, vol. 28, part I. 1976. Athens: University of Georgia Press.

Colonial Records of the State of Georgia, vol. 28, part II. 1979. Athens: University of Georgia Press.

Concord Town Records, 1732–1820. 1894. Concord: Republican Press Association.

A Copy of the Poll List, of the Election for Representatives for the City and County of New-York; Which Election Began on Monday the 7th day of March, and ended on Friday the 11th, of the same Month, in the Year of our Lord MDCCLXVIII. 1880a. New York: Francis Hart & Co.

A Copy of the Poll List, of the Election for Representatives for the City and County of New-York; Which Election Began on Monday the 23d day of January, and ended on Friday the 27th, of the same Month, in the Year of our Lord MDCCLXIX. 1880b. New York: Francis Hart & Co.

A Copy of the Poll List, of the Election for Representatives for the City and County of New-York; Which Election Began on Tuesday the 17th day of February, and ended on Thursday the 19th, of the same Month, in the Year of our Lord MDCCLXI. 1880c. New York: Francis Hart & Co.

Copy of the Old Records of the Town of Duxbury, Mass., from 1642 to 1770. 1893. Plymouth: Avery & Doten.

Correspondence of the Colonial Governors of Rhode Island, 1723–1775. 1902. Boston: Houghton, Mifflin and Company.

Correspondence of William Shirley, Governor of Massachusetts and Military Commander in America, 1731–1760, vol. I. 1912. New York: Macmillan.

The Documentary History of the State of New York, vol. III. 1850. Albany: Weed, Parsons & Co.

The Documentary History of the State of New York, vol. IV. 1851. Albany: Charles Van Benthuysen.

Documents and Records Relating to the Province of New Hampshire, from the Earliest Period of Its Settlement: 1623–1686, vol. I. 1867. Concord: George E. Jenks.

Documents and Records Relating to the Province of New Hampshire, from 1692 to 1722, vol. III. 1869. Manchester: John B. Clarke.

Documents and Records Relating to the Province of New Hampshire, from 1749 to 1763, vol. VI. 1872. Manchester: James M. Campbell.

Documents and Records Relating to the Province of New-Hampshire, from 1764–1776, vol. VII. 1873. Nashua: Orren C. Moore.

Documents and Records Relating to Towns in New Hampshire, vol. IX. 1875. Concord: Charles C. Pearson.

Documents Relating to the Colonial History of the State of New Jersey, vol. I. 1880. Newark: Daily Journal.

Documents Relating to the Colonial History of the State of New Jersey, vol. III. 1881. Newark: Daily Advertiser Printing House.

Documents Relating to the Colonial History of the State of New Jersey, vol. IV. 1882. Newark: Daily Advertiser Printing House.

Documents Relating to the Colonial History of the State of New Jersey, vol. VI. 1882. Newark: Daily Advertiser Printing House.

Documents Relating to the Colonial History of the State of New Jersey, vol. X. 1886. Newark: Daily Advertiser Printing House.

Documents Relating to the Colonial History of the State of New Jersey, vol. XI, vol. I 1704–1739. 1894. Patterson: Press Printing and Publishing Co.

Documents Relating to the Colonial History of the State of New Jersey, vol. XVII, vol. V 1756–1768. 1892. Trenton: John L. Murphy Publishing Co.

Documents Relating to the Colonial History of the State of New Jersey, vol. XIX, vol. III 1751–1755. 1897. Patterson: Press Printing and Publishing Co.

Documents Relating to the Colonial History of the State of New Jersey, vol. XXVI, vol. VII 1768–1769. 1904. Patterson: Call Printing and Publishing Co.

Documents Relating to the Colonial History of the State of New York, vol. XIV. 1883. Albany: Weed, Parsons and Company.

Documents Relating to the History of the Early Colonial Settlements Principally on Long Island, with a Map of Its Western Part, Made in 1666. 1883. Albany: Weed, Parsons and Company.

Documents Relative to the Colonial History of the State of New York, vol. III. 1853. Albany: Weed, Parsons and Company.

Documents Relative to the Colonial History of the State of New York, vol. V. 1855. Albany: Weed, Parsons and Company.

Documents Relative to the Colonial History of the State of New York, vol. VI. 1855. Albany: Weed, Parsons and Company.

Documents Relative to the Colonial History of the State of New York, vol. VII. 1856. Albany: Weed, Parsons and Company.

Documents Relative to the Colonial History of the State of New York, vol. VIII. 1857. Albany: Weed, Parsons and Company.

The Early Records of Groton, Massachusetts. 1880. Cambridge: University Press.

The Early Records of Lancaster, Massachusetts. 1884. Lancaster: W. J. Coulter.

Early Records of Londonderry, Windham, and Derry, N. H., 1719–1762. 1908. Manchester: Manchester Historic Association.

Early Records of the Town of Dedham, Massachusetts, 1672–1706, vol. 5. 1899. Dedham: Dedham Transcript Press.

Early Records of the Town of Lunenburg, Massachusetts, Including that Part which is Now Fitchburg, 1719–1764. 1896. Fitchburg: Sentinel Printing Company.

Early Records of the Town of Portsmouth. 1901. Providence: E. L. Freeman & Sons.

Early Records of the Town of Providence, vol. III. 1893. Providence: Snow & Farnham.

Early Records of the Town of Providence, vol. VIII. 1895. Providence: Snow & Farnham.

Early Records of the Town of Providence, vol. XI. 1896. Providence: Snow & Farnham.

Early Records of the Town of Providence, vol. XIII. 1897. Providence: Remington Printing Co.

Early Records of the Town of Providence, vol. XV. 1899. Providence: Snow & Farnham.

Early Records of the Town of Warwick. 1926. Providence: E. A. Johnson Company.

Early Records of the Town of Worcester. Book II. 1740–1753. 1880. Worcester: Worcester Society of Antiquity.

Early Town Records of Newcastle, Maine, from January 24, 1756 to January 6, 1779. 1914. Damariscotta: n.p.

Extract from the Journal of the Honourable House of Representatives. 1731. Boston: Thomas Fleet.

Extracts from the Records of Colchester, with Some Transcripts. 1864. Hartford: Case, Lockwood and Company.

Fourth Report of the Record Commissioners. 1880. Boston: Rockwell and Churchill.

At the General Assembly of the Governor and Company of the English Colony of Rhode-Island and Providence Plantations in New-England in AMERICA, begun and held at South-Kingston within and for said Colony, on the last Wednesday in October, in the Twenty first Year of the Reign of his most Sacred Majesty, George the Second, by the Grace of GOD, King of Great Britain, France and Ireland, Defender of the Faith, &c. 1747. Newport: Ann Franklin.

Grants, Concessions, and Original Constitutions of the Province of New Jersey. 1758. Philadelphia: W. Bradford.

"Hartford Town Votes, volume I, 1636–1716" in *Collections of the Connecticut Historical Society*, vol. VI. 1897. Hartford: Connecticut Historical Society.

Historical Abstract of the United States, Colonial Times to 1970, Part 2. 1975. Washington, DC: U.S. Bureau of the Census.

Historical Memoranda Concerning Persons and Places in Old Dover, N. H., vol. I. 1900. Dover: n.p.

To the Honourable GEORGE CLARKE, Esq; Lieut. Governour and Commander in Chief of the Province of New-York, &c. 1737. New York: John Peter Zenger.

Huntington Town Records, Including Babylon, Long Island, N. Y., 1688–1775. 1888. Huntington: Long Islander Print.

Index of Colonial and State Laws of New Jersey Between the Years of 1603 and 1903 Inclusive. 1905. Camden: Sinnickson Chew & Sons.

Journal and Votes of the House of Representatives of the Province of Nova Cesarea, or New Jersey, in the First Sessions of Assembly, Began at Perth Amboy, the 10th Day of November, 1703. 1872. Jersey City: John H. Lyon.

Journal of the Commons House of Assembly, October 6, 1757–January 24, 1761. 1996. Columbia: South Carolina Department of Archives and History.

Journal of the Commons House of Assembly of South Carolina for the Session Beginning September 20, 1692, and Ending October 15, 1692. 1907. Columbia: Historical Commission of South Carolina.

Journal of the Commons House of Assembly of South Carolina, June 2, 1724–June 16,

1724. 1944. Columbia: Joint Committee of Printing, General Assembly of South Carolina.

Journal of the General Assembly of His Majesty's Province of New-Hampshire, Being the Whole Proceedings thereof, to their Dissolution. 1762. Portsmouth: Daniel Fowle.

Journal of the Honourable House of Representatives, of His Majesty's Province of the Massachusetts-Bay in New-England. 1754. Boston: Samuel Kneeland.

Journal of the Honorable House of Representatives, Of His Majesty's Province of the Massachusetts-Bay in New-England, Begun and held at Boston, in the County of Suffolk, on Wednesday the Thirty-First day of May, Annoque Domini, 1769. 1769. Boston: Edes and Gill.

Journal of the Honourable House of Representatives, of His Majesty's Province of the Massachusetts-Bay in New-England, Begun and Held at Boston, upon Wednesday the Twenty-Ninth day of May, Annoq, Domini, 1728. 1728. Boston: Bartholomew Green and Samuel Kneeland.

Journal of the Honourable House of Representatives, of His Majesty's Province of the Massachusetts-Bay in New-England, Begun and Held at Boston, upon Wednesday the Twenty-Sixth day of May, Annoq, Domini, 1725. 1725. Boston: Bartholomew Green and Samuel Kneeland.

Journal of the Honourable House of Representatives, Of His Majesty's Province of the Massachusetts-Bay in New-England Begun and held at Boston, in the County of Suffolk, on Wednesday the Thirtieth day of May, Annoque Domini, 1739. 1739. Boston: Samuel Kneeland.

Journal of the Honourable House Of Representatives of His Majesty's Province of the Massachusetts-Bay in New-England, Begun and held at Boston, in the County of Suffolk, on Wednesday the Thirtieth day of May, Annoque Domini, 1750. 1750. Boston: Samuel Kneeland.

Journal of the Honourable House Of Representatives of His Majesty's Province of the Massachusetts-Bay in New-England, Begun and held at Boston in the County of Suffolk, on Wednesday the Thirtieth Day of May, Annoque Domini, 1753. 1753. Boston: Samuel Kneeland.

Journal of the Honourable House of Representatives, of His Majesty's Province of the Massachusetts-Bay, in New-England, Begun and held at Concord, in the County of Middlesex, on Wednesday the Thirtieth Day of May, Annoque Domini, 1764. 1764. Boston: Green and Russell.

Journal of the Honourable House of Representatives, of His Majesty's Province of the Massachusetts-Bay, in New-England, Begun and held at Boston, in the County of Suffolk, on Wednesday the Thirty-first Day of May, Annoque Domini, 1758. 1758. Boston: Samuel Kneeland.

Journal of the Honourable House of Representatives, Of His Majesty's Province of the Massachusetts-Bay in New-England, Begun and Held at Boston, in the County of Suffolk, on Wednesday the Twenty-Eighth day of May, Annoque Domini, 1740. 1740. Boston: Samuel Kneeland.

Journal of the Honourable House of Representatives, of His Majesty's Province of the Massachusetts-Bay in New-England, Begun and held at Boston, in the County of Suffolk, on Wednesday the Twenty-eighth Day of May, Annoque Domini, 1755. 1755. Boston: Samuel Kneeland.

Journal of the Honourable House of Representatives, Of His Majesty's Province of the Massachusetts-Bay, in New England, Begun and held at BOSTON, in the County of Suffolk, on Wednesday the Twenty-eighth Day of May, Annoque Domini, 1766. 1766. Boston: Green and Russell.

Journal of the Honourable House of Representatives, Of His Majesty's Province of the Massachusetts-Bay in New-England, Begun and Held at Boston, in the County of Suffolk, on Wednesday the Twenty-fifth day of May, Annoque Domini, 1748. 1748. Boston: S. Kneeland and T. Green.

Journal of the Honourable House of Representatives, of His Majesty's Province of the Massachusetts-Bay, in New-England, Begun and held at Boston, in the County of Suffolk, on Wednesday the Twenty-fifth Day of May, Annoque Domini, 1757. 1757. Boston: Samuel Kneeland.

Journal of the Honourable House of Representatives, of His Majesty's Province of the Massachusetts-Bay, in New-England, Begun and held at Boston, in the County of Suffolk, on Wednesday the Twenty-fifth Day of May, Annoque Domini, 1763. 1763. Boston: Green and Russell.

Journal of the Honorable House Of Representatives of His Majesty's Province of the Massachusetts-Bay in New-England, Begun and held at Boston in the County of Suffolk on Wednesday the Twenty-ninth Day of May, Annoque Domini, 1751. 1751. Boston: Samuel Kneeland.

Journal of the Honourable House of Representatives, of His Majesty's Province of the Massachusetts-Bay, in New England, Begun and Held at Boston, in the County of Suffolk, on Wednesday the Twenty-Ninth Day of May, Annoque Domini, 1765. 1765/1766. Boston: Green and Russell.

Journal of the Honourable House of Representatives, of His Majesty's Province of the Massachusetts-Bay, in New-England, Begun and held at Boston, in the County of Suffolk, on Wednesday the Twenty-seventh Day of May, Annoque Domini, 1761. 1761. Boston: Samuel Kneeland.

Journal of the Honourable House of Representatives, of His Majesty's Province of the Massachusetts-Bay, in New-England, Begun and held at Boston, in the County of Suffolk, on Wednesday the Twenty-sixth Day of May, Annoque Domini, 1756. 1756. Boston: Samuel Kneeland.

Journal of the House of Assembly. 1755. New Bern: James Davis.

Journal of the House of Burgesses, of the Province of North-Carolina. 1749. New Bern: James Davis.

Journal of the House of Representatives. 1717. Boston: B. Green.

Journal of the House of Representatives for his Majestie's Province of New-York in America. 1695. New York: William Bradford.

Journal of the House of Representatives of the Province of New-Hampshire. 1745. Boston: J. Bushell, B. Allen, and J. Green.

Journal of the Legislative Council of the Colony of New-York. Began the 9th Day of April, 1691; and Ended the 27 of September, 1743. 1861. Albany: Weed, Parsons & Company.

Journal of the Votes and Proceedings of the General Assembly of Her Majesties Colony of Nova-Casarea or New Jersey, in America. 1711. New York: William Bradford.

Journal of the Votes and Proceedings of the General Assembly of His Majesty's colony of New-York, in America. 1737. New York: John Peter Zenger.

Journal of the Votes and Proceedings of the General Assembly of His Majesty's colony of New-York, in America. 1738. New York: John Peter Zenger.

Journal of the Votes and Proceedings of the General Assembly of His Majesty's colony of New-York, which began the 23d of July, 1728. 1728. New York: William Bradford.

Journal of the Votes and Proceedings of the General Assembly of the Colony of New-York, which began the 27th of March, 2739 [sic]. 1739. New York: William Bradford.

Journal of the Votes and Proceedings of the General Assembly of His Majesty's Colony of New-York, began the Twenty Ninth Day of August, 1739. 1739. New York: William Bradford.

Journal of the Votes and Proceedings of the General Assembly of His Majesty's Colony of New-York, begun the 11th Day of Sept. 1740. 1740. New York: William Bradford.

Journal of the Votes and Proceedings of the General Assembly of the Colony of New-York. 1743. New York: James Parker.

Journal of the Votes and Proceedings of the General Assembly of the Colony of New-York. 1773. New York: H. Gaine.

Journal of the Votes and Proceedings of the General Assembly of the Colony of New-York, Began the 4th of April, 1769, and ended by Prorogation, the 20th of May following. 1769. New York: Hugh Gaine.

Journal of the Votes and Proceedings of the General Assembly of the Colony of New-York; Began the 6th of January, 1774, and ended by Prorogation, the 19th of March following. 1774. New York: Hugh Gaine.

Journal of the Votes and Proceedings of the General Assembly of the Colony of New-York, Began the 7th of January, 1772, and ended by prorogation, the 24th of March following. 1771. New York: H. Gaine.

Journal of the Votes and Proceedings of the General Assembly of the Colony of New-York. Began the 8th Day of November, 1743; and Ended the 23d of December, 1765, vol. II. 1766. New York: Hugh Gaine.

Journal of the Votes and Proceedings of the General Assembly of the Colony of New-York; Began the 10th of January, 1775, And adjourned the 3d April, to the 3d May following. 1775. New York: Hugh Gaine.

Journal of the Votes and Proceedings of the General Assembly of the Colony of New-York, Began the 11th of December, 1770, and ended by prorogation, the 4th of March 1771. 1771. New York: Hugh Gaine.

Journal of the Votes and Proceedings of the General Assembly of the Colony of New-York, Began the 21st of November, 1769, and ended by prorogation, the 27th of January 1770. 1770. New York: Hugh Gaine.

Journal of the Votes and Proceedings of the General Assembly of the Colony of New-York, Began the 27th of October, 1768, and ended, by dissolution, the 2nd of January, 1769. 1769a. New York: Hugh Gaine.

Journal of the Votes and Proceedings of the General Assembly of the Colony of New-York, begun the 14th Day of April, 1741. 1741. New York: William Bradford.

Journal of the Votes and Proceedings of the General Assembly of the Colony of New-York, begun the 15th Day of Sept. 1741. 1741. New York: William Bradford.

Journal of the Votes and Proceedings of the House of Representatives of the Province of Pennsylvania. 1728. Philadelphia: Andrew Bradford.

Journal of the Votes and Proceedings of the House of Representatives of the Province of Pennsylvania. 1729. Philadelphia: Andrew Bradford.

Journals of the Board of Trade and Plantations, Vol. 8, January 1742–December 1749. 1931. London: His Majesty's Stationery Office.

Journals of the Commons House of Assembly of South Carolina for the Two Sessions of 1698. 1914. Columbia: Historical Commission of South Carolina.

Journals of the House of Burgesses of Virginia 1619–1658/59. 1915. Richmond: The Colonial Press.

Journals of the House of Burgesses of Virginia 1659/60–1693. 1914. Richmond: The Colonial Press.

Journals of the House of Burgesses of Virginia 1695–1696, 1696–1697, 1698, 1699, 1700–1702. 1913. Richmond: Library Board, Virginia State Library.

Journals of the House of Burgesses of Virginia 1702/3–1705, 1705–1705, 1710–1712. 1912. Richmond: Library Board, Virginia State Library.

Journals of the House of Burgesses of Virginia 1712–1714, 1715, 1718 1720–1722, 1723–1726. 1912. Richmond: The Colonial Press.

Journals of the House of Burgesses of Virginia 1727–1734 1736–1740. 1910. Richmond: The Colonial Press.

Journals of the House of Burgesses of Virginia 1742–1747 1748–1749. 1909. Richmond: The Colonial Press.

Journals of the House of Burgesses of Virginia 1752–1755 1756–1758. 1909. Richmond: The Colonial Press.

Journals of the House of Burgesses of Virginia 1758–1761. 1908. Richmond: Library Board, Virginia State Library.

Journals of the House of Burgesses of Virginia 1761–1765. 1907. Richmond: Library Board, Virginia State Library.

Journals of the House of Burgesses of Virginia 1766–1769. 1906. Richmond: Library Board, Virginia State Library.

Journals of the House of Burgesses of Virginia 1770–1772. 1906. Richmond: Library Board, Virginia State Library.

Journals of the House of Representatives of Massachusetts 1715–1717. 1919. Boston: Massachusetts Historical Society.

Laws of the Government of New-Castle, Kent, and Sussex, Upon Delaware, vol. I. 1763. Wilmington: James Adams.

Laws of New Hampshire Including Public and Private Acts and Resolves and the Royal Commissions and Instructions, with Historical and Descriptive Notes, and an Appendix, vol. one. 1904. Manchester: John B. Clarke.

Laws of New Hampshire Including Public and Private Acts and Resolves and the Royal Commissions and Instructions, with Historical and Descriptive Notes, and an Appendix, vol. two. 1913. Concord: Rumford Printing Company.

Laws of New Hampshire Including Public and Private Acts and Resolves, Royal Commissions and Instructions, Notes and Appendix, vol. three. 1915. Bristol: Musgrove Printing House.

The Laws of the Province of Maryland, Collected into one Volumn, by Order of the Governour and Assembly, of the said Province, At a General Assembly begun at St. Mary's the 10th Day of May, 1692 and continued by several Assemblies to the Year 1718. 1718. Philadelphia: Andrew Bradford.

Laws of the State of Delaware, from the Fourteenth Day of October, One Thousand Seven

Hundred, to the Eighteenth Day of August, One Thousand, Seven Hundred and Ninety-Seven, vol. I. 1797. New Castle: Samuel and John Adams.

Manual of the Corporation of the City of New York. 1865. New York: Edmund Jones & Co.

Minutes of the Common Council of the City of Philadelphia. 1704 to 1776. 1847. Philadelphia: Crissy & Markley.

Minutes of the Common Council of New York, 1675–1776, vol. II. 1905. New York: Dodd Mead and Company.

Minutes of the Common Council of New York, 1675–1776, vol. III. 1905. New York: Dodd Mead and Company.

Minutes of the Common Council of New York, 1675–1776, vol. IV. 1905. New York: Dodd Mead and Company.

Minutes of the Common Council of New York, 1675–1776, vol. V. 1905. New York: Dodd Mead and Company.

Minutes of the Provincial Council of Pennsylvania, from the Organization to the Termination of the Proprietary Government, vol. I. 1838. Harrisburg: Theophilus Fenn.

Minutes of the Provincial Council of Pennsylvania, from the Organization to the Termination of the Proprietary Government, vol. III. 1840. Harrisburg: Theophilus Fenn.

Miscellaneous Provincial and State Papers, 1725–1800, vol. XVIII. 1890. Manchester: John B. Clarke.

Muddy River and Brookline Records, 1634–1838. 1875. Boston: J. E. Farwell & Co.

New York Red Book Containing the Portraits and Biographies of the U.S. Senators, Governor, State Officers and Members of the Legislature. 1909. Albany: J. B. Lyon.

North Carolina Government, 1585–1979: A Narrative and Statistical History. 1981. Raleigh: North Carolina Department of the Secretary of State.

Official Letters of Alexander Spotswood, Lieutenant-Governor of the Colony of Virginia, 1710–1722, vol. II. 1885. Richmond: Virginia Historical Society.

Official Records of Robert Dinwiddie, Lieutenant-Governor of the Colony of Virginia, 1751–1758, vol. I. 1883. Richmond: Virginia Historical Society.

Old Records of the Town of Fitchburg, Massachusetts, 1764–1789, vol. 1. 1898. Fitchburg: Sentinel Printing Company.

Pennsylvania Archives, vol. I. 1852. Philadelphia: Joseph Severns & Co.

Pennsylvania Archives, vol. II. 1853. Philadelphia: Joseph Severns & Co.

Pennsylvania Archives, second series, vol. VII. 1890. Harrisburg: E. K. Meyers.

Pennsylvania Archives, second series, vol. IX. 1880. Harrisburg: Lane S. Hart.

Pennsylvania Archives, fourth series, vol. I. 1900. Harrisburg: Wm. Stanley Ray.

Pennsylvania Archives, fourth series, vol. III. 1900. Harrisburg: Wm. Stanley Ray.

Pennsylvania Archives, sixth series, vol. XI. 1907. Harrisburg: Harrisburg Publishing Co.

Pennsylvania Archives, eighth series, vol. II. 1931. Harrisburg: Bureau of Publications.

Proceedings in Parliament, 1614. 1988. Philadelphia: American Philosophical Society.

A Proclamation. 1701. New York: W. Bradford.

Public Records of the Colony of Connecticut, Prior to the Union with the New Haven Colony, May 1665. 1850. Hartford: Brown & Parsons.

Public Records of the Colony of Connecticut, from August, 1689, to May, 1706. 1868. Hartford: Case, Lockwood and Brainard.

Public Records of the Colony of Connecticut, from October, 1706, to October, 1716, with the Council Journal from October, 1710 to February, 1717. 1870. Hartford: Case, Lockwood and Brainard.

Public Records of the Colony of Connecticut, from May 1717, to October, 1725 with the Council Journal from May, 1717 to April, 1726. 1872. Hartford: Case, Lockwood and Brainard.

Public Records of the Colony of Connecticut, from May, 1726, to May, 1735, Inclusive. 1873. Hartford: Case, Lockwood and Brainard.

Public Records of the Colony of Connecticut, from October, 1735 to October, 1743, Inclusive. 1874. Hartford: Case, Lockwood and Brainard.

Public Records of the Colony of Connecticut, from May, 1762 to October, 1767, Inclusive. 1881. Hartford: Case, Lockwood and Brainard.

Public Records of the Colony of Connecticut, from May, 1768 to May, 1772. 1885. Hartford: Case, Lockwood and Brainard.

Records of the Colony of New Plymouth in New England. Court Orders: 1633–1640. 1855a. Boston: William White.

Records of the Colony of New Plymouth in New England. Court Orders: 1651–1661. 1855b. Boston: William White.

Records of the Colony of New Plymouth in New England. Court Orders: 1661–1668. 1855c. Boston: William White.

Records of the Colony of New Plymouth in New England. Laws: 1623–1682. 1861. Boston: William White.

Records of the Colony and Plantation of New Haven, from 1638 to 1649. 1857. Hartford: Case, Tiffany and Company.

Records of the Colony of Rhode Island and Providence Plantations, in New England, vol. I. 1856. Providence: A. Crawford Greene and Brother.

Records of the Colony of Rhode Island and Providence Plantations, in New England, vol. II. 1857. Providence: A. Crawford Greene and Brother.

Records of the Colony of Rhode Island and Providence Plantations, in New England, vol. IV. 1859. Providence: Knowles, Anthony & Co.

Records of the Colony of Rhode Island and Providence Plantations, in New England, vol. V. 1860. Providence: Knowles, Anthony & Co.

Records of the Colony of Rhode Island and Providence Plantations, in New England, vol. VI. 1861. Providence: Knowles, Anthony & Co.

Records of the Colony of Rhode Island and Providence Plantations, in New England, vol. VII. 1862. Providence: A. Crawford Greene.

Records of the Governor and Company of the Massachusetts Bay in New England, vol. I. 1853. Boston: William White.

Records of the Governor and Company of the Massachusetts Bay in New England, vol. II. 1853. Boston: William White.

Records of the Governor and Company of the Massachusetts Bay in New England, vol. III. 1854. Boston: William White.

Records of the Governor and Company of the Massachusetts Bay in New England, vol. IV—Part I. 1854. Boston: William White.

Records of the Governor and Company of the Massachusetts Bay in New England, vol. IV—Part II. 1854. Boston: William White.

Records of the Governor and Company of the Massachusetts Bay in New England, vol. V. 1854. Boston: William White.

Records of the Town of Braintree. 1886. Randolph: Daniel H. Huxford.

Records of the Town of Cambridge (Formerly Newtowne) Massachusetts, 1630–1703. 1901. Cambridge: University Press.

The Records of the Town of Hanover, New Hampshire, 1761–1818. 1905. Concord: Rumford Printing Co.

Records of the Town of Jamaica, Long Island, New York, 1656–1751, vol. I. 1914. Brooklyn: Long Island Historical Society.

Records of the Town of Newark, New Jersey, from its Settlement in 1666, to its Incorporation as a City in 1836. 1864. Newark: Daily Advertiser Office.

Records of the Town of Plymouth, vol. I. 1889. Plymouth: Avery & Doten.

Records of the Town of Plymouth, vol. II. 1892. Plymouth: Avery & Doten.

Records of the Town of Plymouth, vol. III. 1903. Plymouth. Memorial Press.

Records of the Towns of North and South Hempstead, Long Island, N. Y. 1896. Jamaica: Long Island Farmer Print.

Records of the Virginia Company of London, vol. III. 1933. Washington, DC: Government Printing Office.

Report of the Record Commissioners of the City of Boston, Containing the Boston Records from 1660 to 1701. 1881. Boston: Rockwell and Churchill.

Report of the Record Commissioners of the City of Boston, Containing the Boston Records from 1700 to 1728. 1883. Boston: Rockwell and Churchill.

Report of the Record Commissioners of the City of Boston, Containing the Boston Records from 1729 to 1742. 1885a. Boston: Rockwell and Church.

Report of the Record Commissioners of the City of Boston, Containing the Boston Town Records, 1742 to 1757. 1885b. Boston: Rockwell and Church.

Report of the Record Commissioners of the City of Boston, Containing the Boston Town Records, 1758 to 1769. 1886. Boston: Rockwell and Church.

Report of the Record Commissioners of the City of Boston, Containing the Boston Town Records, 1770 through 1777. 1887. Boston: Rockwell and Church.

Report of the Record Commissioners of the City of Boston, Containing the Records of Boston Selectmen, 1701 to 1715. 1884. Boston: Rockwell and Church.

Report of the Record Commissioners of the City of Boston, Containing the Records of Boston Selectmen, 1716 to 1736. 1885. Boston: Rockwell and Church.

Report of the Record Commissioners of the City of Boston, Containing the Records of Boston Selectmen, 1742–3 to 1753. 1887. Boston: Rockwell and Church.

Report of the Record Commissioners of the City of Boston, Containing the Records of Boston Selectmen, 1764 through 1768. 1889. Boston: Rockwell and Church.

The Revised Ordinances of the City of Norfolk, to Which are Prefixed the Original Charter of the Borough, and the Amended Charter of 1845 Creating the Borough into a City, and a Collection of Acts and Parts of Acts of the General Assembly, Relating to the City. 1866. Norfolk: Office of the Daily Old Dominion.

The Second Book of Records of the Town of Southampton, Long Island, N. Y., with other Ancient Documents of Historic Value. 1877. Sag-Harbor: John H. Hunt.

Second Report of the Record Commissioners of the City of Boston; Containing the Boston Records, 1634–1660, and the Book of Possessions, 2nd ed. 1881. Boston: Rockwell and Churchill.

State Records of North Carolina vol. XXV. 1906. Goldsboro: Nash Brothers.

The Statutes at Large; Being a Collection of all the Laws of Virginia, from the First Session of the Legislature, in the Year 1619, vol. I. 1809. Richmond: Samuel Pleasants, Junior.

The Statutes at Large; Being a Collection of all the Laws of Virginia, from the First Session of the Legislature, in the Year 1619, vol. II. 1823. New York: R. & W. & G. Bartow.

The Statutes at Large; Being a Collection of all the Laws of Virginia, from the First Session of the Legislature, in the Year 1619, vol. III. 1823. Philadelphia: Thomas Desilver.

The Statutes at Large; Being a Collection of all the Laws of Virginia, from the First Session of the Legislature, in the Year 1619, vol. IV. 1820. Richmond: Franklin Press.

The Statutes at Large; Being a Collection of all the Laws of Virginia, from the First Session of the Legislature, in the Year 1619, vol. V. 1819. Richmond: Franklin Press.

The Statutes at Large; Being a Collection of all the Laws of Virginia, from the First Session of the Legislature, in the Year 1619, vol. VII. 1820. Richmond: Franklin Press.

Statutes at Large of Pennsylvania from 1682 to 1801, vol. II. 1896. Harrisburg: Clarence M. Busch.

Statutes at Large of Pennsylvania from 1682 to 1801, vol. III. 1896. Harrisburg: Clarence M. Busch.

Statutes at Large of Pennsylvania from 1682 to 1801, vol. IV. 1897. Harrisburg: Clarence M. Busch.

Statutes at Large of Pennsylvania from 1682 to 1801, vol. V. 1898. Harrisburg: Wm Stanley Ray.

Statutes at Large of Pennsylvania from 1682 to 1801, vol. VI. 1899. Harrisburg: Wm Stanley Ray.

Statutes at Large of Pennsylvania from 1682 to 1801, vol. VII. 1900. Harrisburg: Wm Stanley Ray.

Statutes at Large of South Carolina, vol. second. 1837. Columbia: A. S. Johnson.

Statutes at Large of South Carolina, vol. third. 1838. Columbia: A. S. Johnson.

Statutes at Large of South Carolina, vol. fourth. 1838. Columbia: A. S. Johnson.

Town of Weston, Records of the First Precinct, 1746–1754, and of the Town, 1754–1803. 1893. Boston: Alfred Mudge & Son.

Town Records of Dudley, Massachusetts, 1732–1754. 1893. Pawtucket: Adam Sutcliffe Co.

Town Records of Dudley, Massachusetts, 1754–1794. 1894. Pawtucket: Adam Sutcliffe Co.

Town Records of Manchester, from the Earliest Grants of Land, 1636, When a Portion of Salem until 1736, as Contained in the Town Records of Salem, Second and Third Book of the Records of the Town of Manchester. 1889. Salem: Salem Press Publishing and Printing Co.

Town Records of Manchester, from 1718 to 1769, as Contained in the "Commoners Records," and the "Fourth Book of Town Records," 1736 to 1786, vol. II. 1891. Salem: Salem Press Publishing and Printing Co.

Town Records of Salem, Massachusetts, vol. I. 1868. Salem: The Essex Institute.

Town Records of Salem, Massachusetts, vol. II. 1913. Salem: The Essex Institute.

Town Records of Salem, Massachusetts, vol. III. 1934. Salem: The Essex Institute.

Town Records of Topsfield, Massachusetts, vol. I. 1917. Topsfield: Topsfield Historical Society.

Town Records of Topsfield, Massachusetts, vol. II. 1920. Topsfield: Topsfield Historical Society.

Votes and Proceedings of the General Assembly of the Colony of New-York (April). 1744. New York: James Parker.

Votes and Proceedings of the General Assembly of the Colony of New-York (July). 1744. New York: James Parker.

Votes and Proceedings of the General Assembly of the Colony of New-York (November, 1744). 1745. New York: James Parker.

Votes and Proceedings of the General Assembly of the Province of New-Jersey. 1740. Philadelphia: B. Franklin.

Votes and Proceedings of the General Assembly of the Province of New-Jersey (April). 1745. Philadelphia: William Bradford.

Votes and Proceedings of the General Assembly of the Province of New-Jersey (September). 1745. Philadelphia: William Bradford.

Votes and Proceedings of the General Assembly of the Province of New-Jersey (February 1745–1746). 1746. Philadelphia: William Bradford.

Votes and Proceedings of the General Assembly of the Province of New-Jersey (May). 1746. Philadelphia: William Bradford.

Votes and Proceedings of the General Assembly of the Province of New-Jersey. 1748. Philadelphia: William Bradford.

Votes and Proceedings of the General Assembly of the Province of New-Jersey. 1749. Philadelphia: William Bradford.

Votes and Proceedings of the General Assembly of the Province of New-Jersey. 1750. Philadelphia: William Bradford.

Votes and Proceedings of the General Assembly of the Province of New-Jersey (February). 1755. Woodbridge: James Parker.

Votes and Proceedings of the General Assembly of the Province of New-Jersey (July). 1755. Philadelphia: William Bradford.

Votes and Proceedings of the General Assembly of the Province of New-Jersey (December). 1755. Philadelphia: William Bradford.

Votes and Proceedings of the General Assembly of the Province of New-Jersey (May). 1756. Woodbridge: James Parker.

Votes and Proceedings of the General Assembly of the Province of New-Jersey (March). 1757. Woodbridge: James Parker.

Votes and Proceedings of the General Assembly of the Province of New-Jersey (March [*sic*] May). 1757. Woodbridge: James Parker.

Votes and Proceedings of the General Assembly of the Province of New-Jersey (August). 1757. Woodbridge: James Parker.

Votes and Proceedings of the General Assembly of the Province of New-Jersey (October). 1757. Woodbridge: James Parker.

Votes and Proceedings of the General Assembly of the Province of New-Jersey (March). 1758. Woodbridge: James Parker.

Votes and Proceedings of the General Assembly of the Province of New-Jersey (July). 1758. Woodbridge: James Parker.

Votes and Proceedings of the General Assembly of the Province of New-Jersey (March). 1760. Woodbridge: James Parker.

Votes and Proceedings of the General Assembly of the Province of New-Jersey (October). 1760. Woodbridge: James Parker.

Votes and Proceedings of the General Assembly of the Province of New-Jersey. 1765. Burlington: James Parker.

Votes and Proceedings of the General Assembly of the Province of New-Jersey. 1769. Woodbridge: James Parker.

Votes and Proceedings of the General Assembly of the Province of New-Jersey, Held at Amboy on Friday the Second of October, 1741. 1741. Philadelphia: B. Franklin.

Votes and Proceedings of the General Assembly of the Province of New-Jersey, Held at Burlington on Friday the Twenty-Second of June 1744. 1744. Philadelphia: William Bradford.

Votes and Proceedings of the General Assembly of the Province of New-Jersey. Held at Burlington on Thursday the Twentieth of August 1746. 1746. Philadelphia: William Bradford.

Votes and Proceedings of the General Assembly of the Province of New-Jersey held at Trenton on Friday the Ninth of May 1746. 1746. Philadelphia: William Bradford.

Votes and Proceedings of the General Assembly of the Province of New-Jersey held at Burlington on Thursday the 24th of January 1750–1. 1751. Philadelphia: William Bradford.

Votes and Proceedings of the General Assembly of the Province of New-Jersey, held at Perth-Amboy on Monday the 20th of May 1751. 1751. Philadelphia: W. Bradford.

Votes and Proceedings of the General Assembly of the Province of New-Jersey, held at Perth-Amboy on Monday the 20th of May 1751. 1751. Philadelphia: W. Bradford.

Votes and Proceedings of the General Assembly of the Province of New-Jersey, held at Perth-Amboy on Saturday the 25th of January 1752. 1752. Philadelphia: W. Bradford.

Votes and Proceedings of the General Assembly of the Province of New-Jersey, Begun at Perth-Amboy, Wednesday April 17, 1754, and adjourn'd to Elizabeth-Town, Thursday April 25, 1754. 1754. Woodbridge: James Parker.

Votes and Proceedings of the General Assembly of the Province of New-Jersey: At a Sessions begun and holden at Perth-Amboy, October 1, 1754. 1754. Woodbridge: James Parker.

Votes and Proceedings of the General Assembly of the Province of New-Jersey: At a Sessions begun and holden at Elizabeth-Town, April 7, 1755. 1755. Woodbridge: James Parker.

Votes and Proceedings of the General Assembly of the Province of New-Jersey: At a Session held at Elizabeth-Town, by Adjournment, March 9th, 1756, and continued till the 16th Day of the same Month, and then Adjourned to the 7th day of April following. 1756. Philadelphia: William Bradford.

Votes and Proceedings of the General Assembly of the Province of New-Jersey, At a Session held at Perth-Amboy, began March 8, 1759, and then prorogued to the 17th day of April following. 1759. Woodbridge: James Parker.

Votes and Proceedings of the General Assembly of the Province of New-Jersey, which began the 27th of October, 1738. 1738. New York: John Peter Zenger.

Votes and Proceedings of the House of Representatives of the Government of the Counties of New-Castle, Kent, and Suffolk, upon Delaware, at a Session of Assembly Held at New-Castle the Twenty-First Day of October (the Twentieth being Sunday) 1765. 1770. Wilmington: James Adams.

Votes and Proceedings of the House of Representatives of the Province of Pennsylvania. Beginning the Fourth Day of December, 1682, vol. the First. 1752. Philadelphia: B. Franklin and D. Hall.

Votes and Proceedings of the House of Representatives of the Province of Pennsylvania. Beginning the Fourteenth Day of October, 1707, vol. the Second. 1753. Philadelphia: B. Franklin and D. Hall.

Votes and Proceedings of the House of Representatives of the Province of Pennsylvania, vol. [the First] Part the Second. 1752. Philadelphia: B. Franklin and D. Hall.

Votes and Proceedings of the House of Representatives of the Province of Pennsylvania, Met at Philadelphia, on Saturday the Fourteenth of October, Anno Dom. 1732, and continued by Adjournments. 1732. Philadelphia: B. Franklin.

Votes and Proceedings of the House of Representatives of the Province of Pennsylvania, Met at Philadelphia, on the Fourteenth of October, Anno Dom. 1738, and continued by Adjournments. 1738. Philadelphia: B. Franklin.

Votes and Proceedings of the House of Representatives of the Province of Pennsylvania, Met at Philadelphia, on the Fifteenth of October, Anno Dom. 1739, and continued by Adjournments. 1739. Philadelphia: B. Franklin.

Votes and Proceedings of the House of Representatives of the Province of Pennsylvania, Met at Philadelphia, on the Fourteenth of October, Anno Dom. 1741, and continued by Adjournments. 1741. Philadelphia: B. Franklin.

Votes and Proceedings of the House of Representatives of the Province of Pennsylvania, Met at Philadelphia, on the Fourteenth of October, Anno Dom. 1742, and continued by Adjournments. 1743. Philadelphia: B. Franklin.

Votes and Proceedings of the House of Representatives of the Province of Pennsylvania, Met at Philadelphia, on the Fifteenth of October, Anno Dom. 1744, and continued by Adjournments. 1745. Philadelphia: B. Franklin.

Votes and Proceedings of the House of Representatives of the Province of Pennsylvania, Met at Philadelphia, on the Fourteenth of October, Anno Dom. 1748, and continued by Adjournments. 1749. Philadelphia: B. Franklin.

Votes and Proceedings of the House of Representatives of the Province of Pennsylvania, Met at Philadelphia, on the Fourteenth of October, Anno Dom. 1749, and continued by Adjournments. 1750. Philadelphia: B. Franklin.

Votes and Proceedings of the House of Representatives of the Province of Pennsylvania, Met at Philadelphia, on the Fourteenth Day of October, Anno Dom. 1750, and continued by Adjournments. 1751. Philadelphia: B. Franklin.

Votes and Proceedings of the House of Representatives of the Province of Pennsylvania, Met at Philadelphia, on the Fifteenth Day of October, Anno Domini 1753, and Continued by Adjournments. 1754. Philadelphia: B. Franklin.

Votes and Proceedings of the House of Representatives of the Province of Pennsylvania, Met at Philadelphia, on the Fourteenth of October, Anno Domini 1754, and Continued by Adjournments. 1755. Philadelphia: B. Franklin.

Votes and Proceedings of the House of Representatives of the Province of Pennsylvania, Met at Philadelphia, on the Fourteenth of October, Anno Domini 1755, and continued by Adjournments. 1756. Philadelphia: B. Franklin.

Votes and Proceedings of the House of Representatives of the Province of Pennsylvania, Met at Philadelphia, on the Fourteenth of October, Anno Domini 1756, and continued by Adjournments. 1757. Philadelphia: B. Franklin.

Votes and Proceedings of the House of Representatives of the Province of Pennsylvania, Met at Philadelphia, on the Fourteenth of October, Anno Domini *1763, and continued by Adjournments.* 1764. Philadelphia, PA: B. Franklin and D. Hall.

Votes and Proceedings of the House of Representatives of the Province of Pennsylvania, Met at Philadelphia, on the Fifteenth of October, Anno Domini *1764, and continued by Adjournments.* 1764. Philadelphia, PA: B. Franklin and D. Hall.

Votes and Proceedings, of the Lower House of Assembly of the Province of Maryland. 1732. Annapolis: William Parks and Edmund Hall.

Votes and Proceedings, of the Lower House of Assembly of the Province of Maryland. 1733. Annapolis: William Parks.

Votes and Proceedings of the Lower House of Assembly of the Province of Maryland. 1735. Annapolis: William Parks.

Votes and Proceedings of the Lower House of Assembly of the Province of Maryland. 1740. Annapolis: Jonas Green.

Votes and Proceedings of the Lower House of Assembly of the Province of Maryland, at a session begun and held August 5, 1745. 1745. Annapolis: Jonas Green.

Votes and Proceedings of the Lower House of Assembly of the Province of Maryland, at a session begun and held March 12, 1745.6. 1746. Annapolis: Jonas Green.

Votes and Proceedings of the Lower House of Assembly of the Province of Maryland. 1746. Annapolis: Jonas Green.

Votes and Proceedings of the Lower House of Assembly of the Province of Maryland. 1747. Annapolis: Jonas Green.

Votes and Proceedings of the Lower House of Assembly of the Province of Maryland. 1748. Annapolis: Jonas Green.

Votes and Proceedings of the Lower House of Assembly of the Province of Maryland. 1749. Annapolis: Jonas Green.

Votes and Proceedings of the Lower House of Assembly of the Province of Maryland. 1750. Annapolis: Jonas Green.

Votes and Proceedings of the Lower House of Assembly of the Province of Maryland. 1752. Annapolis: Jonas Green.

Votes and Proceedings of the Lower House of Assembly of the Province of Maryland. 1753/1754. Annapolis: Jonas Green.

Votes and Proceedings of the Lower House of Assembly of the Province of Maryland. 1755. Annapolis: Jonas Green.

Votes and Proceedings of the Lower House of Assembly of the Province of Maryland. 1757. Annapolis: Jonas Green.

Votes and Proceedings of the Lower House of Assembly of the Province of Maryland. 1759. Annapolis: Jonas Green.

Votes and Proceedings of the Lower House of Assembly of the Province of Maryland. 1762. Annapolis: Jonas Green.

Votes and Proceedings of the Lower House of Assembly of the Province of Maryland. 1768. Annapolis: Anne Catharine Green.

Votes and Proceedings of the Lower House of Assembly of the Province of Maryland. 1771. Annapolis: Anne Catharine Green.

Votes and Proceedings of the Lower House of Assembly of the Province of Maryland. November session, 1769. Being the second session of this Assembly. 1770. Annapolis: Anne Catharine Green.

Votes and Resolves of the Lower House of Assembly, of the Province of Maryland. 1728. Annapolis: William Parks.

Votes of the General Assembly (May). 1747. Philadelphia: William Bradford.

Votes of the General Assembly (November). 1747. Philadelphia: William Bradford.

Votes of the General Assembly of His Majesty's Province of New-York, in America. 1725. New York: William Bradford.

Watertown Records, Comprising the First and Second Books of Town Proceedings with the Land Grants and Possessions, also the Proprietors' Book and the First Book and Supplement of Births Deaths and Marriages. 1894. Watertown: Press of Fred G. Barker.

Watertown Records, Comprising the Third Book of Town Proceedings and the Second Book of Births Marriages and Deaths to the End of 1737, also Plan and Register of Burials in Arlington Street Burying Ground. 1900. Watertown: Press of Fred G. Barker.

Watertown Records, Comprising the Fourth Book of Town Proceedings and the Second Book of Births Marriages and Deaths from 1738 to 1822. 1904. Boston: F. H. Gilson, Company.

Watertown Records, Comprising the Fifth Book of Town Proceedings 1745/6 to 1769 and the Sixth Book of Town Proceedings, 1769 to 1792. 1928. Newton: Graphic Press.

Worcester Town Records, from 1753 to 1783. 1882. Worcester: Worcester Society of Antiquity.

II. NEWSPAPERS AND PERIODICALS

American Weekly Mercury. 1720. "New-Castle, Octob. 24." October 27.

American Weekly Mercury. 1722. "ADVERTISEMENTS." January 9–16.

American Weekly Mercury. 1729. "The Busy-Body." September 18–25.

American Weekly Mercury. 1733a. "Whereas great Complaint is made." September 27-October 4.

American Weekly Mercury. 1733b. "Mr. Bradford." December 14–21.

American Weekly Mercury. 1734. "Philadelphia, October 3." September 26-October 3.

American Weekly Mercury. 1735. "Mr. Bradford." September 18–25.

American Weekly Mercury. 1737. "New-York, September 12." September 8–15.

Boston Evening-Post. 1738. "Boston." May 8.

Boston Evening-Post. 1739. "From the New-York Weekly Journal, March 19, 1738." April 30.

Boston Evening-Post. 1750. "To the Publisher of the Boston Evening-Post." May 7.

Boston Evening-Post. 1754. "Boston. In the House of Representatives, June 18, 1754." June 24.

Boston Evening-Post. 1759. "Some Observations and Remarks relating to the Election of Representatives." May 14.

Boston Evening-Post. 1763. "Mene, Mene, Tekel Upharsin." March 14.

Boston Evening-Post. 1764a. "To the Freeholders, &c." May 14.

Boston Evening-Post. 1764b. "Boston, May 23." May 28.

Boston Evening-Post. 1764c. "Mr. Franklin's Remarks on a late Protest." December 24.

Boston Evening-Post. 1765a. "Boston, Sept. 13, 1765." September 16.

Boston Evening-Post. 1765b. "To Jacob Fowle and William Bourn, Esq'rs, the present Representatives of the Town of Marblehead." October 14.

Boston Evening-Post. 1765c. "At a Meeting of the Freeholders and Other Inhabitants of the Town of Salem." October 28.

Boston Evening-Post. 1765d. "Pembroke, October 21 1765." October 28.

Boston Evening-Post. 1765e. "Boston, November 4." November 4.

Boston Evening-Post. 1767. "BOSTON, May 25." May 25.

Boston Evening-Post. 1768a. "Messi'rs Fleets." August 15.

Boston Evening-Post. 1768b. "Boston, September 5, 1768." September 5.

Boston Evening-Post. 1769a. "Journal of the Times." January 16.

Boston Evening-Post. 1769b. "The Town of Bridgewater." May 29.

Boston Evening-Post. 1770. "To. Mr. Samuel Bachelder, Representative for the Town of Haverhill." October 1.

Boston Evening-Post. 1773a. "To ABRAHAM FULLER, Esq." February 1.

Boston Evening-Post. 1773b. "Proceedings of the Town of Medway." May 17.

Boston Evening-Post. 1773c. "The Town, after passing the above Resolves, voted the following Instructions to their Representative, which passed nemine contradicente." May 24.

Boston Gazette, or Weekly JOURNAL. 1751. "Extract of a Letter, dated Barnstable May 10th 1751." May 14.

Boston Gazette, or WEEKLY ADVERTISER. 1753. "BOSTON." May 22.

Boston Gazette, or WEEKLY ADVERTISER. 1754a. "The Speech of His Excellency WILLIAM SHIRLEY, Esq." June 18.

Boston Gazette, or WEEKLY ADVERTISER. 1754b. "We hear that the Towns" August 20.

Boston Gazette, or WEEKLY ADVERTISER. 1754c. "Boston." September 17.

Boston Gazette, or WEEKLY ADVERTISER. 1754d. "Newbury, September 20, 1754." September 23.

Boston Gazette, or WEEKLY ADVERTISER. 1754e. "Mr. Kneeland." December 31.

Boston Gazette (supplement). 1766a. "To the Inhabitants of the Province of Massachusetts Bay." April 14.

Boston Gazette, and COUNTRY JOURNAL. 1766b. "Boston, July 28." July 28.

Boston-Gazette (supplement). 1773a. "To James Prescott, Esq. Representative of the Town of Groton, and the Districts of Pepperall and Shirley." April 19.

Boston Gazette, and COUNTRY JOURNAL. 1773b. "At a legal Meeting of the Freeholders and other Inhabitants of the Town of Mendon, held by Adjournment from February 10th, to March 1, 1773, it being the Day of our anniversary Town-Meeting for the Election of Town Officers." June 6.

Boston Gazette, and COUNTRY JOURNAL. 1773c. "The proceedings of the Town of Townshend, at a Meeting of the Inhabitants of said Town, legally Assembled at the Publick Meeting-House, in said Town, upon Tuesday the fifth of January 1773, at Eleven of the Clock in the Forenoon." July 26.

Boston Gazette, and COUNTRY JOURNAL. 1773d. "At a legal Meeting of the Freeholders and other Inhabitants of the Town of Westborough, on Friday, the first Day of January, 1773, the following Vote passed, viz." July 26.

Boston Gazette (supplement). 1773e. "At Legal Meeting of the Freeholders and other Inhabitants of the Town of Harvard, on Monday March 1st, by adjournment from the 18th of February, last." August 30.

Boston News-Letter. 1765. "Boston, October 24." October 24.

Boston Post Boy. 1754. "Custom-House, Rhode Island, Sept. 20." September 23.

Boston Post-Boy & Advertiser. 1763. "The following Gentlemen are returned to represent the Several Towns, viz." May 30.

Boston Post-Boy, &c. Extraordinary. 1765a. "To Mr. Henry Herrick." November 4.

Boston Post-Boy, &c. Extraordinary. 1765b. "The Following are INSTRUCTIONS voted by the Town of Newbury-Port, at a legal Meeting of the Freeholders and other Inhabitants of said Town, October 21, 1765, and given to Dudley Atkins, Esq., their Representative." November 4.

Boston Post-Boy, &c. Extraordinary. 1765c. "At a Meeting of the Freeholders and other Inhabitants of the Town of Ipswich, assembled on this 21st Day of October, 1765, Voted that the following Instructions be given to Dr. John Calef, Representative of said Town, for his Conduct at the next Meeting of the General Assembly." November 4.

Boston Post-Boy & Advertiser. 1765d. "At a Meeting of a large Assembly of the respectable Populace in New-London the 10th of Decem. 1765, the following Resolves were unanimously come into." December 16.

Boston Post Boy. 1769. "Boston, May 29." May 29.

Boston Weekly News-Letter. 1747. "Ipswich, May 15." May 21.

Boston Weekly News-Letter. 1735. "Dorchester, May 5." May 1–8.

Boston Weekly News-Letter. 1769. "At a Town Meeting Held at Brooklyn, by Adjournment, the 30th Day of May, 1769." June 8.

Boston Weekly Post-Boy. 1741. "Woburn, May 5." May 11.

Connecticut Courant. 1765a. "A COPY of the Instructions, given by the Freemen of the Town of HARTFORD, to their Deputies." September 23.

Connecticut Courant. 1765b. "NEW-HAVEN, September 20." September 23.

Connecticut Courant. 1768. "To the PRINTERS." August 29.

Connecticut Courant. 1770. "From the *New York Gazette*." March 5.

Connecticut Gazette; and Universal Intelligencer. 1774. "PROVIDENCE, August 13; At a Town-Meeting held at Providence, convened by Warrant, on the 12th Day of August, 1774." August 19.

Connecticut Gazette; and Universal Intelligencer. 1775. "Middletown, Octo. 18, 1775." November 10.

Dunlap's Pennsylvania Packet. 1775. "To the FREEHOLDERS and others, qualified to elect Members of Assembly for the County of Chester." September 25.

Essex Gazette. 1768a. "From the New-Hampshire Gazette." May 2–9.

Essex Gazette. 1768b. "NEW-YORK, Nov, 24." December 6–13.

Essex Gazette. 1769a. "Monday, May 8." May 2–9.

Essex Gazette. 1769b. "Monday, May 23." May 16–23.

Essex Gazette. 1773a. "The Committee of Correspondence have received the following Votes and Resolves of the large and respectable town of IPSWICH." January 12–19.

Essex Gazette. 1773b. "The Following are the Instructions from the Town of Petersham to Capt. Ephraim Doolittle, their Representative, voted unanimously at the later Meeting." January 19–26.

Essex Gazette. 1773c. "The Committee also Reported the following INSTRUCTIONS to the Representatives of this Town." March 16–23.

Essex Gazette. 1773d. "Danvers, March 7, 1773." April 13–20.

Essex Gazette. 1773e. "At a legal meeting of the freeholders and other inhabitants of the town of Beverly, assembled by adjournment from the 21st day of December last past, to this 5th day of January, 1773." April 13–20.

Essex Gazette. 1773f. "SALEM, My 25." May 18–25.

Essex Gazette. 1774. "At a Meeting of the Freeholders of the Town of Beverly, on the 26th Day of September, 1774. September 27-October 4.

Gentleman's Magazine. 1768. "Ballad on the GENERAL ELECTION." March.

Georgia Gazette. 1764. "Georgia." October 11."

Georgia Gazette. 1765. "Boston, in New-England, Sept. 28." October 24.

Georgia Gazette. 1768a. "Georgia." April 20.

Georgia Gazette. 1768b. "To Mrs. Heriot Crooke." May 11.

Georgia Gazette. 1768c. "Georgia." July 6.

Georgia Gazette. 1769. "SAVANNAH, October 25." October 25.

Independent Reflector. 1753. "Of Elections, and Election-Jobbers." July 5.

Maryland Gazette. 1745. "ADVERTISEMENTS." August 9.

Maryland Gazette. 1747a. "Mr. Green." May 12.

Maryland Gazette. 1747b. "Annapolis." July 21.

Maryland Gazette. 1749. "Annapolis." April 19.

Maryland Gazette. 1750a. "Annapolis." January 31.

Maryland Gazette. 1750b. "Annapolis." May 30.

Maryland Gazette. 1750c. "In Pursuance to the Order of the honourable the Lower House of Assembly, at their Session in May last, the following Bill, which did not Pass into a Law is here inserted, viz." July 25.

Maryland Gazette. 1750d. "The Honourable the Lower House of Assembly, at their last Sitting, Ordered, That the following Bill, which was put off for the Consideration of the next Session of Assembly, should be published in one or more of the *Maryland* Gazettes." August 1.

Maryland Gazette. 1750e. "Conclusion of the Bill, entituled, An Act for the better Encouragement of Learning within this Province, which was begun in our last." August 8.

Maryland Gazette. 1751a. "Annapolis." June 5.

Maryland Gazette. 1751b. "Annapolis." December 18.

Maryland Gazette. 1752a. "To the Honourable the Lower House of Assembly; the humble Petition of *John Paca*, *Walter Tolly*, *William Smith*, and *John Matthews*, of *Baltimore* County, Gentlemen." February 13.

Maryland Gazette. 1752b. "Annapolis." March 12.

Maryland Gazette. 1752c. "Annapolis." April 23.

Maryland Gazette. 1753a. "To his Excellency HORATIO SHARPE, Esq." October 11.

Maryland Gazette. 1753b. "NOTICE is hereby given." October 11.

Maryland Gazette. 1754a. "To the Printer of the MARYLAND Gazette." October 24.

Maryland Gazette. 1754b. "ANNAPOLIS." December 19.

Maryland Gazette. 1755a. "To Mr. Jonas Green." March 6.

Maryland Gazette. 1755b. "ANNAPOLIS, July 3." July 3.

Maryland Gazette. 1755c. "ANNAPOLIS, August 7." August 7.

Maryland Gazette. 1756a. "The Subscriber." August 7.

Maryland Gazette. 1756b. "ANNAPOLIS, Sept. 16." September 16.

Maryland Gazette. 1757. "To the Worshipful John Goldsborough, Mathew Tilghman, Pollard Edmondson and *—— ——, Esquires, Representatives for Talbot County in the General Assembly of Maryland." February 10.

Maryland Gazette. 1758a. "By the UPPER HOUSE of ASSEMBLY, December 16, 1757." January 5.

Maryland Gazette. 1758b. "Mr. Green." August 24.

Maryland Gazette. 1759a. "ANNAPOLIS, January 12." January 12.

Maryland Gazette. 1759b. "NEW-YORK, January 15." January 25.

Maryland Gazette. 1760. "ANNAPOLIS, October 9." October 9.

Maryland Gazette. 1761. "ANNAPOLIS, November 12." November 12.

Maryland Gazette. 1764a. "ANNAPOLIS, December 13." December 13.

Maryland Gazette. 1764b. "ANNAPOLIS, December 20." December 20.

Maryland Gazette. 1765a. "From the Boston Evening Post, August 19." September 5.

Maryland Gazette. 1765b. "The Freemen of the Town of Newport, at a Meeting held on the third Instant, Unanimously Voted, That the following Instructions should be given to the Gentlemen who represent them in the General Assembly, viz." September 26.

Maryland Gazette. 1765c. "A Copy of the REMONSTRANCE of the Freeholders and Freemen of Anne-Arundel County, to Messeurs Worthington, Hammond, Hall, and Johnson, their Representatives in Assembly; accompanied with some Instructions to them." October 24.

Maryland Gazette. 1767. "To the FREEHOLDERS and FREE-VOTERS in ANNE-ARUNDEL COUNTY." December 3.

Maryland Gazette. 1768a. "ANNAPOLIS, June 16." June 16.

Maryland Gazette. 1768b. "ANNAPOLIS, July 14." July 14.

Maryland Gazette. 1770. "Supplement to the Maryland Gazette." November 29.

Maryland Gazette. 1771a. "To the PRINTER." February 7.

Maryland Gazette. 1771b. "ANNAPOLIS." October 17.

Maryland Gazette. 1771c. "ANNAPOLIS." November 21.

Maryland Gazette. 1773a. "To the GENTLEMEN, FREEMEN, and VOTERS of the City of ANNAPOLIS." May 13.

Maryland Gazette. 1773b. "ANNAPOLIS, May 20." May 20.

Maryland Gazette. 1773c. "To the FIRST CITIZEN." May 20.

Maryland Gazette. 1773d. "To BRUTUS." May 20.

Maryland Gazette. 1773e. "To the FIRST CITIZEN." June 10.

Maryland Gazette. 1773f. "To Charles Ridgely, Thomas Cockey Dye, Aquila Hall, and Walter Tolley, Esqs." June 17.

Maryland Gazette. 1773g. "To the PUBLICK." July 29.

Maryland Gazette. 1773h. "To JOHN HAMMOND, Esquire." September 9.

Maryland Gazette. 1773i. "To the Electors of Anne-Arundel county." November 4.

Massachusetts Gazette. 1765. "To STEPHEN HALL, Esq." October 24.

Massachusetts Gazette and the Boston News-Letter. 1766. "We hear from Charlestown." August 21.

Massachusetts Gazette and Boston News-Letter. 1767. "Having occasionally met with the Resolves of a Committee chosen and appointed the Town of Medfield." December 31.

Massachusetts Gazette and Boston News-Letter. 1768. "Medfield, January 5, 1768."
    January 7.

Massachusetts Gazette and the Boston Weekly News-Letter. 1772. "AT a Meeting of the
    Freeholders and other Inhabitants of the Town of Charlestown, legally Assem-
    bled on 7th December, 1772, and continued by Adjournment to the 28th of said
    Month." December 31.

Massachusetts Gazette and the Boston Weekly News-Letter. 1773a. "The said Commit-
    tee reported the following INSTRUCTIONS to their Representative, viz. 'To
    SIMON ESTES, Esq.'" January 14.

Massachusetts Gazette (supplement). 1773b. "At a Legal Meeting of the Freeholders
    and other Inhabitants of the Town of Medfield, on the 28th Day of December,
    1772, and continued by Adjournment to the Eleventh Day of January, 1773."
    March 25.

Massachusetts Gazette and the Boston Weekly News-Letter. 1774. "AT a Town-Meeting
    held in MARSHFIELD, the 31st of January, 1774, NATHANIEL RAY." Feb-
    ruary 3.

Massachusetts Spy. 1770. New-Haven, September 28." October 11 to 13.

Massachusetts Spy Or, Thomas's Boston Journal. 1772. "To Capt. William Heath, Rep-
    resentative of the Town of Roxbury, in General Assembly." November 26.

Massachusetts Spy Or, Thomas's Boston Journal. 1773a. "At a legal meeting of the free-
    holders and other inhabitants of the town of GLOUCESTER, qualified for
    voting, by adjournment, on the 28th day of December, Anno Domini. 1772."
    January 14.

Massachusetts Spy Or, Thomas's Boston Journal. 1773b. "At a meeting of the freehold-
    ers and other inhabitants of the town of DEDHAM, duly warned and legally
    assembled, at the meeting-house in the first precinct, on Monday the 4th day of
    January, A. D. 1773." January 14.

Massachusetts Spy Or, Thomas's Boston Journal. 1773c. "Our committee of correspon-
    dence have received the following letter from the Town of YORK." January 14.

Massachusetts Spy Or, Thomas's Boston Journal. 1773d. "The following proceedings of
    the town of BOLTON, have been received by the Committee of Correspon-
    dence in this town." January 14.

Massachusetts Spy Or, Thomas's Boston Journal. 1773e. "Proceedings of the Town of
    LEICESTER." February 11.

Massachusetts Spy Or, Thomas's Boston Journal. 1773f. "At a meeting of the Town of
    LYNN, legally assembled on the 6th of January, A.D. 1773." February 25.

Massachusetts Spy Or, Thomas's Boston Journal. 1773g. "Friday, March 12." March 18.

Massachusetts Spy Or, Thomas's Boston Journal. 1773h. "Wednesday, March 17." March 18

Massachusetts Spy Or, Thomas's Boston Journal. 1773i. "Wednesday, June 16." June 17.

Newport Mercury. 1764a. "GIDEON WANTON, jun." April 16.

Newport Mercury. 1764b. "To the Freemen of the Town of Newport." April 16.

Newport Mercury. 1765. "At a Town-Meeting of the Town of Little-Compton, in
    the Colony of Rhode-Island, on the 27th Day of August, 1765." September 2.

Newport Mercury. 1768. "BALLAD on the General Election." August 22–29.

Newport Mercury. 1774a. "To the FREEMEN of the town of Newport." April 18.

Newport Mercury. 1774b. "The subscriber presents his regards to the freemen of the
    town of Newport." April 18.

Newport Mercury. 1774c. "Newport, May 2." May 2.

Newport Mercury. 1774d. "At a town meeting held at Providence, on the 17th day of May, 1774, called by warrant." June 13.

New-England Courant. 1726. "Boston, January 15." January 15–22.

New-England Weekly Journal. 1729a. "Boston." March 17.

New-England Weekly Journal. 1729b. "Boston." May 19.

New-England Weekly Journal. 1740. "Cambridge, May 19." May 20.

New-Hampshire Gazette. 1762. "To the Freeholders." January 15.

New-Hampshire Gazette. 1765. "Portsmouth." December 27.

New-Hampshire Gazette and Historical Chronicle. 1770. "At the Annual Meeting of the Town of EXETER March 26, 1770." April 13.

New-Hampshire Gazette and Historical Chronicle. 1774a. "TAXATION, without REPRESENTATION, is subversive of our constitutional LIBERTY." March 18.

New-Hampshire Gazette and Historical Chronicle. 1774b. "To the independent Freeholders of the Town of Portsmouth." March 25.

New-Hampshire Gazette and Historical Chronicle. 1774c. "To the ELECTORS of REPRESENTATIVES for the Town of Portsmouth." March 25.

New-Hampshire Gazette and Historical Chronicle. 1775. "To the Hon. JOHN FENTON, Esq." February 24.

New-London Gazette. 1765. "Instructions given by the Town of Norwich, on the 10th Day of September, 1765, to their Representatives in General Assembly." September 13.

New-London Gazette. 1766. "A Meeting of the Freemen of the Town of Windham, on the 9th of September, A. D. 1766, it was voted (neminecontradicente) that the following Instructions be given to the Representatives chosen to represent us, at the General Assembly, to be held at New-Haven, in October next." October 31.

New-London Gazette. 1768. "Instructions of the Freemen of the Town of Lebanon, in Connecticut, to Major William Williams, and Capt. William Symmes, Representatives of said Town, at the General Assembly to be holden at Hartford, the second Thursday in May next." April 29.

New-London Gazette. 1769. "Instructions from the Freemen of the Town of Norwich, to their Representatives, Sept. 12, 1769." September 22.

New-York Evening Post. 1747a. "TO the Freeholders and Freemen, of the City and County of NEW-YORK." January 11.

New-York Evening Post. 1747b. "To C. C. Esq." January 25.

New York Gazette Revived in the Weekly Post-Boy. 1747a. "Extract from the Votes of the General-Assembly of New-York." October 12.

New York Gazette Revived in the Weekly Post-Boy. 1747b. "A MESSAGE from his Excellency the Honourable George Clinton, Captain General and Governor in Chief of the Province of New-York, &c. To the General Assembly of said Province, on Tuesday the 13th of October, 1747." October 19.

New York Gazette Revived in the Weekly Post-Boy. 1747c. "By His Excellency the Honourable GEORGE CLINTON, Captain General and Governor in Chief of the Province of New-York, &c." October 26.

New York Gazette Revived in the Weekly Post-Boy. 1747d. "Die Martis, 17th of October, 1747." November 2.

New York Gazette Revived in the Weekly Post-Boy. 1747e. "Extract from the Votes of the General Assembly of New-York." November 23.

New York Gazette Revived in the Weekly Post-Boy. 1747f. "To the Freeholders and Freemen of the City and County of New-York." November 30.

New York Gazette Revived in the Weekly Post-Boy. 1747–48. "An Address to the Freeholders and Freemen of the Cities and Counties of New-York, on Occasion of the ensuing Elections for Representatives in General Assembly." January 18.

New York Gazette Revived in the Weekly Post-Boy. 1749. "Mr. Parker." May 22.

New York Gazette Revived in the Weekly Post-Boy. 1750a. "To the Freeholders and Freemen of the City and County of New-York." September 3.

New York Gazette Revived in the Weekly Post-Boy. 1750b. "NEW-YORK, September 3." September 3.

New York Gazette Revived in the Weekly Post-Boy. 1751. "To the Freeholders and Electors of the Several Counties and Corporations of the Province of New-Jersey." March 18.

New York Gazette Revived in the Weekly Post-Boy. 1752a. "To the Freeholders and Freemen of the City and County of New-York." January 27.

New York Gazette Revived in the Weekly Post-Boy. 1752b. "At a grand Meeting at the Niew Zale van Cajapham, in the Out-Ward of the City of New-York on the [blank] Day of January, 1752." February 3.

New York Gazette Revived in the Weekly Post-Boy. 1752c. "Extract of a Letter from Queen's County, dated 15th Feb. 1752." February 3.

New-York Gazette. 1761a. "New-York, January 21, 1761." February 2.

New-York Gazette. 1761b. "A Report having been industriously propagated." February 2.

New-York Gazette. 1761c. "William Bayard, Begs Leave to inform the PUBLICK." February 2.

New-York Gazette. 1761d. "PURSUANT to His Majesty's Writ." February 2.

New-York Gazette. 1761e. "New-York, February 23." February 23.

New-York Gazette. 1764. "God Save the King." March 5.

New-York Gazette, or Weekly Post-Boy. 1768a. "To the Freeholders and Freemen of the City and County of New-York." February 15.

New-York Gazette; and the Weekly Mercury. 1768b. "City of New-York, February 11, 1768." February 22.

New-York Gazette; and the Weekly Mercury. 1768c. "To the Freeholders and Freemen, of the City of New-York." February 22.

New-York Gazette; and the Weekly Mercury. 1768d. "The Farmer's Letter, No. 12, Must be Deferred till another Opportunity, to make Room for the following Address to the Public." February 29.

New-York Gazette; and the Weekly Mercury. 1769a. "To the Freeholders and Freemen of the City and County of New-York." January 9.

New-York Gazette, or Weekly Post-Boy. 1769b. "It is expected that Writs will very soon be issued for the Election of Members for a New Assembly." January 9.

New-York Gazette, or Weekly Post-Boy. 1769c. "Zur Nach Right." January 16.

New-York Gazette; and the Weekly Mercury. 1769d. "A Seasonable Advertisement to the Freeholders and Freemen of the City of New-York, and all the real Friends to Liberty and Lovers of their Country." January 16.

New-York Gazette; and the Weekly Mercury. 1769e. "Colony of New York, Queen's County." April 17.

New-York Gazette; and the Weekly Mercury. 1769f. "To John De Noyellis and Samuel Gale, Esqrs, Members of the General Assembly for the County of Orange." November 27.

New-York Gazette; and the Weekly Mercury. 1770a. "NEW-YORK, January 1." January 8.

New-York Gazette; and the Weekly Mercury. 1770b. "To JOHN CRUGER, JAMES JAUNCEY, JAMES DE LANCEY, and JACOB WALTON, Esquires, Representatives in General Assembly, for the City and County of New-York." January 8.

New-York Gazette, or Weekly Post-Boy. 1770c. "On the Nature of Representation; and the Right of instructing our Representatives." January 8.

New-York Gazette, or Weekly Post-Boy. 1770d. "The following Sheet of the West Chaster County Instructions, signed by 282 Freeholders, was some Time ago delivered to Mr. Thomas." January 8.

New-York Gazette; and the Weekly Mercury. 1770e. "An ACT that all Elections to be held or made for the Election of Representatives to sit in General Assembly for the Colony of New-York, shall be by Ballot only." January 15.

New-York Gazette; and the Weekly Mercury. 1770f. "New-York, Jan. 22. January 22.

New-York Gazette; and the Weekly Mercury. 1770g. "To the Public." January 22.

New-York Journal; or the General Advertiser. 1768a. "New-York, Feb. 8th 1768." February 18.

New-York Journal; or the General Advertiser. 1768b. "Mr. Holt." February 18.

New-York Journal; or the General Advertiser. 1768c. "To the Freeholders and Freemen of the City and County of New-York." February 25.

New-York Journal; or the General Advertiser. 1768d. "New-Jersey, February 19th, 1768." February 25.

New-York Journal; or the General Advertiser. 1769a. "To the Freeholders and Freemen, of the City and County of New-York." January 12.

New-York Journal; or the General Advertiser. 1769b. "These may certify." January 12.

New-York Journal; or the General Advertiser. 1769c. "NEW-YORK, January 12." January 12.

New-York Journal; or the General Advertiser. 1769d. "The EXAMINER, No. I." January 12.

New-York Journal; or the General Advertiser. 1769e. "WHEREAS, on the late Examination before the honourable House of Assembly." January 19.

New-York Journal; or the General Advertiser. 1769f. "NEW-YORK, February 2." February 2.

New-York Journal; or the General Advertiser. 1769g. "Colony of New-York, Queen's County." April 17.

New-York Journal; or The General Advertiser. 1774. "New-Jersey." December 15.

New-York Mercury. 1753. "Extract from the Votes of the General Assembly of the Colony of New-York." November 12.

New-York Mercury. 1756. "The following Piece is taken from a Supplement to the Pennsylvania Journal of March 25, 1756, and inserted here by DESIRE." April 5.

New-York Mercury. 1758. "New-York, December 22, 1758." December 23.

New-York Mercury. 1761a. "New-York, January 21, 1761." January 26.

New-York Mercury. 1761b. "William Bayard, Begs Leave to inform the PUBLICK." February 16.

New-York Mercury. 1764. "From Flushing we are assured." May 14.

New-York Mercury. 1765. "To John Cruger, Phillip Livingston, Leonard Lispenard, and William Bayard, Esqrs, Representatives in the General Assembly, of the Freemen and Freeholders of the City and County of New York." December 2.

New-York Mercury. 1766. "To John Cruger, Phillip Livingston, Leonard Lispenard, and William Bayard, Representatives in the General Assembly, of Freemen and Freeholders of the City of New York." June 30.

New-York Weekly Journal. 1733a. "ADVERTISEMENTS." January 21.

New-York Weekly Journal. 1733b. "Westchester, October 29th, 1733." October 5.

New-York Weekly Journal. 1734a. "I Find Mr. Bradford's Writers and inclin'd to renew their Correspondence." June 10.

New-York Weekly Journal. 1734b. "Mr. Zenger." October 7.

New-York Weekly Journal. 1734c. "Goshen, August 21, 1734." October 7.

New-York Weekly Journal. 1737a. "Mr. Zenger." May 23.

New-York Weekly Journal. 1737b. "The Votes and Proceedings of the General Assembly of this Province." June 20.

New-York Weekly Journal. 1737c. "Some necessary Precautions, worthy to be considered by all English Subjects, in their Election of Members, to Represent them in General Assembly." July 18.

New-York Weekly Journal. 1737d. "A Word in Season." September 5.

New-York Weekly Journal. 1738a. "Precautions worthy to be consider'd in the Choice of Representatives in General Assembly." March 5.

New-York Weekly Journal. 1743. "New-York." October 24.

New-York Weekly Journal. 1750. "EASTCHESTER, August 27, 1750." September 3.

The North-Carolina Magazine; or Universal Intelligencer. 1764. "Lately Published." November 2–9.

Pennsylvania Chronicle, and Universal Advertiser. 1767. "To the Freeholders, and others, Electors for the City and County of Philadelphia." September 14–21.

Pennsylvania Chronicle, and Universal Advertiser. 1768a. "Philadelphia." August 1–8.

Pennsylvania Chronicle, and Universal Advertiser. 1768b. "To our 'patriotic' Freemen, the Promoters of Town-Meetings." August 15–22.

Pennsylvania Chronicle, and Universal Advertiser. 1769. "Mr. Goddard." October 16–23.

Pennsylvania Evening Post. 1776. "Mr. Towne." April 27.

Pennsylvania Gazette. 1742. "It being asserted in a printed Paper." September 23.

Pennsylvania Gazette. 1746. "Just published, and sold by B. Franklin." December 30.

Pennsylvania Gazette. 1748. "Just published and to be sold by the Publishers hereof." November 11.

Pennsylvania Gazette. 1754a. "To the Printers of the Pennsylvania Gazette." September 19.

Pennsylvania Gazette. 1754b. "Annapolis, November 28." December 19.

Pennsylvania Gazette. 1755. "Philadelphia." August 21.

Pennsylvania Gazette. 1773. "To the respectable Farmers, Tradesmen, Mechanics and others, Electors for the City and County of Philadelphia." September 22.

Pennsylvania Packet; and the General Advertiser. 1772. "Philadelphia, Oct. 21." October 26.

Providence Gazette; and Country Journal. 1763a. "In the House of Deputies." April 2.

Providence Gazette; and Country Journal. 1763b. "To the Printer of the Providence Gazette, and Country Journal." November 12.

Providence Gazette Extraordinary. 1765. "At a Town Meeting of the Town of PROVIDENCE, in the Colony of RHODE-ISLAND, on the thirteenth Day of August, 1765." August 24.

Providence Gazette; and Country Journal. 1768. "ANECDOTE." July 2.

Providence Gazette; and Country Journal. 1773a. "Rehoboth, May 26, 1773." June 19.

Providence Gazette; and Country Journal. 1773b. "PROVIDENCE, September 11." September 11.

Providence Gazette; and Country Journal. 1773c. "PROVIDENCE, October 23." October 23.

Providence Gazette; and Country Journal. 1774. "Providence. October 1." October 1.

South-Carolina Gazette. 1732a. "To the several Worthy Electors of Members of Assembly for the Parish of St. Philip's Charlestown." March 10–17.

South-Carolina Gazette. 1732b. "CHARLESTOWN, March 24." March 17–24.

South-Carolina Gazette. 1735. "CHARLESTOWN, April 12." April 5–12.

South-Carolina Gazette. 1736a. "To the Author of the Daily Journal." October 16–23.

South-Carolina Gazette. 1736b. "CHARLESTOWN, November 6." October 30-November 6.

South-Carolina Gazette. 1736c. "To the Electors of the Parishes of St. Philip's Charlestown, St. John's in Colleton County, St Thomas & St Dennis." November 6–13.

South-Carolina Gazette. 1736d. "CHARLES-TOWN." November 6–13.

South-Carolina Gazette. 1741. "To the Electors for the Parish of St. Philip Charles-Town." October 31-November 7.

South-Carolina Gazette. 1747–48. "To the Freeholders of the Province of SOUTH-CAROLINA." December 28-January 6.

South-Carolina Gazette. 1748. "By His Excellency JAMES GLEN, Esquire, Captain-General, Governor, and Commander in Chief, in and over His Majesty's Province of South-Carolina." October 31-November 7.

South-Carolina Gazette. 1749. "CHARLES-TOWN, April 10." April 7–10.

South-Carolina Gazette. 1751. "CHARLES-TOWN, December 2." December 6.

South-Carolina Gazette. 1752. "CHARLES-TOWN, January 22." January 22.

South-Carolina Gazette. 1754a. "CHARLES-TOWN, Nov. 7." November 7.

South-Carolina Gazette. 1754b. "CHARLES-TOWN, Nov. 14." November 14.

South-Carolina Gazette. 1757. "The Humble ADDRESS of the Commons House of Assembly of the said Province." June 23.

South-Carolina Gazette. 1758. "To the Electors of St. John's Parish, Colleton County." December 1–8.

South-Carolina Gazette. 1759. "CHARLES-TOWN, August 11." August 8–11.

South-Carolina Gazette. 1760a. "AN ACT." May 24–31.

South-Carolina Gazette. 1760b. "AN ACT, to prevent the export of grain and other provisions." June 10–14.

South-Carolina Gazette. 1760c. "CHARLES-TOWN, October 11." October 4–11.

South-Carolina Gazette. 1760d. "To the Electors of the Parish of St. John, Colleton County." October 4–11.

South-Carolina Gazette. 1760e. "CHARLES-TOWN, October 25." October 18–25.

South-Carolina Gazette. 1760f. "CHARLES-TOWN, November 15." November 8–15.

South-Carolina Gazette. 1761. "CHARLES-TOWN, December 26." December 19–26.

South-Carolina Gazette. 1762a. "CHARLES-TOWN, January 30." January 23–30.

South-Carolina Gazette. 1762b. "To the Electors of St. John's Parish, Colleton County." February 13–20.

South-Carolina Gazette. 1762c. "To the Freeholders and Electors of the parish of Prince-George, Winyah." March 20–27.

South-Carolina Gazette. 1762d. "CHARLES-TOWN, October 23." October 16–23.

South-Carolina Gazette. 1762e. "CHARLES-TOWN, December 18." December 18.

South-Carolina Gazette. 1763a. "A LETTER 'To _____ and the rest of the electors in St. John's parish, Colleton county,' as inserted, by the desire of the parishioners, in the South-Carolina Weekly Gazette of the 5th of January last, published by Mr. Robert Wells." January 29–February 5.

South-Carolina Gazette. 1763b. "To the Gentlemen Electors of the Parish of St. Paul, Stono." January 29-February 5.

South-Carolina Gazette. 1765a. "CHARLES-TOWN, January 30, 1765." January 26-February 2.

South-Carolina Gazette. 1765b. "The Portrait of a good Senator." February 16–23.

South-Carolina Gazette. 1765c. "COPY of the Instructions, given by the Town of Providence, on the 13th of August, 1765, to their Deputies in General Assembly." October 5–12.

South-Carolina Gazette. 1768a. "To Every Freeholder in the Province." September 26.

South-Carolina Gazette. 1768b. "CHARLES-TOWN, October 3." October 3.

South-Carolina Gazette. 1768c. "CHARLES-TOWN, October 10." October 10.

South-Carolina Gazette. 1768d. "CHARLES-TOWN, October 17." October 17.

South-Carolina Gazette. 1769a. "CHARLES-TOWN, March 9." March 9.

South-Carolina Gazette. 1769b. "Mr. Timothy." November 30.

South-Carolina Gazette. 1772. "From the South Carolina Gazette, Sept. 15." November 12.

Virginia Gazette. 1738. "A Writ is order'd." November 3.

Virginia Gazette (Purdie and Dixon). 1766a. "Mess. Purdie & Dixon, Please insert the Following in your next." October 17.

Virginia Gazette (Purdie and Dixon). 1766b. "An Address of the Freeholders of James City County to LEWIS BURWELL, Esq." October 30.

Virginia Gazette (Purdie and Dixon). 1768. "To the free and independent ELECTORS of the borough of NORFOLK." November 10.

Virginia Gazette (Rind). 1769a. "To THOMAS HARRISON, and JAMES SCOTT, Esquires." April 27.

Virginia Gazette (Rind). 1769b. "WILLIAMSBURG, August 3." August 3.

Virginia Gazette (Purdie and Dixon). 1771. "To Mess. Purdie & Dixon." April 11.

Virginia Gazette (Rind). 1774a. "Mrs. Rind." April 7.

Virginia Gazette (Purdie and Dixon). 1774b. "VIRGINIA." June 30.

Virginia Gazette (Purdie and Dixon). 1774c. "WILLIAMSBURG, June 30." June 30.

Virginia Gazette (Purdie and Dixon). 1774d. "Mr. Purdie." July 7.

Virginia Gazette (Purdie and Dixon). 1774e. "WILLIAMSBURG, July 7." July 7.

Virginia Gazette (Rind). 1774f. "Friday, July 15." July 14.

Virginia Gazette (Rind). 1774g. "WILLIAMSBURG, July 14." July 14.

Virginia Gazette (Rind). 1774h. "Here follow the RESOLVES entered into by different counties in Virginia." July 21.

Virginia Gazette (Rind). 1774i. "Proceedings of Virginia." July 28.

Virginia Gazette (Rind). 1774j. "Further Proceedings of Virginia." August 4.

III. OTHER PUBLICATIONS

An Account of the Rise, Progress, and Consequences Of the two late Schemes Commonly call'd the Land-Bank or Manufactory Scheme and the Silver Scheme, in the Province of the Massachusetts-Bay. 1744. Boston: n.p.

Adams, Charles Francis. 1850. *The Works of John Adams, Second President of the United States*, vol. II. Boston: Charles C. Little and James Brown.

An Address to the Freeholders and Inhabitants of the Province of Massachusetts-Bay, in New England. 1751. Boston: n.p.

An Address to the Freeholders of Dutchess County. 1769. New York: n.p.

An Advertisement having appeared. 1769. n.p.

Advertisement. Province of Massachusetts-Bay. 1754. Boston: S. Kneeland and T. Green.

Advice and Information to the Freeholders and Freemen of the Province of Pensilvania. 1727. Philadelphia: Andrew Bradford.

Advice to the Free-holders and Electors of Pennsylvania, &c. 1735. Philadelphia: Andrew Bradford.

Agrippa, Cornelius. 1751. *Appendix to Massachusetts in Agony*. Boston: Daniel Fowle.

Allen, James. 1679. *New-Englands choicest Blessing And the Mercy most to be desired by all that with well to this People*. Boston: John Foster.

Allen, Myron O. 1860. *The History of Wenham, Civil and Ecclesiastical, from its Settlement in 1639, to 1860*. Boston: Bazin & Chandler.

Allen, W. C. 1918. *History of Halifax County*. Boston: Cornhill Company.

Allen, Wilkes. 1820. *The History of Chelmsford, from its Origin in 1653, to the Year 1820*. Haverhill: P. N. Green.

Andros Tracts, vol. third. 1874. Boston: Prince Society.

Arnold, Samuel Green. 1860. *History of the State of Rhode Island and Providence Plantations*, vol. II. New York: D. Appleton & Company.

Arnold, Samuel Greene. 1876. *An Historical Sketch of Middletown, R. I., from Its Organization in 1743, to the Centennial Year, 1876*. Newport: John P. Sanborn Co.

Assembly. 1772. Philadelphia: n.p.

Atkinson, Joseph. 1878. *The History of Newark, New Jersey, being a Narrative of Its Rise and Progress, from the Settlement in May, 1666, by Emigrants from Connecticut, to the Present Time*. Newark: William B. Guild.

Babson, John J. 1860. *History of the Town of Gloucester, Cape Ann, Including the Town of Rockport.* Gloucester: Procter Brothers.

"Bacon's Rebellion. William Sherwood's Account." 1893. *Virginia Magazine of History and Biography* 1:167–74.

Bailey, Raymond C. 1979. *Popular Influence upon Public Policy: Petitioning in Eighteenth-Century Virginia.* Westport: Greenwood.

Bailey, Sarah Loring. 1880. *Historical Sketches of Andover (Comprising the Present Towns of North Andover and Andover), Massachusetts.* Boston: Houghton, Mifflin and Company.

Bailyn, Bernard. 1967. *The Ideological Origins of the American Revolution.* Cambridge: Belknap Press.

Bailyn, Bernard. 1968. *The Origins of American Politics.* New York: Alfred A. Knopf.

Baird, Charles W. 1871. *Chronicle of a Border Town: History of Rye, Westchester County, New York, 1660–1870.* New York: Anson D. F. Randolph and Company.

The Ballator. 1768. New York: n.p.

Banks, Charles Edward. 1911. *The History of Martha's Vineyard, Dukes County, Massachusetts,* vol. I. Boston: George H. Dean.

Banks, Charles Edward. 1911. *The History of Martha's Vineyard, Dukes County, Massachusetts,* vol. II. Boston: George H. Dean.

Barry, John S. 1853. *A Historical Sketch of the Town of Hanover, Mass.* Boston: Samuel G. Drake.

Barry, William. 1847. *A History of Framingham, Massachusetts, from 1640 to the Present Time.* Boston: James Munroe and Company.

Batinski, Michael C. 1987. *The New Jersey Assembly, 1738–1775.* Lanham, MD: University Press of America.

Batinski, Michael C. 1996. *Jonathan Belcher, Colonial Governor.* Lexington: University Press of Kentucky.

Beach, Joseph Perkins. 1912. *History of Cheshire, Connecticut from 1694 to 1840.* Cheshire: Lady Fenwick Chapter, D. A. R.

Beer, Samuel H. 1957. "The Representation of Interests in British Government: Historical Background." *American Political Science Review* 51:613–50.

Bell, Charles H. 1888. *History of the Town of Exeter, New Hampshire.* Boston: J. E. Farwell & Co.

Belknap, Jeremy. 1831. *The History of New-Hampshire,* vol. I. Dover: S. C. Stevens and Ela & Wadleigh.

Belknap, Jeremy. 1812. *The History of New-Hampshire,* vol. II. Dover: O. Crosby and J. Varney.

Benedict, William A., and Hiram A. Tracy. 1878. *History of the Town of Sutton, Massachusetts, from 1704 to 1876.* Worcester: Sanford & Company.

Bicknell, Thomas Williams. 1898. *A History of Barrington, Rhode Island.* Providence: Snow & Farnham.

Bigelow, E. Victor. 1898. *A Narrative History of the Town of Cohasset, Massachusetts.* Boston: Press of Samuel Usher.

Biglow, William. 1830. *History of Sherburne, Mass. from Its Incorporation, M DC LXXIV, to the end of the Year M DCCC XXX.* Milford: Ballou & Stacy.

Billings, Warren M. 2004. *A Little Parliament: The Virginia General Assembly in the Seventeenth Century*. Richmond: Library of Virginia, Jamestown 2007/ Jamestown-Yorktown Foundation.

Bishop, Cortlandt F. 1893. *History of Elections in the American Colonies*. New York: Columbia College.

Blackstone, William. 1771. *Commentaries on the Laws of England*, vol. I. Philadelphia: Robert Bell.

The Bland Papers: Being a Section from the Manuscripts of Colonel Theodorick Bland, Jr. of Prince George County, Virginia, vol. I. 1840. Petersburg: Edmund & Julian C. Ruffin.

Bliss, Leonard, Jr. 1836. *The History of Rehoboth, Bristol County, Massachusetts*. Boston: Otis, Broaders, and Company.

Bliss, William Root. 1896. *Quaint Nantucket*. Boston: Houghton, Mifflin and Company.

Bonomi, Patricia U. 1971. *A Factious People: Politics and Society in Colonial New York*. New York: Columbia University Press.

Bonomi, Patricia Updegraff. 1966. "Political Patterns in New York City: The General Assembly Election of 1768." *Political Science Quarterly* 81:432–47.

Booth, Henry A. 1904. "Springfield during the Revolution." In *Papers and Proceedings of the Connecticut Valley Historical Society*, vol. II. Springfield: Connecticut Valley Historical Society.

Borden, William. 1746. *An Address to the Inhabitants of North-Carolina*. Williamsburg, VA: William Parks.

Bourne, Edward E. 1875. *The History of Wells and Kennebunk from the Earliest Settlement to the Year 1820, at which Time Kennebunk was Set Off, and Incorporated*. Portland: B. Thurston & Company.

Boyer, Paul S. 1964. "Borrowed Rhetoric: The Massachusetts Excise Controversy of 1754." *William and Mary Quarterly* 21:328–51.

Brodhead, John Romeyn. 1853. *History of the State of New York, First Period, 1609–1664*. New York: Harper & Brothers.

Brodhead, John Romeyn. 1871. *History of the State of New York*, second vol. New York: Harper & Brothers.

Brooks, Charles. 1855. *History of the Town of Medford, Middlesex County, Massachusetts, from its First Settlement, in 1630, to the Present Time, 1855*. Boston: James M. Usher.

Brown, Robert E. 1955. *Middle-Class Democracy and the Revolution in Massachusetts, 1691–1780*. New York: Cornell University Press.

Brown, Robert E., and B. Katherine Brown. 1964. *Virginia 1705–1786: Democracy or Aristocracy?* East Lansing: Michigan State University Press.

Bull, Sidney A. 1920. *History of the Town of Carlisle, Massachusetts, 1754–1920*. Cambridge: Murray Printing Company.

Burgh, James. 1774. *Political Disquisitions: Or, an Enquiry in Public Errors, Defects, and Abuses*. London: E. and C. Dilly.

Burt, Henry M. 1898. *The First Century of the History of Springfield, the Official Records from 1636 to 1736*, vol. I. Springfield: Henry M. Burt.

Burt, Henry M. 1899. *The First Century of the History of Springfield, the Official Records from 1636 to 1736*, vol. II. Springfield: Henry M. Burt.

Bushman, Richard L. 1985. *King and People in Provincial Massachusetts*. Chapel Hill: University of North Carolina Press.

Butler, Caleb. 1848. *History of the Town of Groton, Including Pepperell and Shirley, from the First Grant of Groton Plantation in 1655*. Boston: T. R. Marvin.

A Card. 1768. New York: John Holt.

The Case of the Manor of Livingston, and the CONDUCT of the Honourable House of ASSEMBLY, towards it, considered. 1769. New York: John Holt.

Caulkins, Frances Manwaring. 1860. *History of New London, Connecticut*. Hartford: Case, Lockwood and Company.

Caulkins, Frances Manwaring. 1874. *History of Norwich, Connecticut*. Hartford: Case, Lockwood and Company.

"Causes of Discontent in Virginia, 1676." 1894. *Virginia Magazine of History and Biography* 2:166–73.

"Causes of Discontent in Virginia, 1676 (continued)." 1895a. *Virginia Magazine of History and Biography* 2:289–92.

"Causes of Discontent in Virginia, 1676 (continued)." 1895b. *Virginia Magazine of History and Biography* 2:380–92.

Chaffin, William L. 1886. *History of the Town of Easton, Massachusetts*. Cambridge: John Wilson and Son.

Chamberlain, Mellen. 1908. *A Documentary History of Chelsea, Including the Boston Precincts of Winnisimmet, Rumney Marsh, and Pullen Point, 1624–1824*, vol. II. Boston: Massachusetts Historical Society.

Champagne, Roger. 1963. "Family Politics versus Constitutional Politics: The New York Assembly Elections of 1768 and 1769." *William and Mary Quarterly* 20:57–79.

Chandler, Julian A. C. 1901. *The History of Suffrage in Virginia*. Baltimore: Johns Hopkins Press.

Chandler, Seth. 1883. *History of the Town of Shirley, Massachusetts, from its Early Settlement to A. D. 1882*. Fitchburg: Blanchard & Brown.

"Charles City County Grievances, 1676." 1895. *Virginia Magazine of History and Biography* 3:132–47.

Chase, Frederick. 1891. *A History of Dartmouth College and the Town of Hanover, New Hampshire*. Cambridge: John Wilson and Son.

Chase, George Wingate. 1861. *The History of Haverhill, Massachusetts, from its First Settlement, in 1640, to the Year 1860*. Lowell: Stone & Huse.

Clark, George Faber. 1859. *A History of the Town of Norton, Bristol County, Massachusetts, from 1669 to 1859*. Boston: Crosby, Nichols, and Company.

Clarke, George Kuhn. 1912. *History of Needham, Massachusetts, 1711–1911*. Cambridge: University Press.

Clarke, Mary Patterson. 1943. *Parliamentary Privilege in the American Colonies*. New Haven: Yale University Press.

City of New-York, ss. January 6th, 1769. 1769. New York: n.p.

Cobbett's Parliamentary History of England, vol. VIII. 1811. London: T. C. Hansard.

Cobbett's Parliamentary History of England, vol. IX. 1811. London: T. C. Hansard.

Coffin, Joshua. 1845. *A Sketch of the History of Newbury, Newburyport, and West Newbury, from 1635 to 1845*. Boston: Samuel G. Drake.

Colegrove, Kenneth. 1920. "New England Town Mandates." *Publications of the Colonial Society of Massachusetts* 21:411–49.

A Collection of Interesting, Authentic Papers Relative to the Dispute between Great Britain and America. 1777. London: J. Almon.

Collections of the Maine Historical Society, vol. III. 1853. Portland: Brown Thurston.

Collections of the South Carolina Historical Society, vol. V. 1897. Richmond: William Ellis Jones.

Collections, Topographical, Historical and Biographical, Relating Principally to New-Hampshire, vol. I. 1831. Concord: M. E. & J. W. Moore.

The Colonial Virginia Register. 1902. Albany: Joel Munsell's Sons.

Conroy, David W. 1995. *In Public Houses: Drink & the Revolution of Authority in Colonial Massachusetts.* Chapel Hill: University of North Carolina Press.

Considerations on the Election of Counsellors, Humbly Offered to the Electors. 1761. Boston: n.p.

A Contrast: Read my Fellow Citizens, and judge for yourselves. 1769. New York: n.p.

Cooper, Christopher A., and Lilliard E. Richardson Jr. 2006. "Institutions and Representational Roles in American State Legislatures." *State Politics and Policy Quarterly* 6:174–94.

Cooper, Francis Hodges. 1916. *Some Colonial History of Beaufort County, North Carolina.* Chapel Hill: University of North Carolina.

Copeland, Alfred. 1892. *A History of the Town of Murrayfield.* Springfield, MA: Clark W. Bryan & Company.

Corey, Deloraine Pendre. 1899. *The History of Malden, Massachusetts, 1633–1785.* Cambridge: University Press.

Correspondence between William Penn and James Logan, Secretary of the Province of Pennsylvania, and Others. 1872. Philadelphia: B. Lippincott & Co.

Cothren, William. 1854. *History of Ancient Woodbury, Connecticut, from the First Indian Deed in 1659 to 1854.* Waterbury: Bronson Brothers.

Crafts, James M. 1899. *History of the Town of Whately, Mass, Including a Narrative of Leading Events from the First Planting of Hatfield: 1661–1899.* Orange: D. L. Crandall.

Crowell, Robert. 1868. *History of the Town of Essex, from 1634 to 1868.* Springfield: Samuel Bowles & Co.

Cuddihy, William J. 2009. *The Fourth Amendment: Origins and Original Meaning, 602–1791.* New York: Oxford University Press.

Currier, John J. 1896. *"Ould Newbury": Historical and Biographical Sketches.* Boston: Damrell & Upham.

Currier, John J. 1902. *History of Newbury, Mass., 1635–1902.* Boston: Damrell & Upham.

Currier, John J. 1906. *History of Newburyport, Mass., 1764–1905.* Newburyport: John J. Currier.

Cushing, Caleb. 1826. *The History and Present State of the Town of Newburyport.* Newburyport: E. W. Allen.

Daggett, John. 1894. *A Sketch of the History of Attleborough from its Settlement to the Division.* Boston: Samuel Usher.

Daniels, Bruce C. 1979. *The Connecticut Town: Growth and Development, 1735–1790.* Middletown: Wesleyan University Press.

Daniels, George F. 1892. *History of the Town of Oxford, Massachusetts*. Worcester: Chas. Hamilton.

D'Anvers, Caleb. 1737. *The Craftsman*, vol. X. London: R. Franklin.

Davis, Charles Henry Stanley. 1870. *History of Wallingford, Conn., from its Settlement in 1670 to the Present Time*. Wallingford: Mount Tom Printing House.

Davis, T. E. 1904–5. "Hendrick Fisher." *Proceedings of the New Jersey Historical Society* 4:129–46.

Day, Alan, and Katherine Day. 1971. "Another Look at the Boston 'Caucus.'" *Journal of American Studies* 5:19–42.

Deane, Samuel. 1831. *History of Scituate, Massachusetts, from its First Settlement to 1831*. Boston: James Loring.

Defence of Injur'd Merit Unmasked. 1771. United States: n.p.

DeForest, Heman Packard. 1891. *The History of Westborough, Massachusetts*. Part 1: *The Early History*. Cambridge: John Wilson and Son.

Denison, Frederic. 1878. *Westerly (Rhode Island) and Its Witnesses, for Two Hundred Years, 1626–1876*. Providence: J. A. & R. A. Reid.

"Depositions of Jireh Bull and Thomas Paine, 1699." 1885. *Rhode Island Historical Magazine* 6:155–56.

A Dialogue Shewing What's therein to be found. 1725. Philadelphia: Samuel Keimer.

The Diaries of George Washington, 1748–1799, vol. I. 1925. Boston: Houghton Mifflin Company.

"Diaries of John Hull, Mint-Master and Treasurer of the Colony of Massachusetts Bay." 1857. *Transactions and Collections of the American Antiquarian Society* 3:109–316.

Diary and Letters of His Excellency Thomas Hutchinson, Esq., Captain-General and Governor-in-Chief of His Late Majesty's Province of Massachusetts Bay in North America. 1884. Boston: Houghton, Mifflin, & Co.

The Diary of Colonel Landon Carter of Sabine Hall, 1752–1778, vol. I. 1965. Charlottesville: University Press of Virginia.

Diary of John Adams. 1763. http://www.masshist.org/digitaladams/archive/doc?id =D9&bc=%2Fdigitaladams%2Farchive%2Fbrowse%2Fdiaries_by_number. php

Diary of Matthew Patten of Bedford, N. H. 1903. Concord: Rumford Publishing Company.

"Diary of Samuel Sewall." Vol. I: "1674–1700." 1878. *Collections of the Massachusetts Historical Society*, fifth ser., 5:1–509.

"Diary of Samuel Sewall." Vol. II: "1700–1714." 1879. *Collections of the Massachusetts Historical Society*, fifth ser., 6:1–440.

"Diary of Samuel Sewall." Vol. III: "1714–1730." 1882. *Collections of the Massachusetts Historical Society*, fifth ser., 7:1–410.

Dickinson, H. T. 1995. *The Politics of the People in Eighteenth-Century Britain*. New York: St. Martin's.

Dickinson, H. T. 2007. "The Representation of the People in Eighteenth-Century Britain." In *The Realities of Representation*, ed. Maija Jansson. New York: Palgrave Macmillan.

Dinkin, Robert J. 1977. *Voting in Provincial America*. Westport: Greenwood Press.

Doggett, Samuel Bradlee. 1930. *Seth Bullard of Walpole, Massachusetts.* Norwood: Plimpton Press.

Dorchester Antiquarian and Historical Society. 1859. *History of the Town of Dorchester, Massachusetts.* Boston: Ebenezer Clapp, Jr.

Douglass, William. 1755. *A Summary, Historical and Political, of the First Planting, Progressive Improvements, and Present State of the British Settlements in North-America,* vol. I. London: R. Baldwin.

Douglass, William. 1755. *A Summary, Historical and Political, of the First Planting, Progressive Improvements, and Present State of the British Settlements in North-America,* vol. II. London: R. Baldwin.

Dow, Joseph. 1893. *History of the Town of Hampton, New Hampshire,* vol. I. Salem: Salem Press Publishing and Printing Co.

Drake, Francis S. 1878. *The Town of Roxbury.* Boston: Alfred Mudge and Son.

Drake, Samuel Adams. 1880. *History of Middlesex County, Massachusetts,* vol. II. Boston: Estes and Lauriat.

Draper, James. 1841. *History of Spencer from its Earliest Settlement to the Year 1841.* Worcester: Spooner and Howland.

Dulany, Daniel. 1765. *Considerations on the Propriety of Imposing Taxes in the British Colonies, For the Purpose of raising a Revenue, by Act of Parliament.* North-America [Annapolis]: A North-American [Jonas Green].

Dutchess County Historical Society. 1921. *Year Book.* Dutchess County, NY: Dutchess County Historical Society.

The Eclipse. 1754. Boston: n.p.

Ellis, Charles M. 1847. *The History of Roxbury Town.* Boston: Samuel G. Drake.

English Advice To the Freeholders &c. of the Province of the Massachusetts-Bay. 1722. Boston: James Franklin.

Eulau, Heinz, and Paul D. Karps. 1977. "The Puzzle of Representation: Specifying Components of Responsiveness." *Legislative Studies Quarterly* 2:233–54.

The Examiner, No. II. 1769. New York: n.p.

"'Fare Weather and Good Helth': The Journal of Cesar Rodeney, 1727–1729." 1962. *Delaware History* 10:33–70.

Felt, Joseph B. 1827. *The Annals of Salem, from its First Settlement.* Salem: W. & S. R. Ives.

Felt, Joseph B. 1834. *History of Ipswich, Essex, and Hamilton.* Cambridge: Charles Folsom.

A Few Observations on the Conduct of the General Assembly of New-York, for some years past, addressed to the Freemen and Freeholders of the city and province. 1768. New York: n.p.

Folsom, George. 1830. *History of Saco and Biddeford, with Notices of Other Early Settlements, and of the Proprietary Governments in Maine.* Saco: Alex C. Putnam.

Ford, Paul Leicester, ed. 1902. *The Journals of Hugh Gaine, Printer,* vol. I. New York: Dodd, Mead & Company.

Franklin, Benjamin. 1921. *Autobiography of Benjamin Franklin.* New York: Macmillan.

Freedom the First Blessing. 1754. Boston: Thomas Fleet.

Freeman, Samuel. 1821. *An Appendix to the Extracts from the Journals Kept by the Rev.*

Thomas Smith, Late Pastor of the First Church of Christ in Falmouth, in the County of York, (Now Cumberland). Portland: A. Shirley.

To the Freeholders and Freemen of the City of New-York. 1769. New York: n.p.

To the Freeholders and Freemen of the City and County of New-York. 1768. New York: John Holt.

To the Freeholders and Freemen of the City and County of New-York. 1769a. New York: n.p.

To the Freeholders and Freemen, of the City and County of New-York. 1769b. New York: John Holt.

To the Freeholders and Freemen of the City and County of New-York. 1769c. New York: n.p.

To the Freeholders, and Freemen, of the City and County of New-York. 1770. New York: John Holt.

To the Freeholders and Freemen of the City and County of New-York, in Communion with the Reformed Dutch Church. 1769. New York: n.p.

To the Freeholders and Freemen, of the City and County of New-York. The Querist, No. II. 1769. New York: n.p.

To the Freeholders, and Freemen, of the City and Province of New-York. 1769. New York: n.p.

To the Freeholders and Other Electors for the City and County of Philadelphia, and Counties of Chester and Bucks. 1764. Philadelphia: B. Franklin and D. Hall.

To the Freeholders and other Electors of Assembly-Men, for Pennsylvania. 1765. Philadelphia: Anthony Armbrister.

To the Free-Holders Of the Province of Pennsylvania. 1742. Philadelphia: William Bradford.

To the Freeholders of the Town of Boston. 1760. Boston: n.p.

Freeman, Frederick. 1860. *The History of Cape Cod.* Boston: Geo. C. Rand & Avery.

To the FREEMEN of PENNSYLVANIA, and more especially to those of the City and County of PHILADELPHIA. 1755. Philadelphia: n.p.

An die Freyhalter der Stadt und County. 1764. Philadelphia: Anton Armbrüster.

Friedman, Bernard. 1965. "The New York Assembly Elections of 1768 and 1769: The Disruption of Family Politics." *New York History* 46:3–24.

Frothingham, Richard, Jr. 1845. *The History of Charlestown, Massachusetts.* Boston: Charles C. Little and James Brown.

Fox, Charles J. 1846. *History of the Old Township of Dunstable.* Nashua, NH: Charles T. Gill.

Gage, Thomas. 1840. *The History of Rowley.* Boston: Ferdinand Andrews.

Gleason, J. Philip. 1961. "A Scurrilous Colonial Election and Franklin's Reputation." *William and Mary Quarterly* 18:68–84.

The Good of the Community impartially considered, in a Letter to a Merchant in Boston; in Answer to one received respecting the Excise-Bill. 1754. Boston: n.p.

Goss, Elbridge Henry. 1891. *The Life of Colonel Paul Revere,* vol. II. Boston: Joseph George Cupples.

Green, Samuel. 1894. *An Historical Sketch of Groton, Massachusetts.* Groton: n.p.

Greene, Jack P., ed. 1961. "South Carolina's Colonial Constitution: Two Proposals for Reform." *South Carolina Historical Magazine* 62:72–81.

Greene, Jack P. 1963. *The Quest for Power: The Lower Houses of Assembly in the Southern Royal Colonies, 1689–1776*. New York: Norton.

Greene, Jack P. 1979. "Character, Persona, and Authority: A Study of Alternative Styles of Political Leadership in Revolutionary Virginia." In *The Revolutionary War in the South*, ed. W. Robert Higgins. Durham: Duke University Press.

Greene, Jack P. 1981. "Legislative Turnover in British America, 1696 to 1775: A Quantitative Analysis." *William and Mary Quarterly* 38:442–63.

Griffith, Henry S. 1913. *History of the Town of Carver, Massachusetts*. New Bedford: E. Anthony & Sons.

Griffith, Lucille. 1970. *The Virginia House of Burgesses, 1750–1774*. Rev. ed. University: University of Alabama Press.

Grubb, F. W. 1990. "Growth of Literacy in Colonial America: Longitudinal Patterns, Economic Models, and the Direction of Future Research." *Social Science History* 14:451–82.

Haight, Elizabeth S. 1984. "The Northampton Protest of 1652: A Petition to the General Assembly from the Inhabitants of Virginia' Eastern Shore." *American Journal of Legal History* 28:364–75.

Hancock, John. 1722. *Rulers Should Be Benefactors*. Boston: B. Green.

Hannaford, Jeremiah Lyford. 1852. *History of Princeton, Worcester County Massachusetts*. Worcester: C. Buckingham Webb.

Hanson, J. W. 1848. *History of the Town of Danvers, from its Early Settlement to the Year 1848*. Danvers: Courier Office.

Harlow, Ralph Volney. 1917. *The History of Legislative Methods in the Period Before 1825*. New Haven: Yale University Press.

Hasbrouck, Frank. 1909. *The History of Dutchess County, New York*. Poughkeepsie: S. A. Matthieu.

Hasse, A. R. 1903. "The First Published Proceedings of an American Legislature." *The Bibliographer* 2:240–42.

Haw, James. 2002. "Political Representation in South Carolina, 1669–1794: Evolution of a Lowcountry Tradition." *South Carolina Historical Magazine* 103:106–29.

Hazan, Henry A. 1883. *History of Billerica, Massachusetts*. Boston: A. Williams and Co.

Historical Memoirs from 16 March 1763 to 9 July 1776 of William Smith. 1956. New York: Colburn & Tegg.

History of Barnstable County, Massachusetts. 1890. New York: H. W. Blake.

History of Bristol County, Massachusetts, vol. I. 1883. Philadelphia: J. W. Lewis & Co.

A History of Brookline, Massachusetts, from the First Settlement of Muddy River until the Present Time. 1906. Brookline: Brookline Press Company.

History of the College of William and Mary from its Foundation, 1660, to 1874. 1874. Richmond: J. W. Randolph & English.

History of Concord, New Hampshire, from the Original Grant in Seventeen Hundred and Twenty-Five to the Opening of the Twentieth Century, vol. I. 1903. Concord: Rumford Press.

History of the Connecticut Valley in Massachusetts, vol. II. 1879. Philadelphia: Louis H. Everts.

History of Cumberland Co., Maine. 1880. Philadelphia: Everts & Peck.

History of Essex County, Massachusetts, vol. II. 1888. Philadelphia: J. W. Lewis & Co.

History of Middlesex County, Connecticut. 1884. New York: J. B. Beers & Co.

History of Middlesex County, Massachusetts, vol. II. 1890. Philadelphia: J. W. Lewis & Co.

History of Middlesex County, Massachusetts, vol. III. 1890. Philadelphia: J. W. Lewis & Co.

History of Middlesex County, Massachusetts, Containing Carefully Prepared Histories of Every City and Town in the County, vol. I. 1880. Boston: Estes and Lauriat.

History of Middlesex County, Massachusetts, Containing Carefully Prepared Histories of Every City and Town in the County, vol. II. 1880. Boston: Estes and Lauriat.

History of Newport County, Rhode Island. 1888. New York: L. E. Preston.

History of Norfolk County, Massachusetts. 1884. Philadelphia: J. W. Lewis & Co.

History of Plymouth County, Massachusetts, vol. I. 1884. Philadelphia: J. W. Lewis & Co.

History of Weymouth, Massachusetts, vol. II. 1923. Boston: Wright & Potter Printing Company.

History of Worcester County, Massachusetts, vol. II. 1889. Philadelphia: J. W. Lewis & Co.

History of Worcester County, Massachusetts, Embracing a Comprehensive History of the County from its First Settlement to the Present Time, vol. II. 1879. Boston: C. F. Jewett and Company.

History of York County, Maine. 1880. Philadelphia: Everts & Peck.

Hobart, Aaron. 1839. *An Historical Sketch of Abington, Plymouth County, Massachusetts*. Boston: Samuel N. Dickinson.

Hodgman, Edwin R. 1883. *History of the Town of Westford, in the County of Middlesex, Massachusetts, 1659–1883*. Lowell: Morning Mail Company.

Hubbell, Jay B., and Douglass Adair. 1948. "Robert Munford's 'The Candidates.'" *William and Mary Quarterly* 5:217–57.

Hudson, Alfred Sereno. 1889. *The History of Sudbury, Massachusetts, 1638–1889*. Boston: R. H. Blodgett.

Hudson, Charles. 1862. *History of the Town of Marlborough, Middlesex County, Massachusetts, from Settlement in 1657 to 1861*. Boston: Press of T. R. Marvin & Son.

Hudson, Charles. 1913. *History of the Town of Lexington, Middlesex County, Massachusetts, from its First Settlement to 1868*, vol. I. Boston: Houghton Mifflin Company.

Hulme, Harold. 1929. "The Sheriff as a Member of the House of Commons from Elizabeth to Cromwell." *Journal of Modern History* 1:361–77.

Hume, David. 1760. *Essays and Treatises on Several Subjects*, vol. I. London: A. Millar.

Huntington, Samuel P. 1966. "Political Modernization: America vs. Europe." *World Politics* 18:378–414.

Huntoon, Daniel T. V. 1893. *History of the Town of Canton, Norfolk County, Massachusetts*. Cambridge: John Wilson and Son.

Hutchinson, Thomas. 1765. *The History of the Colony of Massachuset's Bay, from the Settlement Thereof in 1628, until Its Incorporation with the Colony of Plimouth, Province of Main, &c. by the Charter of King William and Queen Mary in 1691*. London: M. Richardson.

Hutchinson, Thomas. 1767. *The History of the Province of Massachusets-Bay, from the*

Charter of King William and Queen Mary in 1691, Until the Year 1750. Boston: Thomas and John Fleet.

Hutchinson, Thomas. 1828. *The History of the Province of Massachusetts Bay, from 1749 to 1774, Comprising a Detailed Narrative of the Origin and Early Stages of the American Revolution.* London: John Murray.

Hyde, Charles M. 1879. *Historical Celebration of the Town of Brimfield, Hampden County, Mass.* Springfield: Clark W. Bryan Company.

"Instructions to Berkeley, 1642." 1895. *Virginia Magazine of History and Biography* 2:281–88.

Jackson, Francis. 1854. *A History of the Early Settlement of Newton, County of Middlesex, Massachusetts.* Boston: Stacy and Richardson.

Jameson, E. O. 1886. *The History of Medway, Mass., 1713–1885.* Providence: J. A. & R. A. Reid.

Jansson, Maija. 2007. "Realities of Representation: State Building in Early Modern Europe and European America." In *The Realities of Representation*, ed. Maija Jansson. New York: Palgrave Macmillan.

Jewell, Malcolm E. 1982. *Representation in State Legislatures.* Lexington: University Press of Kentucky.

John Adams diary 9 [electronic edition]. 1763. *Adams Family Papers: An Electronic Archive.* Massachusetts Historical Society. http://www.masshist.org/digitaladams/.

John Adams diary 13 [electronic edition]. 1766. *Adams Family Papers: An Electronic Archive.* Massachusetts Historical Society. http://www.masshist.org/digitaladams/.

Jones, Elias. 1902. *History of Dorchester County, Maryland.* Baltimore: Williams & Wilkins Company Press.

Jordan, David W. 1987. *Foundations of Representative Government in Maryland, 1632–1715.* New York: Cambridge University Press.

Jordan, John W. 1897. "James Burnside of Northampton County, Pennsylvania." *Pennsylvania Magazine of History and Biography* 21:117–18.

Journal Kept by William Williams of the Proceedings of the Lower House of the Connecticut General Assembly, May 1757 Session. 1975. Hartford: Connecticut Historical Society.

The Journal of Nicholas Cresswell, 1774–1777. 1924. New York: Dial Press.

Judd, Sylvester. 1863. *History of Hadley.* 1863. Northampton: Metcalf & Company.

Kalm, Peter. 1770. *Travels into North America*, vol. I. Warrington: William Eyres.

Kammen, Michael G. 1966. "Virginia at the Close of the Seventeenth Century: An Appraisal by James Blair and John Locke." *Virginia Magazine of History and Biography* 74:141–69.

Kammen, Michael. 1969. *Deputyes and Libertyes.* New York: Alfred A. Knopf.

Kellogg, Louise Phelps. 1904. "The American Colonial Charter." In *Annual Report of the American Historical Association for the Year 1903*, vol. I. Washington, DC: Government Printing Office.

Kelly, Paul. 1984. "Constituents' instructions to Members of Parliament in the eighteenth century." In *Party and Management in Parliament, 1660–1784*, ed. Clyve Jones. Leicester: Leicester University Press.

Kingsbury, J. D. 1883. *Memorial History of Bradford, Mass.* Haverhill: C. C. Morse & Son.

Kip, William Ingraham. 1872. *The Olden Time in New York*. New York: G. P. Putnam & Sons.

Kirby, John B. 1970. "Early American Politics—The Search for Ideology: An His-toriographical Analysis and Critique of the Concept of 'Deference.'" *Journal of Politics* 32:808–38.

Klain, Maurice. 1955. "A New Look at the Constituencies: The Need for a Recount and a Reappraisal." *American Political Science Review* 49:1105–19.

Kolp, John G. 1992. "The Dynamics of Electoral Competition in Pre-Revolutionary Virginia." *William and Mary Quarterly* 49:652–74.

Kukla, Jon. 1985. "Order and Chaos in Early America: Political and Social Stability in Pre-Restoration Virginia." *American Historical Review* 90:275–98.

Kukla, Jon. 1989. *Political Institutions in Virginia, 1619–1660*. New York: Garland.

Labaree, Leonard Woods. 1930. *Royal Government in America*. New Haven: Yale University Press.

Labaree, Leonard Woods. 1935. *Royal Instructions to British Colonial Governors, 1670–1776*, vol. I. New York: D. Appleton-Century Company.

Lamson, Daniel S. 1913. *History of the Town of Weston, Massachusetts, 1630–1890*. Boston: Geo. H. Ellis Co.

Larned, Ellen D. 1874. *History of Windham County, Connecticut*, vol. I. Worcester: Charles Hamilton.

Lease, Owen C. 1950. "The Septennial Act of 1716." *Journal of Modern History* 22:42–47.

Leder, Lawrence H. 1963. "The New York Elections of 1769: An Assault on Privi-lege." *Mississippi Valley Historical Review* 49:675–82.

Leder, Lawrence H. 1966. "The Role of Newspapers in Early America 'In Defense of Their Own Liberty.'" *Huntington Library Quarterly* 30:1–16.

Leonard, Joan de Lourdes. 1948. "The Organization and Procedure of the Penn-sylvania Assembly, 1682–1776 II." *Pennsylvania Magazine of History and Biogra-phy* 72:376–412.

Leonard, Joan de Lourdes. 1954. "Elections in Colonial Pennsylvania." *William and Mary Quarterly* 11:385–401.

Leonard, Mary Hall. 1907. "The Revolutionary War." In *Mattapoisett and Old Roch-ester, Massachusetts*. New York: Grafton Press.

A Letter from a Gentleman in Philadelphia, to a Freeholder in the County of Northamp-ton. 1757. Philadelphia: n.p.

A Letter from a Gentleman to his Friend, Upon the Excise-Bill now under Consideration. 1754. Boston: n.p.

A Letter to B. G. from one of the Members of the Assembly of the Province of New-Jersey, dissolved March 15. 1738,9. 1739. Philadelphia: Benjamin Franklin.

A Letter to the Common People of the Colony of Rhode Island. 1763. Providence: William Goddard.

A Letter to the Freeholders and other Inhabitants of the Massachusetts-Bay, relating to their approaching Election of Representatives. 1739. Newport: Ann Franklin.

A Letter to the Freeholders and other Inhabitants of the Massachusetts-Bay, Relating to their approaching Election of Representatives. 1749. Boston: Rogers and Fowle.

A Letter to the Freeholders and other Inhabitants of this Province, qualified to vote for Representatives in the ensuing Election. 1742. Boston: n.p.

A Letter to the Freeholders and Qualified Voters, Relating to the Ensuing Election. 1749. Boston: Rogers and Fowle.

The Letter to the Free-Holders of the Province of Pennsylvania, Continued. 1743. Philadelphia: n.p.

A Letter to the Freemen and Freeholders of the Province of New-York, Relating to The Approaching Election of their Representatives. 1750. New York: n.p.

Letters and Diary of John Rowe, Boston Merchant, 1759–1762, 1764–1779. 1903. Boston: W. B. Clarke.

Letters and Papers of Benjamin Franklin and Richard Jackson, 1753–1785. 1947. Philadelphia: American Philosophical Society.

The Letters and Papers of Cadwallader Colden, vol. VIII. 1937. New York: New York Historical Society.

The Letters and Papers of Cadwallader Colden, vol. IX. 1937. New York: New York Historical Society.

Letters and Papers Relating to the Provincial History of Pennsylvania, with some Notices of the Writers. 1855. Philadelphia: Crissy & Markley.

"Letters of the Byrd Family (Continued)." 1929. *Virginia Magazine of History and Biography* 37:28–33.

"Letters of James Logan to Thomas Penn and Richard Peters." 1911. *Pennsylvania Magazine of History and Biography* 35:264–75.

Letters to Washington and Accompanying Papers, vol. II. 1899. Boston: Houghton, Mifflin and Company.

Letters to Washington and Accompanying Papers, vol. III. 1901. Boston: Houghton, Mifflin and Company.

Lewis, Alonzo. 1829. *The History of Lynn.* Boston: Press of J. H. Eastburn.

Lewis, Isaac Newton. 1905. *A History of Walpole, Mass.* Norwood: Plimpton Press.

Liberty. 1769. New York: John Holt.

Lichtenstein, Gaston. 1910. *When Tarboro was Incorporated; also Reverend James Moir, Edgecombe Changes her County Seat, and Germantown, Pennsylvania.* Richmond: Capitol Printing Company.

Lincoln, C. H. 1899. "Representation in the Pennsylvania Assembly Prior to the Revolution." *Pennsylvania Magazine of History and Biography* 23:23–34.

Lincoln, Charles Z. 1906. *The Constitutional History of New York from the Beginning of the Colonial Period to the Year 1905, Showing the Origin, Development, and Judicial Construction of the Constitution,* vol. III. Rochester: Lawyers Co-operative Publishing Company.

Lincoln, Solomon, Jr. 1827. *History of the Town of Hingham, Plymouth County, Massachusetts.* Hingham: Caleb Gill Jr. and Farmer and Brown.

The Literary Diary of Ezra Styles, D. D., LL. D. 1901. New York: Charles Scribner's Sons.

Livingston, Edwin Brockholst. 1910. *The Livingstons of Livingston Manor.* New York: Knickerbocker Press.

Longmore, Paul K. 1995. "From Supplicants to Constituents: Petitioning by Virginia Parishioners, 1701–1775." *Virginia Magazine of History and Biography* 103:407–42.

Lossing, Benson J. 1860. *The Life and Times of Philip Schuyler.* New York: Sheldon & Company.

Main, Gloria L., and Jackson T. Main. 1999. "The Red Queen in New England?" *William and Mary Quarterly* 56:121–50.

Main, Jackson Turner. 1966. "Government by the People: The American Revolution and the Democratization of the Legislatures." *William and Mary Quarterly* 23:391–407.

Main, Jackson Turner. 1973. *Political Parties before the Constitution.* Chapel Hill: University of North Carolina Press.

Many of the Electors of the Two, to The Electors of the Four. 1739. New York: John Peter Zenger.

Marvin, Abijah P. 1879. *History of the Town of Lancaster, Massachusetts.* Boston: J. E. Farwell & Co.

McAlister, J. 1989. "Colonial America, 1607–1776." *Economic History Review* 42:245–59.

McCleskey, Turk. 2012. "Quarterly Courts in Backcountry Counties of Colonial Virginia." *Journal of Backcountry Studies* 7:47–57.

McCrone, Donald J., and James H. Kuklinski. 1979. "The Delegate Theory of Representation." *American Journal of Political Science* 23:278–300.

McKinley, Albert Edward. 1905. *The Suffrage Franchise in the Thirteen English Colonies in America.* Philadelphia: Ginn & Co.

Memoirs of the Life and Peregrinations of the Florentine Philip Mazzei, 1730–1816. 1942. New York: Columbia University Press.

MERCHANTS'-HALL. 1768. New York: John Holt.

Merrill, Joseph. 1880. *History of Amesbury.* Haverhill: Franklin P. Stiles.

Merritt, Richard L. 1963. "Public Opinion in Colonial America: Content-Analyzing the Colonial Press." *Public Opinion Quarterly* 27:356–71.

Metcalf, John G. 1880. *Annals of the Town of Mendon, from 1659 to 1880.* Providence: E. L. Freeman & Co.

Miller, Elmer I. 1907. *The Legislature of the Province of Virginia.* New York: Columbia University Press.

Miller, Warren E., and Donald E. Stokes. 1963. "Constituency Influence in Congress." *American Political Science Review* 57:45–56.

The Mode of Elections Considered. 1769. New York: n.p.

Mombert, J. I. 1869. *An Authentic History of Lancaster County, in the State of Pennsylvania.* Lancaster: J. E. Barr & Co.

The Monster of Monsters. 1754. Boston: Zachariah Fowle.

The Montresor Journals. 1882. New York: New-York Historical Society.

Morgan, Edmund S. 1988. *Inventing the People.* New York: Norton.

Morris Morris' Reasons for His Conduct, in the Present Assembly, in the Year. 1728. Philadelphia: Andrew Bradford.

Morse, Abner. *A Genealogical Register of the Inhabitants and History of the Towns of Sherborn and Holliston.* 1856. Boston: Press of Damrell & Moore.

Mr. Jauncey heartily thanks his worthy Friends in this City. 1769. New York: n.p.

Munford, Robert. 1798. *A Collection of Plays and Poems, by the Late Col. Robert Munford, of Mecklenburg County, in the State of Virginia.* Petersburg: William Prentis.

Myers, Albert Cook, ed. 1904. *Hannah Logan's Courtship.* Philadelphia: Ferris & Leach.

Narratives of New Netherlands, 1609–1664. 1909. New York: Charles Scribner's Sons.

Nash, Gilbert. 1885. *Historical Sketch of the Town of Weymouth, Massachusetts, from 1622 to 1884*. Boston: Alfred Mudge & Son.

Nason, Elias. 1877. *A History of the Town of Dunstable, Massachusetts, from its Earliest Settlement to the Year of Our Lord 1873*. Boston: Alfred Mudge & Son.

Ne quid falsi dicere andeat, ne quid veri non andeat. 1734. New York: Andrew Bradford.

Newcomb, Benjamin H. 1995. *Political Partisanship in the American Middle Colonies, 1700–1776*. Baton Rouge: Louisiana State University Press.

"New York Broadsides, 1762–1779." 1899. *Bulletin of the New York Public Library* 3:23–33.

New-York, March 8, 1768. 1768. New York: n.p.

New-York, January 4, 1769. 1769. New York: n.p.

New-York, January 6th, 1769. 1769. New York: n.p.

New-York, January 9, 1769. 1769. New York: John Holt.

Nichols, Gilbert M. 1902. "Freetown, Mass., 1683–1780." In *A History of the Town of Freetown, Massachusetts*. Fall River: J. H. Franklin & Company.

"Notes and Queries." 1898. *Pennsylvania Magazine of History and Biography* 22:368–90.

Nourse, Henry S. 1894. *History of the Town of Harvard, Massachusetts*. Harvard, MA: Warren Hapgood.

Observations and Reflections On the Present State of the Colony of Rhode-Island, In which the Cooper's Letter is particulary taken Notice of—Addressed to the FREEMEN of the said Colony. 1763. Newport: Samuel Hall.

Observations on Mr. Justice Livingston's Address to the House of Assembly, In Support of his Right to a SEAT. 1769. New York: John Holt.

Observations on the Reasons, Lately Published, for the malicious Combination of several Presbyterian Dissenters, and a few principal Men of some other Congregations, who have been led blindfolded into an ungenerous Confederacy, for opposing the Re-Election of the late worthy Members of the GENERAL ASSEMBLY, and thereby prevent their obtaining the only Honour that can sufficiently Reward their late spirited Prosecution of the INSTRUCTIONS given them by the united Voice of the People. 1769. New York: n.p.

The Occasionalist. 1768. New York: n.p.

Olson, Alison G. 1992. "Eighteenth-Century Colonial Legislatures and Their Constituents." *Journal of American History* 79:543–67.

Olson, Alison. 2001. "Monster of Monsters and the Emergence of Political Satire in New England." *Historical Journal of Massachusetts* 29:1–21.

Orcutt, Samuel. 1880. *The History of the Old Town of Derby, Connecticut, 1642–1880*. Springfield: Press of Springfield Printing Company.

Orcutt, Samuel. 1882. *History of the Town of New Milford and Bridgewater, Connecticut, 1703–1882*. Hartford: Case, Lockwood and Brainard Company.

Orcutt, William Dana. 1893. *Good Old Dorchester*. Cambridge: John Wilson & Son.

Paige, Lucius R. 1883. *History of Hardwick, Massachusetts*. Boston: Houghton, Mifflin and Company.

Paige, Lucius R. 1877. *History of Cambridge, Massachusetts*. Boston: H. O. Houghton and Company.

Palfrey, John Gorham. 1840. *A Discourse Pronounced at Barnstable on the Third of September, 1839, at the Celebration of the Second Centennial Anniversary of the Settlement of Cape Cod*. Boston: Ferdinand Andrews.

The Papers of Henry Laurens. Vol. 4: *Sept. 1, 1763–Aug. 31, 1765.* 1974. Columbia: University of South Carolina Press.

The Papers of Sir William Johnson, vol. I. 1921. Albany: University of the State of New York.

The Papers of Sir William Johnson, vol. III. 1921. Albany: University of the State of New York.

The Papers of Sir William Johnson, vol. IV. 1925. Albany: University of the State of New York.

The Papers of Sir William Johnson, vol. VI. 1928. Albany: University of the State of New York.

The Papers of Sir William Johnson, vol. VII. 1931. Albany: University of the State of New York.

Papers Read before the Lancaster County Historical Society, Friday, January 2, 1920. 1920. Lancaster: Lancaster County Historical Society.

Parmenter, C. O. 1898. *History of Pelham, Mass. from 1738 to 1898, including the Early History of Prescott.* Amherst: Press of Carpenter & Morehouse.

Parsons, Langdon B. 1905. *History of the Town of Rye, New Hampshire, from its Discovery and Settlement to December 31, 1903.* Concord: Rumford Printing Co.

Partridge, George F. 1919. *History of the Town of Bellingham, Massachusetts, 1719–1919.* Bellingham: Town of Bellingham.

Passages from the Diary of Christopher Marshall, Kept in Philadelphia and Lancaster During the American Revolution. Vol. I: 1839–1849. Philadelphia: Hazard & Mitchell.

Patterson, Samuel C., Ronald D. Hedlund, and G. Robert Boynton. 1975. *Representatives and Represented.* New York: John Wiley & Sons.

Pease, Charles Stanley. 1917. *History of Conway (Massachusetts), 1767–1917.* Springfield: Springfield Printing and Binding Company.

Pepper, C., Jr. 1846. *Manor of Rensselaerwyck.* Albany: J. Munsell.

Perley, Sidney. 1880. *The History of Boxford, Essex County, Massachusetts, from the Earliest Settlement Known to the Present Time.* Boston: Franklin Press.

Perry, Elizabeth A. 1886. *A Brief History of the Town of Glocester, Rhode Island.* Providence: Providence Press Company.

Peter Oliver's Origin & Progress of the American Rebellion, a Tory View. 1961. San Marino: Huntington Library.

Petyt, William. 1739. *Jus Parliamentarium: or the Ancient Power, Jurisdiction, Rights and Liberties, of the Most High Court of Parliament, Revived and Asserted.* London: John Nourse.

Phelps, Noah A. 1845. *History of Simsbury, Granby, and Canton, from 1642 to 1845.* Hartford: Case, Tiffany and Burnham.

Phillips, Hubert. 1921. *The Development of a Residential Qualification for Representatives in Colonial Legislatures.* Cincinnati: Abington.

Pierce, Frederick Clifton. 1879. *History of Grafton, Worcester County, Massachusetts, from its Earliest Settlement by the Indians in 1647 to the Present Time, 1879.* Worcester: Chas. Hamilton.

Pierce, Josiah. 1862. *A History of the Town of Gorham, Maine.* Portland: Foster & Cushing and Bailey and Noyes.

Pitkin, Hanna Fenichel. 1967. *The Concept of Representation.* Berkeley: University of California Press.

A PLEA for the Poor and Distressed, Against the BILL for granting an Excise upon Wines and Spirits distilled, sold by Retail, or consumed within this Province, &c. 1754. Boston: n.p.

The Plot. By Way of a Burlesk, To turn F——n out of the Assembly; between H. and P. Proprietary Officers, being two of the WISER Sort. 1764. Philadelphia: Anthony Armbruster.

Pole, J. R. 1962. "Historians and the Problem of Early American History." *American Historical Review* 67:626–46.

Pole, J. R. 1966. *Political Representation in England and the Origins of the American Republic.* London: Macmillan.

A Political Creed for the Day. 1768. New York: James Parker.

Porritt, Edward. 1903. *The Unreformed House of Commons: Parliamentary Representation before 1832*, vol. I. Cambridge, MA: University Press.

Porritt, Edward. 1911. "Barriers against Democracy in the British Electoral System." *Political Science Quarterly* 26:1–31.

Potter, Elisha R. 1842. *Considerations on the Questions of the Adoption of a Constitution and Extension of Suffrage in Rhode Island.* Boston: Thomas H. Webb & Co.

Pownall, Thomas. 1766. *The Administration of the Colonies.* 3rd ed. London: J. Dodsley and J. Walter.

Pratt, Enoch. 1844. *A Comprehensive History, Ecclesiastical and Civil, of Eastham, Wellfleet and Orleans, County of Barnstable, Mass.* Yarmouth: W. S. Fisher and Co.

Precedents of Proceedings in the House of Commons, vol. II. 1818. London: Luke Hansard and Sons.

Price, Kent C. 1985. "Instability in Representational Role Orientation in a State Legislature: A Research Note." *Western Political Quarterly* 38:162–71.

Purvis, Thomas L. 1986. *Proprietors, Patronage, and Paper Money: Legislative Politics in New Jersey, 1703–1776.* New Brunswick: Rutgers University Press.

Quincy, Josiah, Jr. 1915–16. "Journal of Josiah Quincy, Junior, 1773." *Massachusetts Historical Society Proceedings* 49:424–81.

Randall, James G. 1916. "The Frequency and Duration of Parliaments." *American Political Science Review* 10:654–82.

Read, Benjamin. 1892. *The History of Swanzey, New Hampshire, from 1734 to 1890.* Salem: Salem Press Publishing and Printing Co.

Reed, Jonas. 1836. *A History of Rutland.* Worcester: Mirick & Bartlett.

Register of Pennsylvania. 1830. "Historical Notes Relating to Lancaster County." January 9.

Rehfeld, Andrew. 2009. "Representation Rethought: On Trustees, Delegates, and Gyroscopes in the Study of Political Representation and Democracy." *American Political Science Review* 103:214–30.

Reid, John Phillip. 1989. *The Concept of Representation in the Age of the American Revolution.* Chicago: University of Chicago Press.

The Relapse. 1754. Boston: n.p.

The Remonstrance of Several of the Representatives for several Counties of the Province of New-York being Members of the present Assembly. 1698. New York: William Bradford.

The Review. 1754. Boston: n.p.

Rich, Shebnah. 1883. *Truro–Cape Cod, or Land Marks and Sea Marks*. Boston: D. Lothrop and Company.

Richards, Lysander Salmon. 1901. *History of Marshfield*. Plymouth: Memorial Press.

Rider, Sidney S. 1889. *An Inquiry Concerning the Origin of the Clause in the Laws of Rhode Island (1719–1783) Disfranchising Roman Catholics*. Providence: E. A. Johnson & Co.

Rivers, William James. 1856. *A Sketch of the History of South Carolina to the Close of the Proprietary Government by the Revolution of 1719*. Charleston: McCarter & Co.

Roads, Samuel, Jr. 1880. *The History and Traditions of Marblehead*. Cambridge: Riverside Press.

Rosenthal, Alan. 2004. *Heavy Lifting*. Washington, DC: CQ Press.

Rupp, I. Daniel. 1844. *History of Lancaster County*. Lancaster, PA: Gilbert Hills.

Rushworth, John. 1682. *Historical Collections of Private Passages of State*. London: J. A. for Robert Boulter.

Salley, A. S., Jr. 1898. *The History of Orangeburg County, South Carolina, from its First Settlement to the Close of the Revolutionary War*. Orangeburg: R. Lewis Berry.

Sanford, Enocii. 1870. *History of Raynham, Mass., from its First Settlement to the Present Time*. Providence: Hammond, Angell & Co.

As a Scandalous Paper, Stiled, An Answer to the foolish Reason for re-choosing the Old Members, &c. 1769. New York: n.p.

Scharf, J. Thomas. 1886. *History of Westchester County, New York, Including Morrisania, Kings Bridge, and West Farms, Which Have Been Annexed to New York*, vol. I. Philadelphia: L. E. Preston & Co.

Schenck, Elizabeth Hubbell. 1889. *The History of Fairfield, Fairfield County, Connecticut, from the Settlement of the Town in 1639 to 1818*, vol. I. New York: Elizabeth Hubbell Schenck.

Schutz, John A. 1997. *Legislators of the Massachusetts General Court, 1691–1780*. Boston: Northeastern University Press.

Scudder, Horace E. 1880. "Life in Boston in the Colonial Period." In *The Memorial History of Boston, Including Suffolk County, Massachusetts*, ed. Justin Winsor. Boston: Ticknor and Company.

A Seasonable Advertisement to the Freeholders and Freemen of the City of New-York, and all the real Friends to Liberty and Lovers of their Country. 1769. New York: John Holt.

The Secret Diary of William Byrd of Westover, 1709–1712. 1941. Richmond: Dietz Press.

Sedgwick, Theodore, Jr. 1833. *A Memoir of the Life of William Livingston, Member of Congress in 1774, 1775, and 1776; Delegate to the Federal Convention of 1787, and Governor of the State of New-Jersey from 1776 to 1790*. New York: J. & J. Harper.

Sewall, Samuel. 1868. *The History of Woburn, Middlesex County, Mass., from the Grant of its Territory to Charlestown, in 1640, to the Year 1860*. Boston: Wiggin and Lunt.

Sheldon, George. 1895. *A History of Deerfield, Massachusetts*, vol. I. Greenfield: E. A. Hall & Co.

Sheldon, Hezekiah Spencer. 1879. *Documentary History of Suffield, in the Colony and*

Province of the Massachusetts Bay, in New England, 1660–1749. Springfield: Clark W. Bryan Company.

Shonnard, Frederic, and W. W. Spooner. 1900. *History of Westchester County, New York, from its Earliest Settlement to the Year 1900.* New York: New York Historical Company.

Six Arguments Against Chusing Joseph Galloway An Assemblyman in the ensuing Election: Addressed to himself by one heretofore his Friend. 1766. Philadelphia: William and Thomas Bradford.

Smith, J. E. A. 1869. *The History of Pittsfield, (Berkshire County,) Massachusetts, from the Year 1734 to the Year 1800.* Boston: Lee and Shepard.

Smith, John Montague. 1899. *History of the Town of Sunderland, Massachusetts, which Originally Embraced within Its Limits the Present Towns of Montague and Leverett.* Greenfield: E. A. Hall & Co.

Smith, S. F. 1880. *History of Newton, Massachusetts.* Boston: American Logotype Company.

Smith, Sir Thomas. [1583] 1906. *De Republica Anglorum.* Cambridge: Cambridge University Press.

Smith, W. Roy. 1903. *South Carolina as a Royal Province, 1719–1776.* New York: Macmillan.

Smith, William. 1829. *The History of the Late Province of New-York, from its Discovery to the Appointment of Governor Colden in 1762,* vol. II. New York: New-York Historical Society.

Some necessary Precautions, worthy to be considered by all English Subjects, their Election of Members to Represent them in General Assembly. 1727. Philadelphia: Andrew Bradford.

Some Observations on the Bill, intitled, "An Act for granting to His Majesty an Excise upon Wines, and Spirits distilled, sold by Retail or consumed within this Province, and upon Limes, Lemons, and Oranges." 1754. Boston: Thomas Fleet.

Some Records of Sussex County, Delaware. 1909. Philadelphia: Allen, Lane & Scott.

"Somerset Patriotism Preceding the Revolutionary War." 1916. *Somerset County Historical Quarterly* 5:241–47.

Squire, Peverill. 2012. *The Evolution of American Legislatures: Colonies, Territories, and States, 1619–2009.* Ann Arbor: University of Michigan Press.

Squire, Peverill, and Keith E. Hamm. 2005. *101 Chambers: Congress, State Legislatures, and the Future of Legislative Studies.* Columbus: Ohio State University Press.

Squire, Peverill, and Gary Moncrief. 2015. *State Legislatures Today: Politics under the Domes.* 2nd ed. Lanham, MD: Rowman & Littlefield.

Stackpole, Everett S. 1903. *Old Kittery and Her Families.* Lewiston: Press of Lewiston Journal Company.

Standard History of Essex County, Massachusetts, Embracing a History of the County from its First Settlement to the Present Time, with a History and Description of its Towns and Cities. 1878. Boston: C. F. Jewett & Company.

Staples, William R. 1843. *Annals of the Town of Providence, from Its First Settlement, to the Organization of the City Government, in June, 1832.* Providence: Knowles and Vose.

Stearns, Ezra S. 1906. *History of Plymouth New Hampshire*, vol. I. 1906. Cambridge: University Press.

Steiner, Bernard Christian. 1897. *A History of the Plantation of Menuckatuck and of the Original Town of Guilford, Connecticut, Comprising the Present Towns of Guilford and Maidson*. Baltimore: Friedenwald Company.

Stephens, A. J. 1838. *The Rise and Progress of the English Constitution: The Treatise of J. L. De Lolme, LL. D.*, vol. I. London: John W. Parker.

Stevens, William B. 1891. *History of Stoneham, Massachusetts*. Stoneham: F. L. & W. E. Whittier.

Stiles, Henry R. 1904. *The History of Ancient Wethersfield, Connecticut*, vol. I. New York: Grafton Press.

Streeter, Sebastian F. 1876. *Papers Relating to the Early History of Maryland*. Baltimore: John Murphy.

Surrency, Erwin C. 1965. "Revision of Colonial Laws." *American Journal of Legal History* 9:189–202.

Sutherland, Lucy S. 1968. "Edmund Burke and the Relations between Members of Parliament and Their Constituents." *Studies in Burke and His Time* 10:1005–21.

Sydnor, Charles S. 1952. *Gentlemen Freeholders*. Chapel Hill: University of North Carolina Press.

Taswell-Langmead, Thomas Pitt. 1946. *English Constitutional History*. 10th ed. Boston: Houghton Mifflin.

Taylor, Charles J. 1882. *History of Great Barrington, (Berkshire County,) Massachusetts*. Great Barrington: Clark W. Bryan & Co.

Teele, A. K. 1887. *The History of Milton, Mass., 1640–1887*. Boston: Rockwell and Church.

Temple, J. H. 1887. *History of North Brookfield, Massachusetts*. Boston: Rand Avery.

Temple, J. H., and George Sheldon. 1875. *A History of the Town of Northfield, Massachusetts, for 150 Years*. Albany: Joel Munsell.

Thornton, Mary L. 1944. "Public Printing in North Carolina, 1749–1815." *North Carolina Historical Review* 21:181–202.

Tilden, William S. 1887. *History of the Town of Medfield, Massachusetts, 1650–1886*. Boston: Geo. H. Ellis.

Tilghman, Oswald. 1915. *History of Talbot County, Maryland, 1661–1861*, vol. I. Baltimore: Williams & Wilkins Company.

To the Independent Freeholders and Freemen of this City and County. 1770. New York: n.p.

To Morris Morris on the Reasons published for his Conduct in Assembly in the Year 1728. 1728. Philadelphia: Andrew Bradford.

To The Printer. 1739. Boston: n.p.

Tobey, Samuel, and Thomas Andros. 1872. *History of the Town of Berkeley. Mass*. New York: Kilbourne Tompkins.

Tocqueville, Alexis de. 1969. *Democracy in America*. Garden City: Anchor Books.

Tompkins, D. A. 1903. *History of Mecklenburg County and the City of Charlotte, from 1740 to 1903*. Charlotte, NC: Observer Printing House.

A Tooth-Full of Advice. 1768. New York: n.p.

Town of Millbury. 1915. *Centennial History of the Town of Millbury, Massachusetts*. Worcester: Davis Press.

Trumbull, James Russell. 1898. *History of Northampton, Massachusetts, from its Settlement in 1654*, vol. I. Northampton: Press of Gazette Printing Co.

Trumbull, James Russell. 1902. *History of Northampton, Massachusetts, from its Settlement in 1654*, vol. II. Northampton: Gazette Publishing Co.

Tucker, John. 1771. *A Sermon Preached at Cambridge, before his Excellency, Thomas Hutchinson, Esq; Governor: His Honor Andrew Oliver, Esq; Lieutenant-Governor, the Honorable His Majesty's Council, and the Honorable House of Representatives, of the Province of the Massachusetts-Bay in New-England, May 29th 1771*. Boston: Richard Draper.

Tucker, William Franklin. 1877. *Historical Sketch of the Town of Charleston, in Rhode Island, from 1636 to 1876*. Westerly: G. B. & J. H. Utter.

Tully, Alan. 1977. *William Penn's Legacy: Politics and Social Structure in Provincial Pennsylvania, 1726–1755*. Baltimore: Johns Hopkins University Press.

Turner, J. Kelly, and Jno. L. Bridgers Jr. 1920. *History of Edgecombe County, North Carolina*. Raleigh: Edwards & Broughton Printing Co.

"Two Addresses of Conrad Weiser to the German Voters of Pennsylvania." 1899. *Pennsylvania Magazine of History and Biography* 23:516–21.

Tyler, Lyon G. 1893. "Virginia under the Commonwealth." *William and Mary Quarterly* 1:189–96.

An Unanswerable Answer to the Cavils and Objections (Printed, or not Printed, or not worth Printing) Against a Paper lately Published, called Many of the Electors of the TWO to the Electors of the FOUR. 1739. New York: William Bradford.

Van Schaack, Henry C. 1842. *The Life of Peter Van Schaack, LL. D., Embracing Selections from his Correspondence and Other Writings, during the American Revolution and His Exile in England*. New York: D. Appleton.

Veitch, George Stead. 1913. *The Genesis of Parliamentary Reform*. London: Constable & Company.

"Virginia in 1636–'8." 1903. *Virginia Magazine of History and Biography* 10:263–72.

The Voice of the People. 1754. Boston: n.p.

Wadleigh, George. 1913. *Notable Events in the History of Dover, New Hampshire, from the First Settlement in 1623 to 1865*. Dover: Tufts College Press.

Wahlke, John C., Heinz Eulau, William Buchanan, and LeRoy C. Ferguson. 1962. *The Legislative System*. New York: Wiley.

Ward, Andrew H. 1826. *A History of the Town of Shrewsbury*. Worcester: Rogers & Griffin.

Warden, G. B. 1970. "The Caucus and Democracy in Colonial Boston." *New England Quarterly* 43:19–45.

Warner, Samuel. 1890. "Historical Sketch of Wrentham." In *History and Directory of Wrentham and Norfolk, Mass., for 1890*. Boston: Press of Brown Bros.

Warren-Adams Letters, vol. I. 1917. Boston: Massachusetts Historical Society.

Washburn, Emory. 1860. *Historical Sketches of the Town of Leicester, Massachusetts, During the First Century from its Settlement*. Boston: John Wilson and Son.

Waters, Thomas Franklin. 1917. *Ipswich in the Massachusetts Colony*, vol. II. Salem: Newcomb & Gauss.

Waters, Wilson. 1917. *History of Chelmsford, Massachusetts*. Lowell: Courier-Citizen Company.

Wells, Daniel White, and Reuben Field Wells. 1910. *A History of Hatfield, Massachusetts*. Springfield: F. C. H. Gibbons.

Wertenbacker, Thomas J. 1914. *Virginia under the Stuarts, 1607–1688*. Princeton: Princeton University Press.

Wertenbacker, Thomas J. 1958. *Give Me Liberty: The Struggle for Self-Government in Virginia*. Philadelphia: American Philosophical Society.

Weston, Thomas. 1906. *History of the Town of Middleboro, Massachusetts*. Boston: Houghton, Mifflin and Company.

Wheeler, George Augustus, and Henry Warren Wheeler. 1878. *History of Brunswick, Topsham, and Harpswell, Maine*. Boston: Alfred Mudge & Sons.

White, Stephen. 1763. *Civil Rulers Gods by Office, and the Duties of Such Considered and Enforced. A Sermon Preached before the General Assembly of Connecticut, at Hartford, on the Day of their Anniversary Election, May the 12th, 1763*. New London: Timothy Green.

Wilderson, Paul W. 1994. *Governor John Wentworth & the American Revolution*. Hanover, NH: University Press of New England.

Willard, D. 1838. *Willard's History of Greenfield*. Greenfield, MA: Kneeland & Eastman.

Willard, Joseph. 1826. *Topographical and Historical Sketches of the Town of Lancaster, in the Commonwealth of Massachusetts*. Worcester: Charles Griffin.

Williamson, Chilton. 1960. *American Suffrage: From Property to Democracy, 1760–1860*. Princeton: Princeton University Press.

Williamson, William D. *The History of the State of Maine*, vol. I. 1832. Hallowell: Glazier, Masters & Co.

Willis, William. 1865. *The History of Portland, from 1632 to 1864*. Portland: Bailey & Noyes.

Winsor, Justin. 1849. *A History of Duxbury, Massachusetts, with Genealogical Registers*. Boston: Crosby & Nichols.

Winthrop's Journal, "*History of New England*," *1630–1649*, vol. I. 1908. New York: Charles Scribner's Sons.

Winthrop's Journal, "*History of New England*," *1630–1649*, vol. II. 1908. New York: Charles Scribner's Sons.

A Word of Advice. 1768. New York: John Holt.

The Works of the Right Honourable Edmund Burke, vol II. 1792. London: J. Dodsley.

Worthington, Erastus. 1827. *The History of Dedham, from the Beginning of its Settlement in September, 1635 . . . to May, 1827*. Boston: Dutton and Wentworth.

Wright, Otis Olney. 1917. *History of Swansea, Massachusetts, 1667–1917*. Fall River: Dover Press.

Wroth, Lawrence C. 1922. *A History of Printing in Colonial Maryland, 1686–1776*. Baltimore: Typothetae of Baltimore.

Zagarri, Rosemarie. 2000. "Suffrage and Representation." In *A Companion to the American Revolution*, ed. Jack P. Greene and J. R. Pole. Malden: Blackwell.

Zemsky, Robert. 1971. *Merchants, Farmers, and River Gods*. Boston: Gambit.

Index

Adams, John: bill drafting committee, 180; Boston caucus, 111–12; candidate deference, 102; taverners' power, 115

Adams, Samuel, 167

Albany County (NY), 135

Allen, James, 148

Allen, Jerimiah, 45

Allen, William, 51

Amherst (NH), 71, 94

Andros administration, 28

Annapolis (MD), 51, 54, 73, 143, 193; assembly voting process, 42; delegation voting, 225

Anne Arundel County (MD), constituent instructions, 177

Ashford (CT), 75

assembly elections: assembly salaries as issue, 123–27; assessments of incumbents, 150–51; budget issues, 121; campaigning, 114–19; campaign literature, 47, 116–17, 153–56; campaign rhetoric, 116, 155; candidate declinations, 105–7, 108; candidate emergence, 101–12; candidate recruitment, 106–7, 109, 110, 112; candidate qualities, 102–5; candidate slates, 109–12; clergy campaigning, 114–15; competitiveness, 86–87; days and hours, 91–93; election violence, 139–41; election winner rules, 100–101; election writs, 90–91, 160; English comparisons, 30, 31, 32, 34, 38, 39, 41, 42, 45, 48, 49, 63, 125, 127; ethnic politics, 41, 43, 110, 116–17, 139–41, 142, 143, 146, 149–50, 156; formal candidate qualifications, 38–56; formal voter qualifications, 29–37; gubernatorial influence on, 147–49; importance of, 85–86, 113; incumbent reelections, 86, 150, 151, 222–23; incumbent turnover, 86; issue importance, 119–127, 152; lawyer candidates, 103, 153–54; legal limits on, 118; mass democracy characteristics, 29, 38, 56, 231–32; merchant candidates, 103, 153–54; mismanagement of, 92–93; New York City and County 1768 elections, 153–54; New York City and County 1769 elections, 153, 154–57; polling places, 72–73, 74, 93–94; proxy voting, 15, 17, 18–19,

4; selectmen requests, 181; social
status of assembly members, 161;
voter turnout, 134–35; voting
irregularities, 146
Bradford, Andrew, 192, 193, 195
Bradford, William, 192, 195
Braintree (MA): assembly election
competitiveness, 87–88; excise bill,
221–22
Brent, Margaret, 39
Bristol (PA), 93
Brunswick (NC), 33, 42, 73
Bucks County (PA), 83, 93, 110, 160,
197; ballot stuffing, 144; delegation
voting, 230; squirrel bill, 202
Burke, Edmund: Bristol speech, 5–6;
Burkean dilemma, 5–6, 7, 10, 11,
185–89, 233–34
Burlington (NJ), 72, 73
Burlington County (NJ), 139

Calvert, Charles, 80–81
Calvert, Philip, 80
Calvert County (MD), election vio-
lence, 139
Cambridge (MA), 126; assembly
gallery instruction, 190–91; ballot
stuffing, 144; delegation voting,
230; election conduct, 138; excise
bill, 220
The Candidates, 185
Carlisle (MA), 70
Caroline County (VA), 205–6
Carter, Landon, Burkean dilemma,
186–87
Cecil County (MD), 143
Charles City County (VA), 163
Charleston (SC), 72, 108; incumbent
reelections, 150
Chatham (CT), 75
Chelmsford (MA), 161
Chelsea (MA), 68
Chester (PA), 93

Chester County (PA), 83, 93, 160;
delegation voting, 230; incumbent
support, 216; squirrel bill, 202
College of William and Mary, 46;
assembly seat, 62–63
Colleton County (SC), 142
colonial governments: colony boundaries, 58, 79; control over assembly
seats, 58; development of assemblies, 11–26, 27; expanded agendas,
204; legal mechanisms establishing,
3–4; representation in, 4
colonial governors: apportionment
battles, 77–81; assembly salaries
and, 126–27; budget issues and,
121; constituent consultations,
169–70; election schedules, 165–
66; influence on assembly elections,
89, 147–49; information suppres-
sion, 198; patronage powers, 46,
147, 210–12; treating assembly
members, 210
Concord (MA), 52, 70
Connecticut assembly: apportionment, 57, 70, 74–76; charter, 4;
colony boundaries, 58; constituent
consultations, 170; constituent
instructions, 174–76, 181, 182;
delegate orientation in, 16; development, 16; election schedule, 88;
failed manor house, 65; freeholder
voting qualifications, 32; goat bill,
202; lack of journal, 195–96; laws
read publicly, 189, 190; member
character qualifications, 38; member residency requirement, 49, 50,
53; multimember districts in, 57;
New Haven justice of the peace
vote, 199; New Haven merger, 1;
recall of assembly members, 185;
semi-annual elections, 88, 164;
taxes and representation, 75–76;
treating, 131–32; voter qualifications, 36